AYMER DE VALENCE

EARL OF PEMBROKE

1307-1324

AYMER DE VALENCE

EARL OF PEMBROKE
1307–1324

BARONIAL POLITICS IN THE
REIGN OF EDWARD II

J. R. S. PHILLIPS

Lecturer in Medieval History
University College, Dublin

OXFORD
AT THE CLARENDON PRESS
1972

Oxford University Press, Ely House, London W. 1

GLASGOW NEW YORK TORONTO MELBOURNE WELLINGTON
CAPE TOWN IBADAN NAIROBI DAR ES SALAAM LUSAKA ADDIS ABABA
DELHI BOMBAY CALCUTTA MADRAS KARACHI LAHORE DACCA
KUALA LUMPUR SINGAPORE HONG KONG TOKYO

PRINTED IN GREAT BRITAIN
AT THE UNIVERSITY PRESS, OXFORD
BY VIVIAN RIDLER
PRINTER TO THE UNIVERSITY

TO MY MOTHER

Preface

SINCE the publication in 1914 of T. F. Tout's *Place of the Reign of Edward II* and in 1918 of J. C. Davies's *Baronial Opposition to Edward II* the reign of Edward II has suffered from comparative neglect. Their work was of very great importance at the time and has deeply influenced all subsequent work on the period, in particular by the assumption that there was a consistent baronial opposition to the monarchy based on the constitutional doctrine of baronial control over the King's government. It will, however, be argued in the course of this book that this is an extremely misleading view because it oversimplifies the very complex nature of political life during the reign and does not allow sufficiently for the personal element in the activities and attitudes of individual magnates.

The purpose of the present book is to attempt to clarify the course and significance of English politics in the reign of Edward II through a study of the career of one important magnate. It is not, however, intended as a biography, since the available materials will not permit such an approach, and the Earl of Pembroke has been chosen rather to illustrate the problems of the period from the point of view of a magnate who was for most of his career closely associated with the monarchy and with the making and performance of royal policy. In this sense Pembroke represents the opposite side of the coin to Thomas of Lancaster, the King's opponent. Detailed coverage of the period starts in 1312, when Pembroke first became of real individual importance, and continues down to his death in 1324. This means that some of the problems of the early part of the reign have not been treated exhaustively and that those of the very end of the reign have been omitted entirely, except for certain pointers to the future. In addition to tracing Pembroke's share in the politics of the reign some discussion has also been included on the structure of his retinue and on his land holdings, although lack of evidence, especially in the latter case, does not allow of any very detailed conclusions.

The last word is far from having been said about the reign

of Edward II. For example, the history of royal transactions with the Italian bankers and of the financial stringency which hampered the making and pursuit of any consistent policy towards the Scots remains to be worked out. Other serious omissions are the study of English government policy towards Ireland during the reign and an examination of the activities of the Elder and Younger Despensers. I hope eventually to do some research into these latter two aspects of the reign. An important contribution has, however, been made since the completion of this book by Dr. J. R. Maddicott's study, *Thomas of Lancaster, 1307–1322* (Oxford, 1970), which will do much to alter the traditional orthodoxies on the period. Dr. Maddicott and I agree on the essential point that there was no baronial opposition to Edward II in the sense in which this term has previously been used, but naturally we differ on many matters of detail. I do not, for example, agree with his view of the constitutional propriety of Lancaster's behaviour, nor do I accept his conclusion on the alleged 'middle party' of the Earl of Pembroke, the non-existence of which in any form is indeed one of the central parts of my argument. On the other hand his work is a most valuable contribution to understanding of the period and the differences between our interpretations serve to underline the amount of research which has still to be done. Since Dr. Maddicott's book was published when my own was already complete, I have not attempted to make any comments on questions of detailed interpretation in the substance of my own work.

This book is based on a thesis which was submitted to the University of London for the degree of Doctor of Philosophy in the autumn of 1967. In carrying out the research and the later revision I have received help from many quarters. I should especially like to thank Mr. Anthony Tomkinson of Royal Holloway College, London, who supervised the original thesis, for his patient and stimulating criticism. Any merits in the finished work owe much to him. Dr. E. B. Fryde of the University College of Wales, Aberystwyth, and Mr. T. B. Pugh of the University of Southampton have also been generous with their advice and comments. I also benefited from discussions of the period with Dr. J. R. Maddicott when we were both postgraduate students. Our conclusions are however, entirely independent, since we decided not to refer to each other's researches so as to provide two separate and complementary accounts of the many controversial problems of the reign. My colleagues in the Department of Medieval History at University College, Dublin, have helped me considerably by their comments. The staff of many libraries and archives have been of great help, especially those of the Public Record Office, the British Museum, the Bodleian Library, and the National Library of Wales. The documents reproduced in the appendices are published with the permission of the Controller of H.M. Stationery Office[1] and of the Librarian of the Bodleian Library.[2] The outlines of the lordships of Pembroke and Haverford which are included in Map 1 are taken from the *Historical Map of South Wales and the Border in the Fourteenth Century* by W. Rees (London, 1933) with the permission of the Ordnance Survey. The outline of the commote of Ystlwyf which also appears in Map 1 is taken from *Welsh Administrative and Territorial Units* by M. Richards (Cardiff, 1969) by permission of the University of Wales Press. I should also like to thank the authorities of Royal Holloway College, London, and the R.A.F. Benevolent Fund for assistance while I was doing my research and the History and Law Committee of the Board of Celtic Studies of the University of Wales for the appointment that made it possible for me to complete my work. Miss Elizabeth Danbury, who is studying the military activities of the household of Edward II, has kindly read my final typescript in search of errors of fact and barbarisms in style. For those that remain I take full responsibility.

J. R. S. P.

University College, Dublin
December 1970

---

[1] P.R.O., E. 101/68/2/42D; S.C. 1/49/39; E. 163/4/6; C. 49/4/27; S.C. 1/63/183.
[2] Bodleian, Dugdale MS. 18, f. 80; Dodsworth MS. 8, f. 262.

Contents

List of Tables and Maps

Abbreviations

Ann. Lond.: *Annales Londonienses*, in *Chronicles of the Reigns of Edward I and Edward II*, vol. 1, ed. W. Stubbs, R.S. (London, 1882).
Ann. Paul.: *Annales Paulini*, in ibid.
Bain: *Calendar of Documents relating to Scotland, 1272–1357*, ed. J. Bain, 2 vols. (Edinburgh, 1884–7).
B.B.C.S.: *Bulletin of the Board of Celtic Studies*.
B.I.H.R.: *Bulletin of the Institute of Historical Research*.
Blaneford: *Annales of Henry Blaneford*, ed. H. T. Riley, R.S. (London, 1866).
B.M.: British Museum.
Bridlington: *Gesta Edwardi de Carnarvon of a Canon of Bridlington*, in *Chronicles of the Reigns of Edward I and Edward II*, vol. 2, ed. W. Stubbs, R.S. (London, 1883).
The Bruce: *The Bruce of John Barbour*, ed. W. M. Skeat, Early English Text Society, 2 vols. (London, 1870, 1889).
The Brut: *The Brut*, ed. F. Brie, Early English Text Society, 2 vols. (London, 1906–8).
C. Ch. R.: *Calendar of Charter Rolls*.
C. Ch. Warr.: *Calendar of Chancery Warrants*.
C. Cl. R.: *Calendar of Close Rolls*.
C.F.R.: *Calendar of Fine Rolls*.
C.P.R.: *Calendar of Patent Rolls*.
C. Papal Letters: *Calendar of Papal Letters*.
C. Treaty Rolls: *Calendar of Treaty Rolls*.
Cal. I.P.M.: *Calendar of Inquisitions Post Mortem*.
Cal. Inquis. Misc.: *Calendar of Inquisitions Miscellaneous*
Cat. Anc. Deeds: *Catalogue of Ancient Deeds*.
D.N.B.: *Dictionary of National Biography*.
E.H.R.: *English Historical Review*.
Econ. Hist. R.: *Economic History Review*.
F.: *Foedera Conventiones Litterae et Cuiuscunque Generis Acta Publica*, ed. Th. Rymer, Record Commission Edition (London, 1816–30).
Flores: *Flores Historiarum*, ed. H. R. Luard, R.S. (London, 1890).
Fordun: *Johannis de Fordun Chronicon Gentis Scotorum*, ed. W. F. Skene (Edinburgh, 1871–2).
G.E.C.: *Complete Peerage*, ed. G. E. Cokayne, new edn. (London, 1910–59).
G.R.: *Gascon Rolls*.
Hist. Anglicana: *Historia Anglicana of Thomas Walsingham*, ed. H. T. Riley, R.S. (London, 1863–4).
Hist. Dunelm. Scriptores Tres: *Historiae Dunelmensis Scriptores Tres*, ed. J. Raine, Surtees Society, vol. 9 (Edinburgh, 1839).
Knighton: *Chronicon Henrici Knighton*, ed. J. R. Lumby, R.S. (London, 1889–95).

Lanercost: *Chronicon de Lanercost*, ed. J. Stevenson, Bannatyne Club, vol. 65 (Edinburgh, 1839).

Le Baker: *Chronicon Galfridi le Baker of Swynbroke*, ed. E. M. Thompson (Oxford, 1889).

Melsa: *Chronicon Monasterii de Melsa*, ed. E. A. Bond, 3 vols., R.S. (London, 1866–8).

Murimuth: *Continuatio Chronicarum of Adam Murimuth*, ed. E. M. Thompson, R.S. (London, 1889).

N.L.W.: National Library of Wales.

P.W.: *Parliamentary Writs and Writs of Military Summons, Edward I and Edward II*, ed. F. Palgrave, Record Commission (London, 1827–34).

Polychronicon: *Polychronicon of Ranulph Higden*, ed. C. Babington and J. R. Lumby, R.S. (London, 1865–86).

P.R.O.: Public Record Office.

R.S.: Rolls Series.

Reg. Baldock: *Registrum Radulphi de Baldock, etc., Bishops of London*, ed. R. C. Fowler, Canterbury and York Series, vol. 7 (London, 1911).

Reg. Gandavo: *Registrum Simonis de Gandavo, Bishop of Salisbury*, ed. C. T. Flower and M. C. B. Dawes, Canterbury and York Series, vol. 40 (London, 1934).

Reg. Greenfield: *Register of William Greenfield, Archbishop of York, 1306–15*, ed. W. Brown and A. Hamilton Thompson, Surtees Society, vols. 145, 149, 151–3 (Durham, 1931–8).

Reg. Orleton: *Registrum Ade de Orleton, Bishop of Hereford*, ed. A. T. Bannister, Canterbury and York Series, vol. 5 (London, 1908).

Reg. Palat. Dunelm.: *Registrum Palatinum Dunelmense*, ed. T. D. Hardy, 4 vols., R.S. (London, 1873–8).

Reg. Sandale: *Registers of John Sandale and Rigaud de Assier, Bishops of Winchester, 1316–23*, ed. F. J. Baigent, Hampshire Record Society (Winchester, 1897).

Reg. Stapledon: *Register of Walter Stapledon, Bishop of Exeter, 1307–26*, ed. F. C. Hingeston-Randolph (London, 1892).

Reg. Swinfield: *Registrum Ricardi de Swinfield, Bishop of Hereford*, ed. W. W. Capes, Canterbury and York Series, vol. 6 (London, 1909).

Rot. Parl.: *Rotuli Parliamentorum, 1272–1326*, ed. J. Strachey and others (London, 1767).

Scalacronica: *Scalacronica of Thomas Gray of Heton*, ed. J. Stevenson, Maitland Club, vol. 40 (Edinburgh, 1836).

Soc. of Antiqs.: Society of Antiquaries of London.

T.R.H.S.: *Transactions of the Royal Historical Society*.

Trivet (Cont.): *Nicolai Triveti Annalium Continuatio*, ed. A. Hall (Oxford, 1722).

Trokelowe: *Annales of John Trokelowe*, ed. H. T. Riley, R.S. (London, 1866).

Vita: *Vita Edwardi Secundi*, ed. N. Denholm-Young (London, 1957).

Vita et Mors: *Vita et Mors Edwardi Secundi*, in *Chronicles of the Reigns of Edward I and Edward II*, vol. 2, ed. W. Stubbs, R.S. (London, 1883).

Introduction

Pembroke's Connections with France and his Place in English Magnate Society

MOST previous research on the reign of Edward II has tended to concentrate attention upon opposition to the monarchy during the periods of major political crisis, one result of this being the relative neglect of the remaining quieter portions of the reign which harboured the seeds of these troubles. This approach has also meant that there has been insufficient study of the individual role of any of the leading political figures. Consequently any attempt to trace the career of one of the important magnates might not only be expected to throw fresh light upon his own activities but also to help fill many of the gaps in our knowledge of the reign of Edward II.[1] The career of Aymer de Valence, the Earl of Pembroke, is especially suitable for this latter purpose, since his continuous involvement in royal affairs until his death in 1324 provides both the opportunity to examine events from the King's side of the fence and the record evidence with which to do so. A second reason for studying Pembroke is that earlier writers have produced a picture of him as a skilful political leader which needs to be tested in the light of further research.

Because Aymer de Valence held the English earldom of Pembroke and spent his entire career in English service it is easy to forget that in origin he was almost entirely French and that he retained very close links with France throughout his life. Before going on to discuss the details of his career in England it will, therefore, be helpful to examine these French connections.

As the grandson of Hugh X, Count of La Marche and Angoulême, Aymer de Valence was a member of the Lusignan family which was the leading family in their part of France and

---

[1] Since the completion of this book one major gap has been filled by Dr. J. R. Maddicott's study of Thomas of Lancaster, the opponent of Edward II and often a rival of Pembroke: *Thomas of Lancaster, 1307–1322* (Oxford, 1970).

　　　　　B

of ancient importance both in France and overseas.[1] Their connection with England was the result of the marriage of Hugh X and Isabella of Angoulême, the widow of King John of England, and the migration to England in 1247 of their sons, William, Guy, and Aymer, at the invitation of their half-brother Henry III. In the same year one of these brothers, William de Valence, was given as his wife Joan de Munchensy, the granddaughter of

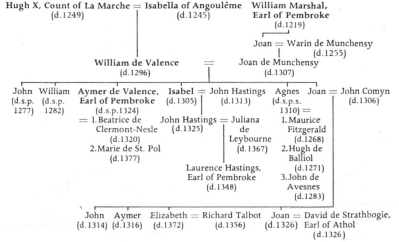

TABLE I. Descent of Aymer de Valence from the Lusignan Counts of La Marche and Angoulême and from the Marshal Earls of Pembroke

the great William Marshal, Earl of Pembroke, and heiress to the lordship of Pembroke in the partition of the lands of Anselm, the last Marshal Earl of Pembroke. Joan's lands, together with others granted to him by Henry III, and the courtesy title of Earl of Pembroke gave William de Valence a place in English society which formed the basis of his long and often stormy career in English politics and in the service of the Crown, until his death in 1296.[2]

However, William retained a close connection with France through the lands which he still held there. In his will Hugh X of La Marche had made provision for his four younger sons,

---

[1] For the Lusignan family background see the articles by S. Painter in *Speculum*, vols. 30–2 (1955–7).

[2] For their careers see F. R. Lewis, 'William de Valence', *Aberystwyth Studies*, vol. 13 (1935), and H. S. Snellgrove, *The Lusignans in England* (Albuquerque, 1950).

William's share being the four castellanies of Rancon, Bellac, Champagnac, and Montignac.¹ The first three were grouped closely in an area to the north of Limoges within the county of La Marche, Rancon being held from the Bishop of Limoges, while the latter two were held from the abbess of La Règle at Limoges. The fourth castellany, Montignac, lay on the Charente near Angoulême, of which county it formed part, and was held from the Bishop of Angoulême.² Bellac, Champagnac, and Rancon may have remained continuously in William's hands during his lifetime but Montignac at least went through a series of transitions. In 1248 William gave it to his brother Geoffrey and in 1276, after the latter's death, bestowed it upon his eldest son, William, who died in 1282. After William's own death in 1296 his French lands went to his remaining son and heir, Aymer de Valence, who did homage for Montignac in 1300 at about the same time as he did so for Rancon, Bellac, and Champagnac.³ When Aymer died in 1324 his French lands went to one of his coheirs, the Earl of Athol, who resigned his rights there to Aymer's widow in 1332. In 1333 she gave them to the Earl of Richmond as part of an exchange of lands, but on his death in 1334 the lands reverted to her and, so far as is known, they remained in her control until 1372, when they were confiscated by the French Crown and granted to the Duke of Bourbon.⁴

As lord of Montignac Pembroke was therefore a French magnate as well as an English one, and there is some evidence that in the early years of his career Philip IV attempted to make him act in his service. In 1303 and 1304 Aymer was three times summoned to serve in the French campaigns against Flanders.⁵

¹ *Layettes du Trésor des Chartes*, vol. 2, no. 3049. William never held land at Valence from which he took only his name.
² *Inventaire-sommaire des archives départementales de la Haute-Vienne*, series G, p. 19; A. A. Thomas, *Le Comté de la Marche et le Parlement de Poitiers* (Paris, 1910), p. xxix; J. Burias, *Bulletins et mémoires de la Société archéologique et historique de la Charente*, 1955 (1957), pp. 229–33.
³ Burias, loc. cit.; *Inventaire-sommaire des archives départementales de la Haute-Vienne*, series G, p. 19 (the date is printed as 1290 but is certainly an error for 1299/1300); A. A. Thomas, op. cit., pp. xxix–xxx. All the relevant documents on Montignac, 1243–1331, are listed in the *Inventaire-sommaire des archives départemententales de la Charente*, series G, vol. 1, p. 85 (bundle G. 138).
⁴ *C.P.R., 1330–4*, pp. 397, 404; *Titres de la maison ducale de Bourbon* (Paris, 1867–8), nos. 3224, 3235, 3257.
⁵ *Archives historiques du Poitou* (Poitiers, 1881, 1883), vol. 11, no. 5, and vol. 13

There is no evidence that he ever gave personal military service
to the French Crown at this or any later date and it is likely
that he either paid fines in lieu of its performance or that his
French tenants and retainers served in his place.

There was for a time, however, a slight chance that Pembroke
might become a magnate of even greater territorial importance
in France than in England. The details of this episode in his
career have been fully worked out by both French and English
historians and only a brief summary of the main points need
be given here.[1] In 1283 Hugh XIII of La Marche, Angoulême,
and Fougères made a will giving the succession to his brother,
Guiard; but in a second will in 1297 Hugh disinherited his
brother and named as his heir Geoffrey de Lusignan, the
grandson of Hugh X by his third son. In default of Geoffrey
the lands were to go to Aymer de Valence, whose father was
Hugh X's fourth son, and, failing him, to Hugh XIII's nephew,
Renaud de Pons, or Amaury de Craon, a great-grandson of
Hugh X. In 1305 or 1306 Geoffrey de Lusignan died without
an heir, and Aymer would then have had a good chance of succession to the two counties, had not Hugh XIII again changed his
mind in 1302 and placed him fourth in succession instead of
second as before. However, when Hugh XIII died in 1303 his
brother, Guiard, was able to set his wills aside, and with royal
approval succeeded as Count of La Marche and Angoulême.[2]

Aymer's chances of ever succeeding to these lands were therefore extremely remote and they were finally extinguished by the
determination of Philip IV, with whom Count Guiard had put
himself out of favour by his alliance with Edward I of England
in 1305,[3] to the effect that on Guiard's death the two counties
would come into the hands of the French Crown. To ensure
that this would take place Philip IV had begun, even before
Guiard's death in about November 1308, to take action to buy
out the possible claimants to the lands, including Aymer de

nos. 190, 197; *Recueil des Historiens des Gaules et de la France* (Paris, 1894), vol. 23,
pp. 790, 803.

[1] P. Boissonade, *Bulletins et mémoires de la Société archéologique et historique de la
Charente*, 1943 (1948), pp. 140–98; G. W. Watson, *Genealogist*, New Series, vol. 21
(1905), pp. 163–72 and 234–43 (this article includes all the relevant documents
from French sources).

[2] Watson, op. cit., pp. 163–9; *Archives historiques du Poitou*, vol. 58, no. 415.

[3] For the relations between the French monarchy and the Count of La Marche
see P. Boissonade, op. cit.

Valence. On 24 September 1308 an agreement was made at Longpont-près-Montlhéry between the Bishop of Autun, acting for Aymer, and Philip IV's Chancellor, William de Nogaret. This records that Aymer was proposing to press his claim to La Marche, Angoulême, and Fougères against Guiard in the royal court, basing his claim on Hugh XIII's will. Aymer promised that if his case were upheld he would then lay claim to a third of these lands, to include the city of Angoulême and the castles of Lusignan, Cognac, and Merpins, and would then cede all his rights to the French Crown in return for an annual revenue of 1,000 *livres tournois*.[1] The form of the agreement makes it clear that Pembroke had probably undertaken the case at royal instigation and as a means of forwarding royal claims to the lands. When Guiard died shortly afterwards his lands were taken into royal hands, and control, once gained, was not relinquished. With the changed situation, Pembroke's case fell through, and on 17 February 1309 a further agreement between him and Philip IV was made in Paris. In this Pembroke stated that, although he had a claim to La Marche and the other lands, he had been informed by the King's men that the King ought to have them and had therefore after due deliberation decided to cede his rights to Philip IV. In return he was to receive 1,000 *livres*, as in 1308, in exchange for his liege homage. Pembroke's disclaimer was followed by the buying-out by Philip IV of all the other possible claimants.[2] Philip IV appears to have honoured his side of the bargain, since there is a record of Pembroke's receiving his 1,000 *livres* in 1312.[3]

Pembroke's family connections with French society were strengthened by his marriages to the daughters of important French magnates. The first of these was to Beatrice, the daughter of Ralph de Clermont, lord of Nesle in Picardy and Constable of France, and had taken place by 18 October 1295,[4] although they apparently did not live together as man and wife until early in 1297.[5] Very little is known of their married life

---

[1] *Archives Nationales*, J. 374, no. 4 (printed in Watson, op. cit., pp. 170–1).

[2] *Archives Nationales*, J. 374, no. 6 (printed in Watson, op. cit., pp. 171–2, and *Trésor des Chartes*, vol. 1, p. 76); Watson, op. cit., pp. 234–40.

[3] *Trésor des Chartes*, vol. 1, p. 292.

[4] This appears from an account of Aymer's mother, Joan de Valence: E. 101/505/25, m. 2.

[5] Ibid. /26, m. 12: this is when Beatrice left Joan's household.

together and, apart from one unrevealing letter written to Aymer by Beatrice in 1296,[1] there is no surviving correspondence between them. In August 1297, at Aymer's request, Beatrice was assigned a royal house in Marlborough for her to stay in during her husband's absence with the King in Flanders, but in December 1297 she crossed to join Aymer in Flanders. In April 1302 during the Scottish campaign she again went to join her husband.[2] Except for passing references to Beatrice in 1312 and again in 1315, when she recorded that Aymer allowed her £50 a year for her personal expenses, there is no further mention of her until she accompanied the Queen to France in June 1320.[3] In September 1320 she died and was buried at Stratford in London.[4]

There is no record of what lands Beatrice possessed in France, but after her death Aymer became involved in a many-sided family dispute among the heirs of Beatrice's sister, Alice, the lady of Nesle, which probably concerned Beatrice's own possessions. As early as 23 November 1318 Pembroke and his wife had appointed Citard de Penna Varia as their proctor for their French legal affairs and by November 1320 a lawsuit was under way between Pembroke, Jean de Flandre, the new lord of Nesle, and Jean's sisters, Isabelle and Jeanne. At the same time Jean de Flandre was also involved in a case against his two sisters and in November 1321 Jean, Isabelle, Jeanne, and others were concerned together in a suit against their aunt, Isabelle, the lady of Semblançay.[5] Just where Pembroke stood in this frenzy of litigation and what he might gain or lose by it is unfortunately unknown.

Pembroke's second marriage[6] was to Marie de Saint-Pol, the

---

[1] S.C. 1/48/183 (this is identifiable only on internal evidence).

[2] S.C. 8/77/3817; *C. Cl. R., 1296–1302*, p. 58; C. 67/12, m. 1; ibid. /15, m. 11.

[3] B.M., Add. Ch. 19835; E. 42/A.S. 85; B.M., Add. MS. 17362, f. 11.

[4] B.M., Add. MS. 9951, ff. 45v., 2v.

[5] E. 30/53; M. E. Boutaric (ed.), *Les Actes du Parlement de Paris*, 1st series, vol. 2 (Paris, 1867), pp. 337, 342–3, 397, 399. For details of the relationships of the family of Clermont-Nesle see Boutaric, op. cit., p. 537, and A. Du Chesne, *Histoire de la maison de Chastillon sur Marne* (Paris, 1621), pp. 306–7.

[6] Some writers also refer to an alleged marriage between Pembroke and an unnamed daughter of the Count of Bar. The story can be traced back via Gough's *Sepulchral Monuments* (London, 1786), vol. 1, part 2, p. 88, and W. Dugdale's *The Baronage of England* (London, 1675), vol. 1, p. 778, to R. Brooke, *Catalogue of the Succession of the Kings, Princes, etc., from the Norman Conquest to 1619* (London, 1619), p. 181 (no source given). The marriage is in fact fictitious, but the original

daughter of Guy de Châtillon, Count of Saint-Pol and Butler of France, who, like Aymer, was of distinguished ancestry and related to many of the leading families of France.[1] Their marriage took place in Paris in July 1321 and she brought with her 500 *livres* in rents, and the lands of Tours-en-Vimeu, Thièvre, Oreville, and Freacans in the Pas-de-Calais area.[2] On Pembroke's death in 1324 Marie began a long and interesting independent career of over fifty years until her own death in 1377, during which time she remained faithful to her husband's memory.[3] Pembroke's tomb in Westminster Abbey is one of the finest there, and there was once also a chantry, founded by his wife in his memory, which now forms part of the chapel of St. John.[4] The same purpose lay behind Marie's foundation of Denny Abbey in Cambridgeshire[5] and in 1347 of Pembroke College in Cambridge, one of whose scholars, James Nicholas of Dacia, later composed an ingenious but historically worthless poem on Aymer's life.[6]

Apart from these details of Pembroke's tenure of French lands and his two French marriages, there is little surviving material on this side of his life. There are occasional glimpses, for

cause of the error is unknown, unless it is a very garbled echo of Pembroke's imprisonment at Bar in 1317.

[1] For her family background and relations see A. Du Chesne, op. cit., pp. 275–85, and H. Jenkinson, *Archaeologia*, vol. 66 (1915), pp. 402–3.

[2] *Ann. Paul.*, p. 291; Du Chesne, op. cit., p. 285. There is a very early story that on the day of their marriage Marie de Saint-Pol's husband, Pembroke, was killed in a tournament: *Collectanea of John Leland*, vol. 5, p. 199 (1770 edition). The origin of this has not been traced but may be linked with the real death of a later Earl of Pembroke, John Hastings, in a tournament in 1389.

[3] For her later life see the very interesting article by H. Jenkinson, 'Mary de Sancto Paulo, Foundress of Pembroke College, Cambridge', *Archaeologia*, vol. 66 (1915), and the manuscript life of her by Dr. Gilbert Ainslie, Master of Pembroke College, Cambridge (1847).

[4] See L. E. Tanner, 'The Countess of Pembroke and Westminster Abbey', *Pembroke College, Cambridge Annual Gazette*, vol. 33, Dec. 1959. She also installed a memorial window to her husband in the new church of the Grey Friars in London: *Monumenta Franciscana*, R.S. (London, 1858), vol. 1, pp. 514, 517.

[5] See W. Dugdale, *Monasticon Anglicanum* (London, 1817–30), vol. 6, part 3, pp. 1548–53.

[6] B.M., Cotton MS. Claudius A. XIV. Two devotional books which once belonged to Marie de Saint-Pol survive as B.M., Royal MS. 16. E. V (*Miroir de l'Âme*) and as Cambridge Univ. MS. Dd. V. 5 (a breviary; see vol. 5, p. 585, of catalogue). A copy of a chronicle on the Crusades which had belonged to Marie de Saint-Pol was once in the library of Charles V of France: L. Delisle, *Recherches sur la librairie de Charles V, Roi de France, 1337–80* (Amsterdam, 1967), part 1, p. 52, and part 2, p. 169.

example, of Pembroke's dealings with the Paris draper and burgess, Étienne Marcel, which suggest the latter may have been one of Pembroke's chief business agents in France. In 1307 Marcel paid 902 *livres parisis* to a representative of Pembroke in Paris; in May 1309 Pembroke wrote from Avignon ordering him to pay £50 sterling to John Vanne; in another letter of 1309, written from Rancon, Pembroke thanked Marcel for buying a £200 horse for him from Étienne Barbeut, asked him to send his wife a gift of cloth, and also forwarded a letter from the lord of Coucy and a memoir on some business with one of his wife's relatives, William de Flandre; and in 1312 Marcel received a sum of 1,000 *livres tournois* on his behalf.[1] On the administration of Pembroke's lands in Poitou practically the only information consists of two letters to Henry de Stachesden, his Receiver there, in July 1313.[2]

Despite the lack of evidence, it is still essential to stress the personal importance of Pembroke's links with France. At the same time these have a more general importance, since they also added considerably to his value as a diplomat for the English Crown. He made visits to France or travelled through the country in 1307 to 1308, 1309, 1312, on three occasions in 1313, in 1315, 1317, 1320, 1321, and in 1324. Except in 1320 and 1321, all these visits were diplomatic ones, and it was entirely appropriate that his death should have taken place in June 1324 while he was on yet another royal mission to the French court.

However, the career of William de Valence had already determined that his descendants would live and make their own careers in an English environment, despite their close connections across the Channel. It is also necessary therefore to examine the place which his son, Aymer de Valence, occupied in English magnate society. Since Aymer was his father's third son his early years are obscure. Neither the date nor the place of his birth is known, but it is most likely that he was born between 1270 and 1275.[3] The first reference to his existence,

---

[1] *Cat. Anc. Deeds*, vol. 5, p. 197; S.C. 1/50/56 and 57; *Trésor des Chartes*, vol. 1, p. 292.

[2] E. 163/4/1/1; S.C. 1/50/58. See also Appendix 1 for list of Pembroke's known officials in France.

[3] The date can roughly be calculated from the statements of Aymer's age in the *Inquisitions post mortem* of the four people from whom he inherited his lands, William

on 24 May 1282, shows that as a younger son he was originally intended for an ecclesiastical career like his notorious uncle and namesake, Aymer de Valence, Bishop of Winchester, in the reign of Henry III.[1] Only three weeks later, on 16 June 1282, William de Valence's eldest surviving son and heir, William de Valence the Younger, was killed in a battle at Llandeilo in Wales, so that his younger brother, Aymer, became the heir to the earldom of Pembroke.[2] Nothing further is known about Aymer until he accompanied his father on an embassy to meet French envoys at Cambrai early in 1296.[3] This visit to France proved to be the last action in the long career of William de Valence, who died on 16 May the same year at his manor of Brabourne in Kent.[4] Aymer now inherited his father's lands in Poitou and was known as lord of Montignac, until the death of his mother Joan, the aged Countess of Pembroke, in September 1307 also brought him the palatine lands and title of the earldom of Pembroke.[5]

When Aymer de Valence became Earl of Pembroke in 1307 he joined a select group of ten other English earls. The veteran among them was Henry de Lacy of Lincoln, who was aged fifty-six in 1307 and had a long and distinguished career already behind him, but was also to play an important part in national politics until his death in 1311. Next came Robert de Vere of Oxford, aged fifty, who lived on until 1331 but had little discernible role in the events of Edward II's reign. At the age of about forty-one John of Brittany, the Earl of Richmond, was another comparative veteran, who had just succeeded to his

de Valence, Joan de Valence, Agnes de Valence, and Denise de Vere. See Chapter V of J. C. Russell's *British Medieval Population* (Albuquerque, 1948) for a discussion of the problems posed by this type of evidence.

[1] This appears from a letter of that date asking the Pope to provide him with benefices to support his future career: S.C. 1/13/204; *C. Cl. R., 1279–88*, p. 188. The letter also clearly implies that he was literate.

[2] *Annales Cambriae*, p. 106. William de Valence's sons were John, who died in childhood in 1277, William (d.s.p. 1282), and Aymer (d.s.p. 1324).

[3] *Archives historiques du Poitou*, vol. 58, no. 374.

[4] D.L. 42/12, f. 57*v*.; E. 101/505/25, m. 9. The account of his death in the *D.N.B.*, vol. 21, p. 376, is incorrect and that in *G.E.C.*, vol. 10, p. 381, note *a*, is incomplete.

[5] He is sometimes incorrectly referred to as Earl of Pembroke before 1307. Since the palatine lands of the earldom were Joan de Valence's own inheritance and she also had dower from the English lands of her husband, Aymer did not yet control much territory in England and had none in Wales or Ireland.

earldom and survived until 1334. He was to be consistently associated with the King but had very little independent importance.

These three earls were followed by a group of younger men headed by Guy de Beauchamp of Warwick, then in his early thirties, who was to die in 1315. By then he had become one of the most bitter of Edward II's opponents. Humphrey de Bohun of Hereford was about thirty-one, and pursued a chequered career which brought him now into the ranks of the King's opponents and then back to Edward II's support, until his death at Boroughbridge in 1322 in arms against the King and the Despensers. Thomas Earl of Lancaster was twenty-nine or thirty in 1307 and the holder of the earldoms of Leicester and Derby as well as Lancaster. Through his marriage to the daughter and heiress of Henry de Lacy he also acquired the earldoms of Lincoln and Salisbury in 1311, which made him the most powerful magnate in England. He was a constant source of opposition to his cousin Edward II, whom he loathed and despised, and has aptly been described as 'the supreme example of the over-mighty subject whose end must be either to destroy or be destroyed'.[1] In the event it was he who was destroyed after his defeat at Boroughbridge in 1322. After Thomas of Lancaster there were four even younger men. Piers Gaveston, the new Earl of Cornwall and boon companion of the King, was twenty-three, the same age as the King. Although of noble birth, Gaveston was in the terms of the English earls a foreign upstart, and this fact, together with his personal arrogance and over-close relations with the King, ensured that he would become the source and focus of grave political disturbance between 1307 and his execution in 1312. Edmund FitzAlan of Arundel was twenty-two in 1307 and, despite his early connections with the King's opponents, was to spend most of the reign in association with the King until his execution in 1326 as a supporter of the Younger Despenser. FitzAlan's brother-in-law, John de Warenne Earl of Surrey, who was a year younger at twenty-one, had just succeeded to the earldom which he held until 1347. Warenne was one of the three earls who did not join the Ordainers in 1310 (the other two were the Earl of Oxford and, inevitably, Gaveston) and played no major part

[1] M. McKisack, *The Fourteenth Century, 1307–1399* (Oxford, 1959), p. 69.

in English politics. In general he was to be found among the royal circle of magnates, but this can be accounted for as much by his personal feuds with the Earl of Lancaster as by any royalist leanings he may have had. The youngest of the group was Gilbert de Clare, aged only sixteen, who was allowed by Edward II to succeed to his earldom of Gloucester in that year. Gilbert remained consistently loyal to his royal uncle until his death at Bannockburn in 1314. His posthumous influence was, however, considerable because of the political battles which accompanied and followed the partition of his lands among his three sisters and their husbands. Last of all, the Earl of Pembroke himself was in his early or mid-thirties and of an age with Warwick, Lancaster, and Hereford. By 1307 he already had much diplomatic experience and had commanded royal armies in Scotland with mixed success. As the following chapters will try to show he was to be a close associate of the King until his death in 1324, except for one brief flirtation with Edward II's opponents between 1310 and 1312. In his political, governmental, diplomatic, and military activities Pembroke was to be one of the busiest earls during the reign.

To this list of English earls in 1307 should be added Gloucester's father-in-law, Richard de Burgh, Earl of Ulster, already a veteran of nearly fifty, who played a passing role in English affairs in the middle of the reign. Ireland also supplied a newcomer in the form of John de Bermingham, who was created Earl of Louth in 1319 as a reward for his defeat of Edward Bruce, and who became a follower of the Younger Despenser in 1321.[1] Four new English earls were created during Edward II's reign. The King's two half-brothers, Thomas of Brotherton and Edmund of Woodstock, became Earls of Norfolk and Kent in 1312 and 1321 respectively, years when royalist earls were in short supply. Norfolk was only twelve in 1312 and Kent was aged twenty at the time of his creation. Neither was of any real political significance. In 1322 Andrew de Harcla was made Earl of Carlisle after his contribution to the defeat of Lancaster at Boroughbridge, but was executed in the following year when he tried to negotiate with the Scots on his own initiative. The

---

[1] He made an indenture with the Younger Despenser on 28 May 1321, and soon after was forced to flee to Normandy by Despenser's opponents: Bodleian, Dugdale MS. 18, f. 39*v*.; S.C. 8/59/2917.

remaining addition was Hugh Despenser the Elder, who became Earl of Winchester in 1322 after the King had destroyed his own and Despenser's opponents.

The second-rank magnates are too numerous to discuss in detail and they were not in any case for the most part of any great importance in their own right. Of those who were, the most obvious example is the Elder Despenser mentioned above. Already aged forty-six in 1307 and with long experience in royal service, he was to become one of the most prominent and hated of the King's close associates in the early years of the reign. For reasons which are obscure but which may well have been personal, Despenser was a particular *bête noire* of the Earl of Lancaster. In the later years of the reign, and particularly after 1318, Despenser's importance owed a great deal to the growing influence of his son, Hugh Despenser the Younger. The Younger Despenser, who was only in his early twenties at the beginning of the reign, is the classic example of a man on the make who succeeded in making it. Having risen to power as a royal favourite in the manner typical of Edward II's reign, he became after 1322 the most powerful man in the kingdom, until he and his father were both destroyed in the upheaval of 1326. Another family combination of an elder and a younger man was that of the Mortimers. Roger Mortimer of Chirk was already an established figure in 1307 and was to be a loyal supporter of the Crown for most of the reign, until he joined in the revolt against the Despensers in 1321. But of far greater significance was his young nephew, Roger Mortimer of Wigmore, aged twenty in 1307, whose career was formed under Edward II. He too was loyal to the King until the 1321 revolt. Ironically, after the fall of the Despensers which he helped to engineer in 1326, he became a royal favourite on an even grander scale through his liaison with Edward II's widow Isabella and in 1330 met the same fate as his former opponents. Another important baronial figure was Bartholomew de Badlesmere, who began his career in the service of the Earl of Gloucester, and after reputedly leaving him to his death at Bannockburn entered royal service, where he rose fast. Like many others his opposition to the Despensers proved his undoing and he was executed in 1322. Lastly there are three other men who should be mentioned in passing, Roger Damory, Hugh

Audley the Younger, and William de Montacute. These were all young men of no importance early in the reign, who became royal favourites by early in 1317, the first two also becoming men of substance through royally sponsored marriages.

Despite Pembroke's close connections with France, he was by no means untypical of the leading English magnates of his time. There were in fact many of the English nobility who still had Continental links either through birth, marriage, or the tenure of land. The King himself was the prime example, being the son of a Castilian princess and the husband of a French one, and also, as Duke of Aquitaine, being the most powerful of the vassals of the French monarchy. Among the English earls the Earl of Richmond was the son of Duke John of Brittany and the brother of Arthur II and represented the latest link in the traditional connection between Brittany and the earldom of Richmond. He appears to have held no land in his native Brittany.[1] Piers Gaveston, the new Earl of Cornwall, was the son of Arnaud de Gabaston, a nobleman from Béarn in Gascony, and held land in Gascony by grant from Edward II.[2] Thomas of Lancaster's mother was Countess of Champagne and Brie and his youngest brother John was lord of Beaufort in Champagne. After John of Lancaster's death in 1317 Beaufort passed to his elder brother Henry, the future Earl of Lancaster and Leicester. Henry of Lancaster's French associations were also increased by his second marriage in about 1323 to Alix, the daughter of the famous Jean de Joinville, Seneschal of Champagne. The mother of the Earl of Hereford was the daughter of Enguerrand de Fiennes, lord of Guisnes, and his wife was the widow of Count John of Hainault, Holland, and Zeeland. The Earl of Surrey's wife was the daughter of Count Henry of Bar in the Empire while his brother-in-law, Edmund FitzAlan of Arundel, was the grandson through his mother of Tomasso Marquis of Saluzzo in Piedmont. Henry de Lacy of Lincoln was the grandson of an earlier Marquis of Saluzzo, Manfred III. Among the baronage Henry de Beaumont, a prominent magnate in the early years of Edward II's reign, was a younger son of Louis de Brienne, Vicomte of Beaumont in Maine and himself a younger son of John de Brienne, King

[1] See I. Lyubimenko, *Jean de Bretagne, Comte de Richmond* (Lille, 1908).
[2] See A. A. Taylor, 'The Career of Peter of Gaveston', M.A. (London, 1939).

of Jerusalem and Emperor of Constantinople. Lastly Roger Mortimer of Wigmore, the future Earl of March, was married to Joan de Geneville, whose father Piers de Geneville was a nephew of Jean de Joinville and whose mother Joan was the daughter of Count Hugh XII of La Marche and Angoulême and therefore also related to the Earl of Pembroke. In 1323 Geoffrey, a younger son of Roger Mortimer, inherited his mother's French lands and became lord of Couhé in Poitou, where he founded a junior line of the Mortimer family.[1]

In addition to these links with France and other parts of the Continent there were also several marriage connections among the earls of Edward II's reign. The most important of these were Thomas of Lancaster's marriage to Alice, the daughter of the Earl of Lincoln; the Earl of Arundel's to the sister of the Earl of Surrey; and the Earl of Cornwall's in 1309 to the Earl of Gloucester's sister Margaret. Gilbert de Clare of Gloucester was himself doubly linked with Richard de Burgh of Ulster by his own marriage to the earl's daughter Maud de Burgh and by that of the earl's son John de Burgh to Gilbert's sister Elizabeth de Clare. The Earl of Cornwall's marriage was designed to aid his naturalization as an established member of English magnate society, and during the reign there are several other cases of the way in which a good marriage could help in the rise from relative obscurity. The best example is that of the Gloucester heiresses who eventually in 1317 each received a share of their dead brother's inheritance. Eleanor de Clare married the Younger Despenser in 1306, at a time when she was not expected to have any great prospects of her own. After Gilbert de Clare's death in 1314 his other two sisters became valuable properties to be bestowed only on men trusted by the King. Gaveston's widow Margaret de Clare and John de Burgh's widow Elizabeth were therefore safely married off in 1317 to two of the King's current favourites, Hugh Audley the Younger and Roger Damory. Other marriages had political significance when they were contracted or were to acquire it later. It was certainly no accident that the Earl of Arundel chose to marry his son Richard to the Younger Despenser's daughter Isabel in February 1321 at a time when Despenser

[1] See G. W. Watson, 'Geoffrey de Mortemer and his Descendants', *Genealogist*, new series, vol. 22 (1906).

was rapidly becoming a very powerful figure. The marriage of Bartholomew de Badlesmere's daughter Elizabeth to Edmund, the eldest son of Roger Mortimer of Wigmore, in 1316 marked at the time Badlesmere's growing importance among the baronage, but became of greater significance in 1321 and 1322 when Badlesmere was associated with the Mortimers and other opponents of the Despensers. Similarly the marriage of Maurice de Berkeley's son Thomas to Margaret, the daughter of Roger Mortimer of Wigmore, in 1319 initially marked a change in

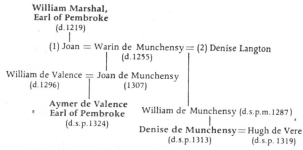

TABLE II. The relationship between Aymer de Valence and Denise de Munchensy

Maurice's social orbit but, as in Badlesmere's case, had political consequences in 1321.

As already seen, the Earl of Pembroke's personal relationships were with France rather than England, but he had a number of connections with the British Isles through the marriages of his sisters. Isabel de Valence married John Hastings of Abergavenny, whose son, another John Hastings, was for long one of Pembroke's retainers, and whose grandson Laurence Hastings was to be Aymer de Valence's eventual successor in 1339 as Earl of Pembroke. His sister Agnes married successively Maurice FitzGerald, an Irish magnate, Hugh de Balliol from Scotland, and John d'Avesnes, son of the Countess of Hainault. As she left no surviving heir her lands passed to Aymer in 1309. Pembroke's third sister Joan de Valence married John Comyn of Badenoch, who was murdered by his rival Robert Bruce in 1306. Their eldest son, another John Comyn, died fighting in Pembroke's retinue at Bannockburn in 1314 and one of their daughters, Joan, married David de Strathbogie Earl of Athol. Pembroke's cousin Denise de Munchensy, whose lands he inherited in 1313, was married to Hugh de Vere, brother of the Earl of Oxford.

One feature of Pembroke's background which he shared with several of the leading magnates was his family relationship to the King. Aymer de Valence's father had been Henry III's half-brother, and hence he was Edward II's cousin. The Earl of Richmond's mother Beatrice was a daughter of Henry III, making him Edward II's first cousin, as was Thomas of Lancaster through his father Edmund of Lancaster, Edward I's younger brother. The Earl of Hereford was Edward II's brother-in-law through his marriage to Edward I's daughter Elizabeth; the Earl of Gloucester's mother Joan of Acre was also a daughter of Edward I, so that Gilbert de Clare was the King's nephew; and the Earl of Surrey's wife Joan de Bar was Edward II's niece. Similarly, when Gaveston, the Younger Despenser, the Younger Audley, and Roger Damory married the Earl of Gloucester's sisters, they too were joining the royal circle. In effect most of the leading figures in the political crises of the reign were related in one way or another to the monarchy.

As an earl Aymer de Valence was already one of a very small group of magnates, and it would naturally be interesting to know how he compared with his fellows in landed and movable wealth. Until the hazardous business of studying baronial incomes has been carried much further no very reliable answers can be given to this question, but there are none the less a few pieces of evidence which give a general indication of the answer. At his death in 1324 Pembroke's lands in England, Wales (which he probably visited only rarely), and Ireland (which he may never have visited), were valued at about £3,000. But there is no indication of what his actual revenue was in practice, so this figure should not be taken too literally.[1] His French lands probably also made a considerable contribution to his revenues, but there is no evidence to clarify this problem.[2] Pembroke's wealth would have been considerable, were it not for the fact that he was suffering from financial stringency at the end of his life, as a result of a heavy ransom he had been forced to agree to in 1317 and possibly also because of delays in the

[1] The available evidence on Pembroke's lands is discussed in Chapter VIII.

[2] In addition to the revenues from his hereditary French lands there were also the 1,000 *livres tournois* a year which he received from the French monarchy in return for giving up his claims to La Marche and Angoulême.

payment of royal debts to him. As regards the Earl of Cornwall, a tentative estimate of £4,000 has been made for the value of his lands.[1] When the Earl of Hereford made his will in 1319 he believed himself to be sufficiently wealthy to be able to leave £2,000 to each of his four younger sons to purchase lands or marriages and 1,000 marks to his son-in-law Hugh de Courtenay.[2] The survey of the Earl of Arundel's lands made after his execution in 1326 is too incomplete to give a reliable idea of their value, but a sum of £524 in cash belonging to him was found in Chichester cathedral.[3] The most wealthy of the magnates in the period before 1322 were certainly the Earl of Lancaster, whose revenue in the year 1313 to 1314 was £6,661. 17s. 11d., and the last Clare Earl of Gloucester, whose lands were extended at £6,532. 5s. 7¾d. before their partition in 1317.[4] At the end of the reign there was no one to compare with the two Despensers, whose revenues from land and stores of cash may have exceeded those of any other magnate of the period, except perhaps the Earl of March at the beginning of Edward III's reign. The Despensers however were untypical, in that much of their wealth came from royal gifts and the extortion of land and property from other people and was not inherited as in the cases of Lancaster or Gloucester. After the Elder Despenser's death in 1326 money totalling £2,800 was found at two of his manors,[5] while his son had £5,886. 7s. 8d. deposited with the Italian banking firm of the Peruzzi at the end of 1324.[6] Surveys of the Despensers' lands made after their fall in 1326 have also survived, which, although incomplete, give some idea of their landed wealth. The Elder Despenser had lands in England alone worth at least £2,500, together with movable goods (not including the sums of money just mentioned) of over £3,000.[7] The Younger Despenser had English lands worth

---

[1] A. A. Taylor, op. cit., pp. 110, 128.

[2] T. H. Turner, 'The Will of Humphrey de Bohun, Earl of Hereford and Essex', *Archaeological Journal*, vol. 2 (1845), p. 346.

[3] E. 142/33, m. 3d.; C. 47/3/53/7. This figure is quoted by E. B. Fryde in 'The Deposits of the Younger Despenser with Italian Bankers', *Econ. Hist. R.*, 2nd series, vol. 3 (1950–1), p. 358.

[4] J. F. Baldwin, 'The Household Accounts of Henry Lacy and Thomas of Lancaster', *E.H.R.*, vol. 42 (1927), p. 198; J. C. Ward, *The Estates of the Clare Family, 1066–1317*, Ph.D. (London, 1962), p. 281.

[5] E. B. Fryde, op. cit., p. 358; E. 142/33, mm. 5, 10.

[6] E. B. Fryde, op. cit., p. 348.   [7] E. 142/33.

about £2,000, plus other lands there not valued and vast holdings in South Wales, which would have increased the total very considerably. His movable goods, excluding his money deposits with Italian bankers, came to around £2,500.[1] It must be emphasized that most of these figures are tentative and should be treated as evidence of the scale of wealth rather than as exact information.

In his studies of the magnates during the Wars of the Roses Mr. K. B. McFarlane has already pointed out the frequency with which magnate inheritances were diverted through lack of male heirs for reasons other than execution and warfare.[2] It is therefore interesting to see how far the same phenomenon operated in the reign of Edward II, when a number of prominent magnates also met violent deaths. At the beginning of the reign there were eleven English earls. The Earl of Richmond was unmarried and his inheritance passed to his nephew the Duke of Brittany. The Earl of Pembroke had one illegitimate son, who died before him, but no issue by either of his marriages, and his lands were divided up among the heirs of his two sisters Isabel and Joan. The Earl of Lincoln left only a daughter, who took her inheritance to her husband the Earl of Lancaster, who in turn left no direct heirs when he died in 1322, so that his lands passed to his brother Henry of Lancaster. Lancaster died violently, but he had been estranged from his wife since 1317 and his chances of an heir were therefore slim in any case. The Earl of Surrey had two illegitimate sons, but no heirs by his wife, from whom he unsuccessfully tried to obtain a separation, and his lands eventually went to his sister's son by the Earl of Arundel. The Earl of Cornwall left only a daughter when he was executed in 1312, but his lands were forfeited to the Crown, a fact which reduced any chance of their inheritance by a son even if he had one. The Earl of Gloucester's infant son had predeceased him when he was killed at Bannockburn in 1314. Gloucester left three sisters to divide his inheritance, but had he lived there is a reasonable chance that he would have had a male heir. The extinction of the Clare Earls of Gloucester can therefore be attributed to the effects of

[1] E. B. Fryde, op. cit., pp. 348–9; E. 142/33. My calculations of these figures agree generally with those of Dr. Fryde, although not always exactly.

[2] K. B. McFarlane, 'The Wars of the Roses', *Proceedings of the British Academy*, vol. 50 (1964), pp. 115–17.

war. The Earl of Oxford left no son when he died in 1331 and was succeeded by his nephew. Of the eleven earls only three had male heirs to succeed them. The Earl of Warwick died naturally in 1315, leaving a son Thomas de Beauchamp as a minor in royal custody; the Earl of Hereford was killed at Boroughbridge in 1322 and his lands forfeited, but he had five sons, the eldest of whom, John de Bohun, eventually succeeded him in 1327. The same is true of the Earl of Arundel's execution and forfeiture in 1326, since his son Richard FitzAlan was restored to the earldom in 1330. Of the earls created later in the reign the Earls of Winchester and Carlisle were both executed and forfeited their estates, the Earl of Kent was executed in 1330 leaving a son, and his brother the Earl of Norfolk died in 1338 without a male heir. Perhaps we should also add Roger Mortimer of Wigmore, the Earl of March, who was executed and forfeited in 1330, but whose grandson regained the earldom in 1354. All told, therefore, the effects of war and execution determined the fate only of the earldoms of Cornwall and Gloucester, plus those of Winchester and Carlisle among the new creations. As in the fifteenth century infertility and other natural hazards were far more potent than either the sword or the axe.

Taken as a whole the leading magnates of the reign of Edward II were a motley group, lacking any individuals of outstanding ability, a fact which may have been due in part to the youth and inexperience of many of them. The most able and constructive was certainly the veteran Earl of Lincoln, who appears to have tried to steer a steady course between opposition to the King's favourite Gaveston and loyalty to the King himself. No one else could both, as he did, have played an important part in the events which preceded the election of the Ordainers in 1310, and also have been appointed as Keeper of the Realm by the King in the same year during Edward II's absence in Scotland. His death in 1311 was a grave blow to the future political stability of England. Of the earls who were most adamant in their hostility to the King, Thomas of Lancaster was a man of great pretensions but of little ability. When in office he showed himself to be incompetent, and out of it he was for much of the time a lonely and petulant critic of the King and his favourites, with little or no idea of what he really

wanted, and a man who irritated the other earls as much as he
infuriated the King. He was not in reality the leader of a united
reformist and constitutional opposition as he has usually been
depicted. He and his cousin Edward II were alike, since both
lacked any talent for government and statesmanship. Lancaster's death brought him popular sanctification, but he was
no Simon de Montfort and his peers knew it. Lancaster's constant colleague and ally, Guy de Beauchamp of Warwick,
whose son Thomas was named after Lancaster, was possessed
of a greater ruthlessness in political action than any of his
fellows, as his role in the death of Gaveston showed. His early
death in 1315 may be counted as fortunate for the King. Of the
rest, the Earl of Hereford had some ability as a political leader,
as he proved by his role in the revolt of 1321, but he was not
outstanding; the Earl of Surrey and his brother-in-law Edmund
FitzAlan of Arundel were trimmers ready to accommodate
themselves to whoever was in power; the Earls of Richmond
and of Oxford were nonentities; the Earl of Gloucester died
too young for any talents he might have had to show themselves. Whatever capacities the Earl of Cornwall possessed in
the military or administrative spheres, he had a unique ability
for creating enemies and paid the price. The Elder Despenser,
the future Earl of Winchester, and his son Hugh Despenser the
Younger are both excellent examples of ability misapplied to
self-seeking and destructive ends. The royal favourites who
arose in the middle of the reign, Roger Damory, Hugh Audley
the Younger, and William de Montacute, no doubt had their
good points; but they were men of crude and overweening
ambition, whose actions nearly precipitated civil war in 1317
and made a peace settlement very difficult in 1318. Roger
Mortimer of Chirk is a rather shadowy figure, who appears to
have been swept along by the tide of events, but his nephew
Roger Mortimer of Wigmore came to prominence as a leader
of the revolt of 1321, and after 1322 became the most important
member of the opposition to the King and the Despensers which
triumphed in 1326. He must definitely be counted as one of the
abler men of the period, although this was not initially obvious.
Lastly there is Bartholomew de Badlesmere, whose rise in royal
service after the death of his original master, the Earl of
Gloucester, probably owed much to his ability. Although not

socially of the front rank, he was certainly one of the leading political figures between about 1316 and 1321, when his career was finally vitiated and he himself destroyed by the enmity towards him of both the King and Lancaster.

In this undistinguished company the Earl of Pembroke appears as a man of moderation and loyalty to the King, who had definite capacities as an administrator, diplomat, and perhaps even as a military commander. But the present study is not intended to portray Pembroke as a 'good thing' or as a remarkable political leader. In the long run, as later chapters will try to show, he was a man of modest talents, whose ability was not up to the demands placed upon it by the crises of the reign of Edward II. This rather gloomy picture of Pembroke and the other magnates should not however be seen as too personal a condemnation of them. They were probably not much better or worse than their counterparts at other times, and their reputation suffers in part through their misfortune in living during the reign of a king like Edward II, rather than in that of an Edward III, who knew both the importance of good relations with his magnates and also how to cultivate their support.

Past historians, viewing this crisis-ridden reign, have tended to imply that the English magnates of the period formed, apart from a few favourites, a united opposition to Edward II, with a coherent plan of reform. However, this description does not do justice to the delicate network of personal relations, interests, and patronage from which the association between the magnates and the monarchy was formed, and which in the end made up most of what we choose to call politics.[1] The reality was far more complex than this traditional oversimplified view, and the period can only be understood by treating the magnates as individuals with different interests, whose political attitudes to the Crown and to each other often altered with circumstances. None the less something did go gravely wrong with the political structure of England between 1307 and 1326, and this book is an attempt to find out why, using the career of the Earl of Pembroke as a point of concentration and focus.

---

[1] Professor V. H. Galbraith's comments on the nature of medieval politics in his review article, 'A New Life of Richard II', *History*, vol. 26 (1941–2), pp. 228–31, can very aptly be applied to the reign of Edward II.

I

The Formation of a Career, 1296 to June 1312

THE chief aim of this book is to assess the part played by the Earl of Pembroke in the crises of the reign of Edward II. This makes it necessary to omit any detailed treatment of his activities in the latter part of the reign of Edward I, interesting as these are. Instead this period is examined to show the factors that shaped his early career and helped to determine its pattern in later years. However, evidence on Pembroke's share in the politics of the first years of the new reign is sparse and for this reason full coverage is not attempted of such problems as the Coronation Oath of 1308 and the growth of the opposition to Gaveston between 1308 and 1310. It was not until the spring of 1312 that Pembroke emerged clearly and unequivocally as a leading political figure and from then until his death in 1324 it becomes possible to examine in detail both his own career and the political problems with which he was associated.

The career of Aymer de Valence effectively began after his father's death in June 1296,[1] although he had to wait a further eleven years before his mother's death in 1307 brought him the palatine lands and title of Earl of Pembroke. In the meantime, as lord of Montignac he began to make a name for himself in Edward I's wars and in the royal diplomacy for which his French connections made him especially suited.

His first independent public action was his participation in Edward I's campaign of 1297 in Flanders, where he commanded a retinue of forty-nine, having apparently been knighted just before he left England.[2] Aymer was one of the few substantial magnates to accompany the King, and his retinue was the largest of the non-household contingents, while

[1] Shortly afterwards he visited the King in Scotland between 23 Aug. and 2 Oct. to discuss problems arising from the disposal of his father's property: E. 101/505/25, m. 17; ibid. /26, m. 1.

[2] E. 101/6/28. His knighting is implied by his mother's request for an aid from her tenants in Sept. 1297: E. 101/505/27, m. 1.

one of his bannerets, Thomas de Berkeley, acted as constable of the army following the Earl of Hereford's refusal to serve in this capacity.[1] In the event there was little military activity in Flanders, but Aymer was able to serve in other ways, which included the supervision of the English fleet at Sluys.[2] He also took part, with the Archbishop of Dublin and others, in the negotiations which preceded the truce made with France at Groslingues on 23 November. One of the French envoys on this occasion was Aymer's father-in-law Ralph de Clermont, the Constable of France.[3]

Too much should not be made out of Aymer de Valence's support of Edward I in the crisis year of 1297, since he was still young and inexperienced and carried no political weight. None the less the Flemish expedition had an important part in forming the pattern of his career, since his close association with and support of the monarchy was to continue for the rest of Edward I's reign and during that of Edward II until his death in 1324. The only exception to this was his alliance with the Ordainers between 1310 and 1312, but it will be suggested that he was still basically loyal even during this period when he was apparently in opposition to the King. Aymer's father William de Valence had spent fifty years in the service of his half-brother Henry III and his nephew Edward I, so that loyalty to the monarchy was an entirely natural attitude for his son. The 1297 campaign was therefore an indication of Aymer's future political role, just as it also foreshadowed in essence his other roles as military leader, royal adviser, and diplomat.

During the next ten years much of Aymer de Valence's time was spent either on royal embassies to France or in the Scottish wars. This period of his career, however, lies outside the scope of the present study, and it may be summarized briefly. In May 1299 he was appointed as an envoy to make a French marriage treaty on behalf of the King, and for further French negotiations in 1301, 1302, and 1303. In 1304 he was commissioned to

    [1] See N. B. Lewis, 'The English Forces in Flanders in 1297', in *Studies in Medieval History Presented to F. M. Powicke* (Oxford, 1948). Berkeley was a former retainer of William de Valence and had made an indenture with Aymer just before the campaign: E. 101/68/1/1. Many of Aymer's retinue were in fact Berkeley's men: E. 101/6/28; C. 67/12, mm. 8–2; B.M., Add. MS. 7965, ff. 68–68*v*.
    [2] S.C. 1/47/76.
    [3] *F.*, vol. 1, pp. 881–2. A report on their negotiations is in S.C. 1/45/104B.

supervise the expenses of Prince Edward's proposed mission to do homage for Aquitaine.[1] Aymer served regularly in the Scottish campaigns, taking part in the Falkirk campaign of 1298 and in the battle itself.[2] He was again in Scotland in 1299, was present at the siege of Caerlaverock in July 1300, and also served in 1301 and 1302. As early as August 1301 his services in Scotland had been such that Edward I gave him the castle and barony of Bothwell, assessed at a value of £1,000.[3] In 1303 he acted as leader of the host and Lieutenant South of the Forth, and in April 1306, after the murder of his brother-in-law John Comyn by Robert Bruce, Aymer was appointed Lieutenant and Captain of the North with wide powers to harry the Scots. The following June he routed Bruce at Methven, but was himself defeated by Bruce at Loudoun Hill in May 1307.[4] During the years 1297 to 1307 Aymer had thus built up a very substantial record of valuable and loyal service to the King.

It is impossible to say what contact Aymer had with the young Prince Edward during the Scottish campaigns, but two letters written to him by Edward in July and August 1306, when both men were in Scotland, suggest they were at least on good terms and that Edward was ready to defer to his cousin's advice on the conduct of military operations. Edward's correspondence of 1304 and 1305 does not, on the other hand, show Aymer as a prominent member of his circle.[5] However, on his deathbed in July 1307 Edward I reputedly charged Aymer, the Earls of Lincoln and Warwick, and Robert Clifford with the future welfare of his son, which 'thai granted him with god wille'.[6] This again emphasizes the special position of trust Aymer had acquired under Edward I.

[1] *F.*, vol. 1, pp. 904, 940, 942, 967; *C.P.R., 1292–1301*, p. 580; *C. Cl. R., 1302–7*, p. 81.   [2] See E. 101/6/39, mm. 2, 3.
   [3] C. 67/14, m. 11; ibid. /15, m. 16; N. H. Nicolas, *The Siege of Caerlaverock* (London, 1828), p. 17; *Cal. of Documents relating to Scotland, 1272–1357*, vol. 2, nos. 1214, 1280.
   [4] S.C. 1/48/116; ibid. /31/33; *F.*, vol. 1, p. 983; G. W. S. Barrow, *Robert Bruce and the Community of the Realm of Scotland* (London, 1965), pp. 215–16. Aymer's conduct of operations in 1306 is illuminated by a series of letters addressed to him by Edward I: S.C. 1/47/77–91.
   [5] S.C. 1/49/2, 3; *Letters of Edward Prince of Wales, 1304–5*, ed. H. Johnstone, Roxburghe Club, vol. 194 (Cambridge, 1931).
   [6] *The Brut*, ed. F. Brie (London, 1906–8), vol. 1, p. 202. This is the source of W. Pakington's later account in *Collectanea of John Leland*, vol. 1, p. 461.

Aymer's services to the monarchy continued after Prince Edward's accession on 8 July 1307. On 30 August he was appointed Keeper of Scotland, agreeing to stay there until 2 February 1308; but on 13 September he was replaced by the Earl of Richmond and left Scotland by royal licence on 12 October.[1] There is no reason to compare Aymer's removal with that of Walter Langton, the former Treasurer, and to suppose that his supercession was the result of a loss of royal favour or, as has been suggested, that it turned him into a royal opponent.[2] Aymer was replaced solely because he was needed for the more urgent business of helping to negotiate the terms of the contract for Edward II's marriage to Isabella, the daughter of Philip IV of France.

On 6 November the Earl of Pembroke, as Aymer de Valence had just become,[3] was appointed to undertake this new task, together with the Bishops of Durham and Norwich, the Earl of Lincoln, and others. He and his colleagues were in France by the end of November and remained there until they returned briefly in mid-January to meet the King at Dover and escort him to Boulogne for his marriage.[4] Pembroke therefore missed the Wallingford tournament on 2 December at which Edward II's Gascon favourite, Piers Gaveston the new Earl of Cornwall, antagonized the other earls who took part and began to form the future baronial opposition against himself and the King.[5] Pembroke escaped this particular strain on his loyalty but it was nevertheless apparent that, even without the aggravating effect of Gaveston's conduct, reform was urgently needed to end causes of grievance against the royal administration,

---

[1] *F.*, vol. 2, pp. 4, 6; B.M., Add. MS. 35093, f. 3*v*.; E. 101/373/23, f. 2. See also P. M. Barnes and C. W. S Barrow, 'The Movements of Robert Bruce between September 1307 and May 1308', *Scottish Historical Review*, vol. 49 (April 1970), p. 47.

[2] J. C. Davies, *The Baronial Opposition to Edward II* (Cambridge, 1918), p. 111.

[3] His mother, the Countess of Pembroke, died in September. He received his lands on 27 Oct.: *C.F.R., 1307–19*, p. 6.

[4] *F.*, vol. 2, pp. 11–12. Pembroke probably arrived at Boulogne on 25 Nov. at the same time as a section of the royal household which was sent ahead of the King to make arrangements for his marriage: E. 101/624/15, m. 1. Pembroke was in the King's company at Dover on 15 Jan. and presumably crossed to Boulogne with him on 21 Jan. 1308: E. 101/373/6, m. 2.

[5] *Vita Edwardi Secundi*, ed. N. Denholm-Young (London, 1957), p. 2. Henceforward cited as *Vita*. *Trokelowe*, p. 65, says that Pembroke was present but misdates the tournament to after the Coronation in Feb. 1308.

such as the abuse of the royal rights of purveyance. The real question at issue was whether a group of magnates sympathetic to the new King could induce him to undertake reforms of his own free will or whether pressure would instead come from other less friendly magnates, whose determination would be strengthened by hatred of Gaveston. This was the background to an important document drawn up at Boulogne on 31 January 1308 a few days after Edward II's marriage there and shortly before his return to England.

This document exists in two transcripts among the Dugdale manuscripts in the Bodleian, an original copy which was in the Earl of Lancaster's archives in 1322 having apparently not survived.[1] It was referred to by Dugdale himself in his *Baronage*, but its text appears to be unknown to modern writers except Mr. N. Denholm-Young.[2] It is drawn up as letters patent of the Bishop of Durham, the Earls of Lincoln, Surrey, Pembroke, and Hereford, Robert Clifford, Payn Tybetot, Henry de Grey, John Botetourt, and John de Berwick. They declared that since they were bound by fealty to preserve the King's honour and the rights of his Crown, they had agreed by common assent to do all within their legal power to protect and maintain his honour. They also promised to redress and amend everything that had been done 'avant ces heurs' against the King's honour and rights as well as all oppressions against his people 'que ont este fait et uncore se font de jour en jour'. All swore to uphold the agreement and gave the Bishop of Durham powers to excommunicate anyone who broke it.

Denholm-Young suggests the agreement was linked with the new form of Coronation Oath introduced a few weeks later, but admits that the connection is not obvious, and sees it as a possible reaction to Gaveston's appointment as Regent. In fact any connection with the Oath is very unlikely. Those who framed the document had in mind the long-standing administrative abuses committed by royal officers, especially during the previous reign, matters which all sections of political opinion

---

[1] Bodleian, Dugdale MS. 18, ff. 1v., 80; D.L. 41/1/37, m. 7. See the full text in Appendix 4.

[2] W. Dugdale, *Baronage* (London, 1675), vol. 1, p. 183, note. Davies, op. cit., p. 34, and B. Wilkinson, *Constitutional History of Medieval England*, vol. 3 (London, 1958), p. 68, mention Dugdale's note. A few lines are quoted by N. Denholm-Young in *History and Heraldry, 1254–1310* (Oxford, 1965), pp. 130–1.

could agree needed reform. Who actually inspired this agreement is unknown but the most likely candidates are the Bishop of Durham or the Earl of Lincoln, both of them men of long experience. The tone of the document's references to the King appears friendly, and the omission of any mention of Gaveston,[1] although his actions certainly added to the urgency of the situation, may have been meant to spare the King embarrassment. It is implausible that the parties to the agreement would have chosen Boulogne to draw up such a document, when the King was present and would know of their actions, if they had been his opponents.[2] The Bishop, Lincoln, Pembroke, and John de Berwick had also just negotiated the King's marriage contract, Clifford was Marshal of the royal household, and Berwick was a royal clerk. Neither is there anything in the earlier careers of Pembroke or any of the other leading parties to suggest that at this time they were likely to be anything but loyal to the King. The Bishop had been one of Edward I's closest advisers and, although he fell out with the King in 1302, was on very cordial terms with Prince Edward and predictably returned to favour after his accession. Lincoln also had a long record of royal service[3] and, although later a prominent Ordainer, was one of the few earls to stay with Edward after 1310. It may also not be fanciful to connect the presence of

[1] The Earls of Lincoln, Surrey, Hereford, and Pembroke had all witnessed Gaveston's creation as Earl of Cornwall at Dumfries on 6 August 1307 and had presumably then approved of it: *F.*, vol. 2, p. 2. Lincoln's approval is confirmed by the author of the *Vita*, p. 1.

[2] There is no necessary reason for supposing either that Edward II was kept in ignorance of what was being done at Boulogne or that pressure was being brought to bear upon him. It is more likely that the King had shown signs of willingness to consider reform. Most of the matters at issue were the result of administrative practices developed in the reign of Edward I and already complained about then, so that Edward II could not be held personally responsible for them and would not lose face by agreeing to amend them. Unfortunately events in England moved so swiftly after the King's return that it was impossible to test the Boulogne agreement in practice. Because all later demands for reform were made by the opponents of the King and were coupled with attempts to remove Gaveston, Edward II was no longer capable of agreeing to changes unless they were forced upon him.

[3] See C. M. Fraser, *A History of Antony Bek* (Oxford, 1957), pp. 211–14. Bek and Lincoln were among the first to do homage to Edward II at Carlisle after his father's death and were reputedly added to Edward II's council soon after his accession: D.L. 34/12; B.M., Harleian MS. 530, f. 8 (Dunmow chronicle). Lincoln's part in the events of 1307 to 1311 was a very important one, which still requires close examination. Lincoln appears to have turned against Gaveston in 1308 more in sorrow than in anger: *Vita*, p. 4.

Pembroke, Lincoln, and Clifford with Edward I's charge to them of the previous July. There can be little doubt that, both before the King left England and while he was at Boulogne, there was much evidence of the rising force of baronial opposition within England, and the natural conclusion is that, in making the Boulogne agreement, Pembroke and his colleagues were consciously aligning themselves for the time being upon the side of the King. Their hope was that, if the King would agree to the reform of abuses in the royal administration which the King's opponents would soon be demanding, they would be able to prevent the political situation from getting out of control and so be able to achieve their primary purpose of preserving the honour and rights of the King.

Whatever the immediate purpose of the Boulogne agreement and the hopes of its authors, the confused events of the following months soon swallowed it up. By April 1308 relations between the King and magnates had deteriorated to such an extent that the latter were openly demanding that Gaveston should be exiled. The passions that were generated by these events are well illustrated in a letter by an unknown author written on 14 May, four days before Edward II agreed to Gaveston's exile. After reporting that the French King had sent the Abbot of Saint-Germain-des-Prés and three knights to put pressure on Edward II to accept the demands of Gaveston's opponents, the writer added a rumour that Philip IV and his sister, Edward I's widow, had sent £40,000 to the Earls of Lincoln and Pembroke for their expenses in proceeding against Gaveston.[1] There is little doubt that Pembroke must have at least accepted the necessity of Gaveston's exile, but this document would suggest he took a leading role in the movement. It is true that a great deal remains obscure both about developments in 1308 in general and about Pembroke's place in them, and it is evident that in such a situation the political alignments of individual magnates were likely to be very fluid;[2] but it is also true that

[1] Lincoln, Dean and Chapter Muniments, D. II/56/1, no. 39. I owe this reference to Dr. J. R. Maddicott.

[2] Because there is so little evidence of Pembroke's activities at the critical moments early in 1308 any detailed discussion of the problem of the Coronation Oath is best omitted. No new material has come to light to help clarify the problem. My own impression is that the importance of the oath has been greatly exaggerated and I am inclined to agree with the views of H. G. Richardson in his

the rumours contained in this letter do not fit what else is known of Pembroke at this period. Other evidence suggests that Pembroke was still on good terms with the King. In November 1308 Edward assisted Pembroke in recovering a debt at the Exchequer and gave him the important lordship of Haverfordwest in Pembrokeshire; in March 1309 the King also approved his purchase of Hertford and gave him diplomatic help in business he was prosecuting at the court of Philip IV of France.[1] If it would appear from all this that the King was trying to win Pembroke over by making valuable concessions,[2] then there is also the awkward fact that in March 1309 Pembroke went on a royal embassy to Avignon, together with the Earl of Richmond and Bishops of Worcester and Norwich, to ask the Pope to reverse Archbishop Winchelsey's excommunication of Gaveston.[3] This was achieved on 25 April and led directly to Gaveston's return to England at the end of June.[4] If Pembroke really had been one of Gaveston's most prominent opponents in 1308 then he had made a remarkable volte-face. On the whole it seems more likely that up to this point Pembroke's sympathies still lay with the King as they had done at Boulogne in January 1308.

article 'The English Coronation Oath', in *Speculum*, vol. 24 (1949), and with Professor M. McKisack in *The Fourteenth Century*, p. 6. Generally speaking it is unwise to assume that in a period of fast-moving events the opposition which faced Edward II in April 1308 was necessarily fully formed two months earlier in February. The chronicles do not suggest Pembroke was a leader of the anti-Gaveston movement in 1308.

[1] E. 368/79, m. 28*d*.; *C.P.R., 1307–13*, pp. 145, 153; *G.R., 1307–17*, no. 208.

[2] M. McKisack in *The Fourteenth Century*, p. 7, suggests the King was trying to conciliate a number of the magnates during 1308 and 1309. This is probably true in some instances even if it is not in Pembroke's case. Gaveston's removal may in itself have contributed to a more peaceful atmosphere. Edward II's household account roll for this period gives interesting evidence of a number of magnates having social dealings with the King. For instance, on 22 Sept. he was visited by the Earls of Surrey and Lancaster, on 24 Nov. 'many magnates' dined with the King, between 19 Feb. and 3 Mar. 1309 the Earls of Lincoln, Richmond, and Gloucester dined with him, as did the Earl of Hereford on 1 June: Bodleian, MS. Latin Hist. C. 5, mm. 3, 4, 7, 10.

[3] *F.*, vol. 2, p. 68. Pembroke's account for this mission ran between 6 Mar. and 17 July: E. 101/372/23. He was still at Avignon on 15 and 24 May and then returned to England, making a short stay at his estates at Rancon in Poitou in June: *G.R., 1307–17*, no. 260; *Trésor des Chartes*, vol. 1, no. 1343; S.C. 1/50/56, 57.

[4] *Reg. Swinfield*, Canterbury and York Series, vol. 6 (London, 1909), p. 451. Gaveston arrived in Chester from Dublin on 27 June: Bodleian, MS. Latin Hist. C. 5, m. 10.

On the other hand there is no doubt that Pembroke's attitude did alter radically between Gaveston's return to England and the opening of the Parliament of February 1310. The order of 7 February 1310 forbidding Pembroke, Lancaster, Hereford, and Warwick to bring armed retainers to this assembly is a clear indication of the changed situation, and shows how some of the prominent future Ordainers were already acting together.[1] One major reason for Pembroke's new alignment was the royal government's admitted failure to implement the reforms agreed upon at Stamford in August 1309.[2] Pembroke's adherence to the Boulogne agreement of 1308 had been an attempt to achieve reform from within the royal circle but, with the obvious failure of this approach, he could hardly refuse to support any fresh moves for reform, even if these were backed by magnates such as Lancaster and Warwick who were personally hostile to the King. The second reason was certainly Gaveston's arrogant behaviour since his return, symbolized by his abusive references to Pembroke and other magnates, one writer even describing Pembroke as his chief enemy.[3] In 1309 Pembroke's loyalty to the King had overcome his antipathy to Gaveston. Pembroke's adherence to the Ordainers in 1310 is thus explicable, but in view of the earlier course of his career, it is reasonable to suggest that he still remained basically loyal to the King and believed he had no alternative course of action. The election on 20 March[4] of the moderate Pembroke as the first of the Ordainers, together with the Earl of Lincoln, may indeed have been intended to reassure Edward. However, unlike his fellow Ordainers, Lincoln, Gloucester, and Richmond, Pembroke did not continue to serve the King while acting as an Ordainer. This may have been caused by Gaveston's continued presence as well as a desire not to compromise his value as a reformer by seeming too close to the King. But it does not follow that his attitude to the King was the same as that of the extreme Ordainers like Lancaster or Warwick. It would be wrong to see the Ordainers as a solidly knit group, and there were indeed

[1] *C.P.R., 1307–13*, p. 207.   [2] See *C. Cl. R., 1307–13*, p. 189: 10 Dec. 1309.
[3] See *Historia Anglicana of Thomas Walsingham*, ed. H. T. Riley (London, 1863), vol. 1, p. 115, for Gaveston's description of Pembroke as Joseph the Jew; *Lanercost*, p. 218. See also *Vita*, p. 11.
[4] *P.W.*, vol. 2, part 1, p. 43. A notarial certificate of 17 Mar. relating to the appointment of the Ordainers survives as B.M., Cotton Charter XVI. 58.

probably as many points of view as there were Ordainers. It is also most important to realize that in 1310 Pembroke and others were united as much by loyalty to their fellow magnates as by other reasons.

For the next two years Pembroke was to be closely associated with the work of the Ordainers,[1] but it is significant that the King continued to value his advice and was unwilling at first to accept the fact of his opposition. On 16 June 1310 Edward wrote asking him to attend a Council meeting at Westminster on Scotland, a subject in which he was well experienced, and personally appealed to him to serve in the coming Scottish campaign. Despite Pembroke's refusal, Edward appealed again on 4 July, even offering to send four of his councillors to meet him at Leicester.[2] However, this attempt to weaken Pembroke's resolve was no more successful than Hereford's efforts to detach Warenne from the King a little later.[3] Nor did Pembroke and several other Ordainers answer the military summons for 8 September in person, although they did observe the letter of their obligations by sending token forces, Pembroke's contingent being ten men representing five fees.[4]

Instead of going to Scotland, Pembroke remained in London to begin the work of reform. Little is known of his role as an Ordainer during the following twelve months, except that in February 1311 he, Lancaster, Hereford, and Warwick were said to be in process of deciding certain matters, which at least suggests that these four earls took the leading part in drafting the Ordinances. Pembroke and his three colleagues were still busy in London in July[5] and witnessed the final publication of the Ordinances on 27 September, while Pembroke was also

---

[1] Pembroke had withdrawn to Hertford by 10 Apr.: *Cat. Anc. Deeds*, vol. 4, p. 35. On 24 May the King gave authority to the Earls of Gloucester, Lincoln, Richmond, and Arundel to give safe conducts to Pembroke, Hereford, and Warwick to visit him at Kennington: *C.P.R., 1307–13*, p. 228. There is no evidence on what happened at this meeting if it took place.

[2] S.C. 1/49/6, 7. In the first letter Edward II told Pembroke that the Earls of Gloucester, Surrey, Cornwall, and Richmond had all agreed to go to Scotland. On 4 July the King proposed to send the Bishop of London, the Earls of Lincoln and Richmond, and Robert Clifford to meet Pembroke at Leicester on 26 July.

[3] D.L. 34/8 (probably dated 23 Jan. 1311).

[4] *Ann. Lond.*, p. 174; *Vita*, p. 11; C. 47/5/8. Hereford, Warwick, and Lancaster sent military service representing 5, 5, and 8 fees: ibid.

[5] *Ann. Lond.*, p. 174; C. 47/22/10/10; F. M. Powicke and C. R. Cheney, *Councils and Synods* (Oxford, 1964), vol. 2, part 2, p. 1314.

present at the appointment of new sheriffs in October.[1] Gaveston's unauthorized return from exile at the end of 1311 led to a fresh crisis, which Archbishop Winchelsey tried to resolve by calling a council of prelates and magnates to meet at St. Paul's on 13 March 1312.[2] Part of the council's business was to try to prevent Walter Langton, whom the King had appointed as Treasurer contrary to the Ordinances, from presiding at the Exchequer. Pembroke, Hereford, and John Botetourt were deputed to do this and succeeded in their task on 3 and 4 April.[3]

But for present purposes the council's most important decision was the appointment of Pembroke and the Earl of Surrey, John de Warenne, to pursue and capture Gaveston. Pembroke's known moderation and previous possession of royal confidence, and the fact that Warenne had remained an active royal supporter and had joined the Ordainers at this juncture only through the Archbishop's personal persuasion, made the two earls the ideal choice for this role. Gaveston's most violent enemies, Lancaster, Warwick, and Hereford,[4] probably wished to reassure the King as to Gaveston's safety if he were captured and may even have envisaged the necessity of arresting him in the King's presence. In the event this decision proved a momentous one for the King and Gaveston, for the Ordainers, and most of all for Pembroke himself.

The pursuit of Gaveston approached its climax on 5 May when he left Tynemouth for the castle of Scarborough where the King had decided to place him for safety.[5] Soon afterwards Pembroke and his companions, Warenne, Henry Percy, and Robert Clifford, caught up with him and by 17 May the siege of Scarborough was well under way.[6] Gaveston's isolation from royal help was ensured by the presence between Scarborough and Knaresborough, where the King was staying, of the Earl of Lancaster, who also sent troops to the siege.[7]

[1] *Stats. of Realm*, vol. 1, p. 167; E. 368/82, m. 2 (schedule).
[2] *Reg. Gandavo*, Canterbury and York Series, vol. 40 (London, 1934), pp. 418–19. Pembroke was certainly present by 25 Mar.: *Cat. Anc. Deeds*, vol. 5, p. 163.
[3] E. 159/85, m. 52. Printed in J. C. Davies, op. cit., pp. 551–2.
[4] *Ann. Lond.*, pp. 203–4; *Trokelowe*, p. 74; *Vita*, pp. 22–3.
[5] *C. Cl. R., 1307–13*, p. 460. Lancaster had entered Newcastle close by Tynemouth on the previous day: ibid. Gaveston was given custody of Scarborough on 4 Apr.: *C.P.R., 1307–13*, p. 454.
[6] *C. Cl. R., 1307–13*, p. 460. For a detailed account of the siege see A. A. Taylor, op. cit.   [7] *Vita*, pp. 23–4; S.C. 8/205/10204.

Gaveston was therefore forced to surrender on 19 May after agreeing to terms with Pembroke, Warenne, and Percy.

Accounts of the events prior to Gaveston's surrender conflict. A writer hostile to the King, and to Pembroke's own apparently leading part in the affair, says that Gaveston sent messengers to ask for the King's aid when his position became desperate, that the King then summoned Pembroke secretly, and by persuasion and a £1,000 bribe made him agree to protect Gaveston. The *Vita* also says the King took the initiative in offering detailed terms, but that Gaveston himself was responsible for actually winning Pembroke over to their acceptance, a view that the *Annals of London* also support.[1] The truth is hard to determine, but the King certainly remained in contact with Gaveston by letter during the siege[2] and so may well have taken a personal part in the negotiations. The charge of corruption against Pembroke is unlikely and can be rejected, but either Pembroke or one of his retainers probably did visit the King at York. The fairly mild surrender terms suggest that they were made in return for some clear assurances by the King.

Two copies of Gaveston's surrender terms are known, so its details are not in any doubt.[3] Pembroke, Warenne, and Percy promised on behalf of the community of the realm to take Gaveston to St. Mary's Abbey, York,[4] where they would show their agreement with him to the King and to Lancaster or his representative. If the King were not willing to continue negotiations over Gaveston's future with the prelates, earls, and barons between then and 1 August following, Pembroke and his colleagues promised to restore Scarborough to Gaveston and to guarantee his safety until that date. All three agreed to forfeit all their property if any harm came to Gaveston, who in turn promised not to try and persuade the King to alter any

---

[1] *Flores*, vol. 3, p. 150; *Vita*, p. 24; *Ann. Lond.*, p. 204.

[2] B.M., Cotton MS. Nero C. VIII, ff. 88, 107*v*. (these are royal household accounts).

[3] *Ann. Lond.*, pp. 204–6; *Litterae Cantuarienses*, ed. J. B. Sheppard, R.S. (London, 1887–9), vol. 3, pp. 388–93 (this is derived from Canterbury Register I, ff. 365*v*.–366, which is the probable source of the text in another Canterbury MS., B.M., Harleian MS. 636, f. 233).

[4] In Taylor, op. cit., p. 333, Everwyk (York) is misread as Warwick. An interesting detail in the surrender agreement is the use by Pembroke, etc., of the phrase 'la Cummunalte du reaume Dengleterre' in a context where it can only refer to the magnates.

points in the agreement. Given good faith on both sides a solution might have been possible, but the history of Gaveston's previous exiles made mutual suspicion far more likely.

Pembroke did, however, try to carry out the terms, and by 26 May he, Warenne, and Percy had joined the King at York, where they stayed until at least 28 May. Gaveston was probably with them in accordance with their agreement, although there is no mention of him. If Lancaster or an envoy appeared at this point, his presence is unrecorded. It is possible, as the writer of the *Vita* claims, writing with hindsight, that Pembroke had negotiated on his own initiative and without consulting the other magnates,[1] and that Lancaster did not feel bound by the agreement. But it is difficult to believe this, since Lancaster's proximity to Scarborough during the siege could easily have allowed him to influence the surrender terms, and Pembroke could at the very least hardly have avoided informing him of what was happening. This would apply equally if the St. Paul's council had in fact given Pembroke full powers to negotiate a surrender. Lancaster could certainly not have pleaded ignorance of the terms as an excuse for not appearing at York. In any case Gaveston's surrender was only provisional, pending a final agreement by all the magnates, and Pembroke could not therefore be accused of making a full settlement without authority.

With or without Lancaster, there probably were discussions at York between Pembroke and the King, since a *colloquium* is said to have been held at which Edward promised to satisfy all the earls' demands, while Pembroke, Warenne, and Percy renewed their oaths to forfeit their land if any harm came to Gaveston.[2] The impression that serious efforts were being made to implement the surrender terms is strengthened by the summons on 3 June of a Parliament to meet at Lincoln on 8 July,[3] within the period laid down in the surrender. At the end of the York meeting Gaveston was put in Pembroke's personal custody, perhaps at the latter's request, to be taken south for greater safety,[4] and the two men set out early in June.

---

[1] C. 53/98, m. 2; *Vita*, p. 24.
[2] *Trokelowe*, p. 76.
[3] *P.W.*, vol. 2, part 1, p. 72.
[4] *Trokelowe*, p. 76; *Vita*, p. 24; *Murimuth*, p. 17; *Flores*, vol. 3, pp. 150, 336.

The placing of Gaveston in Pembroke's custody was not in itself a breach of the Scarborough agreement, which required his safe keeping till 1 August, but it may have been enough to arouse suspicions in the minds of some of the other magnates, who were unwilling to trust any undertaking by the King and Gaveston, and who no doubt remembered Pembroke's previous loyalty to the King. The decision to take Gaveston south and to place him in Wallingford, which was a part of the Cornwall earldom and had been restored to Gaveston in February 1312,[1] may have crystallized such suspicions, through the fear that he might successfully defy the magnates in a castle situated close to several royal fortresses and hence more easily defensible than Scarborough had been. In such an atmosphere what followed is understandable.

Pembroke and his prisoner travelled south until on 9 June they reached Deddington in Oxfordshire, at that time held in part by the Younger Despenser and therefore probably a safe place. Pembroke then left him and a few retainers at the house of the rector and went to visit his wife at his manor of Bampton about twenty miles away.[2] All this time the King had kept in constant touch with Gaveston.[3] On the morning of 10 June the Earl of Warwick came to Deddington, captured Gaveston, and took him to Warwick; and he was executed nearby on 19 June.[4]

It seems likely that Warwick was acting on his own initiative in capturing Gaveston. After he lodged him in Warwick castle he then awaited the arrival of Lancaster, Hereford, and Arundel before taking further action. The magnates present then assured one another of their mutual support in the proposed execution and its possible consequences. On 18 June, the day before the execution, John Botetourt gave his approval of Gaveston's capture and intended death, while Warwick and Lancaster gave Hereford separate guarantees in return for his support.[5]

---

[1] *Trokelowe*, p. 76; *C. Ch. R., 1300–26*, p. 131; *C.P.R., 1307–13*, p. 429.

[2] *Ann. Lond.*, p. 206; *Flores*, vol. 3, p. 151; H. M. Colvin, *A History of Deddington* (London, 1963), pp. 33–4.

[3] B.M., Cotton MS. Nero C. VIII, ff. 86, 105.

[4] *Ann. Lond.*, pp. 206–7. Details of Gaveston's capture are confirmed in letters patent of John Botetourt on 18 June: Bodleian, Dugdale MS. 15, p. 293; Bodleian, Tanner MS. 90, p. 1. See Taylor, op. cit., for an account of the execution.

[5] Bodleian, Laud Misc. MS. 529, f. 104; Bodleian, Dugdale MS. 15, p. 293; Bodleian, Tanner MS. 90, p. 1; D.L. 25/1982; D.L. 34/13.

Several writers hint at suspicions that Pembroke deliberately connived at Gaveston's capture,[1] but in view of his later conduct this interpretation must be rejected. Pembroke probably did not realize that Warwick was pursuing him or that he was so close behind him, and his separation from Gaveston at Deddington can at worst be described as an act of extreme foolishness.

Between 10 and 19 June Pembroke tried to regain custody of Gaveston and to vindicate his own reputation. Pembroke's plea to the Earl of Gloucester to help him avoid permanent disgrace and the forfeiture of his lands received the comfortless reply that Warwick had acted with Pembroke's counsel and aid,[2] and that he should negotiate more carefully in future. He then appealed to the clerks and burgesses of the university and town of Oxford to help him recover Gaveston or at least to recognize the justice of his case and clear him of suspicion; but both groups refused all help.[3]

Gaveston's death marked a clear turning-point in Pembroke's career. His first prompt reaction was to abandon his fellow Ordainers, Gaveston's executioners. Together with Warenne, he went over to unequivocal support of the King, while the other party to Gaveston's surrender, Henry Percy, equally definitely joined the King's opponents.[4] From 1312 to 1324 Pembroke was to be a constant and trusted ally of the King and, especially in the two years after 1312, often took a leading part in the royal administration. The circumstances of Gaveston's death and the slur cast upon his reputation were undoubtedly Pembroke's prime motive for rejoining the King. But it is also clear that Pembroke was returning to his natural loyalty, which his record of royal service from 1297 to 1309 had already made evident. Gaveston's presence had probably been the major reason for the break in Pembroke's personal relations with the King after 1310, and his removal, even by peaceful means, would have led to an eventual resumption of that connection.

---

[1] *Trokelowe*, p. 76; *Vita*, p. 26; *Melsa*, vol. 2, p. 327; *Vita et Mors*, p. 298.

[2] Gloucester meant the St. Paul's assembly in March when the earls had bound themselves to capture Gaveston: *Vita*, p. 22. The Earl of Gloucester was in the Tewkesbury area in early June: *C.P.R., 1307–13*, p. 223.   [3] *Vita*, pp. 25–6.

[4] *Ann. Lond.*, p. 208; *Flores*, vol. 3, p. 336 (Warenne's support of the Ordainers dated only from March); D.L. 25/1900 (Percy's bond with Hereford on 3 July).

Although in future years Pembroke remained loyal to the concept of reform contained in the Ordinances, the behaviour of the other Ordainers could be regarded as ending his loyalty to them as fellow magnates. With Pembroke's departure the Ordainers were split irrevocably. For his own part the King, who was no doubt delighted to see his enemies divided and regain the services of an experienced and proven man, accepted Pembroke back with alacrity.[1]

[1] *Ann. Lond.*, p. 208.

II

The Armed Truce
June 1312 to October 1313

THE period between the death of Gaveston in June 1312 and
the settlement of October 1313 by which Gaveston's opponents
were formally pardoned for their share in his pursuit and
execution was one of great tension. Negotiations to try to resolve the crisis began in the late summer of 1312 and achieved
some outward success in the preliminary peace treaty between
the King and his baronial enemies in December 1312. But in
reality both sides were still very wary and were not wholly
sincere in their attempts to reach agreement, so that the possibility of further violence remained. The negotiations dragged
on in this atmosphere until the autumn of 1313, when a final
peace was made more from exhaustion than from conviction.
Accordingly Gaveston's death still cast a shadow over English
politics after 1313. The part played in these events by the Earl
of Pembroke was a considerable one, although it is not always
possible to follow it in precise detail. None the less there is
sufficient evidence to show that Pembroke had now become one
of the most important political figures in the country.

The events immediately after Gaveston's death and Pembroke's change of allegiance are obscure. Pembroke and
Warenne had apparently rejoined the King in Lincolnshire by
6 July and then travelled south with him via Pembroke's own
castle of Hertford, reaching Westminster on 14 July.[1] The
opposition magnates are said to have gathered at Worcester at
the end of June.[2] For the moment, then, both sides remained
aloof, uncertain as to the next step.

During July and August 1312 open warfare remained a possibility, and the magnates remained in arms for their own safety.

[1] C. 53/98, m. 2; E. 101/375/8, f. 27; ibid. /374/17.
[2] *Vita*, p. 29. Warwick was in the area in late June and Hereford and Percy
were certainly there on 3 July: B.M., Add. MS. 28024, ff. 122, 122v. (Beauchamp
Cartulary); D.L. 25/1900.

On the King's side there was a heated debate over whether to fight or negotiate. The hostile *Flores* says the King was guided by treacherous and evil advisers, foremost among whom was Pembroke. The usually well-informed and more balanced *Vita* takes a similar view, saying that the King was supported in his wish to destroy Gaveston's killers by Pembroke, who had good reason to do so, by the Elder Despenser, Henry de Beaumont, Edmund Mauley, and by Gaveston's retainers. Others pointed out the danger of the King being captured or of a Scottish invasion if civil war broke out, but are said to have been over-ruled.[1] If he had wanted to fight, the King would certainly have had the retinues of Pembroke, Warenne, Despenser, and Beaumont, as one writer claims. The total figure of 1,000 men-at-arms given by the same author is greatly exaggerated, but additional foot soldiers were collected in August in the counties around London, as well as a number of men who were brought from Ponthieu.[2] It is impossible fully to confirm or deny the chroniclers' accounts of Pembroke's conduct at this time. He had ample reason to be embittered against Lancaster, Warwick, Hereford, and their supporters, and may briefly have been tempted to vindicate himself in battle. But it must be remembered that the chroniclers were likely to view in a sinister light the behaviour of someone who was regarded as having betrayed the baronial cause. It also appears that they were wrong in thinking that the King was planning war, as Parliament had been resummoned on 8 July to meet on 20 August,[3] and the small scale of the forces collected suggests they were only an insurance against the opposition forces which would be brought to Parliament.[4] Support of a moderate and cautious policy of this kind would be more in keeping with what is known of Pembroke's character than a desire for a violent solution, whatever the provocation. The most suggestive evidence as to his probable pacific attitude, however, lies in the

[1] *Vita*, pp. 29–32. The *Vita* refers to Pembroke *cuius intererat comites debellare*. *Flores*, vol. 3, p. 336.

[2] Ibid., p. 337; *C.P.R., 1307–13*, p. 486; E. 101/375/8, f. 38v.

[3] *P.W.*, vol. 2, part 1, p. 74.

[4] The southern half of the country at least was still in a disturbed state. The King and Warenne both explained to Pembroke by letter at this time that Warenne had had to organize the defences of Sussex against possible attack from the men of the Earl of Arundel, William de Braose, and Archbishop Winchelsey who were then returning home through the area: S.C. 1/50/63; ibid. /49/8 and 103.

major part he took in the royal diplomatic offensive launched early in August, by which the King hoped to outmanoeuvre his opponents by diplomatic rather than military means.

The first steps in this new policy took place after Pembroke had joined the King at Dover on 4 August at the latter's request.[1] The next few days saw a flurry of activity. On 4 August it was decided to send John Benstede to summon Hereford, Warwick, and Lancaster to appear unarmed at Westminster on 27 August to discuss the Ordinances which they were declared to have issued to the King's loss and prejudice.[2] On 6 August powers were given for three envoys to visit the Pope, no doubt in order to obtain his support against the opposition magnates, but also to try and make the King financially secure by starting to negotiate a great papal loan. On the same date letters were sent to Philip IV of France on behalf of Pembroke himself and Henry de Beaumont whom Edward II was proposing to send to France to explain weighty but unspecified business.[3] Their business was also explained to two papal envoys, who were then waiting in France for a chance to enter England. Pembroke and Beaumont left for France on 6 August and returned to rejoin the King on 17 August, bringing with them two of Philip IV's clerks, William de Novo Castro and Raymond de Suspiriano.[4] The likely purpose of Pembroke's mission was to ask Philip IV to send an envoy to mediate between Edward II and his opponents, and also to invite the two papal envoys to cross to England. But Edward also had a more specific aim than this: he wanted assistance to revoke or annul the Ordinances.

Although Pembroke was concerned in organizing and carrying out the diplomacy of August 1312, the King's attitude to the Ordinances as revealed then in fact represented a policy pursued since 1311. As early as 12 October 1311, only two days

[1] S.C. 1/49/8; ibid. /50/63. Pembroke and his wife had been in London on 20 July and he and Warenne dined with the King at Westminster on 23 July: B.M., Add. Ch. 19835; E. 159/85, m. 70; E. 101/374/17.

[2] *C.P.R., 1307–13*, p. 489; *P.W.*, vol. 2, part 1, p. 88; E. 101/375/8, f. 7. Benstede met Lancaster near Blackburn on 19 Aug.: E. 101/309/18.

[3] *F.*, vol. 2, pp. 175, 196, 205.

[4] *C. Papal Letters, 1305–42*, pp. 104, 107; E. 101/375/8, ff. 7, 9. The latter was almost certainly Mr. Raymond Subirani, who entered Edward II's service on 15 Aug. and was closely concerned in royal diplomacy, together with Pembroke, over the following year: ibid., f. 10.

after the general publication of the Ordinances, the King had sent Robert de Newenton and William de Lughtebergh to the Pope and seven English representatives at the Council of Vienne to deliver a protestation asking for the Ordinances to be annulled if they should prove prejudicial to him.[1] These or later envoys also took a letter asking the Pope to absolve the King from his oath to uphold the Ordinances and to send envoys to England.[2]

A further royal embassy went to the Curia in February 1312 and was still there in May when Clement V appointed Cardinal Arnold of St. Prisca and Bishop Arnold of Poitiers to try to make peace in England, giving them specific powers to annul the Ordinances.[3] A secret royal mission had also been sent to France between 15 May and 2 June, probably to make similar requests.[4] The King's moves in August 1312 were thus a continuation of existing policy, and his offer to the Ordainers in March to discuss the Ordinances was certainly only a cover for his real ambition to destroy them entirely and to have Gaveston's latest exile revoked. Gaveston's death probably only strengthened this ambition, and the tone of his references to the Ordinances in the summons to Lancaster and his allies on 4 August does not suggest any intention to compromise.[5] It is in fact clear that just as the Ordainers in 1310 consciously remembered the precedents of 1258, so the King in his turn hoped for a repeat of the Mise of Amiens of 1264 and of Clement V's action in 1305.

For Pembroke to be involved in a policy seeking the destruction of the Ordinances may appear paradoxical after it has been suggested that he still accepted the need for reform, but there was an enormous difference between what the King may have wanted and what could in practice be achieved. No one would have appreciated more than Pembroke himself that the King's aims were political nonsense, and that to attempt to

---

[1] B.M., Cotton MS. Nero C. VIII, ff. 55, 55*v*. The English representatives were the Archbishop of York, the Bishops of London, Winchester, and Carlisle, Otto de Grandison, Amanieu d'Albret, Mr. Adam de Orleton.

[2] *Liber Epistolaris of Richard of Bury*, ed. N. Denholm-Young, Roxburghe Club (Oxford, 1950), p. 104: undated but before 14 May 1312. See *C. Papal Letters, 1305–42*, p. 104.

[3] B.M., Cotton MS. Nero C. VIII, f. 57; *C. Papal Letters, 1305–42*, pp. 103, 104, 106, 117. [4] B.M., Cotton MS. Nero C. VIII, f. 58.

[5] *C. Cl. R., 1307–13*, p. 451; *C.P.R., 1307–13*, p. 489; *P.W.*, vol. 2, part 2 Appendix, p. 53.

return to the pre-1310 situation would be a sure way of producing civil war. The only hope of a peaceful settlement was through negotiation with the mediation of papal, French, or other envoys, such as Pembroke's French mission had been intended to provide. None the less, Pembroke's part in carrying out such royal policies, whether or not he fully accepted their aims, can only have compromised him still further in the eyes of the opposition.

Pembroke's importance to the King at this time can be judged from the fact that Edward kept him fully informed of English developments and his own movements while he was in France and expected Pembroke to do likewise, despite the short time he was away. On 7 August Edward wrote from Dover enclosing a letter from Sir Dougal MacDowel giving news of events in Scotland. He added that he would leave for Winchelsea and Pevensey on 8 August to gather news from those areas and asked Pembroke to send him his news as quickly as possible. Another letter of the same date instructed Pembroke and Beaumont to request a safe conduct from Philip IV for his valet, Gerald Dauro. On 9 August the King wrote again to say that, although he was still at Dover, he was leaving for Winchelsea the next day. He promised to write again as soon as he received any further news and again enjoined Pembroke to keep in close touch. There are records of further letters on 10 and 12 August, the latter being in reply to one from Pembroke himself.[1] In a letter of 16 August the King asked Pembroke to come to Faversham on the morning of 17 August to hear his decisions on certain matters. What these were is unknown, but they were probably connected with the news brought to the King by John Sandal on the road between Canterbury and Faversham and which, the King told Pembroke, concerned other affairs in which Pembroke was soon to be involved.[2]

These plans for Pembroke's future employment may have been connected with the first attempts to negotiate between the King and his opponents, which were made in late August, at about the time of the King's return to Westminster for the planned opening of Parliament on 20 August.[3] When negotia-

---

[1] S.C. 1/49/10, 9, 11; E. 101/375/8, ff. 41, 27v.   [2] S.C. 1/49/12.
[3] The King was back at Westminster from 21 Aug. until his departure for Windsor on 17 Sept.: E. 101/375/2, m. 2.

tions started a prominent part was played by the Earls of Gloucester and Richmond, who were uniformly regarded as mediators by the chroniclers.[1] This is borne out by the series of safe conducts issued for the opposition envoys from 28 September and by the peace treaty of 20 December itself, in which the two earls are regularly described in this way.[2] They were also closely associated as mediators with the two papal envoys who reached London on 29 August and with the French envoy, Philip IV's half-brother Louis of Évreux, who arrived on 13 September.[3] The Earl of Gloucester was well equipped for this role, since on the one hand he had been an Ordainer and had sworn the previous March to uphold the Ordinances, while on the other he was also the King's nephew and had continued to serve him while an Ordainer.[4] The Earl of Richmond was a loyal supporter of the King throughout the reign, but politically was a complete nonentity and therefore unlikely to cause offence to either side. Although an Ordainer, he had been in France on diplomatic business from August 1310 until some time earlier in 1312 and, like Gloucester, his reputation had not been affected by the events surrounding Gaveston's death.[5] In addition to these two earls and the foreign envoys, some of the English prelates probably also took some part as mediators,[6] a role which they were to play with notable effect in later crises of the reign. In the later negotiations after 28 September the magnates were represented by Hereford, Robert Clifford, John Botetourt, John de Heselarton, Adam de Herwynton, and Lancaster's steward, Michael de Meldon. Although twice provided with conducts to attend the negotiations, Lancaster and Warwick kept away from London and apparently took no personal part at all.[7] The King's envoys

---

[1] *Trokelowe*, p. 78; *Flores*, vol. 3, p. 337; *Ann. Lond.*, p. 210; *Vita*, p. 33.

[2] *C.P.R., 1307–13*, pp. 498–516: safe conducts dated 28 Sept., 8 Oct., 6 Nov., 11 Nov., 16 Dec.; *F.*, vol. 2, p. 192 (December treaty).

[3] *Ann. Paul.*, pp. 271–2. They are named in the safe conducts given above.

[4] *Ann. Lond.*, p. 210; *Vita*, p. 23. See also M. Altschul, *A Baronial Family in Medieval England: The Clares* (Baltimore, 1965), pp. 161–3.

[5] See I. Lyubimenko, *Jean de Bretagne, Comte de Richmond* (Lille, 1908), for an outline of his career.

[6] See K. Edwards, 'The Political Importance of the English Bishops during the Reign of Edward II', *E.H.R.*, vol. 59 (1944), pp. 324–5.

[7] *C.P.R., 1307–13*, pp. 498–509. Lancaster's known movements during the negotiations are: Croxden, Staffs., 9 Oct. (B.M., Cotton MS. Faustina B. VI,

were Pembroke himself, Hugh Despenser, and Nicholas de Segrave.[1]

Tentative discussions with the magnates may have begun on 23 August, when Gloucester passed through London with his retinue.[2] The exact sequence of events in these early meetings is unknown, but the district most involved in them was apparently St. Albans, where Gloucester, and later the papal envoys as well, stayed in order to be close to the magnates. The baronial army was approaching London by 3 September, when the Bishops of Norwich and Bath and Wells, the Earl of Richmond, and two others were ordered to prohibit Lancaster, Warwick, and Hereford from appearing armed before the King, and by 8 September it had reached Ware in Hertfordshire.[3] It is not known how formal the earliest meetings were, but it is likely that each side was merely sounding out the other's opinion. Predictably the magnates made the upholding of the Ordinances a pre-condition of any agreement. An attempt by the papal envoys to send clerks with papal letters to the magnates at Wheathampstead was rebuffed on the facetious grounds that England already had enough clerks capable of negotiating.[4] Reference is also made to negotiations held before 28 September at Markyate near St. Albans,[5] but without mention of the results. Altogether little or nothing seems to have been achieved in these early stages.

In the meantime Pembroke and other royal advisers were dealing with a potentially dangerous situation within the city of London itself. On 20 September, after the King's departure for Windsor, Pembroke, Despenser, Edmund Mauley the Steward, Nicholas de Segrave the Marshal of the Household, and John Crombwell the Keeper of the Tower, went to Guildhall to ask

f. 79v.: Croxden Abbey chronicle); Melbourne, Derby, 10 Nov. (D.L. 25/2262); Leicester, 3 and 6 Dec. (D.L. 25/2254, 308).

[1] *Ann. Lond.*, pp. 221–2. These three were associated as early as 4 Aug. when a letter which they had sealed containing unspecified royal business was sent to the Earl of Surrey for his seal to be added and for eventual transmission to the Bishop of Lincoln: E. 101/375/8, f. 40v.

[2] *C. Cl. R., 1307–13*, p. 475.

[3] *Trokelowe*, p. 78; *C.P.R., 1307–13*, p. 490; *P.W.*, vol. 2, part 1, p. 88. Lancaster and Warwick were evidently still present in early September.

[4] *Trokelowe*, pp. 77–8.

[5] *C.P.R., 1307–13*, p. 498. These negotiations probably account for the Bishop of Norwich's presence at St. Albans on 24 Sept.: Norfolk and Norwich Record Office, Register of John Salmon, f. 48.

for further security for the holding of the city against the King's enemies. The citizens replied that they had already given their word and need do no more, and then produced a list of complaints against the courts of the Steward and Marshal and the actions of Crombwell, as well as on other matters. Pembroke and his colleagues promised to deal with these questions at Westminster the following day, but as they were leaving Guildhall a rumour spread that they were planning to arrest the Mayor and aldermen, and they barely escaped without injury.[1] That night Crombwell sent the Tower garrison to attack the Tower ward, to which the citizens responded by destroying the wall of an enclosure next to the Tower and arresting Crombwell's men. When the next day the Mayor appeared before the Council at Westminster to hear the promised replies to the city's complaints, Pembroke and his fellow councillors accused the citizens of having seditiously attacked the enclosure by the Tower in order to break open the Tower prison and loot the royal treasury. But although the Mayor held an inquiry into the incident, no answer was apparently ever made to the citizens' own charges against royal officials.[2] Pembroke and his colleagues were thus faced with a hostile and possibly pro-Lancastrian city close to Westminster, as well as with the baronial army encamped in Hertfordshire, and it was to avoid the possible conjunction of the two that on 30 September Pembroke ordered the raising of 1,000 foot in Kent and Essex and on 5 October stated that, despite their safe conducts, the baronial negotiators were not to be allowed to stay in or even pass through the city.[3]

These troubles coincided with the start of what appear to have been the first serious attempts to negotiate between the King and the magnates, and may even have hastened their beginning by emphasizing the dangers of the situation. A particular stimulus may have been provided by the presence in the

[1] *Ann. Lond.*, pp. 215–16; *Ann. Paul.*, p. 272; Pembroke and his colleagues luckily had an armed escort. For a full analysis of these events in London, see G. A. Williams, *Medieval London, from Commune to Capital* (London, 1963), pp. 271–4. According to the witness list of a royal charter of 20 Sept. Pembroke, Segrave, and Mauley were also at Windsor on that date, but this is scarcely possible: Swansea Corporation Records (on deposit at University College, Swansea).

[2] *Ann. Lond.*, p. 217; *Ann. Paul.*, p. 272. The author of the *Annals of London* cannot of course be regarded as an impartial witness to these incidents.

[3] *C.P.R., 1307–13*, p. 498; *C. Cl. R., 1307–13*, p. 481; *F.*, vol. 2, p. 181.

King's company on 15 September of the French and papal envoys and on 16 September of the Earl of Gloucester and others, while Pembroke visited the King at Windsor on 26 September.[1] On 28 September the first safe conducts for Hereford and the other baronial envoys were issued at the request of the three foreign envoys and the Earls of Gloucester and Richmond, and were renewed at intervals as each expired.[2] It is, however, possible that the issuing of conducts was an inducement by the King, and that his opponents had not yet formally agreed to negotiate, since on 30 September the papal and French envoys in London wrote to Hereford and the other four baronial representatives enclosing letters from the King proposing a meeting. They stated that they would be staying in London until a date suggested by the King, and that if Hereford and his colleagues came to London within that period they would find them at the Temple prepared to discuss the contents of the King's letters. Hereford evidently did respond to this invitation, and it is likely that the subsequent negotiations took place at the Temple which, although it was then in royal hands, could be regarded as a neutral point between the city of London and Westminster.[3]

Unfortunately it is impossible to provide any detailed chronology for the negotiations between September and their conclusion in December, but the survival of several documents relating to them at least makes it feasible to say what issues were raised and how they were finally resolved. These documents, none of which bears a date, are the *Prima tractatio ad pacem confirmandam*, a list of royal objections to the Ordinances, and the *Rationes Baronum*.[4]

As its title suggests the *Prima tractatio* belongs to an early stage in the negotiations, as also do the objections to the Ordinances, and the two can therefore be conveniently dis-

---

[1] E. 101/375/2, m. 3.

[2] *C.P.R., 1307–13*, pp. 498–507.

[3] D.L. 36/2/208. Clifford stayed at his hospice next to St. Dunstan's, Fleet St.: E. 403/164, m. 2.

[4] *Ann. Lond.*, pp. 210–15. Stubbs's marginal date of July 1312 for the *Prima tractatio* and the objections to the Ordinances appears to be a guess which is not supported by other evidence. The *Rationes Baronum* are taken from Vatican Instrumenta Miscellanea, 5947 which is published as *Edward II, the Lords Ordainers and Piers Gaveston's Jewels and Horses*, ed. R. A. Roberts, Camden 3rd series, vol. 41 (London, 1929).

cussed together. It is possible that both documents were produced during preliminary talks at Markyate and elsewhere in late August or early September, but this is by no means certain and it is more satisfactory to treat them as an early stage in the negotiations after September.

The objections to the Ordinances can quickly be dismissed. These were drawn up by the two French clerks who returned to England with Pembroke in August and represent the culmination in the King's efforts to destroy the Ordinances. The document is so legalistic in tone and so unrealistic politically that it need not be considered in detail. It could never have formed a basis for negotiations since it invited the barons to agree to an unconditional surrender. Predictably it was rejected out of hand by the magnates, who claimed that the Ordinances were legally valid and must be upheld.[1] With this rebuff the King's hopes of having the Ordinances revoked finally evaporated.

The *Prima tractatio* is, however, a more important document, as well as being a more difficult one to interpret. It may even be an immediate reply to the document just discussed. The *Prima tractatio* first states that because the Earls of Gloucester, Lancaster, Richmond, Pembroke, Warenne, Hereford, Warwick, and Arundel had heard that the King *est engrossi devers eux*, they were willing, if the King gave them sufficient security and agreed to receive them as his lieges, to come to Westminster humbly to beg his pardon. They also offered to provide 400 men-at-arms for six months at their own expense for the next Scottish campaign and to persuade Parliament to grant an aid for the same purpose, as well as to restore all Gaveston's goods seized at Newcastle. In return the King was to promise to maintain the Ordinances, remove all evil councillors, return all seized lands, and release all persons illegally imprisoned.[2] These terms have certain similarities with the treaty of 20 December, but the immediate interest of the *Prima tractatio* lies

---

[1] *Ann. Lond.*, pp. 211–15. The two clerks who drew up the document were evidently William de Novo Castro and Raymond de Suspiriano: E. 101/375/8, f. 9. Both were present at the making of the 20 Dec. treaty: *F.*, vol. 2, pp. 191–2. This identification is to be preferred to that of H. G. Richardson, who suggests that the objections were produced by two other French clerks, Gerard de Curton and Rich. Tybetot, who were also present on 20 Dec. but who probably came to England with Louis of Évreux in September: 'The English Coronation Oath', *Speculum*, vol. 24 (1949), p. 69.

[2] *Ann. Lond.*, pp. 210–11.

in the apparent association of eight earls representing the whole range of political opinion, from the royal supporters Pembroke and Warenne, the mediators Gloucester and Richmond, to the King's opponents Lancaster, Warwick, Hereford, and Arundel. It is just possible that in the autumn of 1312 all the earls were prepared to co-operate in presenting terms to the King and to join in seeking pardon for their actions against Gaveston as if they were all equally guilty. But in view of the completeness of the commitment of Pembroke and Warenne to the King, and of the bitterness between them and Lancaster and the other opposition magnates resulting from Gaveston's death, it is hard to believe that such an act of baronial solidarity could have taken place. One possible explanation of the form of the *Prima tractatio* is that it was a draft treaty put forward by the Earls of Gloucester and Richmond as a basis for further negotiation. But the most probable answer is that it was presented by the opposition themselves. This suggestion fits the account given in the *Vita*, whose author states that at some point the King asked his opponents to draw up a list of their demands and that they then did so, asking for the confirmation of the Ordinances and pardons for Gaveston's death. The King's reaction to these demands, and so we may suppose to the *Prima tractatio*, was to accept all the Ordinances except for those concerning finance, to agree to pardon the earls, but to refuse to accept that Gaveston should be declared a traitor to prevent his widow or daughter from claiming possession of his lands. Edward remained adamant on this last point and proceeded to try to wear out his opponents by dragging out the negotiations.[1] Allowing for the difficulties raised by the lack of a clear chronology for the negotiations, the details in the *Prima tractatio* and the *Vita* probably do give a reasonable idea of the issues involved.

However, further light is thrown on the negotiations prior to the December treaty by the third document, the *Rationes Baronum*, and by some other materials associated with it. A brief explanation is needed since the *Rationes* form part of a report on the negotiations of 1312 and 1313 which was sent to the Pope by his two envoys. The first twelve membranes of the report refer wholly to events in 1313, but the next three mem-

[1] *Vita*, p. 37.

branes, which include the *Rationes,* can be dated to 1312, since they also contain a copy of the treaty of 20 December 1312 and refer to problems which were not issues in 1313 but which do fit the context of late 1312.[1] The *Rationes* show first of all that the magnates were dissatisfied with the security and safe conduct which they said the King claimed to have offered them *propter necessitatem* during the Parliament which met at the end of 1312.[2] They argued that this implied that the King had acted under compulsion and that the Parliament in which the safe conduct had been issued could not in any case properly be held without the magnates, who refused to attend without proper security. The form of security was also deficient because it implied that they had murdered Gaveston and not executed him as an enemy of the King and the realm. The barons' continued insistence on the removal from court of certain objectionable persons is also shown in a list of twenty names inserted close to the *Rationes.*[3] The peace treaty which finally emerged on 20 December is therefore all the more interesting in the light of these statements and demands.

The treaty was formally made in the presence of Pembroke and the other royal negotiators, the mediators, and the baronial envoys.[4] Under its terms the barons were to come to Westminster to receive the King's pardon, Gaveston's jewels and horses were to be restored to royal envoys at St. Albans on 13 January, and a Parliament, for which a form of security for the barons was included, was to be summoned for 18 March. All offences committed against Gaveston were to be pardoned, and in return no action was to be taken against Gaveston's followers. The barons also promised that the coming Parliament would discuss the granting to the King of an aid for the Scottish war and would also consider measures to ensure that no one brought armed retainers to future Parliaments. The King also promised to inquire into the rights of Lancaster's retainer Gruffydd de la Pole in his dispute with the King's

---

[1] *Edward II, the Lords Ordainers, and Piers Gaveston's Jewels and Horses.*

[2] Parliament met on 20 Aug., was prorogued on 28 Aug. until 30 Sept., and ended on 16 Dec.: *P.W.,* vol. 2, part 2, pp. 72–80 and Appendix, p. 53.

[3] *Edward II, the Lords Ordainers, and Piers Gaveston's Jewels and Horses,* pp. 15–17.

[4] Texts of the treaty appear in ibid., pp. 17–21; *F.,* vol. 2, pp. 191–2; *Ann. Lond.,* pp. 221–5; C. 81/83/2572A; Lambeth MS. 1213, pp. 27–31; B.M., Cotton MS. Claudius E. VIII, ff. 256v.–257v. (text of chronicle of Adam Murimuth).

chamberlain John Charlton, to investigate the seizure of the property of another Lancastrian knight Fulk Lestrange, and to restore the lands of Henry Percy. The treaty was however only a partial agreement and not a final settlement, as a comparison of its terms with the *Prima tractatio* makes clear. The two documents both include the baronial promise to request pardon and to take part in a Scottish campaign, but in the really fundamental points they are quite different. The December treaty made no mention of the Ordinances, and had no reference to the baronial description of Gaveston as the King's enemy or to their demand for the removal of evil councillors. It was therefore a considerable paper victory for the King, but it could hardly be supposed that these major issues would not be heard of again. Much would also depend on how the terms of the treaty were performed, and it was in any case possible that Lancaster and Warwick would refuse to accept its conditions, since the treaty was to be sent to them for their approval and their reply then sent back to the papal envoys and the Earls of Gloucester and Richmond.

So far as the Earl of Pembroke was concerned the December treaty could have been regarded as a satisfactory compromise, despite its provisional nature. His position as a principal royal negotiator must certainly have made his part in the negotiations which preceded the treaty a very important one, but there is unfortunately no way of assessing his detailed contribution. On the other hand, there is a great deal of record evidence to suggest that his influence on royal policy and involvement in the routine of government were both considerable at the end of 1312.

During this period many government orders were described as being issued upon Pembroke's information and there is no reason to doubt that his was the dominant influence behind them. Some are of a routine nature but others are of political importance. On 20 and 25 July Warenne was rewarded for his change of side by the restoration of two manors in Northamptonshire and of the honour of High Peak, which had been resumed under the Ordinances. On 27 July Lancaster's knight, Robert Holand, was removed from the custody of Beeston in Cheshire, and had also been replaced as Justice of Chester by 27 November.[1] On 30 July Bartholomew de Badlesmere, one of

[1] *C.F.R., 1307–19*, p. 140; *C.P.R., 1307–13*, p. 482; *C. Ch. R., 1300–26*, p. 202.

Gloucester's retainers, was reappointed Constable of Bristol, while on 31 July Pembroke ordered the arrest of Henry Percy, his partner in Gaveston's surrender, who had joined the opposition. Early in September John de Segrave the Elder was made Keeper of the Forest beyond the Trent and Constable of Nottingham, and Nicholas de Segrave, the Marshal of the Household, received custody of Orford in Suffolk and £60 a year.[1] Gaveston's former castle of Knaresborough was committed to William de Vaux on 13 September and on 20 September Gaveston's widow was given the county of Rutland and Oakham castle. John Sandal was made acting Treasurer on 4 October; the Justice of Wales, Roger Mortimer of Chirk, who had stayed loyal to the King throughout the 1312 crisis, was given letters of protection on 6 November to return to Wales; and on 14 November Hugh Despenser the Elder was granted wardships and marriages worth 3,000 marks in payment of a debt from the Wardrobe.[2] These represent only the more important decisions in which Pembroke was concerned, but are enough to show clearly both his own influence and some of the detailed consequences of the political upheaval of 1312.

In the closing months of 1312 Pembroke, as one might expect, remained in close contact with the King, and is known to have visited him at Windsor on 26 September, 4 October, and 16 November, at Chertsey on 30 November, and at Westminster on 16 December.[3] At other times the King corresponded regularly with the Council at Westminster, and there exists a series of eleven such letters dated between 5 October and 18 December and covering a very wide variety of topics. These range from an assignment of £300 of land to Odyn Bruart, orders to harass Lancaster's retainer Gruffydd de la Pole in every possible legal way, the payment of 3,000 marks to the Earl of Lincoln's executors, the repayment of debts to a royal merchant Anthony Pessagno, and instructions to try to remedy the Household's shortage of money, to letters referring to Elias de Tyngewyk's widow, Alexander de Compton a keeper of former Templar manors, Nicholas Audley's wife, the seizure of

---

[1] *C.P.R., 1307–13*, pp. 483, 486, 490, 506; *C.F.R., 1307–19*, pp. 144–5.
[2] *C.P.R., 1307–13*, pp. 493, 497, 501, 507, 509.
[3] E. 101/375/2, mm. 3, 4, 5; E. 368/95, m. 15*d*.

a royal ship in Picardy, and to the King's clerk Boniface de Saluciis. A letter of 17 December requested Pembroke to act on information brought by a royal valet and may be connected with the treaty negotiations which were then in their final stages.[1]

All these letters were addressed in the first instance to Pembroke himself, sometimes in association with Hugh Despenser the Elder. When this evidence is taken in conjunction with the large number of orders issued on his information, and his part in the diplomacy of August 1312, in the King's relations with the city of London in September, and in the negotiations with the opposition magnates, it is a clear indication of the authority Pembroke had acquired by the end of 1312. By this time Pembroke had become the virtual head of the Council.

Pembroke was also on close terms with the King at a purely personal level. In November 1312 for example the King gave Pembroke a number of falcons which had belonged to Gaveston. This was an unimportant action in a material sense, but was significant since the King would have been unlikely to give away his former favourite's possessions to someone he did not trust and respect. An episode of a similar kind occurred in January 1313 when, in reply to a request from Pembroke for the grant of a wardship, the King told him that he regarded all that Pembroke possessed as if it were his own and was only sorry that his request was such a small one.[2] There is little doubt that Pembroke could have used his position of trust and authority to his own advantage if he had wished to do so. One of his retainers, Maurice de Berkeley, was given custody of the town of Gloucester at his request and two others, William de Cleydon and Thomas de Berkeley, received small grants on his information, but this was all. Pembroke's only personal acquisition was the gift of the New Temple in London on 15 December.[3] Pembroke's conduct thus compares very favourably with that of Gaveston before him and of the Younger Despenser later in the reign.

Pembroke's administrative activities continued unabated

[1] S.C. 1/45/169–73 (5, 29 Oct.; 23, 24, 25 Nov.); ibid. /49/13–17 (21 Oct.; 3, 17, 20 Nov.; 18 Dec.); ibid. /49/54 (17 Dec.).

[2] E. 101/375/8, f. 45; S.C. 1/49/21.

[3] *C.P.R., 1307–13*, p. 480; *C.F.R., 1307–19*, pp. 146, 158; *C. Ch. R., 1300–26*, p. 203.

after the making of the December treaty. On 30 December Pembroke, the Chancellor, and acting Treasurer went to the house of the Carmelites in London to inform the Mayor and aldermen of London of the Council's decision to levy a tallage on the city. Pembroke was probably also present on 10 January when the aldermen appeared before the Council to offer a loan from the city in place of a tallage.[1] On 3 January the King wrote asking Pembroke and Despenser to attend to some business of the Count of Foix in Gascony.[2] Shortly after this Pembroke became involved in an incident concerning the royal merchant and banker Anthony Pessagno of Genoa, an episode which in passing throws some light on public opinion about the royal government. On 13 January the King ordered Pembroke to arrange the payment to Pessagno of debts owing to him from the Wardrobe. He was also asked to investigate the behaviour of John Bedewynd as Sheriff of Cornwall, from which office he was removed on the same date at Pembroke's instance, and as purchaser of tin in Cornwall before Pessagno's appointment to that post the previous October. On 19 January Bedewynd appeared at the Exchequer before Pembroke and John Sandal the acting Treasurer, when Pessagno reported that Bedewynd had declared in the county court at Lostwithiel that the King's councillors were untrustworthy and had advised him badly over Pessagno's appointment as purchaser of tin.[3] Pessagno's affairs also occupied Pembroke on 14 January, when he was asked to see that Pessagno received rapid payment of a debt payable to him in Gascony.[4]

However, Pembroke's main concern at this time was the complex series of problems which arose during January and February 1313 out of the attempts to implement the terms of the December treaty. On 16 December, four days before the final agreement, a general safe conduct until 3 June was issued for Lancaster and his supporters to move freely about the country, and on 18 December Henry Percy's lands were restored until the coming Parliament. On 26 December John de

---

[1] *Cal. of Letter-Books*, D., pp. 305–6.

[2] S.C. 1/49/18.

[3] *C.F.R., 1307–19*, pp. 147, 160–1; S.C. 1/45/174; E. 159/86, m. 76d. The outcome of this episode is unknown.

[4] S.C. 1/45/175. A fragmentary letter of Jan. 1313 from Edward II to Pembroke which also refers to Pessagno exists as S.C. 1/63/193.

Grey, John Wogan, and Alan la Zouche were instructed to examine Gruffydd de la Pole's complaints about the royal seizure of his lands,[1] but the commission went beyond the terms of the treaty since the justices were also ordered to deal with complaints against de la Pole by the King's chamberlain John Charlton and by Roger Trumwyn.[2] The seizure of Fulk Lestrange's lands was also brought within the terms of this commission on 31 December. On 7 January John Sandal and Ingelard Warley were appointed to receive Gaveston's property at St. Albans and on 8 January Parliament was summoned, as had been agreed, for 18 March.[3] Almost at once, however, fresh difficulties began to appear in the way of a settlement and Pembroke immediately became involved in finding solutions to them.

In late December or early January the Earl of Hereford wrote to the papal envoys in London enclosing a complaint by Henry Percy that one of his knights had been imprisoned by royal officials contrary to the treaty. The knight concerned was apparently Edmund Darel, whom John Mowbray the Sheriff of York had imprisoned at Tickhill. When the chief papal envoy, Cardinal Arnold, showed Hereford's and Percy's letters of complaint to the Chancellor, who was then in London, the latter replied that nothing could be done to free Darel without first consulting the King. The Cardinal then sent one of his chaplains with the letters to the King at Windsor.[4] The King reacted on 4 January by summoning Pembroke to discuss the matter at Windsor on 7 January,[5] and on the morning of 8 January Pembroke told the chaplain that he would be in London on 14 January to give the King's answer. On 10 January, however, Hereford sent one of his clerks to tell the

[1] *C.P.R., 1307–13*, pp. 516, 546–7; *P.W.*, vol. 2, part 1, p. 93.

[2] For the background to this problem which erupted at every national crisis, see R. Owen, 'Welsh Pool and Powys-Land', *Collections relating to Montgomeryshire*, vol. 29 (1896), pp. 257–60, and M. C. Jones, 'The Feudal Barons of Powys', ibid., vol. 1 (1868).

[3] *C.P.R., 1307–13*, p. 546; *F.*, vol. 2, p. 194; *P.W.*, vol. 2, part 1, p. 80.

[4] *Edward II, the Lords Ordainers and Piers Gaveston's Jewels and Horses*, Camden 3rd series, vol. 41 (1929), ed. R. A. Roberts, pp. 1, 4, 2, 8, 4. The information from which the present account of these negotiations has been built up does not appear in chronological order in the original document which is chiefly composed of correspondence from the parties involved.

[5] S.C. 1/49/19.

Cardinal that, unless Darel were released at once, the magnates would conclude that the King's safe conducts were worthless and would therefore refuse to restore Gaveston's property on 13 January. Pembroke finally came to London on 15 January and after some discussion with him, the Cardinal stayed on until the following day to allow Pembroke to have further discussions with other royal councillors and with some of the Cardinal's clerks.[1] Afterwards, on 17 January, Pembroke returned to Windsor at the King's request[2] to report on his meetings in London, and, after considering the case with the King, Darel's release on mainprize until 9 February was ordered on 18 January.[3]

Meanwhile Darel's imprisonment had given the opposition magnates an excellent excuse for not carrying out their promises made in December, and, in particular, Lancaster and Warwick were provided with a reason for not approving the treaty. More immediately, however, Darel's imprisonment had had the effect threatened, since on 13 January the magnates had not come to St. Albans to return Gaveston's goods to the King's envoys, Sandal and Warley. The envoys remained there without effect until 15 January, when, in righteous indignation, they drew up before witnesses a formal protestation which they then conveyed to the Cardinal. In these proceedings Hereford seems to have acted as a mediator between the King and the magnates, since in reply to the Cardinal's reproof at the baronial failure to come to St. Albans, he said that he had asked Lancaster, Warwick, and Clifford, for their own honour and the common good, to restore Gaveston's goods as soon as possible and added that when he next met them he would do all in his power to persuade them to observe the terms of the treaty.[4]

Darel's release did not in fact do anything to relieve the new

[1] Camden 3rd series, vol. 41, pp. 4, 2, 5.

[2] S.C. 1/49/20.

[3] *C. Cl. R., 1307–13*, p. 504. Much of the detail on the negotiations for Darel's release comes from a report by the Cardinal to the Earl of Hereford on 20 Jan.: Camden 3rd series, vol. 41, pp. 4–6. In the edition of Vatican Instrumenta Miscellanea, 5947, printed in Camden 3rd series, vol. 41, there is an order for Darel's release dated on 2 Jan.: ibid., p. 2. If correct this document would create great difficulty in working out the sequence of events up to 18 Jan. Fortunately, however, another transcript of the Vatican document in the Public Record Office (P.R.O. 31/9/59, f. 50) shows that 2 Jan. is a misreading for 18 Jan.

[4] Camden 3rd series, vol. 41, pp. 2–7.

crisis. Further issues outstanding between the King and his opponents were revealed when, soon after 13 January, Lancaster sent his chaplain Hugh Skillehare from Pontefract to the Cardinal with a further long list of complaints and demands to be passed on orally to the King. Lancaster said he was ready, with the advice of the other magnates, to return Gaveston's goods to the King, but the offer contained a major regression, since Lancaster now referred to Gaveston as an enemy of the King and the realm and described the restoration of his property as if it were the forfeit of a felon's goods to the crown.[1] This point which had been a leading issue in the 1312 negotiations, had been shelved in the December treaty and its revival alone would make the treaty for all practical purposes a dead letter. That Lancaster and his colleagues had legally executed Gaveston was an admission that the King refused to make. Lancaster went on to demand that the justices whom the King had appointed under the terms of the treaty to hear the complaints of Gruffydd de la Pole and Fulk Lestrange should be replaced by others before 23 February, since, he claimed, neither John Wogan nor Alan la Zouche was impartial, the one having taken part in the original seizure of de la Pole's lands and the other being a retainer of John Charlton, de la Pole's opponent. Lancaster also demanded the removal of the men-at-arms appointed by the King to keep the peace, who, he said, had been arresting his men, and their replacement by royal officials as was usual in time of peace. Lancaster added several minor complaints, asking for justice to be done to the Lady of Everingham and Henry Percy, parson of Werram, as well as in a dispute between Sir William de Ros of Wark and one of Lancaster's retainers. Lancaster finally stated through his envoy that he and Warwick were planning to meet other magnates before 23 February to discuss the terms of the treaty before giving their approval.[2] There is little doubt, however, that approval would really be governed by the King's acceptance of Lancaster's fresh demands.

On receipt of Lancaster's complaints the papal envoys sent the details to the Earls of Gloucester and Richmond, asking

---

[1] Camden 3rd series, vol. 41, p. 7.
[2] Ibid., pp. 7–9. There is no evidence that Lancaster and Warwick ever did hold such a meeting.

them to come to London. At the same time Hereford was also invited to London. After Gloucester's arrival he and the envoys together considered the next step and decided that they should meet members of the royal Council to discuss the answers to be made to Lancaster. This was done, and the King was represented in the talks that followed by Pembroke, the Elder Despenser, and John Sandal. Pembroke and his colleagues ignored the item in Lancaster's demands which described Gaveston as a felon and enemy of the King, on the technical grounds that it contained no request for them to answer,[1] but in reality because they probably did not want to destroy all chance of agreement by formally raising the issue. Lancaster's lesser demands were dealt with without difficulty. The councillors replied that if anyone had indeed been imprisoned in breach of the treaty prompt orders would be given for his release. Similarly they dismissed the complaints relating to William de Ros and the Lady of Everingham, saying that these should be settled by due legal process. Lancaster's second article, his demand that de la Pole's case should be examined by fresh justices, proved far more difficult to solve, so much so that the Earl of Hereford for one despaired of any satisfactory solution. This was because Pembroke and the other councillors declared that there was no evidence to justify the charges against the justices and that if there had been any doubts about them, these should have been raised at the time of their appointment. They were, however, willing for Alan la Zouche to be removed from the commission, but said they could do nothing without consulting the King first. Hugh Despenser finally agreed to put the matter to the King after persuasion by the papal envoys,[2] who themselves met the King at Sheen on 29 January at Pembroke's invitation.[3] But no reply had been received from the King when the envoys reported to Lancaster on 8 February on the course of their meetings with the Council. Two other matters also remained unresolved: the restoration of Gaveston's property and the confirmation by Lancaster and Warwick of the December treaty. Accordingly on 10 February the papal

[1] Ibid., pp. 15, 10, 15, 12, 9. Gloucester and Richmond continued to act as mediators as they had done in 1312.

[2] Ibid., pp. 9–12.

[3] S.C. 1/49/21. The letter makes it clear that the original suggestion for a meeting with the King came from Gloucester.

envoys wrote to Lancaster, Warwick, Hereford, John Botetourt, and Robert Clifford to announce that they were sending
the Bishop of St. Davids, Mr. Walter de Thorp, and two of
their chaplains to discuss these questions.[1]

With the departure of this mission the focus of the continuing mediation between the King and the opposition moved
from London further north, possibly to Kenilworth.[2] In the
instructions to their messengers the papal envoys laid a heavy
burden of responsibility upon Lancaster and his fellows, saying
that by their failure to restore Gaveston's goods in accordance
with the treaty, they were harming the King's honour and
endangering the kingdom, already threatened by the Scots
and disturbances in Gascony, as well as causing unease to the
Pope and French King. They were also told that if they continued their behaviour, the King would be justified in acting
against them. This pressure seems to have been successful, since
on 27 February Hereford, Clifford, and Botetourt delivered
Gaveston's jewels and other goods to the Bishop of Worcester
and John Sandal and received acquittance for them.[3] However,
the mission, which had probably returned by 16 March,[4] left
unsettled the question of Lancaster's and Warwick's confirmation of the December treaty as a whole.

The state of relations between the King and the opposition
at this time is summed up in a document which the latter sent
to the King after the beginning of the Parliament of 18 March.
The document itemizes the points in the December treaty
which had been implemented or on which both sides were
agreed, but also lists those on which agreement had still to be
reached. The earls recalled that they had now restored
Gaveston's jewels and other property, as the treaty required;
they reaffirmed their readiness to come to Westminster to ask
for the King's pardon and their willingness to grant an aid
in Parliament for the Scottish war; and they repeated their
promise not to bring armed followers to Parliaments after their
pardon, since the problems of Henry Percy and Gruffydd de
la Pole were now being settled in accordance with the treaty.

[1] Camden 3rd series, vol. 41, pp. 12–13.
[2] Lancaster was probably there on 16 Feb.: D.L. 25/2253.
[3] Camden 3rd series, vol. 41, pp. 13–15; F., vol. 2, p. 203.
[4] The Bishop of St. Davids was apparently then at Windsor: C. 53/99, m. 8.

The magnates also expressed themselves as satisfied with the King's assurance that after they had been pardoned he would act towards them as a faithful lord.[1] Tacitly they also returned to the form of the treaty by the omission of any words describing Gaveston as a felon or a royal enemy, in contrast to Lancaster's articles of the previous February.[2] This in itself would do much to produce a settlement. On the other hand the magnates demanded a fuller form of acquittance for their restoration of Gaveston's goods than they had been given in February, and they objected to the form of pardon to them as Gaveston's enemies which had been offered in December since it would then appear that they had extorted it from the King, contrary to his Coronation Oath and their homage to him. Instead they included a new form of pardon which was to be held in the custody of the Archbishop of Canterbury, the Bishops of London and Chichester, and the Earls of Gloucester, Richmond, and Arundel, until the magnates had made their submission. The magnates also declared that there was no need to give special pardons to Gaveston's former adherents, since, they said, only the King would have the power to bring any suit against them. Their failure to appear in person at the Parliament of 18 March they attributed to the fact that the summons had not been made in the usual form, and they therefore asked for a correct form of summons so that they might make their submission.[3] The King's objections to this document probably centred on the demand that Gaveston's followers should not be specially pardoned. This was probably because, if the King agreed to it, there might then be a demand for their exile under the terms of the Ordinances. Apart from this point there seems to have been relatively little to prevent an early settlement.

There are some signs that another attempt to achieve one was soon made. On 3 May, at the request of Cardinal Arnold, Louis de Clermont, the newly arrived French envoy, and of the Earls of Gloucester and Richmond, Lancaster and his followers

---

[1] *Ann. Lond.*, pp. 225–9. The document refers to the Parliament as a past event and is therefore datable to between 18 Mar. and 23 May when the next Parliament was summoned. Stubbs's marginal date assigning it to 1312 is thus misleading. An inquiry into the arrest of de la Pole's men had been held by 12 Mar., but his own complaints remained to be settled: *C. Cl. R., 1307–13*, p. 569.

[2] Camden 3rd series, vol. 41, p. 7.

[3] *Ann. Lond.*, pp. 225–9.

were given a safe conduct till 24 June to meet the papal envoys and the King's councillors at Bedford, and on 23 May Parliament was called for 8 July.[1] But there is no evidence that any meetings did take place, and a further six months were to elapse before a settlement was finally made.

As has been seen Pembroke played a leading part in the sequence of negotiation up to 8 February.[2] After that date, however, it became necessary for him to turn his attention to a mission to Paris. One purpose of the mission was to represent the King at the Paris Parlement in business arising out of the Process of Périgueux[3] and in the hearing of appeals made there against English officials in Aquitaine. In November 1312 the Bishop of Exeter had been ordered to prepare the King's defence on these subjects, and on 15 January 1313 a meeting was held at Westminster to discuss them further.[4] A second and more pressing purpose was to answer the appeal made to the Parlement by Amanieu d'Albret following the latter's dispute with the late Seneschal of Gascony, John de Ferrers, which had led to open war between the two in the Duchy in 1312.[5] On 4 February Pembroke, the Bishop of Exeter, and Mr. Thomas Cobham were appointed to be the King's proctors in Paris, being reinforced a few days later by the Chancery's Gascon experts, Masters Richard de Burton, William de Weston, and Henry de Canterbury, as well as by Raymond Subirani. Pembroke, Exeter, and Cobham were given full powers to give answers in Paris on any topic relating to Gascony and, within the Duchy itself, to renew appointments, hold inquiries, and revoke any decisions of the Seneschal which they considered prejudicial to the King.[6] Pembroke himself was also given authority to remove and replace the current Seneschal, Étienne Ferol, and was expected to mediate in the dispute already mentioned involving Amanieu d'Albret, as well as in a problem arising from the custody of the viscounty of Aspre-

[1] *C.P.R., 1307–13*, p. 569; *P.W.*, vol. 2, part 2, p. 94.
[2] See Camden 3rd series, vol. 41, pp. 11–12.
[3] See I. Lyubimenko, op. cit., pp. 80–91, for further details.
[4] *C. Cl. R., 1307–13*, pp. 488, 496; *F.*, vol. 2, p. 190.
[5] *G.R., 1307–17*, no. 834. For further information on Ferrers's attempts to uphold Edward II's ducal rights in Gascony see E. Pole-Stuart, 'Some Aspects of the Political and Administrative History of Gascony, 1303–27', Ph.D. (London, 1927).
[6] *G.R., 1307–17*, nos. 837–41; *C. Cl. R., 1307–13*, p. 567; *C.P.R., 1307–13*, p. 527; Camden 3rd series, vol. 41, pp. 21–2.

mont by the lord of Rouncideval.¹ Most important, however, was the last-minute decision made on 14 February, after Pembroke's departure, that he should arrange a personal meeting between Edward II and Philip IV to resolve outstanding Anglo-French disputes.²

For Pembroke to leave England at a time when the negotiations with the magnates were still in a very critical state, the need to send a mission to Paris and Gascony must have been extremely urgent. There is no doubt that the King was very uncertain as to whether he could spare his services. So serious was the situation in England that on 9 February the papal envoys wrote to tell Philip IV of the dangers to England from internal dissensions and external enemies and to ask Philip to deal promptly with Pembroke's business so that he could return quickly to England where he was badly needed. On top of this plea for haste, the King wrote to Pembroke on 14 February, only a few days after his departure, recalling him to England because royal affairs there were even more pressing.³

Pembroke probably left London on 10 or 11 February, in company with the Bishop of Exeter. Despite his recall, he continued on his way to Paris, which he had reached by 2 March.⁴ The King does not appear to have pressed further for Pembroke's immediate return, and his presence at Westminster cannot again be traced until 28 March,⁵ although he had probably come back some days before that. The mission seems to have had few immediate results, with the very important exception that on 14 March Pembroke made an agreement for Edward II to meet Philip IV at Amiens on 20 May.⁶ The success of such a

---

¹ *G.R., 1307–17*, nos. 834, 836, 844; Camden 3rd series, vol. 41, p. 22.

² *Archives Nationales*, J. 918, no. 18. A copy of this writ is included in B.M., Cotton MS. Julius F. I, f. 45, which is a register of Gascon documents.

³ Camden 3rd series, vol. 41, pp. 21–2; *C.R., 1307–17*, no. 846.

⁴ *C. Cl. R., 1307–13*, p. 567; E. 101/375/8, f. 19; *G.R., 1307–17*, no. 1171; Pembroke's account for the mission began on 3 Feb., the day on which he also received protections for it: E. 101/375/8, f. 15v.; *C.P.R., 1307–13*, pp. 525, 527.

⁵ C. 53/99, m. 7. Pembroke's account ended on 14 Mar. (E. 101/375/8, f. 15v.) but he appears still to have been in Paris on that date: *Archives Nationales*, J. 633, no. 35. The agreement made in Paris on this date may, however, have been performed for Pembroke by proxy, so that he could be back in England before the opening of Parliament due on 18 Mar. The Bishop of Exeter certainly remained in Paris after Pembroke's departure and when he too returned to London on 10 May, Thomas Cobham stayed in France to continue the mission's business: E. 101/375/8, ff. 19, 20. ⁶ *Archives Nationales*, J. 633, no. 35.

meeting in removing causes of Anglo-French dispute would undoubtedly strengthen Edward II's hand in any further negotiations with his English opponents.

After his return to England Pembroke once again became involved in the routine affairs of government. On 8 April for example he was asked by the King to arrange the release of a ship belonging to an English merchant Henry Alard which had been arrested at Calais. Early in May he was concerned with the appointment of Lupus Burgundi and Otto de la Dose to minor official posts in Gascony.[1]

But minor business of this kind was soon overshadowed by the preparations for the King's coming visit to France. At the end of April Philip IV's cousin Louis de Clermont arrived with an invitation for Edward II to attend the knighting of Philip IV's sons at Paris on 3 June.[2] The original intention to meet at Amiens on 20 May was therefore abandoned in favour of Paris. The details of the visit were being worked out by 1 May and on 3 May protections were given to those, including Pembroke and Despenser, who were to accompany the King.[3] One of Pembroke's duties at this time, together with Walter Reynolds, the newly elected Archbishop of Canterbury, John Sandal, and Despenser, was to decide the wages to be paid to the magnates who went with the King. It is significant of Pembroke's special dignity and importance as a royal councillor that, whereas magnates such as the Earl of Richmond and Despenser were paid wages at a fixed daily rate in the usual way, Pembroke instead later received a gift of a flat sum of 1,000 marks, which was also over twice the total amount received by any other magnate.[4]

Final preparations for the visit were discussed at a royal Council held on 20 May[5] and it is clear from this that it was to be more than just a social gathering or a personal meeting between the two kings. Some criticism was being levelled at the King, as he himself recognized, for going to France at a time

---

[1] C. 81/84/2442; S.C. 1/45/176 and 177; *G.R., 1307–17*, nos. 919, 924.

[2] E. 101/375/2, m. 9; *Vita*, p. 38; *C. Cl. R., 1307–13*, p. 579.

[3] *C.P.R., 1307–13*, pp. 579–83; *C. Cl. R., 1307–13*, p. 579.

[4] E. 101/375/8, ff. 11v., 12, 12v., 15. Richmond received 106s. 8d. and Despenser 100s. per day: ibid., ff. 10v. 11v., On other missions and on campaigns Pembroke too was paid wages.

[5] *C. Cl. R., 1307–13*, p. 579.

when the country was still divided internally and menaced by the Scots.[1] But, as has already been shown, the negotiations with the magnates had for the time being ended and there was no immediate prospect of any further meetings, while an attempt to treat with the Scots was at that moment being made by Louis de Clermont and other envoys.[2] The King was in fact going to France at the request both of the Pope and of Philip IV, and his presence there was essential, since the main purpose of his visit was to complete the diplomatic work begun by Pembroke in March and reach a settlement of the major outstanding problems in Anglo-French relations.[3]

The King left for France from Dover on 23 May, accompanied by Pembroke, Richmond, Despenser, and others, and the party reached Paris on 1 June.[4] Pembroke was in close attendance on the King throughout the visit, both in Paris from 1 to 9 June, and at Pontoise from 10 to 30 June, as well as elsewhere.[5] He would certainly therefore have been present at all the ceremonial highlights, the knighting of Philip IV's sons in Paris on 3 June, the taking of the cross and of crusading vows by the two kings in Notre Dame on 6 June, and the banquet with Charles of Valois at the Louvre on 7 June.[6] The activities of some of Pembroke's retainers are also apparent. On 7 June John Merlyn, one of his valets, paid twenty shillings to the King for him to offer at the Crown of Thorns in the Sainte Chapelle in Paris, but, less creditably, on 6 June the King had to pay 6s. 8d. alms to Gerard de Cheveril who had been wounded by members of Pembroke's household at St.-Germain-des-Prés. Pembroke also made use of the occasion to transact some personal business and wrote on 1 and 3 July to Henry de Stachesden, his Receiver in France, about the affairs of his lands in Poitou.[7]

Together with the Bishop of Exeter, the Earl of Richmond,

[1] *C.P.R.*, *1307–13*, p. 588; *Vita*, p. 38.

[2] *F.*, vol. 2, pp. 214–15; E. 101/375/8, f. 15; *Letters from Northern Registers*, ed. J. Raine, R.S. (London, 1883), p. 217.

[3] *P.W.*, vol. 2, part 2, p. 94; *C.P.R.*, *1307–13*, p. 588; *C. Cl. R.*, *1307–13*, p. 583.

[4] *C. Cl. R.*, *1307–13*, p. 583; E. 101/375/2, m. 9.

[5] E. 101/375/8, f. 30v.; ibid. /375/2, mm. 9, 10. Pembroke's constant presence is specifically mentioned in the records.

[6] E. 101/375/8, ff. 20, 30v.; E. 30/1422; *Grandes Chroniques de France*, ed. J. Viard (Paris, 1934), vol. 8, pp. 288–9.

[7] E. 101/375/8, f. 3v.; E. 163/4/1/1; S.C. 1/50/58.

and the clerical experts, Richard de Burton and Henry de Canterbury,[1] Pembroke certainly took a leading part in discussing the problems of Aquitaine, which were the major reason for Edward II's presence. The negotiations ended on 2 July, when Philip IV, as a mark of esteem for Edward's personal visit and taking of the cross, remitted all penalties incurred by Edward II and his subjects in Gascony for alleged offences against France, and also recited his letters patent of 1286 regulating all appeals to Paris by subjects of the Duchy.[2] This was also the means of settling the dispute between the Seneschal and Amanieu d'Albret, who was given £20,000 *tournois* 'for his good services'.[3] Diplomatically therefore the King's visit could be considered highly successful, especially by Pembroke, whose earlier mission had prepared the way. For the moment French goodwill was assured, even though experience showed that Anglo-French agreements on Aquitaine rarely lasted for very long.

These negotiations were so important that the King had to stay in France until their completion, and it was realized that he would not be in England in time to open Parliament on 8 July. On 1 July the Earls of Richmond and Gloucester and two bishops were therefore appointed to open and continue Parliament until the King's arrival.[4] The King finally returned to England on 16 July and reached London on 23 July.[5] Meanwhile Gloucester, Richmond, and some other magnates and prelates had waited in London as instructed, but the opposition magnates gave up and left before the King's return, claiming that the King's advisers had persuaded him to delay his return in order to wear down his opponents. The King, however, still expected as late as 19 July that he would be attending Parliament, since he then advised the Kent justices to postpone all cases involving Pembroke, whose presence at Parliament was urgently needed.[6]

---

[1] E. 101/375/8, f. 16; E. 404/482/22/5. Richmond had earlier taken part in the Process of Périgueux.

[2] *F.*, vol. 2, p. 220; E. 30/52 and 612; C. 47/27/8/29; ibid. /29/7/18; ibid. /30/4/26.   [3] Ibid. /29/7/17; *G.R., 1307–17*, no. 979.

[4] *C.P.R., 1307–13*, p. 594. It had been summoned on 23 May: *P.W.*, vol. 2, part 2, p. 94.

[5] *C. Cl. R., 1313–18*, p. 66; *F.*, vol. 2, p. 222.

[6] *Vita*, p. 42; C. 81/85/2746A. It is not known which opposition magnates attended Parliament.

Altogether the July Parliament seems to have been a complete failure and to have achieved no useful contact with the opposition. But the King's advisers were probably still extremely eager for a Parliament to be held to solve the deadlock between the King and his opponents. On 22 July Pembroke joined the King at Eltham, at the latter's request, and on 26 July, in the presence of Pembroke, Richmond, Despenser, the Bishops of Bath and Wells, Worcester, and Exeter, who probably all shared in the decision, a fresh Parliament was summoned to meet at Westminster on 23 September.[1] The events of the next few weeks are obscure, until on 28 August the King wrote asking Pembroke to meet with other members of the Council at Chertsey on 17 September to discuss the business of the coming Parliament. On the same date the King also requested Philip IV to send his chamberlain Enguerrand de Marigny and the French envoy of 1312, Louis of Évreux, to assist in the negotiations with the magnates.[2]

While on their way to Parliament in mid-September the Earls of Arundel, Lancaster, Gloucester, Hereford, and Warwick met at Brackley, ostensibly to hold a tournament, planned for 19 September, which the King tried to prohibit on 10 and 16 September. Tourneying, however, was only one of their intentions and there can be little doubt that before or after the tournament they met to concert a common baronial approach to the King when they reached Westminster. It is also possible that the King sent Pembroke to find out the magnates' intentions and report them to the Council at Chertsey on 17 September, since on 10 September Pembroke was at Witney, only twenty miles from Brackley.[3]

According to the account in the *Vita*, the magnates came to London on 23 September, the day Parliament was due to begin, but for some time had no contact with the King, who was

---

[1] S.C. 1/49/22; C. 53/100, m. 17; *P.W.*, vol. 2, part 2, p. 114.

[2] S.C. 1/49/23; *F.*, vol. 2, p. 226. The sending of French envoys had probably been discussed when Edward II was in Paris. The two papal envoys had been seeking the return of Louis of Évreux since February 1313: Camden 3rd series, vol. 41, p. 22.

[3] *F.*, vol. 2, pp. 227–8; Hist. MSS. Commission, *Various Collections*, vol. 1, p. 245. If Pembroke did indeed visit Brackley he may also have tried to dissuade the magnates from bringing their retinues to Parliament. The Earl of Gloucester's presence at Brackley suggests he was once again trying to mediate as he had done in 1312 and earlier in 1313.

F

reluctant to meet them. They then demanded that he should fulfil his promises of pardon, and finally under pressure the King gave way.[1] It is not known what demands the magnates made or if they differed in any way from their earlier ones in March, but there was certainly a period of further negotiation and mediation between the magnates' arrival and the King's issue of pardons. The mediation on this occasion was carried out, as in 1312, by the papal envoys and by the Earls of Gloucester and Richmond. Louis of Évreux is also said to have taken part, but this must have been at a late stage of the negotiations, since he and Enguerrand de Marigny were still awaited on 14 October.[2]

The first sign of impending agreement was on 4 October, when the sections of the Ordinances dealing with Henry de Beaumont and his sister Isabella de Vescy were abrogated as being to the King's prejudice.[3] By 14 October the negotiations were sufficiently advanced for the magnates to make a formal submission to the King, and on this date Lancaster, Warwick, Hereford, Arundel, Henry Percy, Robert Clifford, and John Botetourt came before the King at Westminster Hall and asked for and received his pardon. To mark the settlement the Earls dined with the King that night and returned the honour themselves the following night.[4] The opposition magnates attended Parliament for the first time on 15 October[5] and on the next day the King's pardons to them were published. The list was headed by Lancaster, Hereford, Warwick, Percy, Botetourt, and Clifford, with two of Lancaster's chief retainers, Robert de Holand and Gruffydd de la Pole. Warenne also found it advisable to have his name included, presumably because he could be regarded as technically requiring pardon for his share in the pursuit and surrender of Gaveston in 1312. No doubt for the same reason at least eleven of Pembroke's retainers also received pardons, although Pembroke himself, as the King's

[1] *Vita*, p. 43.

[2] Ibid.; *Flores*, vol. 3, p. 337; E. 101/375/9, f. 33.

[3] *C.P.R., 1313–17*, pp. 27, 29.

[4] *Liber de Antiquis Legibus*, ed. Th. Stapleton, Camden Society, vol. 34 (London, 1846), p. 252 (this is a London chronicle); *Vita*, p. 43. The *Flores*, vol. 3, p. 337, says the magnates submitted on 19 Oct. but is certainly mistaken.

[5] *Liber de Antiquis Legibus*, p. 252. This source also says that Parliament itself began on this date, but it had probably met without the opposition magnates since 23 Sept.

leading councillor, evidently did not feel the need to follow suit.[1]

No further decisions emerged from Parliament until the end of October, which suggests that hard bargaining was still in progress. On 30 October the prelates, earls, and barons declared in Parliament that it was the King's prerogative alone to bear arms. This was an important concession, which fulfilled the magnates' promise of the previous December that they would stop bringing their armed retainers to Parliaments once they had received pardon.[2] On 5 November the magnates were given a formal acquittance for their restoration of Gaveston's property, as they had demanded after the first acquittance in February.[3] On 6 November the King confirmed his earlier ordinance giving full pardon to the earls for Gaveston's death, but in return they had to agree to a pardon to Gaveston's former adherents, which they had previously refused to concede.[4] The dispute between Lancaster's two retainers, Gruffydd de la Pole and Fulk Lestrange, and the King's chamberlain John Charlton, which had been a major problem in January and February 1313, was settled by the appointment on 3 November of new justices in place of those of December 1312, and by the pardoning of all three parties on 6 November.[5] Finally, the magnates' promise to grant a subsidy for the Scottish war was fulfilled in the form of a fifteenth and twentieth.[6]

The King should have been well satisfied with this settlement. As in December 1312, the Ordinances were not mentioned,[7] nor was the removal of any royal ministers accepted,[8]

---

[1] *C.P.R., 1313–17*, pp. 21–5. The pardons had been granted in Parliament on 15 Oct.: ibid., p. 26. The Pembroke retainers who received pardons were Richard de Munchensy, William and Percival Simeon, Richard de la Ryvere, William de Faucomberg, John Comyn, Roger Ingpen, John Paynel, Edmund Gacelyn, John Darcy, and John Merlyn.

[2] *C.P.R., 1313–17*, p. 26; *Ann. Lond.*, p. 224.

[3] *C.P.R., 1313–17*, p. 25; *Ann. Lond.*, p. 227.

[4] *C.P.R., 1313–17*, p. 26; *Ann. Lond.*, p. 227.

[5] Camden 3rd series, vol. 41, p. 15; *C.P.R., 1307–13*, pp. 546–7; ibid., *1313–17*, pp. 26, 66.

[6] *Ann. Lond.*, p. 227; *C.P.R., 1313–17*, pp. 49–51.

[7] Except for the clauses concerning Henry de Beaumont which were removed: ibid., pp. 27, 29.

[8] The *Vita*, p. 44, mentions Lancaster's inability to have Despenser removed from the Council.

while Gaveston and his supporters were not referred to as enemies of the King. With these three problems at last removed from politics, at any rate in public, the King had achieved some of the freedom of action within his own kingdom for which Pembroke and his other supporters had been striving since June 1312.

The settlement of October 1313 was basically the same as and an extension of the treaty of December 1312, and, so far as its details were concerned, there was no good reason why it should not have been made earlier. The delay was caused on the one hand by the King's reluctance to give any final pardon to the killers of Gaveston and by his hope that he would succeed in improving the strength of his own position against the opposition by diplomatic means. On the other hand the behaviour of the King's opponents, and especially Lancaster, in raising new causes of dispute with the King in January 1313 does not suggest they were seeking a quick settlement either. At the same time neither side was strong enough to risk a military confrontation, with the result that 1313 was spent in arguing over the details of a settlement which neither could ultimately avoid. Essentially the agreement of October 1313 was a compromise, as it was bound to be under the circumstances of the time, and it was symbolized by the magnates' failure to enforce and the King's inability to destroy the Ordinances. But the personal hostility between Edward II and Lancaster and his allies remained, so that if the political balance changed in the future in favour of one or the other, there was every chance of a further crisis.

As in the case of the treaty negotiations in 1312, it is not possible to define precisely Pembroke's share in the making of the settlement of October 1313. But the evidence that exists to show his close involvement in other royal affairs both in 1312 and 1313 would suggest that his part in the climax of negotiations between the King and his opponents was likely to be considerable. During the latter part of 1312 and 1313 it is apparent that men such as the future Archbishop of Canterbury, Walter Reynolds, the acting Treasurer John Sandal, and Hugh Despenser the Elder were very active members of the royal Council. The evidence available on the Earl of Pembroke, however, makes it clear that he was the most important of the

King's magnate supporters and also the most influential of his advisers. Pembroke's was the guiding hand in the determination and in the execution of royal policy, both in major decisions and in the day-to-day routine of royal government. Pembroke's relations with the King were also very close and were indeed the pre-condition of his influence on policy, but, unlike Gaveston before 1312, he did not possess and probably did not seek a personal ascendancy over the King. Edward II may have been incapable of governing without the strong prop of a reliable man like Pembroke, but he still had to be coaxed from time to time into following a sensible course of action.[1] The King was at the very least capable of dragging his feet, especially when the result was to delay making a public settlement with his hated opponents, Lancaster and Warwick and Gaveston's other enemies. But, with this important limitation, Pembroke was still the chief political figure among the King's associates, and in terms of his own career he was now at a pinnacle of authority which he had never achieved before.

[1] Likely examples of occasions where the King needed a good deal of persuasion are in the decision whether to negotiate with or to fight the magnates in 1312 and in the negotiations over the release of Edmund Darel early in 1313.

III

Partial Eclipse
October 1313 to April 1316

Much of the authority exercised by Pembroke in 1312 and 1313 had derived from his possession of royal confidence. But it was also a product of the relative weakness of the King's opponents, which deprived them of any direct influence in the King's counsels. In this sense Pembroke's importance stemmed from the political stalemate which existed within England and could therefore be affected by any change in the situation. Ironically even the peace settlement at the end of 1313 would probably on its own have contributed to some weakening of Pembroke's position by bringing back into active political life those who had been the King's opponents. It is certainly true, for example, that the Earl of Hereford began to reappear in the royal circle after October 1313.[1] However Pembroke was far more vulnerable to the major alteration in the balance of political power that would inevitably follow a royal reverse. This is what did happen when Edward II's forces were defeated at Bannockburn in June 1314. From then on Pembroke's importance diminished as the King's own freedom of action declined. As a result, much of Pembroke's authority, which had been so great in 1313, had evaporated by the end of 1314 as the King's chief opponents, Lancaster and Warwick, gained in importance. One feature of the changes taking place in 1314 was a fierce quarrel between Pembroke and Lancaster, which illustrates very vividly the personal nature of politics and also provides a sensitive indicator of conditions in the country as a whole. Pembroke was therefore in a state of partial eclipse during 1315 and early 1316 when first Warwick and then Lancaster came to the forefront.

In the months immediately following the 1313 settlement there was not yet any sign of a decline in Pembroke's influence.

[1] See *Vita*, p. 44, and the discussion of the Bannockburn campaign below.

In 1312 and early in 1313 much of his activity, such as in the negotiations with the magnates and the attempts to improve Anglo-French relations, had been intended to help strengthen the King's position and give him greater security. During the same period Pembroke had also taken a prominent part in a number of measures designed to assist the King by relieving the strain on royal finances caused by the continuing political crisis.[1] By the autumn of 1313 these efforts were starting to bear fruit.

In May 1313, for example, a papal envoy to England, Cardinal William Testa, had loaned the King 2,000 marks, and in July at Ibouvillers, during the royal visit to France, Edward II's merchant and banker Anthony Pessagno had borrowed £15,000 on the King's behalf from Enguerrand de Marigny.[2] In both cases Pembroke joined with other royal councillors in guaranteeing repayment of the loans and was indemnified by the King against any loss in the event of non-payment.[3] These two loans, however, were only short-term and were probably raised on the strength of a much more important impending loan from Pope Clement V, which had been under negotiation since August 1312 and in whose inception at that time Pembroke had been closely concerned.[4] Originally the loan had been intended to help the King to hold out against the demands of his opponents and so wear them down. But details of the loan were not finally agreed until 28 October 1313[5] so that it then became a factor in the political situation which followed the 1313 settlement. Under the terms of the loan the Pope agreed to make a private loan to Edward II of 160,000 florins in return for control of the bulk of the revenues of Gascony. Before the loan could be implemented approval was required from Philip IV of France as suzerain of Gascony, and it was for this reason that on 12 December the King, accompanied by Pembroke

---

[1] This is only a very selective account of royal financial affairs.

[2] *C.P.R.*, *1307–13*, pp. 571, 573; ibid., *1313–17*, p. 4.

[3] Ibid., *1307–13*, p. 573; ibid., *1313–17*, p. 102. The indemnity was fortunate for Pembroke, since in Oct. 1313 Testa grew tired of waiting for repayment and appointed proctors to claim the money from Pembroke and his colleagues: E. 329/69.

[4] *F.*, vol. 2, pp. 175–6. The negotiating of this loan has been discussed by Y. Renouard in 'Édouard II et Clément V d'après les rôles gascons', in *Annales du Midi*, vol. 67 (1955), and in *Études d'histoire médiévale*, vol. 2 (Paris, 1968).

[5] *F.*, vol. 2, pp. 231–2; *G.R.*, *1307–17*, no. 1131.

and the Elder Despenser, crossed to Boulogne and met the French King at Montreuil, returning to England on 20 December.[1] The loan agreement was finally confirmed on 20 January 1314 in the King's chamber at Westminster, in the presence of Pembroke and other councillors, and the 160,000 florins, worth £25,000 sterling, were received by Anthony Pessagno on the King's behalf during March.[2]

As one of the chief architects of the negotiations preceding the loan, Pembroke's presence at the formal ceremony of confirmation was appropriate enough. Earlier the same month, on 4 January, he had witnessed another ceremony, with one of his retainers, John Comyn, the acting Treasurer John Sandal, and five others, when the new Archbishop, Walter Reynolds, read out at his inn in Charing Cross the papal bull providing him to Canterbury. Pembroke was also to be present, together with the King, Queen, and a large gathering of other magnates and prelates, at Reynolds's enthronement at Canterbury on 17 February.[3]

Pembroke's main occupation in 1314, in common with the rest of the Council, was the organization of a campaign in Scotland to try to remove the most immediate remaining threat to stability in England. A campaign had already been decided on by 28 November 1313, when the King invited the Scottish magnates and prelates to recognize fealty to him and announced that he would be at Berwick on about 24 June. On 23 December the host was summoned to meet at Berwick on 10 June, but the loss of Roxburgh in February, of Edinburgh in March, and

---

[1] *F.*, vol. 2, pp. 232, 238, 240; *C. Cl. R., 1313–18*, p. 31; *C.P.R., 1313–17*, p. 44; *Trivet (Cont.)*, p. 11. Ostensibly the visit was for a pilgrimage: *F.*, vol. 2, p. 238; *Trivet (Cont.)*, p. 11.

[2] *G.R., 1307–17*, no. 1133; *F.*, vol. 2, pp. 322–4; *C.P.R., 1313–17*, p. 205. Edward II made a further concession to Clement V in return for the loan on 25 Nov. 1313, when he acceded to the Pope's request to allow the Knights Hospitallers to take control of the lands which had formally belonged to the Templars and were then in royal hands. Among those present in the King's green chamber at Westminster on this occasion were Pembroke, the Elder Despenser, Walter Reynolds the Archbishop-elect, and John Sandal the acting Treasurer: E. 30/1368; E. 41/193; E. 135/1/25; S.C. 7/12/12; ibid. /64/20.

[3] *Reg. Sandale*, Hampshire Record Society (Winchester, 1897), xxv, n. 4; *Trivet (Cont.)*, p. 11; *Ann. Paul.*, p. 275; *Trokelowe*, p. 82; C. 53/100, m. 7. Trinity College Cambridge MS. R. 5. 41, f. 112v., which is a Canterbury chronicle, has the details of Reynolds's enthronement but wrongly gives the date as 26 Feb. Extracts from this little-known source are in *Collectanea of J. Leland*, ed. Th. Hearne (London, 1770), vol. 1, p. 272.

the agreement by the constable of Stirling to surrender if not relieved by 24 June,[1] made it necessary to change these plans. By 26 February the King had decided to go to Scotland soon after Easter (7 April) and on 24 March Pembroke was appointed Keeper of Scotland and to act as the King's Lieutenant until the latter's arrival, receiving full powers to do whatever he felt was necessary.[2] Pembroke's part in the campaign was thus intended to be extremely important. He had reached Berwick by 16 April, but was already at work by 3 April when the King wrote, in reply to a request from him, promising that supplies and men would be sent with all speed. On 6 April the King wrote again to announce that he was on his way north and to ask Pembroke to keep him fully informed of progress in arranging the campaign. By 6 June the King had joined Pembroke at Newminster in Northumberland and the campaign was ready to begin.[3]

Despite the settlement of the previous October, the Bannockburn campaign was marked by the failure to take part of four of the leading magnates, the Earls of Lancaster, Warwick, Arundel, and Warenne, a fact which requires some explanation. The earls' argument that the campaign had not been decided upon in Parliament[4] was a transparent excuse, since a Scottish campaign had been implicitly a part of the business of the Parliament of September 1313, which had granted a subsidy for the purpose. The real cause of the absence of Warwick and Lancaster was a fear that if the King were victorious in Scotland he would then turn against them in England,[5] while a royal defeat in their absence would in turn strengthen their hand against the King. Warenne's absence may have been caused partly by his efforts to annul his marriage to the King's niece Joan de Bar, which probably put him on bad terms with the King,[6] but also by fear of the Earl of Lancaster, who was

[1] *F.*, vol. 2, p. 237; *P.W.*, vol. 2, part 2, p. 421. See also G. W. S. Barrow, *Robert Bruce* (London, 1965), pp. 276–8.
[2] *C. Ch. Warr.*, p. 395; *P.W.*, vol. 2, part 1, p. 112.
[3] C. 81/1705/64; S.C. 1/49/26, 27; C. 53/100, m. 4.
[4] *Vita.*, pp. 49–50.
[5] *Knighton*, vol. 1, p. 410. Lancaster stayed at Pontefract during the campaign and Warwick was certainly at Warwick castle early in May: ibid.; B.M., Add. MS. 28024, f. 70.
[6] See F. R. Fairbank, 'The Last Earl of Warenne and Surrey', *Yorks. Arch. Journal*, vol. 19 (1907), pp. 198–9. This may be why Warenne was forced reluctantly

an uncomfortably near neighbour of his in Yorkshire.[1] The Earl of Arundel, who was never noted for independence of spirit, may have been influenced by the example of his brother-in-law Warenne, or, as is more likely, he simply followed what he thought was the more powerful party. Of the magnates who accompanied the King only Hereford's presence is of any special interest. Although a Lancastrian supporter in 1312, his part in persuading Lancaster to accept the peace negotiations of 1312 and 1313 seems to mark him out as a moderate. After the 1313 settlement he remained at court and may even have made an indenture to serve the King in the 1314 campaign.[2]

The details of the campaign and the disaster at Bannockburn on 24 June have been fully worked out elsewhere and do not require repetition.[3] Pembroke's direct participation in the main fighting during the battle seems to have been small. The most detailed account says that the King drew up his division of the army with Sir Giles d'Argentein on one side of him and Pembroke on the other. When defeat became obvious Pembroke seized the King's reins and led him away from the battle against his will, while Argentein rode into the fight and was killed.[4] Many of those captured after the battle were taken at or near the castle of Bothwell, which had technically belonged to Pembroke since 1301.[5] But Pembroke did not apparently go there himself. *The Bruce* states that Maurice de Berkeley, a member of Pembroke's retinue, escaped 'with a great rout of Welshmen', and it is likely that he did so in the latter's company, since the *Lanercost* writer makes the same remark with reference to

to give up the honour of High Peak to the Queen in Feb. 1314: *C.P.R., 1313–17*, p. 38; *C. Cl. R., 1313–18*, p. 38; *C.F.R., 1307–19*, p. 182. Apart from his spectacular change of allegiance in June 1312, when he and Pembroke rejoined the King, Warenne's role in politics at this time was minimal.

    [1] This may explain why Warenne spent June 1314 at his Yorkshire castle of Sandal, which was not far from Pontefract: Lambeth, Register of Walter Reynolds, f. 107.
    [2] *Vita*, p. 44; E. 101/68/2/34 (badly damaged). The *Vita* emphasizes Hereford's reconciliation with the King. He had originally supported Gaveston's execution in 1312 only after firm guarantees from Lancaster and Warwick: D.L. 25/1982; D.L. 34/13.
    [3] The most recent account is in Barrow, op. cit., pp. 301–32.
    [4] *The Bruce*, vol. 1, pp. 264, 317; *Scalacronica*, p. 143.
    [5] *The Bruce*, vol. 1, p. 321; *Melsa*, vol. 2, p. 331; *Lanercost*, p. 227; *Historia Anglicana of Thomas Walsingham*, p. 140; *French Chronicle of London*, Camden Society, vol. 28 (London, 1844), p. 38; *Cal. of Docs. relating to Scotland*, vol. 2, no. 1214.

Pembroke.[1] The *Lanercost* account precedes this point by the statement that a large body of fugitives fled to Carlisle, from which it might be concluded that Pembroke went in the same direction.[2] But this interpretation is unconvincing in view of Pembroke's closeness to the King during the battle, and preference must be given to other accounts which say that Pembroke and other magnates fled with the King to Dunbar and from there sailed to Berwick.[3]

Pembroke is said by some writers to have fled from the battle barefoot and unarmed, only just escaping with his life.[4] His retinue of twenty-two knights and fifty-nine men-at-arms[5] also suffered severely. John Lovel, John Comyn,[6] John de la Ryvere, and William de Vescy[7] were killed, while Thomas de Berkeley senior, Thomas and Maurice the sons of Maurice de Berkeley,[8] John and Nicholas de Kingston, William Lovel, Aymer la Zouche, Thomas and Odo le Ercedekne, and John Mautravers junior were all taken prisoner.[9] As this list refers only to knights it is probable that there were also many casualties among Pembroke's men-at-arms. The exact occasion of these losses is not known but the most likely answer is that Pembroke and his men fought a prolonged rearguard action against the pursuing forces of Sir James Douglas to cover the King's retreat through Linlithgow and Winchburgh on his way to Dunbar.[10] If this is

[1] *The Bruce*, vol. 1, p. 321; *Lanercost*, p. 227.

[2] Ibid. This conclusion is suggested in Barrow, op. cit., p. 331.

[3] *Melsa*, vol. 2, p. 331; *French Chronicle of London*, p. 38; *Lanercost*, p. 227; *Vita*, p. 55; *Scalacronica*, p. 143.

[4] *Ann. Lond.*, p. 231; *Lanercost*, p. 227; *Melsa*, vol. 2, p. 330; *Trokelowe*, p. 85.

[5] Figures built up from material in C. 71/6, mm. 5–1; C. 81/1748/73; ibid. /1728/23; ibid. /1736/23, 24, 47, 48, 54, 56, 59. For details of Pembroke's retinue in this and other campaigns see Appendix 2.

[6] *Ann. Lond.*, p. 231; *Trivet (Cont.)*, p. 15. Lovel is not actually listed among Pembroke's retainers on this occasion but is known to have had close links with him. Comyn was Pembroke's nephew and son of John Comyn of Badenoch.

[7] *Ann. Lond.*, p. 231; *Trivet (Cont.)*, p. 15.

[8] Maurice de Berkeley senior, the son and heir of Thomas de Berkeley senior, is said to have been captured by the *Vita*, p. 55, probably by confusion with his son Maurice. The Berkeley family historian who had access to their records, however, shows that Maurice de Berkeley senior escaped and that his father Thomas was taken prisoner: J. Smyth of Nibley, *Lives of the Berkeleys* (Gloucester, 1883–5), vol. 1, pp. 182–3. *The Bruce*, vol. 1, p. 321, also says that Maurice senior escaped.

[9] *Trivet (Cont.)*, p. 15. This is the fullest casualty list given in a chronicle source. William Lovel and Aymer la Zouche were both free by July 1315: E. 101/15/6.

[10] *The Bruce*, vol. 1, pp. 327–8.

what indeed happened, Pembroke would appear to be the only royal commander to emerge from the disaster with any great credit.

Bannockburn entirely destroyed the favourable conditions created for the King by the 1313 settlement. By 17 July the King had retired to York with Pembroke, Despenser, Henry de Beaumont, and the dead Earl of Gloucester's chief retainer, Bartholomew de Badlesmere, leaving behind a garrison to defend Berwick.[1] On 29 July a Parliament was summoned to meet at York on 9 September, and on 7 September Pembroke and the Bishop of Exeter were authorized to open it in the King's name.[2] Ostensibly called to consider the threat from the Scots, the King's former opponents saw their opportunity and, at Lancaster's insistence, the King was forced to confirm the Ordinances,[3] which by this time had been in abeyance for over two years. There then followed a wholesale removal of royal officers and their replacement by men appointed in the manner stipulated in the Ordinances. John Sandal was appointed as Chancellor and replaced as Treasurer by Walter de Norwich, while the sheriffs of thirty counties, including John Pabenham, the Sheriff of Bedford, and one of Pembroke's retainers, were also removed.[4] But the new appointments were not in reality to the King's disadvantage. John Sandal, for example, was a royal clerk of long standing and had, as acting Treasurer, been very active in royal affairs in 1312 and 1313. Nor is there any obvious sign among the other appointments of men who might be objectionable to the King. What was most offensive to the King was not the character of the new officials but rather the mode and circumstances of their appointment.[5] The York Parliament was, however, only the beginning of the political upheaval which the defeat at Bannockburn brought in its train and the stage was now set for a return to political influence by the most prominent of the former opposition magnates, Lancaster and Warwick.

    [1] C. 53/101, m. 22; *Vita*, p. 57.
    [2] *P.W.*, vol. 2, part 2, p. 126; *C.P.R., 1313–17*, p. 169.
    [3] *Vita*, p. 57; *Lanercost*, p. 229.
    [4] *C. Cl. R., 1313–18*, pp. 197–8; *C.P.R., 1313–17*, p. 178; *C.F.R., 1307–19*, pp. 220–1.
    [5] For a fuller discussion of the York Parliament see T. F. Tout, *The Place of the Reign of Edward II* (2nd edn., Manchester, 1936), pp. 90–2.

For Pembroke the York Parliament and the months which followed marked a decline in his previous importance, which will be discussed later in this chapter. But the Parliament also had a more immediate significance for Pembroke, since it brought the climax of a bitter dispute between himself and Lancaster which had been simmering ever since the peace settlement of October 1313. This was an argument over the possession of the castle and manor of Thorpe Waterville and its associated manors of Aldwincle and Achurch in Northamptonshire, and also over the New Temple in London. Pembroke and Lancaster were the leading parties to this dispute, so that it conveniently symbolizes the political divisions in the country as a whole, with the King's most important magnate sympathizer on one side and his chief opponent on the other. However, the problem was really much more complex than this, since altogether three other persons were also involved: Walter Langton the Bishop of Coventry and Lichfield and former Treasurer; his *familiaris* and right-hand man John Hotot; and William Tuchet, one of Lancaster's bannerets.

The origins of the problem went back to 1298, when Tuchet inherited the demesne lands at Thorpe Waterville of his uncle, William de Luda, Bishop of Ely. At a date between 20 March and 26 December 1300 they passed into the possession of Walter Langton, one of de Luda's executors,[1] as a result of an exchange by which Tuchet gave up Thorpe Waterville in return for the castle of Leinthall in Hereford, and the manors of Preston, Finmere, and Hornington in Buckingham, Oxford, and Essex.[2] However, it appears that Langton had used the powers of his position as royal Treasurer to force Tuchet to make the agreement against his will, since in 1307 Tuchet claimed that he had given up Thorpe Waterville to Langton as a result of an action of novel disseisin taken out against him by Robert de Wickham,[3] at the suggestion and with the financial support of Langton.[4]

---

[1] *C. Ch. Warr.*, p. 94; *C.P.R., 1292–1301*, pp. 439, 540; *C. Ch. R., 1257–1300*, p. 482; ibid., *1300–26*, p. 1.

[2] C.P. 25(1)/285/25/258: dated 27 Jan. 1301 but confirming a prior agreement.

[3] Wickham was an heir of Robert de Waterville, who held Thorpe Waterville until he sold it to Simon de Ellesworth, who in turn sold it to William de Luda: *Henry of Pytchley's Book of Fees*, ed. W. T. Mellows, Northants. Record Soc., vol. 2 (Kettering, 1927), p. 41. Wickham presumably therefore had no good legal claim.

[4] J.I. 1/1344, mm. 2*d*., 13*d*.; E. 13/31, m. 13. See also A. Beardwood, 'The Trial of Walter Langton', *Trans. American Philosophical Association*, vol. 54, part 3 (1964),

Tuchet also fell foul of Langton in 1301, when the latter failed to repay him a debt of £300, and again in 1306, when Langton unsuccessfully tried to force him to give up his manor of Oxinden in Gloucestershire.[1] The exchange of Thorpe Waterville between Tuchet and Langton was legally watertight, but the circumstances in which it was made ensured that at some future date Tuchet would, given a suitable opportunity, try to avenge his wrongs at Langton's hands by regaining possession of Thorpe Waterville by legal or other means.

Langton held Thorpe Waterville until March 1308, when, with his other lands, it was seized by the King after his dismissal as Treasurer, and it then remained in royal hands until restored to him in 1312 when he returned to favour.[2] The fate of Thorpe Waterville is next revealed in July 1313, when Langton's *familiaris*, John Hotot, to whom he had given it for life,[3] brought an action of novel disseisin against William Tuchet. The occasion of the disseisin is not stated, but it is reasonable to suppose that Tuchet, who had unsuccessfully sued before royal justices for Thorpe Waterville's return to him in 1307 after Langton's disgrace,[4] had re-entered it at some time during the disturbances of 1312 when the Ordainers were protesting against Langton's reappointment as Treasurer.[5] It is also likely that, as one of Lancaster's retainers, he had done so with the latter's active support.

Pembroke first entered the picture on 10 November 1313, when he and Tuchet made mutual bonds to the value of £5,000. The purpose of these recognizances was not mentioned, but it is certain from later evidence that they formed part of an exchange of lands whereby Tuchet gave Thorpe Waterville to Pembroke in return for the latter's manors of Moreton and

p. 19. In 1301 Wickham quitclaimed his newly regained control over Thorpe Waterville to Langton: C.P. 25(1)/175/58/398. The material in J.I. 1/1344 and E. 13/31 is the result of inquiries into Langton's conduct held after his dismissal in 1307. It is used in A. Beardwood, op. cit., and has now been edited by the same scholar as Camden, 4th series, vol. 6 (London, 1969).

[1] J.I. 1/1344, mm. 10d. 13,
[2] *C. Cl. R., 1307–13*, p. 28; *C.P.R., 1307–13*, p. 412.
[3] Ibid., pp. 260–1; W. Dugdale, *Monasticon Anglicanum* (London, 1817–30) vol. 5, p. 435; D.L. 25/338. Hotot held land nearby at Clopton: J. Bridges, *The History and Antiquities of Northamptonshire* (London, 1791), vol. 2, pp. 367–9.
[4] *C. Ch. Warr.*, p. 391; J.I. 1/1344, m. 13d.
[5] E. 159/85, m. 52.

Whaddon in Gloucestershire.[1] With its recently fortified manor house and an annual revenue of around £200,[2] Thorpe Waterville was a very valuable acquisition, as well as being close to Pembroke's other Northamptonshire lands at Towcester and those of his retainers, John Hastings, John Pabenham, and John Lovel. Its strategic position in the Midlands, where Lancaster had important holdings,[3] also gave it great importance in the event of any future clash between the King and Lancaster, and it may have been decided for this reason by the King that it would be safer for his chief magnate supporter, Pembroke, to acquire it than to attempt to restore it to the unpopular Langton.[4]

Although Tuchet had been legally compensated by Pembroke for giving up Thorpe Waterville, some pressure had probably been used to make him do so, with the result that on 20 November, only ten days after the transaction, he forcibly entered and seized it back from Pembroke. Although pardoned for the offence on 26 November,[5] at Pembroke's instance and as an inducement to return the lands, Tuchet refused to restore them,[6] and on 3 December Pembroke took preliminary steps to recover possession when a commission was appointed to investigate Tuchet's action.[7] One ominous feature of the situation was that for the first time Lancaster had become directly involved, since it was on his behalf that Tuchet had performed the seizure.[8]

Shortly afterwards measures were taken by the King to provide Pembroke with a clear legal title to Thorpe Waterville by buying out the rights there of Walter Langton, who still remained the legal owner, despite Pembroke's agreement with Tuchet. On 26 January 1314 a conference was held at Windsor, in the presence of the King, Pembroke, Despenser, Sandal, and other councillors, at which Langton agreed on behalf of himself

---

[1] *C. Cl. R., 1313–18*, pp. 80–1; D.L. 42/2, f. 194; *C.F.R., 1307–19*, p. 213.
[2] Bridges, op. cit., vol. 2, p. 367; W. Dugdale, *Monasticon*, vol. 5, p. 435; E. 358/13, mm. 11–12, 48–9.
[3] e.g. Melbourne, Tutbury, Higham Ferrers, Kenilworth, Castle Donington.
[4] Some informal agreement to permit this had probably already been made between Pembroke and Langton.
[5] D.L. 29/1/3, m. 1*d.*; *C.P.R., 1313–17*, p. 44.
[6] Lancaster took action to guard it against counter-attack: D.L. 29/1/3, m. 20*d.*
[7] *C.P.R., 1313–17*, p. 72.
[8] D.L. 29/1/3, m. 1*d.*

and Hotot to give up his rights and grant the lands to the King
or to his assign, who would certainly be Pembroke. He also
promised to quitclaim the lands to the King if he and Hotot
won their action of novel disseisin pending against Tuchet. In
return the King would give him 490 marks in rents and 3,900
marks in cash.[1]

Lancaster meanwhile was making his own arrangements for
Thorpe Waterville's future. On 10 February Tuchet gave seisin
of Thorpe Waterville to Lancaster until 1 August 1315, when
the latter would either re-enfeoff him or give him other lands
of the same value. Tuchet also promised to let Lancaster have
the title deeds if his seisin were ever challenged in a royal court,[2]
these last provisions being made with the actions pending
between Pembroke and Tuchet and Langton and Tuchet in
mind. From being merely a dispute between Tuchet on the one
hand and Langton and Hotot on the other the problem had
thus turned into a direct confrontation between Pembroke and
Lancaster.

It nearly became a military clash as well. On 7 February
the King wrote asking Pembroke to stop collecting men-at-arms
and allow his suit with Lancaster and Tuchet to be settled
legally.[3] On 26 February two messengers from Lancaster came
to the King at Hadley. They accused Pembroke of having purchased the commission of oyer and terminer taken out against
Tuchet,[4] and also claimed that on the day the justices were to
have heard the case at Yardley Hastings, Pembroke's armed
retainers came and prevented Lancaster's and Tuchet's men
from pleading their case. In reply the King promised that the
Council would meet to discuss the matter and again asked Pembroke not to impede the justices.[5] There is little doubt that by
making these charges against Pembroke, Lancaster was trying
to obscure his own interference in the other suit pending over
Thorpe Waterville, that between Langton and Hotot and

  [1] D.L. 25/338.
  [2] D.L. 25/3445, 3446. The first of these documents is undated but is clearly of
the same date as the other.
  [3] S.C. 1/49/24.
  [4] Ibid. /50/86; ibid. /49/25. The commission was that of 3 Dec. 1313: *C.P.R.*,
1313–17, p. 72.
  [5] S.C. 1/49/25; ibid. /50/86. Yardley Hastings belonged to Pembroke's nephew
John Hastings.

Tuchet and himself. The evidence given in Lancaster's own financial records shows that in the early part of 1314 he had spent over £80 in bribes to gain support in this suit. It is also clear that the disturbances at Yardley about which he complained were his doing as much as Pembroke's,[1] and that it was Lancaster's men who prevented the justices there from hearing Langton's and Hotot's plea and threatened to do the same if they attempted to hear the case at Northampton instead.[2] Under such conditions Pembroke can hardly be blamed for gathering men to counteract Lancaster's tactics.

It is unlikely that Lancaster could ever have won against either Pembroke or Langton by a legal judgement, and it was not until Bannockburn had weakened Pembroke's political position that Lancaster was able to obtain legal recognition of his seizure of Thorpe Waterville. On 29 September 1314, during the York Parliament, Pembroke quitclaimed to Lancaster all his rights in Thorpe Waterville and in the New Temple in London,[3] and on 6 October the two earls made a comprehensive agreement in the form of an indenture. Lancaster promised to restore before Christmas the manors of Moreton and Whaddon which Pembroke had given Tuchet in 1313 and to see that Tuchet returned all the muniments relating to them, and undertook to give back all Pembroke's property stored in the New Temple.[4] For his part Pembroke promised to give to Lancaster all the muniments of Thorpe Waterville that he had received from Tuchet,[5] and said that on the day he recovered Moreton and Whaddon[6] he would hand over to Lancaster all the covenants, instruments, and obligations made to the King by Langton and Hotot.[7] Lancaster strengthened his grip on

---

[1] D.L. 29/1/3, mm. 20d., 26d. Lancaster and Tuchet were nearby at Castle Donington in Leicestershire in February, while Pembroke was well distant at Canterbury on 17 Feb.: D.L. 25/3446; C. 53/100, m. 7.

[2] *C.P.R., 1313–17*, p. 141.

[3] D.L. 25/2343; D.L. 42/11, f. 18; B.M., Lansdowne MS. 229, f. 127; Lancaster claimed the New Temple, which the King had given to Pembroke in Dec. 1312, as part of the Leicester earldom. The King confirmed Pembroke's quitclaim on 1 Oct.: D.L. 10/216.

[4] D.L. 42/2, f. 194.

[5] On the same day the King formally asked Pembroke to do this: S.C. 1/49/28.

[6] Tuchet put the manors into the King's hands on 5 Oct. and they were restored to Pembroke on the same day: *C.F.R., 1307–19*, p. 213; *C.P.R., 1313–17*, p. 186.

[7] D.L. 42/2, f. 194. Pembroke did so on 7 Oct.: B.M., Harleian Ch. 43. C. 46.

Thorpe Waterville during 1315 and 1316.[1] In compensation for his losses the King gave Pembroke lands worth £106. 10s. 8¾d. at Hadnock and Little Monmouth in Wales, and, to restore his position in Northamptonshire, gave him custody of two-thirds of the lands of John Lovel of Titchmarsh and left him in control of the royal castle of Rockingham, which he had been given on 18 February 1314 when the threat of a clash with Lancaster was at its height.[2]

But this compensation could not repair the greater damage inflicted upon Pembroke's political and administrative influence by the King's defeat at Bannockburn and Lancaster's victory at the York Parliament. Yet it is also an implicit comment upon Pembroke's behaviour in the days of his power that, whereas the King's opponents now made a renewed attack on unpopular royal counsellors such as Hugh Despenser the Elder and Henry de Beaumont,[3] no such attack was made upon Pembroke. His integrity was such and the King's trust in him so great that, although Warwick and Lancaster were able to force themselves on to the royal Council during the next two years, they could not at the same time exclude Pembroke. Pembroke's career in the royal service therefore continued under the new political conditions created by the events of 1314.

The closing months of 1314 soon exhibited further signs of the changed situation. An early indication of this can be found in the letters on the collection of a clerical tenth which were sent the same day to the Bishops of Bath and Wells and of Exeter by both the King and Lancaster, as if the latter were vetting and approving royal acts.[4] Certain other government decisions at this time were also at least indirectly influenced by Warwick and Lancaster. Shortly before 27 November, for example, the King made a detailed account of his debts to

---

[1] This was done by agreements with John Hotot and William Tuchet. See D.L. 25/2040; ibid. /224; D.L. 36/1/45; C.P. 25(1)/176/66, nos. 243, 247; C.P. 26(1)/2/28 and 29.

[2] *C. Ch. R., 1300–26*, p. 242; *C.P.R., 1307–13*, p. 273; S.C. 8/294/14691; *C.F.R., 1307–19*, p. 212; *C.P.R., 1313–17*, p. 85. John Lovel had been one of Pembroke's retainers. Titchmarsh was next door to Thorpe Waterville. Pembroke's acquisition of Hadnock and Little Monmouth later brought him some difficulties when Lancaster's brother, Henry of Lancaster, complained that they had previously been held from him and that his rights as overlord had been ignored: S.C. 8/56/2770.

[3] *Vita*, pp. 57–8.

[4] Hist. MSS. Comm., *10th Report*, part 3, p. 300; *Reg. Stapledon*, pp. 429–30.

Anthony Pessagno and on 4 December, in response to a demand made at York, the Exchequer was ordered to list all gifts and grants made contrary to the Ordinances since March 1310.[1]

These measures were taken in preparation for the Parliament summoned to meet at London on 20 January 1315.[2] But shortly before it met, there took place on 2 January an event which aptly symbolized the closing of one period of the reign and the start of another. This was the elaborate ceremony attending the final burial of the body of Piers Gaveston at the King's chapel at Langley. The event was attended by the King, the Archbishop, the Chancellor and Treasurer, the royal Justices, four bishops, thirteen abbots, as well as by the Earls of Pembroke and Hereford, Hugh Despenser, Henry de Beaumont, and over fifty knights.[3] Gaveston's murderers Lancaster and Warwick were naturally absent, but Hereford's presence indicates the extent of his return to the royal circle.

When Parliament finally met it continued on the course begun at York. Two of the most objectionable of the King's councillors, Despenser and Walter Langton, were now removed from the Council, steps were taken to reduce Household expenditure,[4] and on 14 February orders were given for the reobservance of the Ordinances, followed on 5 March by instructions to resume grants made since 1310.[5] On the face of it the King's opponents were now in the ascendant. On 15 March Parliament was prorogued until 13 April to allow some of the earls and magnates to return home for Easter, but effectively its business had now ended, since many of them failed to return for the renewed session after Easter.[6]

One magnate who did return, however, was Pembroke. In response to a request by the King at the time of his departure from Parliament, Pembroke sent one of his knights, Sir John Pabenham, to Windsor on 23 March. On 24 March the King wrote asking him not to go any further north from London[7]

---

[1] *C.P.R., 1313–17*, pp. 203–6; *C. Ch. Warr.*, p. 407.

[2] *P.W.*, vol. 2, part 2, p. 136.

[3] B.M., Cotton MS. Cleopatra D. III, f. 56v. (Hales Abbey chronicle); E. 101/375/17, m. 1.   [4] *Vita*, p. 59.

[5] 'Deeds Enrolled on the de Banco Rolls', ed. E. A. Fry (Public Record Office typescript, 1927), p. 58; *C.F.R., 1307–19*, pp. 240, 243–4.

[6] *C. Cl. R., 1313–18*, p. 163; *Trokelowe*, p. 90.

[7] Pembroke may have planned to survey his newly purchased castle of Mitford in Northumberland.

and to be at Westminster on 13 April to give him advice as he had done in the past.[1] This may well be an attempt by the King to use Pembroke to counterbalance the influence of Lancaster and Warwick, but, although it is clear enough proof of the King's continued trust in him, Pembroke's real position can only be shown by an analysis of the political situation of early 1315.

There is a curiously ambivalent quality about the politics of this period, so that it is possible to conclude from the evidence either on the one hand that a new balance of power was working itself out with neither the royal administrators and sympathizers nor the King's opponents having full control, or on the other that for the first time since April 1312 there was something like a united baronial front and that the magnates were discharging what they regarded as their common duty to advise the King.

Both the former chief opposition magnates, Lancaster and Warwick, made frequent appearances as witnesses to royal charters during the London Parliament,[2] and, although this cannot be equated with activity in the making of government decisions, there can be little doubt that such decisions were being made with their likely reaction in mind. In the case of Warwick alone further comment is possible. One contemporary source claims that he was now appointed as head of the Council,[3] and it is certain that Warwick was active as a member of the Council up to at least the first half of June 1315. But it is also evident that others, notably Pembroke, Hereford, the Chancellor, the Treasurer, and the Archbishop, were no less active,[4] and there is no reason to suppose that Warwick was even informally the dominant figure on the Council that Pembroke had been in 1312 and 1313. At the same time it is not entirely clear what was the relationship between Warwick and Lancaster, who did not return to London after the first session of Parliament. It is most probable that Lancaster was content that Warwick, who appears to have had the greater taste for

---

[1] S.C. 1/49/29.   [2] C. 53/101, mm. 5, 6.

[3] *Ann. Lond.*, p. 232. The chronicler is perhaps anticipating Lancaster's formal appointment as head of the Council in 1316. Davies, op. cit., p. 395, dates this reference to Warwick in 1314. Tout in *The Place of the Reign of Edward II* (1936), p. 93, sees Warwick as replacing the incompetent Lancaster. Lancaster had not, however, yet taken any direct part in government and his abilities were still untested.   [4] See *C. Ch. Warr.*, *passim*, and C. 53/101, mm. 1–17.

administrative work,[1] should act for them both on the Council, while he himself exercised his influence from a distance.

Joint magnate activity of one kind was apparent during the London Parliament itself when Pembroke, Hereford, and Lancaster's steward Michael de Meldon, were deputed by the other magnates and prelates to complain at the Exchequer about the levying of scutage on knights' fees for which service had been done in Edward I's Scottish campaigns.[2] But such co-operation during a Parliament in a matter of common interest to Pembroke and others in their capacity as magnates is not strictly comparable to the behaviour of the same individuals in their other capacity as royal councillors, and a few clear examples of this latter form of activity are also required. On 15 March, for instance, the Archbishop, the Chancellor, and Warwick assigned a notary to make a process on Anglo-Scottish relations; on 16 March the King sent instructions to Richmond and Hereford, following advice given by Pembroke, Warwick, and Arundel;[3] and orders issued on 6 and 7 May were made in the presence of the Archbishop, Pembroke, Richmond, Hereford, and Warwick.[4] There are also some signs of Lancaster's intervention at this time in, for example, the granting of a pardon on 17 March, the appointment of a sheriff in Ireland on 20 May, and the granting of safe conducts on the same date for the men of Bristol to discuss their dispute with Bartholomew de Badlesmere, the royal constable of the town.[5]

This evidence does not of itself show which of the two possible explanations of the events of early 1315 is the right one. In a peaceful and undisturbed reign such evidence would suggest a picture of normal baronial co-operation with the King in the work of government, and there would be no very dramatic conclusions to be drawn. But the years preceding 1315 had been so far from normal that a second look at the problem is required. This is not to say that there was no such co-operation, but it is really implausible that magnates who had so recently been bitterly at odds, not only with the King but also among themselves, should suddenly find the means to work together in

---

[1] This is necessarily a somewhat speculative remark.
[2] E. 159/88, m. 144.   [3] E. 101/376/7, f. 18; S.C. 1/45/186.
[4] *C.P.R., 1313–17*, p. 279; S.C. 1/45/186 (endorsement).
[5] *C.P.R., 1313–17*, pp. 263, 289; *C.F.R., 1307–19*, p. 248.

harmony. There are hints that in fact a certain amount of bargaining was going on between the King, his sympathizers, and his opponents. While, for example, the Ordinances were being applied to revoke royal grants and to order a perambulation of the forests, there were at least a few cases of grants that had been revoked in March being restored a month or two later.[1] The evidence in itself is inconclusive, as it often is at a time when there is no spectacular crisis to show what tensions lie concealed beneath the surface. But, armed with a knowledge of the events prior to 1315 and of what was to follow, it seems reasonable to suggest that the emphasis that was laid on the collective responsibility of the Council[2] overlay an uneasy political balance, in which the realignments caused by the events of 1314 were still working themselves out.

This ambiguity makes an assessment of Pembroke's position no easier; but it is at least evident that, while in the early months of 1315 he was still closely involved in the affairs of government, he was not playing any commanding role. In the latter part of the year he continued to be very active but, possibly by accident rather than design, the form taken by his activities tended in practice to push him away from the centre of political developments.

At some time in early May it was decided that Pembroke and the Bishop of Exeter should go to Paris to present a series of petitions relating to Aquitaine.[3] The timing of the mission may have been dictated by a desire to obtain confirmation from the new King of France, Louis X, of his father's agreements on Aquitaine made in 1313. It is also likely that fresh problems had arisen after 1313, since in March 1314 the Queen had gone to Paris with the Earl of Gloucester and others to deliver an earlier set of petitions on the same subject.[4] Pembroke left for

---

[1] *C.P.R., 1313–17*, p. 296; *C.F.R., 1307–19*, pp. 240, 251 (grant to Hugh Audley). The fresh confirmation of the Ordinances and the perambulation of the forest ordered at Lincoln in Jan. 1316 might also imply they had not been fully enforced in 1315.

[2] See, for example, the grant made on 12 Mar. by the King and Great Council: *C.P.R., 1313–17*, p. 264. Many orders were made during May by the King and Council: e.g. ibid., pp. 279, 290.

[3] E. 36/187, p. 53. Edited by G. Cuttino as *The Gascon Calendar of 1322*, Camden, 3rd series, vol. 70 (London, 1949). See items 442–6.

[4] E. 36/187, p. 53; *C.P.R., 1313–17*, p. 85; *C. Treaty Rolls*, p. 207. The Queen's itinerary is given in E. 101/375/9.

France on about 14 May,[1] crossed from Dover to Boulogne,[2] and probably reached Paris before the end of the month. After presenting their petitions, he, the Bishop of Exeter, Anthony Pessagno, and Mr. Henry de Canterbury appeared on 8 June before Louis X and his Council at Vincennes to hear the Bishop of St. Malo give the French replies.[3] The Bishop stated that Louis X agreed that commissioners should be appointed by himself and Edward II to implement the peace treaties between England and France,[4] that written law should continue to be the basis of Edward II's rule in the lands held from the French Crown, as Philip IV had granted in 1313, and that appeals from Aquitaine should be adjourned until the next session of the Paris Parlement or beyond. On behalf of himself and Pembroke, the Bishop of Exeter replied that English commissioners would be appointed as soon as possible, and successfully requested that Louis X should remit his summons to Edward II to send troops to serve in the French campaign in Flanders.[5] On 15 June Louis also remitted punishments for offences committed by English officials in the Duchy, revoked all acts by his own ministers which contravened Philip IV's concessions in 1313, and limited the number of adherents whom Gascon appellants could bring to Paris.[6] In the event, pressure of business in England seems to have prevented English commissioners from being appointed until early in 1316,[7] but the immediate results of Pembroke's and Exeter's efforts were enough to satisfy the King.[8] Pembroke's French mission also provides a further reflection of the political balance of power within England, since, on the day that he and Exeter appeared before the French Council, Lancaster and Warwick were also negotiating on the King's behalf in England between Badlesmere and the citizens of Bristol.[9]

After pausing at his manor of Sutton in Kent on 24 June, Pembroke had returned to Westminster by 1 July.[10] However,

---

[1] One of his retainers received a protection for the mission on this date: *C.P.R.*, *1313–17*, p. 285.
[2] E. 404/483/11/8.   [3] C. 47/27/8/34.
[4] The French did so on 26 June: *F.*, vol. 2, p. 270.
[5] C. 47/27/8/34.
[6] *F.*, vol. 2, pp. 269–70; C. 47/32/11/2.
[7] S.C. 1/37/33. The Bishop of Exeter and the Elder Despenser had been intended to act as commissioners: *C. Ch. Warr.*, p. 423.
[8] S.C. 1/37/33.   [9] Ibid. /35/135 and 135A.
[10] C. 81/1752/56; E. 101/376/7, f. 60.

he soon left again to go to the Marches of Scotland. Pembroke had had a continuing interest in the area since his appointment as Captain between the Trent and Berwick on 10 August 1314[1] and, although he did not remain there himself, he took personal steps in the early part of 1315 to make the region more secure.[2] On 6 February 1315 he acquired a block of territory of value for northern defence when he purchased the castle of Mitford in Northumberland from John de Stuteville for £600, completing the process begun in 1262 when his father bought part of the Mitford lordship for 1,000 marks from its then lord, Roger Bertram.[3] On 18 April Maurice de Berkeley, one of Pembroke's retainers, was appointed by the Council in the presence of Pembroke, the Archbishop, Richmond, and Hereford, to the key post of Keeper of Berwick for one year from 11 May.[4]

It was apparently envisaged as early as 6 May that Pembroke would later be going to the Marches himself,[5] and the details of this were worked out between then and his return from France in July. On 28 May Warwick, Sandal, and Badlesmere were authorized to discuss measures for the defence of the Marches with Lancaster, and on 2 June Sandal left to visit the latter at Kenilworth.[6] Warwick, Sandal, and Lancaster were all at Warwick on 8 and 9 June, when they planned to join the King on 11 or 12 June,[7] and on 20 June it was announced that Pembroke, Badlesmere, Robert de Monthaut, and Richard de Grey were being sent to Newcastle against the Scots.[8] Contracts were made with all four men for their service from 1 July until

---

[1] *P.W.*, vol. 2, part 1, p. 122.

[2] In Jan. 1315 the northern magnates and prelates were also meeting to consider action against the Scots on their own initiative: S.C. 1/35/142 and 142A; *C. Cl. R., 1313–18*, p. 205; *Reg. Greenfield*, vol. 1, no. 359.

[3] E. 163/4/1/2. Licence was given on 16 Feb.: *C.P.R., 1313–17*, p. 254. The agreement was completed on 20 Feb.: *Cat. Anc. Deeds*, vol. 3, A. 4767; B.M., Harleian Ch. 56. F. 40. The 1262 documents are contained in *Cat. Anc. Deeds*, vol. 3, A. 4769–70, 4772–3. Pembroke may well have acquired Mitford with royal backing.

[4] E. 101/68/2/35; Davies, op. cit., Appendix 46. Warwick was apparently absent from Westminster at the time.

[5] He received an advance payment of wages on this date: E. 101/376/11, f. 3.

[6] *C.P.R., 1313–17*, p. 291; *C. Cl. R., 1313–18*, p. 233.

[7] S.C. 1/35/135 and 135A.

[8] *P.W.*, vol. 2, part 1, p. 158. Like Pembroke, these three had already been receiving wages for this duty, Badlesmere since 19 May, Grey since 22 May, Monthaut since 14 June: E. 403/174, mm. 2, 4.

1 November, during which period Pembroke was to receive 4,000 marks for himself and a retinue of 100 men, and the others proportionately less for smaller contingents, making a total of 240 men in all.[1] When finally assembled all four troops were larger than required, Pembroke having 124 men, including 29 knights. The total strength came to 300 men beside Pembroke himself,[2] giving a very valuable mobile force for border defence. Pembroke received further responsibility on 5 July, when he was made Keeper and Lieutenant between the Trent and Roxburgh.[3]

Pembroke's forces assembled at York between 21 and 23 July, but instead of going as intended to defend the border in Northumberland, they were diverted in early August, after reaching Newcastle,[4] to go to the relief of Carlisle, which the Scots had been besieging since 22 July.[5] The force moved east via Barnard's Castle and Kendal,[6] and the news of Pembroke's advance was sufficient to make the Scots break off the siege on 1 August. They were hotly pursued with heavy losses by Andrew Harcla, the commander of Carlisle, aided by Pembroke's men, who by 16 August had followed them as far as Lanercost, north of Carlisle.[7]

On 8 August, as a direct consequence of Bruce's attack on Carlisle, Lancaster was appointed Captain of the royal forces in the area, and Pembroke and his colleagues were told to obey and assist him. It might be understood from this that Lancaster objected to the powers in the Marches given to Pembroke on 5 July[8] and persuaded the King to put Pembroke under his command.[9] But this was probably not the case, since Pembroke's appointment must have been discussed with him when he was examining the situation in the north with Sandal and

[1] E. 101/376/7, ff. 60, 60v.

[2] E. 101/15/6; C. 81/1736/46, 51.

[3] *P.W.*, vol. 2, part 1, p. 159.

[4] E. 101/15/6. They were at Newcastle on 3 Aug. Their movements are worked out from the dates and places of horse losses. The force seems to have moved as a single unit.

[5] *Lanercost*, p. 230.

[6] E. 101/15/6; *Walter of Guisborough*, ed. H. Rothwell, Camden, 3rd series, vol. 89 (London, 1957), p. 397.

[7] *Lanercost*, p. 230; *Vita*, p. 62; E. 101/15/6.

[8] *P.W.*, vol. 2, part 1, pp. 159, 161.

[9] See Davies, op. cit., p. 398; McKisack, op. cit., p. 49.

Warwick in June. It is clear from their respective commissions that Lancaster was put in over-all command of the whole Scottish March in theory, but in practice it seems that they were intended to share the command, with Pembroke in the east around Newcastle and Berwick and Lancaster in the west around Carlisle. The major reason for putting Pembroke under Lancaster's orders on 8 August may have been because the immediate Scottish threat to Carlisle was close to Lancaster's home base and also because Pembroke's forces happened to be in the area at the time.[1]

By 24 August Pembroke and his men had returned to Newcastle on the eastern March, where they remained until about 4 September. From Newcastle they advanced northwards via Alnwick on 7 September,[2] Morpeth on 9 September,[3] and Chatton near Bamburgh on 14 September, devastating the countryside as they went, to prevent an expected Scottish raid into Northumberland.[4] Pembroke then entered Scotland, but was forced to retreat to Longridge near Berwick[5] and was back at Newminster near Morpeth by 1 October.[6] As Pembroke's and Badlesmere's contracts were to expire on 1 November, the King wrote on 18 October to tell them that Henry de Beaumont had been appointed to command the March during the winter in accordance with their advice.[7] Both Pembroke and Badlesmere appear to have rejoined the King by 26 October, but their retinues stayed behind under the supervision of William Felton, and fought a skirmish in which they lost ten horses between them on 31 October at Rothbury near Alnwick.[8]

The payment of Pembroke's 4,000-mark wage for custody of the March appears to have been regular. Half his fee was paid to his receiver William of Lavenham, his chaplain Walter

---

[1] In effect Pembroke and his men were doing Lancaster's job for him.

[2] E. 101/15/6.

[3] S.C. 1/31/147: letter from Earl of Richmond's knight, Bertram de Montboucher.

[4] E. 101/15/6; *Walter of Guisborough*, p. 397; S.C. 1/31/147.

[5] *Walter of Guisborough*, p. 397. Longridge is a likely explanation for *Lomrech* in the text.

[6] E. 101/15/6.

[7] S.C. 1/49/32. The King's only other known letters during this period are those of 18 July and 1 Sept. giving permission for William de Ros junior to stay in Pembroke's company and asking Pembroke to aid the prior of Tynemouth: ibid. /49/30 and 31.

[8] C. 53/102, m. 15; E. 101/376/11, f. 6; E. 101/15/6.

Alexander, and his valet Percival Simeon by 3 July, and a further 1,650 marks by 9 October,[1] which were received by his attorney, William de Cleydon,[2] among others. Similarly, Badlesmere's clerks had been paid 2,100 of his fee of 2,500 marks by 14 October[3] while Monthaut and Grey also received substantial sums. However, these figures may be less satisfactory than they seem. For one thing, these wages might have to be used to pay other troops beside the immediate retinues of the magnates defending the north. In 1315 Pembroke, for example, also had with him at various times about 70 extra men-at-arms, 400 hobelars, and 170 archers.[4] There were probably also delays between the payment of wages by the Exchequer or Wardrobe and the arrival of the money on the March, and in this respect the experiences of Pembroke's retainer, Maurice de Berkeley, as Keeper of Berwick provide a necessary corrective. Although £4,000 were paid out in forty weeks of 1315 and 1316 for use at Berwick, the whole of Berkeley's stay there from April 1315 to about July 1316[5] was punctuated by his pleas of desperation for money and supplies and complaints about the Council's failure to send help.[6] One of Pembroke's colleagues on the March, Richard de Grey, was forced to complain in October 1315 that his wages were in arrears.[7] Despite the best efforts of Pembroke, Berkeley, and others, the state of the Scottish March in 1315 and 1316 was very precarious, partly because of the King's lack of adequate financial resources, but also because of the effects of the exceptionally wet weather in 1315 and the scarcity and high cost of supplies which followed in 1316.[8]

---

[1] E. 101/14/5; E. 101/376/11, ff. 4v., 5; E. 403/176, m. 1.

[2] E. 404/485/20/10; E. 403/174, m. 16; E. 101/376/11, f. 5.

[3] E. 101/14/5; E. 403/174, mm. 7, 16; ibid. /176, m. 2.

[4] E. 101/376/7, ff. 60v.–61v.: the figures fluctuate. Some of these troops may have come from the Irish lordships of Pembroke and others: *P.W.*, vol. 2, part 1, p. 151.

[5] Bain, vol. 3, p. 91; E. 101/14/5.

[6] *C. Ch. Warr.*, pp. 422, 428, 435; Bain, vol. 3, pp. 89–91. But Berkeley could still defeat Bruce's attack on Berwick on 7 Jan. 1316: E. 101/376/7, f. 41v.

[7] E. 404/483/17/7. The Wardrobe Keeper complained in turn that he had no money to pay them. See also S.C. 1/63/189 which reveals a critical shortage of money by the Household in late 1314 after sending money to Berwick.

[8] These problems in defending the Scottish March in 1315 are symptomatic of the wider difficulties during the reign of English defence against Scottish attack. It is clear that shortage of money was one of the major causes of the lack of

During Pembroke's absence in the north important political developments were taking place in the south which involved a further alteration in the balance of political power. As in the months following the York Parliament of 1314, these changes had an effect upon Pembroke's position, and it is necessary to try and trace them in some detail. Earlier in 1315 the most active representative of the King's opponents had been the Earl of Warwick. But by mid-July Warwick's illness had forced his withdrawal from the Council to his castle at Warwick, where he died on 12 August.[1] With the removal of his ally from the Council, Lancaster found it necessary to take a more active role, and the next few months, culminating in the Lincoln Parliament of January 1316, were taken up with the formation of a new relationship between Lancaster, the King, and the most important members of the Council such as Pembroke.

The first stage in this development took place at an assembly of magnates and others which was held in the presence of the King at Lincoln between 30 August and 1 September to consider the state of the realm and other royal affairs.[2] It is possible to trace the presence there of the Keeper of the Privy Seal, the Treasurer, the Archbishop of Canterbury, and Bishops of Norwich and Carlisle, the Earls of Richmond, Hereford, Warenne, and Roger Mortimer of Chirk, as well as of Henry of Lancaster and the Earl of Lancaster himself.[3] The business of this meeting was very largely concerned with Scotland. On 30 August the King announced that, on the advice of Lancaster and the other earls, he had decided to stay in the north of England during the winter and urged the magnates to do the same. On 1 September the clergy were asked to deliver the tenth they had granted for the expenses of the Scots war and orders were given

consistent royal policy towards Scotland. Edward II's financial problems, are, however, so complex that they require a separate detailed examination, which is not possible in the present work. See also H. S. Lucas, 'The Great European Famine of 1315, 1316, and 1317', *Speculum*, vol. 5 (1930).

[1] He was probably back at Warwick by 11 July: B.M., Add. MS. 28024, f. 70. His will is dated there on 28 July, but his death was already expected on 18 July: Bodleian, Dugdale MS. 12, pp. 478–9; *C.F.R., 1307–19*, p. 255. The date of 12 Aug. given for his death in Bodleian, Dugdale MS. 14, p. 53 (copy of John Rous's life of Richard de Beauchamp) is preferable to 10 and 15 Aug. given in *Ann. Lond.*, p. 236 and *Ann. Paul.*, p. 279.
[2] E. 101/376/7, f. 11. The King was at Lincoln from 27 to about 31 Aug.: E. 101/376/27, m. 1.   [3] E. 101/376/7, ff. 11, 11v.; C. 53/102, mm. 16, 17.

for the collection, under the terms of the Statute of Winchester, of men to resist the Scots, while the Bishop of Ely was sent to Ireland to take measures against the Scots invasion there.[1]

Lancaster's individual importance is not obvious at the Lincoln Council itself, but his influence began to grow rapidly afterwards and a situation came into existence in which the King was in frequent contact not only with his Council in London but also with Lancaster, who stayed at Castle Donington in Leicestershire and elsewhere in the Midlands during most of this period.

The full extent of Lancaster's influence is unknown, but there are several examples to show how it was growing. On 4 October the King forwarded to the Chancellor in London a letter from Lancaster dated at Castle Donington on 30 September and asking for an inquiry into the death of one of his valets, with instructions to do as Lancaster requested.[2] A fortnight later on 19 October the King sent William Melton and Hugh Audley from Sawtrey to Castle Donington to ask for Lancaster's advice on difficulties in applying the anti-Scottish measures agreed at Lincoln, and on receiving his replies on 20 October, promptly sent them to the Council.[3] On 25 October another letter from Lancaster, dated at Castle Donington on 23 October and referring to the affairs of the Countess of Warwick, was passed to the Council with instructions for action.[4] In early November the King sent Ingelard de Warley, William de Melton, and William de Montacute from Clipstone to visit Lancaster at Wigan where the latter was suppressing the revolt of his former retainer, Adam Banaster. Lancaster's advice was again sought when the King sent Richard Lovel and Edmund Bacon to see him at the end of November, his replies being received at Clipstone on 7 December.[5]

The year ended with another meeting between the King and the leading magnates held at Doncaster in mid-December and intended, like the assembly at Lincoln in September, to discuss

---

[1] *C. Cl. R.*, *1313–18*, p. 310; *C.P.R.*, *1313–17*, pp. 347, 350; *P.W.*, vol. 2, part 1, pp. 162–3.

[2] S.C. 1/35/155; C. 81/93/3570.

[3] S.C. 1/34/106; *C. Ch. Warr.*, p. 431.

[4] S.C. 1/34/107; *C. Ch. Warr.*, p. 432. The leading councillors then in London were the Archbishop, Chancellor, Treasurer, and Earl of Hereford: ibid., pp. 431–2.

[5] E. 101/376/7, ff. 18, 41.

the state of the realm. Just what the King discussed with Lancaster, Richmond, Hereford, Mortimer of Chirk, and the others present is unknown,[1] but they must certainly have been preparing the ground for the more serious business of the Parliament due to assemble at Lincoln on 27 January 1316.

The effect of these developments at the end of 1315 was to give to Lancaster a new prominence in public affairs, and this inevitably also tended to push Pembroke further into the background. It is difficult to assess the part played by Pembroke in these events, because he was not present at either the Lincoln or Doncaster meetings and his movements in general at the end of 1315 are not known in much detail. But he was apparently in the King's company at Dalby in Lincolnshire on 26 October and was at Clipstone on 16 November,[2] so that he may have been concerned in some of the King's joint dealings with Lancaster and the Council at this time. In mid-November Pembroke probably made a brief return to the north with Badlesmere to release the widow of Robert Clifford, who was held prisoner in Barnard's Castle,[3] and at some time after his return from there went to join the members of the Council in London, where he apparently remained until about 18 January.[4] Pembroke's comparative political eclipse did not affect his close personal relations with the King. On 7 October one of his knights, William de Cleydon, was given custody of Orford castle in Suffolk[5] and on 2 December the King gave to Pembroke as a personal gift the hunting dogs which had belonged to the Earl of Warwick.[6] When Pembroke visited the King at Clipstone in November it was partly in order to discuss private business of his own in France, for which the King offered to send his financial adviser Anthony Pessagno, now a royal knight.[7]

[1] *C.P.R., 1313–17*, p. 421; E. 101/376/7, f. 11; C. 53/102, mm. 14, 15. The King was present from 14 to 18 Dec.: E. 101/376/26, m. 5.

[2] C. 53/102, m. 15; E. 101/376/26, m. 4. Pembroke's nephew John Hastings, the Earl of Hereford, and others were also at Clipstone.

[3] *Bridlington*, pp. 48–9. Badlesmere was appointed to investigate this incident on 16 Nov.: *C.P.R., 1313–17*, p. 422.

[4] E. 101/376/7, f. 17v.; *Cartulary of St. Peter's Gloucester*, vol. 3, R.S. (London, 1867), p. 272; *Cal. of Hereford Cathedral Muniments* (Aberystwyth, 1955), vol. 2, p. 759.

[5] *C.F.R., 1307–19*, p. 262.

[6] E. 101/376/7, f. 83v. At this time the King was also looking after Pembroke's falcons: E. 101/377/4, ff. 1, 1v.

[7] S.C. 1/49/33. Pessagno was knighted on 1 Nov.: E. 101/376/7, f. 41v.

The Lincoln Parliament of January 1316, although nominally called to discuss the threat from the Scots,[1] was to be dominated by the problem of defining the final relation between Lancaster and the royal government. On 27 January, the day of Parliament's opening, Lancaster was still at his castle of Kenilworth, and his continued absence from Lincoln led to the appointment on 8 February of Pembroke and Richmond, with the Bishops of Norwich and Exeter, to act as the King's lieutenants until Lancaster's arrival.[2] Lancaster had arrived in Lincoln by 10 February, but the business of the Parliament did not begin until his attendance on 12 February.[3] After measures dealing with the appointment of sheriffs and the price of victuals, the climax of the Parliament was reached on 17 February, when it was announced that the King had agreed to the enforcement of the Ordinances and to the observation of the perambulations of the forest. It was also announced that because of the King's promise to uphold the Ordinances and to reform the administration of his household and government, Lancaster had accepted the King's request for him to be the head of the Council. No major decisions were to be made without the Council, and councillors who gave bad advice were to be removable in Parliament on the demand of the King and Lancaster. Lancaster's appointment also contained the vital provision that he would be able to discharge himself from the Council without incurring any ill will, if the King did not accept the advice given by him and the Council.[4] It followed naturally from the terms of Lancaster's appointment that at the same time the King also consented to the formation of a commission consisting of the Archbishop, the Bishops of Llandaff, Chichester, Norwich, and Salisbury, the Earls of Pembroke, Hereford, Arundel, Richmond, and Lancaster, and Bartholomew de Badlesmere, who were instructed to consider means of reforming

---

[1] *P.W.*, vol. 2, part 1, p. 168. A detailed account of the Parliament can be found in Davies, op. cit., pp. 408–14.

[2] S.C. 8/71/3534; *P.W.*, vol. 2, part 1, p. 169. The King was at Lincoln from 27 Jan. to 23 Feb.: E. 101/376/26, m. 6.

[3] *B.I.H.R.*, vol. 12, p. 107; *P.W.*, vol. 2, part 1, p. 169.

[4] *P.W.*, vol. 2, part 1, p. 169. See the discussion of the date of Lancaster's appointment in H. Johnstone, 'The Parliament of Lincoln of 1316', *E.H.R.*, vol. 36 (1921). The date is wrongly given as 24 Feb. in Tout, *The Place of the Reign of Edward II* (1936), p. 95.

the realm and the Household as well as the removal from the Household of men whom they regarded as unsuitable.[1]

The King's offer for Lancaster to join the Council was a development from the contacts between the two during the previous autumn, but there is no evidence that such a move was discussed at that time, and it is probable that it was a last-minute arrangement made after Lancaster's attendance at Parliament on 12 February in order to secure his co-operation with the King in the future. But, important as Lancaster's position now was, the names of his colleagues on the reform commission and of the Bishops of Norwich, Chichester, Exeter, and Salisbury, who were added to the Council at the same time,[2] show that in practice he would be working with existing royal councillors and sympathizers and not with any of his own supporters. Lancaster's imposition as head of the Council might appear a revolutionary step, but he would require personal qualities of a high order if he were also to impose himself upon long-established royal sympathizers such as Pembroke.

There are signs that Lancaster was being consulted as early as 26 February, by which date letters referring to Scottish and Irish affairs had been passed to him for comment. But he had not begun his duties with the Council by that date. Nor had he done so by 3 March, when the King forwarded letters on the situation at Berwick to Pembroke, the Archbishop, Chancellor, and Treasurer.[3] On 6 March Lancaster was still at Kenilworth and cannot be traced with the Council in London until 14 March, when he was in the company of the Archbishop, Bishop of Chichester, Pembroke, Richmond, and Badlesmere.[4] On 15 March the King sent two letters from the Constable of France to Lancaster, the Archbishop, and the other members of the Council in London, and other letters were sent to them on 17 and 19 March.[5] On 23 March Lancaster, the Chancellor, Treasurer, and other unnamed magnates of the Council were

---

[1] *Murimuth*, pp. 271–4; *Bridlington*, pp. 50–2.

[2] *P.W.*, vol. 2, part 1, p. 169. Neither Norwich nor Exeter was a newcomer to the Council. See K. Edwards, 'The Political Importance of the English Bishops during the Reign of Edward II', *E.H.R.*, vol. 59 (1944), pp. 320–2, 329–30.

[3] *C. Ch. Warr.*, pp. 435–6.

[4] *Liber Albus of Worcester Priory*, ed. J. M. Wilson, Worcestershire Hist. Soc. (London, 1919), p. 46; C. 53/102, m. 6.

[5] S.C. 1/34/156, 157; ibid. /35/126; ibid. /45/190, 191.

in session at St. Paul's.[1] Shortly afterwards Lancaster left London and on 30 and 31 March he and his banneret, Robert de Holand, were at Langley reporting on the work of the Council, which remained in London.[2] After leaving the King, Lancaster went further north to Kenilworth, which he had reached by 8 April, perhaps intending to spend Easter there. There is, however, no evidence that he rejoined the Council after Easter or at any other time in the following months, and by 28 April he had moved on again to Castle Donington in Leicestershire.[3] Had Lancaster therefore withdrawn from the Council and from an active part in the government by the end of April 1316, only two months after his appointment at Lincoln?

There is no doubt that at some point he did withdraw. In a letter written in July 1317 Lancaster said he had done so because the King was failing to observe the Ordinances, had refused to accept the reform proposals drawn up in London by himself and the reform commission, and was surrounding himself with new favourites.[4] A full assessment of these charges is naturally impossible, but there is at least no prima facie evidence to support them. There is clear evidence during Lancaster's association with the Council of attempts to enforce the Ordinances. Between 6 March and 12 April orders were given for the sheriffs to publish them as often as was necessary for their application, for the resumption of grants made contrary to them, for the prohibition of illegal prises, and for the payment into the Exchequer of the entire receipts of the customs.[5] The proposals made to the King at this time by the reform commission are unknown, but there is nothing to suggest any abrupt rejection of them, and indeed on 17 March the King went so far as to express his complete trust in the Council and to ask them to continue their work as they had begun.[6] Nor is there any evidence that any new royal favourites were yet conspicuous. Even if there were some truth in the charges in

---

[1] *Calendar of the Letter-Books of the City of London, E*, ed. R. R. Sharpe (London, 1903), pp. 59–60.

[2] *C. Ch. Warr.*, p. 440; *C.P.R., 1313–17*, p. 476.

[3] *Liber Albus of Worcester Priory*, p. 46; D.L. 25/1652.

[4] *Murimuth*, p. 275; *Bridlington*, p. 51.

[5] *C. Cl. R., 1313–18*, p. 328; *C.F.R., 1307–19*, pp. 275–7.

[6] S.C. 1/45/190: 'nous nous fioms entierement de vous'. Even allowing for the element of formality in such expressions, there is no indication of impending crisis.

H

relation to the spring of 1316, it is reasonable to suggest that, in making the accusations over a year later, Lancaster was attempting to rationalize his withdrawal in the light of later events.

There is therefore no reason to suppose a sudden and clearly defined cause for Lancaster's withdrawal. But it does appear that the time of his departure can be established as April 1316. The true reasons for his behaviour are likely to have been complex, but the impact of his action, both upon the political scene in general and upon the further career of the Earl of Pembroke in particular, is so important that some explanation must be attempted.

One possible explanation of Lancaster's absence from the Council may be ill health, but at least some passing reference might be expected if this were the case. A second possibility is that, as is commonly alleged, Lancaster was incompetent.[1] It is also true that he had little administrative experience; a contemporary writer noted his habit of leaving even all his own affairs in the hands of others.[2] It might therefore be suggested that he lacked the experience and personal ability needed to act as the head of the Council and deal with the complexities of central government. Lancaster was indeed in the classic position of the reformer who finds that the problems of office are not susceptible to the easy solutions put forward while in opposition. The Ordinances were always an easy reform programme but the inertia of medieval government made their enforcement in practice a much more questionable matter, even supposing that the King and the permanent members of the administration were whole-heartedly in favour of them. When it is remembered that there were also other urgent problems, notably the continuing pressure from the Scots, it can be realized what a burden Lancaster was taking upon himself. It is also probable that Lancaster found difficulty in his relations with his fellow councillors. Although it was quite usual for magnates to take part in the work of the Council, as Pembroke and others had been doing, it was very abnormal for one of them to be formally appointed as its head, and mutual irritation and jealousy were likely to be the result, especially

---

[1] See, for example, Tout, op. cit. (1936), p. 100.
[2] *Polychronicon*, vol. 8, pp. 312–15.

if the leader proved to be incapable of leadership. Frustration at his own incapacity and poor relations with his colleagues may therefore have caused Lancaster's departure from the Council and made him, once he had departed, disinclined to return. It is indeed quite likely that, at least in its early stages, neither the King nor even perhaps Lancaster himself realized that the withdrawal would be final. Fortunately for Lancaster, the condition made at the time of his appointment, which allowed for his possible withdrawal, permitted him to go with some dignity.[1]

Lancaster's withdrawal and the uncertainty as to whether he would return created a new political situation. The period between October 1314 and February 1316 had, as has already been shown, been marked by a gradual change in the balance of power on the King's Council and had culminated in the highly unusual expedient of Lancaster's appointment as its head. Lancaster had now gone, but it was most unlikely that he would choose to remain silent. The problem of his future relations with the King therefore remained, but without the option of a solution like that adopted at Lincoln. The months that followed April 1316 were soon to bring new difficulties, which led England to the verge of civil war and whose resolution required long and tedious negotiations. It also remained to be seen what role the Earl of Pembroke would play. He was still on good terms with the King, and it might be expected that he would once again come into his own.

---

[1] It is possible that Lancaster quarrelled with the King during their interview at Langley at the end of March, but there is no evidence to suggest this.

IV

The Approach to Civil War
April 1316 to November 1317

THIS period was marked by a steady deterioration in the relations between the King and Lancaster, which almost resulted
in the outbreak of civil war in the autumn of 1317. The final
avoidance of this was due in no small measure to the actions of
the Earl of Pembroke, who had by then recovered much of his
lost authority and was once again one of the most prominent
members of the royal Council. Pembroke was not however in
as powerful a position as he had been between the summer
of 1312 and early 1314, since the appearance of new royal
favourites at court added to the complexity of the situation.
These three themes of growing political crisis, the return of
Pembroke to the front rank, and the rise of the favourites are
very closely related and must be treated together. This is also
the period in which the Earl of Pembroke is traditionally
thought to have begun to build up a political following which
historians have called the 'middle party', and there is therefore
all the more reason for examining it in detail. Without a proper
study of what was happening in the eighteen months after
Lancaster left the Council it is impossible to understand either
the problems raised by the 'middle party' interpretation or the
negotiations which preceded the Treaty of Leake in August
1318, both of which will be discussed in the next chapter.

The immediate effect of Lancaster's retirement to his estates
was to create a vacuum at the heart of the royal government,
and in consequence there are signs from the end of April that
a further shift in the political balance was under way. On 1 May
the Chancellor left London for Leicestershire on unspecified
business but almost certainly to see Lancaster, who was then
at Leicester.[1] In the light of the evidence already put forward,
it is likely that he was instructed to find out whether or not

[1] *C. Ch. Warr.*, p. 441; D.L. 42/2, f. 58*v*.

Lancaster intended to return to his place on the Council, and it would seem that he brought back a negative answer, since his mission was promptly followed by a major change in the position of the Earl of Pembroke.

Pembroke had never been excluded from a share in government even during the period of Lancaster's rise to power in late 1315 and his apparent supremacy early in 1316. He was a member of the reform commission appointed at Lincoln and also remained on the Council, with which he can be traced on 3 and 14 March.[1] But so long as Lancaster remained at Westminster Pembroke's own presence was obscured. On the other hand it was reasonable to assume that, if Lancaster departed, Pembroke, as a councillor who had held the trust of the King through a long period of proved and loyal service, would once again come to the forefront of political life. This was precisely what did happen in the spring of 1316.

On 28 April a commission was granted to Pembroke, Bartholomew de Badlesmere, Lancaster, and Robert de Holand to negotiate with the Scots. In its initial form this commission reflects the situation established at Lincoln, with an exact balance between two royal sympathizers, Pembroke and Badlesmere, and two opponents, Lancaster and Holand. On the same day, however, the commission was cancelled and replaced by one addressed to three lesser men, John Walwayn, Jordan Moraunt, and Adam de Swynburn.[2] This may have been caused by uncertainty as to whether Lancaster still intended to co-operate and have been the immediate reason for the Chancellor's visit to Leicestershire on 1 May. But a more suggestive piece of evidence is provided on 11 May when the King wrote to Pembroke saying that he had always found his advice good and profitable and asking him to come to Westminster as soon as possible to help in important business for which his counsel and advice were needed.[3] It is not too fanciful to infer from this that the King was deliberately turning to Pembroke to fill the vacuum caused by Lancaster's abandonment of his office. This reconstruction of the events of April and

[1] *Murimuth*, pp. 271–4; *Bridlington*, pp. 50–2; *C. Ch. Warr.*, p. 436; C. 53/102, m. 6; S.C. 1/35/126.

[2] *C.P.R., 1313–17*, p. 451. No negotiations appear to have followed.

[3] S.C. 1/49/34.

May 1316 is incomplete and bound to be speculative in part, but the crucial point that Lancaster was no longer co-operating with the King seems well established. A further indication that this was so is given by the reappearance on the scene at the end of May of Lancaster's old enemy, Hugh Despenser the Elder, who had been removed from the Council in 1315 on Lancaster's insistence and who would certainly not have returned if Lancaster had been expected to resume his duties.[1]

Pembroke was therefore provided with a new opportunity after two years of relative obscurity. But it did not follow that he would again dominate the Council as he had done in 1312 and 1313, after his dramatic change of allegiance had made him the most valuable of the King's magnate supporters. Except for Lancaster's absence, Pembroke now served on a Council which was essentially unchanged and contained other important men such as the Archbishop of Canterbury, the Bishops of Norwich and Exeter, the Chancellor John Sandal, the Earl of Hereford, and Bartholomew de Badlesmere. Later a trio of new royal favourites was to be added, with very important results for the political stability of England.

Pembroke's renewed importance was soon apparent. As early as 1 May one of his retainers, Maurice de Berkeley, had £600 added to his £1,000 wages for the custody of Berwick, and in June he was appointed to the less burdensome office of Justice of South Wales.[2] On 30 May Pembroke was licensed to hunt in the royal forests and on 17 June John Crosseby, a Chancery clerk who was probably connected with Pembroke, was given a benefice at his instance.[3]

Pembroke's first major service to the King after Lancaster's departure was an attempt to settle the long-standing dispute between Bartholomew de Badlesmere, the Constable of Bristol, and the burgesses of the town.[4] On 13 June the Sheriff of Gloucester, Richard de la Ryvere, who was one of Pembroke's retainers, had arrested several outlaws within Bristol, but his prisoners had been freed by the townspeople and when he returned to execute the arrest he found the town fortified

[1] *Vita*, p. 59; C. 53/102, m. 5*d*.
[2] *C. Cl. R., 1313–18*, p. 288; *C.F.R., 1307–19*, p. 285.
[3] *C.P.R., 1313–17*, p. 468; *C. Cl. R., 1313–18*, p. 343.
[4] For the background see E. A. Fuller, 'The Tallage of 6 Edward II and the Bristol Rebellion, *Trans. Bristol and Gloucs. Arch. Soc.*, vol. 19 (1894–5).

against him. On 20 June Pembroke and three others were appointed to make an inquiry and to punish the community if they refused to return to their loyalty.[1] Pembroke seems not to have left London until shortly after 1 July and, with Badlesmere and Maurice de Berkeley, had reached Keynsham outside Bristol by 7 July.[2] The people of Bristol once again refused to obey royal orders and Pembroke ordered the town to be put in a state of siege, after which he reported on the events to the King by letter, and returned to Westminster with Badlesmere by 11 July.[3] Badlesmere then went back to Bristol with William de Montacute on about 19 July and, with the aid of Roger Mortimer of Wigmore and Maurice de Berkeley, conducted a regular siege, which ended with the town's surrender on 26 July.[4]

Pembroke himself had not joined the siege of Bristol, since on his return to Westminster he found a letter from the King requesting him to go instead to Winchester to urge the monks of St. Swithin's to elect as their new bishop the royal Chancellor John Sandal. Pembroke was the ideal man for the job, since, as the King himself pointed out, he could be expected to do his best to try and achieve what the King wanted.[5] Pembroke left for Winchester soon after 15 July and accomplished his mission when Sandal was duly elected on 26 July.[6]

There are signs that in July Scottish affairs were once more coming to the fore as plans were made for the campaign that was due to start on 10 August. But the holding of a Scottish campaign would be dependent on the goodwill and co-operation of Lancaster, whose influence in the north could make or mar such an operation, and it is likely that his withdrawal in April had been the cause of the postponement in May of the

---

[1] *C.P.R., 1313–17*, p. 489; *C.F.R., 1307–19*, p. 286.

[2] *C. Cl. R., 1313–18*, p. 347; R. Glover, *Nobilitas Politica et Civilis* (London, 1608), p. 150. (Glover's source is an unidentified medieval chronicle.)

[3] *C. Cl. R., 1313–18*, p. 424; C. 53/103, m. 23; *Chartae, Privilegia et Immunitates* (Dublin, 1889), p. 46.

[4] Soc. of Antiquaries MS. 120, f. 19 (Wardrobe Book of 10 Edward II); *Vita*, p. 73; Fuller, op. cit., p. 188.

[5] S.C. 1/49/35, 36: *pur vostre bon procurement nous averoms nostre volunte accomplie*; and . . . *pur lentiere affiance qe nous avoms qe vous mettrez tote foitz peine dacomplir nostre desire*.

[6] B.M., Cotton MS. Galba E. IV, f. 158 (Register of Henry of Eastry); *Reg. Sandale*, Hampshire Record Society (Winchester, 1897), p. 337.

campaign which was then scheduled to begin on 8 July.[1] On 4 August Lancaster was said to be staying to protect the north from the Scots[2] but this was not apparently a sufficient assurance for the campaign to start on 10 August. On 16 August the King reached York on his way north, and there is evidence that between 19 and 24 August Lancaster was also there, in company with the Bishops of Carlisle and Durham, the Earls of Hereford and Warenne, and others.[3] But there is nothing to suggest that Lancaster had returned as head of the Council or that he took part in any administrative activity while he was there. There can be little doubt that the purpose of the meeting was to discuss Scotland, a view which the presence of the two northern bishops would support. Lancaster's co-operation for a campaign was evidently obtained, since on 20 August the army was ordered to meet at Newcastle on 6 October.[4] With this settled, Lancaster withdrew once again to his castle of Pontefract.[5]

Pembroke's part in these proceedings during August is unknown, and his activity in September and early October is scarcely less obscure. He was certainly absent from York at the end of September when John de Sapy was sent to him by the King to inquire about the gathering of his retinue for the war. But he had returned by 10 October when, with Hereford, Badlesmere, and Anthony Pessagno he advised the King to grant Lancaster's request for a pardon for the offences of his retainer, Gruffydd de la Pole, against the royal knight, John Charlton.[6] Lancaster's further co-operation was still therefore being solicited but a new factor was about to appear to destroy this fresh understanding.

On 9 October the Bishop of Durham, Richard Kellaw, died and a complicated struggle then developed in which the King, the Queen, the Earls of Hereford and Lancaster, and last, and most definitely least, the monks of Durham, each had a candi-

---

[1] *F.*, vol. 2, pp. 286, 289. The campaign had originally been summoned at the Lincoln Parliament.

[2] C. 71/9, m. 11.

[3] Soc. of Antiqs. MS. 120, f. 14; C. 53/103, mm. 20, 21. Pembroke does not appear to have been present.

[4] *F.*, vol. 2, p. 295.

[5] Soc. of Antiqs. MS. 120, f. 21; D.L. 42/11, f. 43.

[6] *C.P.R., 1313–17*, p. 548; Soc. of Antiqs. MS. 120, f. 14.

date for election as bishop.[1] On 15 October, Pembroke was at Ripon, preparing to go further north, presumably in connection with the campaign. But before his departure he visited the King at Craike on 17 or 18 October, at the latter's request, to discuss important royal business.[2] He was therefore almost certainly present on 19 October when two monks came from Durham to ask for royal licence to elect a new bishop. Licence was duly given, but it is likely that at the same time Pembroke was commissioned by the King, as in John Sandal's case earlier, to see that either his or the Queen's candidate was successful. Durham proved a harder problem for Pembroke than Winchester had been, and by 28 October Pembroke, with the other interested parties, Hereford and Lancaster, was at Newcastle, en route for Durham.[3] The election took place at Durham on 6 November and its result was awaited in the cathedral by Pembroke and his retainers, John Hastings and John Paynel, by Lancaster with Robert de Holand, by Hereford, and also by Henry de Beaumont, Lancaster's hated opponent, who was there to advance the candidature of his brother Louis, the Queen's nominee. Courageously the monks refused to be influenced and finally chose their own candidate, Henry de Stanford, as bishop. Although the King was ready to accept him, the Queen still insisted on Beaumont's election,[4] and in December the Pope quashed Stanford's election, providing Beaumont to the see in February 1317.[5] With Lancaster's failure to secure his candidate's election and so obtain a major source of influence in the vital border area of Durham and Northumberland, all hope that he might co-operate in a fresh Scottish campaign vanished. The start of the campaign had already been delayed by a month by the Durham election, and now it was abandoned entirely.

[1] *Reg. Palat. Dunelm.*, vol. 2, pp. 834, 1124, 1310; *Hist. Dunelm. Scriptores Tres,* Surtees Soc., vol. 9 (Edinburgh, 1839), pp. 97–9. The candidates were Th. de Charlton (King), Lewis de Beaumont (Queen), J. Kynardston (Lancaster), J. Walwayn (Hereford). [2] C. 81/1706/37; S.C. 1/49/37.
[3] Surtees Soc., vol. 9, Appendix, document no. 95; Soc. of Antiqs. MS. 120, f. 72.
[4] Surtees Soc., vol. 9, pp. 98–9. The editor gives the date of the election as the Feast of St. Leo (28 June), but on other evidence the date must be the Feast of St. Leonard (6 Nov.). This date is accepted by R. Surtees, *History of Durham* (Durham, 1816), vol. 1, p. xxxviii.
[5] John Le Neve, *Fasti Ecclesiae Anglicanae, 1300–1541: Northern Province* (London, 1963), p. 107.

Most important of all was the fact that this episode completed and embittered the breach between the King and
Lancaster which had begun with the latter's withdrawal from
the Council in April. The fresh crisis in their relations is
specially emphasized by the author of the *Vita Edwardi Secundi*,
who was an acute observer of the political scene.[1] In future,
royal policy would have to be decided on the assumption that
Lancaster would take no part in it and would be actively
hostile.

Another result of this final breach with Lancaster was that
Pembroke became of even greater importance than he had been
already since April. After the confrontation at Durham he had
returned to York with the King by 10 November, when he set
about securing the north from the danger of Scottish attack.
On 24 November, with Anthony Pessagno and William de
Montacute, he advised the King on sending an embassy to
negotiate with the Scots, one of the envoys being John d'Eure,
the constable of his castle of Mitford in Northumberland.[2] The
appointment of the Earl of Arundel as Warden of the Scottish
March on 19 November, the arrangements made to defend royal
castles in the area, and the appointments of Roger Mortimer
of Wigmore and Roger Mortimer of Chirk as Justices of Ireland
and North Wales respectively on 23 November probably also
owed much to Pembroke's inspiration.[3]

By 4 December Pembroke had returned to London to join
the other members of the Council, and he soon became deeply
involved in its work. On 4 December the King wrote to Pembroke, the Archbishop, and Chancellor about the envoys who
had just been sent to Scotland, and on 16 December asked him
and his colleagues to advise on the summons to the coronation
of Philip V of France which had just been received. On 13
December Pembroke, Badlesmere, and the Bishop of Ely
appeared before the Council to announce the King's decision
on the partition of the lands of the late Earl of Gloucester.[4]

---

[1] *Vita*, p. 75.

[2] *C. Cl. R., 1313–18*, p. 472; *F.*, vol. 2, p. 302; E. 101/68/2/36.

[3] E. 101/68/2/37; Soc. of Antiqs. MS. 120, ff. 44–6; *C.P.R., 1313–17*, p. 563;
C.F.R., 1307–19, p. 312. The policy seems to have been to create a strong line of
defence in the north to make up for the English inability to go over to the offensive
and fight on Scottish territory.

[4] *C. Ch. Warr.*, p. 450; S.C. 1/35/128, 128A; *Rot. Parl.*, vol. 1, p. 354.

However, Pembroke's greatest preoccupation at the end of 1316 was the organization of an embassy to the newly elected Pope John XXII at Avignon, which Pembroke himself was to lead early in 1317.[1] The part played in this mission by Pembroke would on its own make some consideration of it necessary, but the embassy is doubly interesting since modern historians, especially T. F. Tout and J. C. Davies, have also suggested that during it Pembroke began the formation of his alleged 'middle party'. This latter point is, however, better left to the discussion of the 'middle party' interpretation in the following chapter.

The Avignon mission is also important because it marks a clear change in royal policy. For the time being it was clear that there was no prospect of engaging Lancaster's co-operation, which also implied that it was not possible to counter the Scottish threat by a full-scale campaign for which Lancaster's approval would in practice be essential. It was therefore an appropriate moment for the King's advisers to try to ensure the security of his government by substituting diplomacy for military action in Scotland. It was also suitable because the election of a new pope in August 1316, after a vacancy of over two years, made it possible to enlist papal aid both against the Scots and in solving other urgent problems.

The main purposes of the embassy were threefold: first of all to obtain support against the Scots; secondly to negotiate more favourable terms for the repayment of the loan of 160,000 florins made to Edward II by Clement V in 1314 and so to regain early control of the revenues of the Duchy of Gascony;[2] thirdly to persuade the Pope to allow a delay in Edward II's fulfilment of his crusading oath of 1313 and, if possible, to obtain a grant of clerical taxation, nominally in aid of an eventual crusade.[3] The author of the *Vita Edwardi Secundi* adds that the King's envoys were also to ask the Pope to absolve the King from his oath to observe the Ordinances, as had already

---

[1] For a more detailed account of the mission see Chapter IV, part 1 of my thesis, 'The Career of Aymer de Valence, Earl of Pembroke', Ph.D. (London, 1967/8).

[2] The terms of the loan had proved unsatisfactory almost from the start and several unsuccessful attempts had already been made to alter them: *F.*, vol. 2, pp. 247, 259, 297; E. 101/376/7, f. 12v.

[3] The opinion of the hostile *Flores*, vol. 3, pp. 181–2, that the King wished to use his oath to extract urgently needed cash from the Church is not far from the truth.

been attempted in 1312.[1] There is no other evidence to support this statement, but it cannot be dismissed lightly. If at least the first three aims were achieved the King's difficulties would be greatly relieved, which would make it easier to deal both with the Scots and with his internal opponent, the Earl of Lancaster.

The formal decision to send an embassy to Avignon was apparently taken at York on 24 November and before returning to London Pembroke discussed with the King details of the business to be dealt with by the envoys and the kind of powers that they would need.[2] After he had rejoined the Council early in December Pembroke held similar discussions with them and then sent a royal clerk, Walter de Kemesey, to report to the King.[3] The King was apparently prepared to leave all the details in the hands of Pembroke and his colleagues and on two occasions expressed his full satisfaction with Pembroke's work.[4]

On 16 December the King gave his envoys full powers to renegotiate the terms of repayment of the 1314 loan with the executors of Clement V. Pembroke and Badlesmere, however, regarded this authority as insufficient and wrote asking for the envoys to have power to deal directly with Bertrand de Got, the Marquis of Ancona, who was Clement V's nephew and heir as well as one of his executors. The revised authority was duly given on 21 December.[5] The problem of the King's crusading oath was next to be dealt with. After Pembroke and the Council had written to the King about this in mid-December they were told on 21 December to discuss it among themselves and advise him of the result. On 28 December they replied that Edward II ought to ask for the same period of postponement as the French King, and on 4 January this was also agreed to by the King.[6]

The addition of the Scottish question to the embassy's duties was a rather more complex process. One set of envoys had already been dispatched from York to Scotland on 24 November, the day on which the Avignon mission was also agreed. It

[1] *Vita*, pp. 78–9.   [2] E. 404/1/6; S.C. 1/49/38.
[3] S.C. 1/45/192. While the mission was being prepared the King remained at Nottingham and Clipstone.
[4] Ibid. /49/39; ibid. /45/192: royal letters to Pembroke on 19 and 21 Dec.
[5] *F.*, vol. 2, p. 304; *C. Ch. Warr.*, p. 452.
[6] S.C. 1/45/192; *C. Ch. Warr.*, p. 455; *F.*, vol. 2, p. 309.

was intended that the King's Scottish problems would also be brought up at the papal Curia, but it was apparently felt that there would be too much delay in doing this if the King had to wait until the large-scale embassy to Avignon was fully organized, and on 26 November Richard de Burton and John Benstede were sent off to Avignon for this purpose. No sooner had they left than there was a change of heart by the King and his advisers, who probably reasoned that Burton and Benstede were too junior to make enough impact at Avignon. Early in December they were recalled after reaching Dover, and their task was added to the responsibilities of the much higher-ranking embassy.[1]

The importance which was attached to the Avignon mission can clearly be seen in the care with which it was prepared. Several clerks, for example, were employed to transcribe documents stored in the Tower of London and to copy papal bulls for the use of the envoys. In December a number of royal proctors and other English clerks who were already at Avignon were instructed to give whatever assistance they could to the envoys and at about the same time Pembroke and Badlesmere suggested to the King that his envoys should be allowed to buy support within the Curia itself by granting pensions. The King agreed to this on 4 January.[2] An embassy on this scale would clearly cost a great deal. The King's bankers, the Bardi of Florence, were requested to supply the necessary money and, after consultations with Pembroke, Badlesmere, and others, they advanced a sum of £7,787. 9s. 2d. of which £3,787. 9s. 2d. was earmarked for the expenses of the mission. Out of this sum £1,904 was spent by the King and Queen on presents for the Pope on the advice of Pembroke and his colleagues.[3]

The rank of the royal envoys to Avignon was in keeping with all this expense. All of the envoys were prominent members of the royal Council, and it was clearly felt that any success gained at Avignon would outweigh any possible dangers to the King

---

[1] *F.*, vol. 2, p. 302; Soc. of Antiqs. MS. 120, f. 23*v*. Pembroke's arrival at Westminster with more up-to-date information on royal intentions may account for the envoys' recall.

[2] Soc. of Antiqs. MS. 120, f. 27; *F.*, vol. 2, pp. 305, 308; S.C. 1/45/192; *C. Ch. Warr.*, p. 455.

[3] S.C. 1/45/192; *C.P.R., 1313–17*, p. 608; E. 404/1/6; Soc. of Antiqs. MS. 120, ff. 53*v*., 54.

caused by their absence from England. It was already evident
by 6 December that Pembroke would be one of the envoys,
and the embassy took its final form by 15 December, when its
members were identified as Pembroke, the Bishops of Norwich
and Ely, Bartholomew de Badlesmere, Anthony Pessagno, and
others.[1] The King apparently had some other suggestions, since
on 3 December he wrote asking Pembroke to add Bertrand de
Got to the list of envoys.[2] This was an absurd idea, since
Bertrand was the heir of Clement V and the very man with
whom Pembroke and the others would be negotiating about the
recovery of the Gascon revenues, and it was rejected by Pembroke, one assumes tactfully.

The part played by the Earl of Pembroke in the organization
of the Avignon mission underlines very clearly the extent of his
recovery of authority by the end of 1316. The King's deference
to his advice is very noticeable in the correspondence which
they exchanged on the mission. His close relations with the
King are, however, best expressed in a remarkable letter
addressed to him by Edward II on 19 December. The letter
first of all mentions that Pembroke had left the King some
advice for the conduct of his government during Pembroke's
absence. Just what this advice was is not stated, but Edward
promised to follow it without default. The King then added
a personal touch which must be unique in his relations with
a leading magnate, since he offered to act in person as Pembroke's attorney while he was abroad.[3] Edward's advice and
assistance on anything might be regarded as a mixed blessing,
but his behaviour does indicate his very deep trust in Pembroke. None the less it remained to be seen whether Pembroke
possessed the personal qualities needed to translate the King's
trust into the reality of political leadership. The appearance of
the disruptive influence of three new royal favourites early in
1317 was soon to put him to the test.

The embassy left England in early January 1317 and
reached Avignon in late February or early March.[4] Virtually
nothing is known of what happened after their arrival until

[1] *F.*, vol. 2, pp. 302–4.
[2] S.C. 1/49/38.
[3] Ibid. /49/39. See text in Appendix 4.
[4] Pembroke's account for the mission began on 26 Dec., but he does not appear
to have left on that date: Soc. of Antiqs. MS. 120, f. 24.

the negotiations began to reach a conclusion. On 28 March Pope John XXII agreed to let Edward II postpone his crusade and loaned to him for five years the proceeds of a tenth levied on the English clergy. On 1 April Pembroke, Badlesmere, and the two bishops made a new agreement with Clement V's executors on the repayment of his loan, which would recover control of eighty per cent of the revenues of Gascony for the King.[1] The most important decisions, however, were those made about Scotland, although not in the way intended. On 17 March the Pope appointed Gaucelin d'Eauze and Luke Fieschi, the Cardinals of SS. Marcellinus and Peter and of St. Mary in Via Lata, as envoys to negotiate a peace settlement between England and Scotland, and on 1 May he promulgated a truce between the two countries.[2] Predictably the Scots took no notice either of the papal truce or of his envoys, but the presence in England of the two cardinals proved to be of great importance in 1317 and 1318, when they turned their attention to making a settlement between Edward II and Lancaster. Apart from this one unlooked-for result, Pembroke's mission to Avignon had little permanent value.

The envoys probably left Avignon in late March, but did not apparently travel in company as on the outward journey. On 11 May the Bishops of Norwich and Ely reached London,[3] but the return of the Earl of Pembroke was delayed by a dramatic and totally unforeseen event.

Early in May 1317 Pembroke was travelling homewards between Orléans and Paris when he was waylaid at Étampes by a man variously described as John de la Moiliere or John Lamulher. With his natural son, Henry de Valence, and several of his retainers, he was then taken to somewhere in the County of Bar on the borders of the Empire where he was held to ransom for the enormous sum of £10,400 sterling.[4] The only other significant piece of information readily available is the statement by the author of the *Scalacronica* that Pembroke's captor had once been in the service of the English Crown and had

---

[1] *F.*, vol. 2, pp. 319–20, 322–4. The Gascon problem, however, still took a long time to resolve finally.

[2] Ibid., vol. 2, pp. 347–8; *C. Papal Letters, 1305–42*, p. 127.

[3] Soc. of Antiqs. MS. 120, ff. 23v., 24.

[4] *F.*, vol. 2, p. 329; *C. Papal Letters, 1305–42*, p. 240; G. Mollat (ed.), *Lettres communes de Jean XXII* (Paris, 1909), vol. 5, no. 19750.

a grievance against the King because of arrears in his wages.[1] Otherwise the incident appears at first to be a complete mystery. Fortunately, however, these clues are sufficient, and examination of both English and French sources makes it possible to say who John de la Moiliere was and what were his likely motives. Even so, a good deal about the affair is still uncertain and may never be known.[2]

The basic outline of John de la Moiliere's career is relatively easy to establish. In the first place his real name was Jean de Lamouilly and he came from the village of Lamouilly seven kilometres north of the town of Stenay in the modern French department of the Meuse.[3] As the *Scalacronica* suggests, he did indeed spend some time in England in royal service. He was a royal squire by the end of 1299[4] and in the years that followed saw garrison duty in several English-held castles in Scotland and the north of England. Among the garrison contingents which he commanded at various times were several of his relatives, Henry, Reginald, and Warner de Lamouilly, and at least nine other men whose names indicate that they came from the same general area around the Meuse. Jean de Lamouilly's last positive identification in England is as a member of the garrison of Berwick in June 1312,[5] and he returned to the Continent at some point between then and Pembroke's capture in May 1317. Royal financial records contain several assignments to Jean de Lamouilly between 1312 and 1316 in payment of wages and other sums due from previous years, but they also suggest that there were serious delays in payment.[6] The *Scalacronica* is probably right in saying that

---

[1] *Scalacronica*, p. 144. Adam Murimuth believed Pembroke's captor was one of his own former retainers: *Murimuth*, p. 26.

[2] What follows is a summary of Chapter IV, Part 2 of my original thesis, which contains full references to the material used.

[3] M. L. Liénard, *Dictionnaire topographique de la France: Meuse* (Paris, 1872), p. 123. T. F. Tout, op. cit. (1936), p. 102, suggested he came from a place called Les Molières between Étampes and Versailles. He appears to be the only modern writer to attempt an identification, and it is fair to say that Pembroke's capture is as little known and understood in France as it is in England.

[4] *Liber Quotidianus Garderobae, 28 Edward I*, ed. J. Topham, Society of Antiquaries (London, 1787), p. 322.   [5] Bain, vol. 3, p. 419.

[6] For example, in May 1313 he was assigned the issues of wardships and marriages in payment of £711. 16s. 8d., but in Aug. 1313 the Elder Despenser was given priority for the repayment of money from the same source: *C.P.R., 1307–13*, p. 570; ibid., *1313–17*, pp. 7, 100–1.

in 1317 he was still owed arrears in his wages. The temptation for Jean de Lamouilly to revenge himself against the King by seizing one of his most valued councillors, the Earl of Pembroke, when the latter happened to be passing through France within easy reach, would therefore have been very strong.

Jean de Lamouilly had both a clear motive and the opportunity to take Pembroke prisoner, but this still does not explain how he was able to do so with apparent impunity and successfully extract a ransom from him. One contributory reason was certainly the disturbances in this area of France which followed the disputed succession of Philip V to the French throne in the autumn of 1316.[1] But this is not a sufficient explanation on its own.

The necessary clue is provided by the fact that Pembroke was held prisoner in the County of Bar, which suggests that Jean de Lamouilly had good reason to feel at home there. Jean's home area at Lamouilly was not far from Bar and also appears to have had some feudal dependence upon the county.[2] But Jean de Lamouilly's own personal links with the county were closer still and were probably the original reason for his additional connection with the English Crown. After the marriage in 1293 of Count Henry of Bar and Edward I's daughter Eleanor relations between England and Bar had been very close. In 1299 Henry's brother Jean de Bar entered the service of Edward I[3] at almost the same time that Jean de Lamouilly first appears in the royal Household. This near coincidence in time and the fact that Lamouilly came from a place connected with Bar make it almost certain that he had come to England with Jean de Bar.

For this reason alone the County of Bar would have been

---

[1] For details of this period see P. Lehugeur, *Histoire de Philippe le Long* (Paris, 1897), pp. 61–105.

[2] H. Goffinet, 'Les comtes de Chiny', *Annales de l'Institut archéologique de la province de Luxembourg*, vol 10 (1878), p. 232, vol. 11 (1879), p. 219; M. Gachard, 'Notice d'une collection de documents concernant le comté de Chiny', *Compte-rendu des séances de la Commission royale d'Histoire*, vol. 10 (1869), pp. 117, 131, 139; Jeantin, *Manuel de la Meuse* (Nancy, 1861–3), vol. 2, p. 1018; H. Levallois, 'Recherches à propos d'une liste des vassaux de Bar, de l'an 1311 sur le début du règne du comte Édouard I', *Bulletin mensuel de la Société d'archéologie lorraine et du Musée historique lorrain* (1901), p. 215.

[3] *C.P.R., 1292–1301*, p. 426; C. Moor, *The Knights of Edward I*, Harleian Society (London, 1929–32), vol. 1, p. 40.

a convenient place of refuge for Jean de Lamouilly and his prisoner in 1317, but there are grounds for suspecting that the Count of Bar may have been more than just a benevolent spectator of Jean de Lamouilly's activities. On 10 May 1317 Edward II sent letters requesting assistance in freeing Pembroke to twenty-seven high-ranking people at the French court and along the borders of the Empire.[1] On closer examination of these people and their backgrounds it is apparent that many of them were connected in one way or another with the County of Bar. Those addressed included Count Edward of Bar himself, his uncle Erard de Bar, and sister Joan de Bar. Of the others listed Gaucher de Châtillon, Count of Porcien, Goberd d'Aspremont, Anselm de Joinville, Louis de Looz, Count of Chiny, John Count of Salm, and Sir Peter and Robert de Narcy were all vassals of Bar, while Duke Eudes of Burgundy was the brother-in-law of the Count of Bar and Ralph de Louppy was his close ally.[2] In other words all these people and some of the others as well were in a position to use their influence on the Count of Bar.

This certainly suggests that Edward of Bar knew more about Pembroke's imprisonment than he should have done, and it is even more interesting that he had a motive of his own for at least condoning it. In 1306 Edward of Bar's sister Joan de Bar had married John de Warenne, the future Earl of Surrey, but in 1313 Warenne began proceedings to annul his marriage.[3] At first Edward II took the side of the Countess of Surrey, but in July 1316 the Earl of Surrey surrendered his lands to the Crown, after which they were regranted to him with reversion to his mistress Maud de Neyrford and her two illegitimate sons.[4] In August 1316 the Countess of Surrey left England and was with her brother the Count of Bar by May 1317, the time of Pembroke's capture.[5] Edward of Bar therefore had ample reason for avenging Edward II's slight against his sister by allowing the imprisonment of Pembroke. Pembroke may also

---

[1] *F.*, vol. 2, pp. 329–30.
[2] For detailed analysis with full supporting references see my thesis, pp. 222–7.
[3] *C. Cl. R.*, *1302–7*, p. 321; F. R. Fairbank, 'The Last Earl of Warenne and Surrey', *Yorks. Arch. Journal*, vol. 19 (1907).
[4] Fairbank, op. cit., pp. 199–200; E. 101/376/7, f. 42v.; *C. Cl. R.*, *1313–18*, p. 45; *C.P.R.*, *1313–17*, pp. 483–5, 528–9.
[5] Soc. of Antiqs. MS. 120, f. 49v.; *F.*, vol. 2, pp. 329–30.

unwittingly have given cause for offence himself, since there is some evidence to suggest that one of his tasks while at Avignon earlier in 1317 was to present a petition to the Pope asking for the annulment of Warenne's marriage.[1] Part of the ransom promised by Pembroke may even have been an indirect payment of damages on behalf of Warenne, which Pembroke would later have to recover as best he could.[2]

There is, however, no conclusive proof that the Count of Bar had planned Pembroke's abduction. The most likely sequence of events is that Jean de Lamouilly took advantage of a sudden opportunity to seize Pembroke and that the Count of Bar then gave him protection and in his turn used the occasion to settle his own grievances against Edward II and Warenne. There are still many loose ends to the story, but the evidence that exists shows just how complex such an apparently straight-forward event was.

The capture and imprisonment of Pembroke has its own intrinsic interest as an aspect of Anglo-Continental relations, but it also reveals very clearly the value placed upon Pembroke by Edward II. The absence of Pembroke from England at a time when his presence might be urgently needed was serious, and even the planned absence of himself and his colleagues on the embassy to Avignon was really a calculated risk. When the news of Pembroke's capture reached England Edward II for once acted promptly in an attempt to get him back as quickly as possible. A major diplomatic effort was begun and on 10 May the series of letters already mentioned to leading members of the French court and magnates from the borders of the Empire was sent off. Two royal knights, Ebulo de Montibus and Guy Ferre, were sent to visit the Dukes of Burgundy and Lorraine and twelve other magnates in the area, and a royal clerk, Mr. John Hildesle, left for the papal Curia at Avignon.[3] No one was sent to the French court, but it is likely that

---

[1] In Dec. 1316, just before Pembroke left for Avignon, Warenne gave Pembroke Castle Acre in Norfolk: *C.P.R., 1313–17*, p. 607. There is nothing specifically to connect this transaction with a petition to the Pope, but it is a fair speculation that this was the case.

[2] In Oct. 1317 Warenne granted Stamford and Grantham to Pembroke to be held until he had recovered £4,000 which he had paid on Warenne's behalf while overseas: ibid., *1317–21*, pp. 40, 48. Once again the purpose of the transaction is not stated but the £4,000 may well have been a component of Pembroke's ransom.

[3] *F.*, vol. 2, pp. 329–30; E. 403/180, m. 5; Soc. of Antiqs. MS. 120, f. 27*v*.

Bartholomew de Badlesmere and Anthony Pessagno, who had remained on the Continent after Pembroke's capture, were busy doing what they could in Paris. On 2 June, when Pembroke was still believed to be a prisoner, the King wrote asking for news of him and how best to arrange for his speedy release. Nothing at all is known of just how Pembroke's release was in the end negotiated, but on 17 June one of Pembroke's messengers brought news of his release to the King and was rewarded by being given a gold cup. On the same day the King wrote back to Pembroke expressing his joy at the news of his freedom and asking him to return to England as quickly as possible.[1] Pembroke arrived in London on 23 June accompanied by Badlesmere and Anthony Pessagno and by the French Count of Aumale, who had been sent with him as escort to ensure his safety.[2] By 4 July they had rejoined the King at Northampton and appeared there before the Council on the following day.[3]

The embarrassment caused to Pembroke by his imprisonment did not end with his return to England. He had been forced to agree to pay a ransom of £10,400 and had succeeded in paying £2,500 to secure his immediate release. This amount was quickly repaid to him by the King as compensation for his loss.[4] The remainder he had to raise himself and there is considerable evidence that in 1319 and 1320 Pembroke was being forced to borrow heavily to meet his commitments.[5] To ensure that he would pay the whole of his ransom he had been forced to leave behind six of his retainers as hostages, including his natural son, Henry de Valence. The ransom caused him serious problems for the rest of his life. One of his retainers, Constantine de Mortimer junior, was still held hostage in 1324 and was released only after Pembroke had petitioned the Pope to free him from the oath he had taken to his captor in 1317.[6] There

---

[1] S.C. 1/49/40, 41; Soc. of Antiqs. MS. 120, f. 93.

[2] Soc. of Antiqs. MS. 120, ff. 24, 27v., 54v. It is very likely that Badlesmere reached London on the same date. He closed his account for the mission at Woodstock on 28 June: ibid., f. 24.

[3] E. 368/89, m. 21; E. 101/371/8/30. The Council decided to reward the Count of Aumale for escorting Pembroke to England and he was given a horse, saddle, and £40 in cash. Three of his retainers were also rewarded: E. 101/371/8/30; Soc. of Antiqs. MS. 121, ff. 66v., 28 (Wardrobe Book of 11 Edward II).

[4] *C.P.R., 1317–21*, pp. 6, 9.

[5] For details see discussion in chapter VI.

[6] *C.P.R., 1324–7*, p. 39; *C. Papal Letters, 1305–42*, p. 204.

is little doubt that Pembroke died in debt in 1324, partly as a result of the problems caused by his ransom, and some of his debts were still outstanding when his widow died in 1377.[1]

However, Pembroke's imprisonment and ransom had also had other effects. One was the double postponement on 24 May and 18 June of a Scottish campaign due to start on 8 July, because the King considered that Pembroke's presence would be essential.[2] But of far greater importance was the fact that in Pembroke's absence relations between the King and Lancaster had taken a sharp turn for the worse. How far this would have been prevented if Pembroke's return had not been delayed is debatable, but the lack of his moderating influence at a critical time cannot be ignored. It is therefore necessary to turn next to the political developments in England during Pembroke's absence abroad between January and June 1317 and to consider the situation with which he was faced on his return.

The major problem facing the King and his advisers at the beginning of 1317 was how to deal with the Earl of Lancaster. As already explained, the King and Lancaster were on the worst of terms by the end of 1316, but this situation, which posed a constant threat to the internal stability of the country and gave added incentive to the Scots to attack from without, could not be allowed to continue indefinitely. The problem then was how to regain Lancaster's co-operation with the King or at least his acquiescence in the decisions of the royal government. The solution of making him head of the Council had already been tried and had failed, and in any case much had happened since the Lincoln Parliament to embitter Lancaster still further against the King. None the less the problem had to be tackled, and in one way or another it was to dominate the politics both of 1317 and of 1318.

There is strong evidence that from very early in 1317 attempts were once again being made to make contact with Lancaster. It is possible, though there is no positive proof, that this was partly the result of the advice which the Earl of Pembroke had given to the King before his departure for Avignon.[3] Whatever

---

[1] *Cal. of Wills Proved and Enrolled in the Court of Husting, London,* ed. R. R. Sharpe (London, 1890), part 2, vol. 1, *1358–1410*, pp. 194–6.

[2] E. 101/15/11/4; ibid. /15/14/4.   [3] S.C. 1/49/39.

indirect role Pembroke may have played in these new moves, there were also other members of the Council still in England, such as the Archbishop, the Bishop of Winchester and Chancellor John Sandal, and the Earl of Hereford, who might be expected to try and persuade the King and Lancaster to settle their differences. The important and much studied negotiations that finally achieved this in the Treaty of Leake in August 1318 were in reality the last stages in a process of negotiation that had its origins at this time at the beginning of 1317.

The first evidence of fresh attempts to gain Lancaster's co-operation is associated with two meetings of the royal Council, at Clarendon in February 1317 and at Westminster in April. The first of these Councils had already by 23 January been fixed to meet at Clarendon on 9 February. A formal summons to thirteen of the royal clerks and justices was issued on 28 January, when it was said that the King proposed to meet certain prelates and magnates of the Council to discuss great and arduous affairs touching the King and the state of the realm.[1] Those present at Clarendon between 9 and about 20 February included all the chief members of the Council who had not gone to Avignon with Pembroke, the Archbishop, Chancellor, Treasurer, the Bishops of Salisbury and Exeter, the Earls of Hereford and Norfolk, and the Elder Despenser. Lancaster himself was not present on this occasion, and one writer says specifically that he was not asked to attend; but his interests may have been represented, since his brother, Henry of Lancaster, was at Clarendon during the time of the Council.[2]

During the Clarendon Council itself it was decided that a further meeting would be necessary to discuss the decisions taken at the Council, and on 14 March a formal summons to be at Westminster on 15 April was sent to the Archbishop, the Bishop of Exeter, the Earl of Hereford, the Elder Despenser, and Hugh Despenser the Younger.[3] The most significant point about this second Council is that this time a summons was also sent to Lancaster and his close adherent, Robert de Holand, and to give added force to the summons, two royal envoys,

[1] *C. Ch. Warr.*, p. 460; *C. Cl. R., 1313–18*, p. 451.
[2] C. 53/103, mm. 12–15; *Trivet (Cont.)*, p. 20.
[3] *C. Cl. R., 1313–18*, pp. 449–56, 459.

Robert de la Beche and Robert de Kendale, were sent from Clarendon on 16 March to visit Lancaster at Castle Donington in Leicestershire.[1] Lancaster and Holand had moved to Kenilworth by 4 April, but this was not a prelude to their coming to Westminster and they failed to appear when the Council opened on 15 April.[2] Those present at the Council were, however, determined to try and consult Lancaster and on 21 April they sent Mr. Richard de Burton from Westminster to see him at Castle Donington on behalf of the King.[3] Again there is no sign that Lancaster offered any co-operation. The initial efforts to try to persuade Lancaster to attend the Council had therefore failed, but there can be little doubt either that they were seriously intended or that the Council would try again.

However, any chance that further efforts would have any speedy success was almost at once ruled out by an act of gratuitous folly which opened an even wider breach between the King and Lancaster. This was the abduction of the Countess of Lancaster by John de Warenne, Earl of Surrey, on 9 May at Canford in Dorset. Not unnaturally the abduction was seen by Lancaster as a deliberate plot on the part of the King and his supporters, and one usually well-informed writer implies that it had been planned at the Clarendon Council in February, at which Warenne had been present.[4] At the same time Lancaster's suspicions as to the King's part in the affair were increased by the hostile attitude towards him of certain royal favourites, some of whom were said to have spoken openly of him as a traitor during the Clarendon Council.[5] There is, however, no evidence to support such a clear assertion of cause and effect, and the only link that may safely be suggested between the affair and the King is that knowledge of the hostility to Lancaster of the

---

[1] Ibid., p. 459; Soc. of Antiqs. MS. 120, f. 26. The two envoys returned on 5 Apr.

[2] *C.P.R., 1317–21*, p. 225. The King probably expected a delay in Lancaster's appearance and for this reason appointed Hereford, the Archbishop, and Bishop of Exeter on 13 Apr. to conduct the Council until his own arrival: ibid., *1313–17*, p. 634.

[3] Soc. of Antiqs. MS. 120, f. 25v.: he returned on 2 May.

[4] *Trivet (Cont.)*, pp. 20–1; *Hist. Anglicana*, vol. 1, p. 148; C. 53–103, mm. 12–15. The affair is described as 'primus Concilii ramus apud Clarendoniam tenti': *Trivet (Cont.)*, p. 22. *Flores*, vol. 3, p. 178, also accuses the King of complicity.

[5] *Trivet (Cont.)*, p. 20; *Flores*, vol. 3, p. 178; *Vita*, p. 87; *Hist. Anglicana*, vol. 1, pp. 148, 150.

King and some of his associates may have encouraged Warenne in his intentions. On the whole it is likely that Warenne's abduction of the Countess, who does not appear to have been an unwilling victim, was undertaken by him primarily for personal motives,[1] and it is noticeable later that in the negotiations in 1318 the matter was treated by Lancaster as a private quarrel between him and Warenne and not with the King. However, the known hostility to Lancaster of the royal favourites, even if on this occasion they confined their enmity to words and not deeds, meant that these men had for the first time played an important part in destroying the efforts of other royal associates to gain Lancaster's co-operation. As later events were to show, they would do so again.

The events of May 1317 therefore marked the temporary breakdown of the attempts, perhaps partly inspired by Pembroke, to re-establish contact between the King and Lancaster. On 29 May the King sent one of his knights, Richard Lovel, and a clerk, William Hoo, to see Lancaster, probably to try and placate him,[2] but no other steps to resolve the now critical situation were apparently taken. The next positive move was not made until after Pembroke returned to England at the end of June. He may have had something to do with this, but the main stimulus probably came from the appearance in England of the two papal envoys, Cardinals Gaucelin d'Eauze and Luke Fieschi, who were at Canterbury on 24 June and had reached London by 28 June.[3] Although the cardinals were nominally sent to help Edward II in his relations with the Scots, their prestige could be used to solve the equally pressing problem of the King's relations with Lancaster.

This helps to explain the summons on 1 July of a great Council to discuss royal policy in England, Wales, Scotland, Ireland, and Gascony, which was to meet at Nottingham on 18 July. All the leading members of the Council were sum-

---

[1] In the chronicle of Dunmow, Essex, Warenne is said to have claimed that the Countess had promised to marry him: B.M., Cotton MS. Cleopatra C. III, f. 295v. However, Warenne was at this time deeply involved in trying to marry his mistress, Maud de Neyrford, so that he certainly did not intend to marry the Countess of Lancaster himself.

[2] Soc. of Antiqs. MS. 120, f. 30v.

[3] Trinity College, Cambridge, MS. R. 5. 41, f. 113v. (this is a Canterbury chronicle); Soc. of Antiqs. MS. 120, f. 54.

moned, including Pembroke, Badlesmere, the Archbishop, the Chancellor John Sandal, the new Treasurer the Bishop of Ely, the Bishop of Norwich, the Earl of Hereford, and the Elder and Younger Despensers.[1]

Once again, as in April, Lancaster was also asked to attend and once again he failed to appear.[2] The start of the meeting was delayed for yet another attempt to persuade him to attend, and on 21 July William de Dene delivered two royal letters to Lancaster at Ashburne-in-the-Peak. The first repeated the King's summons to Nottingham, while the second accused Lancaster of gathering armed retainers to disturb the peace.[3] Lancaster's replies are very significant, since they establish the nominal issues of principle which divided him and the King but at the same time reveal the real nature of their quarrel. In reply to the first letter Lancaster claimed that the business of the Nottingham Council ought to be dealt with in Parliament. He then accused the King of ignoring the recommendations made by the reform commission set up at the 1316 Lincoln Parliament, of failing to observe the Ordinances, and in particular of keeping at court, and making gifts to, persons who should have been removed under the Ordinances.[4] This letter is a statement of what may very loosely be called Lancaster's constitutional position and by implication justifies his unwillingness to co-operate with the King since his withdrawal from the Council in April 1316. But his insistence upon observation of the Ordinances, and his particular stress upon the position of certain royal associates and on royal grants of land to them as barriers to a political settlement, also foreshadows very closely the points which he regularly raised during the Leake negotiations in 1318. However, on its own the letter does not fully demonstrate the level of personal hostility and suspicion which really lay behind Lancaster's refusal to come to Nottingham. Reading between the lines, one might deduce that Lancaster was especially hostile to some of the King's close associates, but, to appreciate this point properly, it is necessary to read the account in the *Vita Edwardi Secundi* of Lancaster's verbal message which accompanied his letter. According to this source,

[1] *C. Cl. R., 1313–18*, p. 482; *P.W.*, vol. 2, part 1, p. 197.   [2] Ibid.
[3] *Bridlington*, pp. 50–2; *Murimuth*, pp. 271–4.
[4] Ibid.: details of the King's original letters are contained in Lancaster's replies.

Lancaster said that he had disobeyed the King's summons for fear of plots against him by the King's favourites, who had already shown their hostility towards him and who, he believed, had caused him disgrace and humiliation through the abduction of his wife. Lancaster promised that if these men were expelled from court he would come whenever the King wished.[1] Underlying all Lancaster's talk of the Ordinances, it is apparent that the real problem in 1317 and 1318 was Lancaster's distrust of the King and fear of his favourites.

In reply to the King's second letter Lancaster admitted that he was gathering armed retainers, but claimed he was only doing this in readiness for the planned Scottish campaign, due to begin at Newcastle on 11 August.[2] There is little doubt that his actions again reflected his feeling of insecurity and the possibility of open violence between himself and the King. The King had also taken the precaution of keeping with him John Giffard, John Crombwell, and John de Somery who had recently contracted to serve him with retinues of thirty men each.[3]

Pembroke's movements during the month of July, after his appearance before the Council at Northampton on 5 July,[4] are uncertain. By 13 July he and Badlesmere had left the King on unspecified business concerning John Botetourt, for which the King authorized them to remain away until 20 July. But in the middle of the month ominous news reached the King from Hugh Audley the Elder, that many of the defenders of the Scottish March had abandoned their posts and that the Scots had invaded the country on 8 July; and because of this the King insisted that Pembroke and Badlesmere should be sure to rejoin him on 20 July and should bring with them as many retainers as they could muster.[5]

Lancaster's refusal to attend the Nottingham Council on 18

---

[1] *Vita*, p. 80.

[2] *Bridlington*, pp. 50–2; *Murimuth*, pp. 271–4. There is direct evidence of Lancaster's gathering of forces in indentures for military service made with him by Adam de Swilyngton at Tutbury on 21 June and by Hugh de Meignel at Ashburne-in-the-Peak on 24 July: Bodleian, Dodsworth MS. 94, f. 122v., and Bodleian, Dugdale MS. 18, f. 39v.

[3] Soc. of Antiqs. MS. 121, ff. 28v., 29v., 31.   [4] E. 101/371/8/30.

[5] S.C. 1/49/42. Pembroke had rejoined the King by this date and so was presumably concerned in the discussions which followed Lancaster's failure to appear at Nottingham: C. 53/104, m. 6. On 25 July he was at Radcliffe-on-Trent near

July and the reasons which he gave for it might be expected to end any further immediate attempts to deal with him peacefully. The King was reported to be incensed at his refusal to come, and especially by the demand that he should purge his household, and some of his followers were ready to urge him to pursue Lancaster and either imprison or exile him. Others saw the dangers to the realm which civil war would bring and argued that everything possible should be done to make an agreement with him.[1] However, the gravity of the Scottish threat to the north, which the King had reported to Pembroke on 13 July, also made Lancaster's co-operation more urgent than ever. Despite the emergency, the summons for the Scottish campaign, already delayed twice by Pembroke's imprisonment, was on 28 July again postponed from 11 August to 15 September to give time for further negotiations with Lancaster.[2]

The history of the four months after the abortive Nottingham meeting, August to November 1317, is very complex, but by a careful study of the chronology and available source material it is possible to obtain a picture of the developments in the relations between the King and Lancaster. These few months are also critical for a study of the career of the Earl of Pembroke, since it is at this time that he is supposed to have begun the formal creation of his 'middle party'.

After the conclusion of the Nottingham Council the King moved on to the north towards York, and it was during this period that the first renewed contacts were made with Lancaster. According to the well-informed though unidentified author of the *Continuation of Trivet*, who, together with the writer of the *Vita Edwardi Secundi*, provides most of the detail and chronology of what follows, the King sent solemn envoys to visit Lancaster at Pontefract to try to make peace with him, so that the Scottish campaign could proceed. These envoys are identified as the Archbishops of Canterbury and Dublin, the Bishops of Winchester, Llandaff, Salisbury, Norwich, and Chichester, the Earls of Pembroke and Hereford, and royal bannerets and clerks. The exact date of this mission is not given, apart from the fact that it took place before the King's arrival

Nottingham with a group of his retainers: *Chartae, Privilegia et Immunitates* (Dublin, 1889), p. 47.

[1] *Vita*, pp. 80–1. [2] *P.W.*, vol. 2, part 1, p. 198.

at York,[1] and the most likely date for it is at some point during the King's stay at Lincoln between 18 and 30 August.[2] Circumstantial confirmation of this is provided by the mission of Henry de Pateshull, who was sent to Lancaster on royal business on 18 August, perhaps to announce the mission; by the absence from the witness lists of royal charters of the period of three of those who went to Pontefract, the Archbishop of Canterbury and the Earls of Pembroke and Hereford; and by a royal letter sent to Pembroke and Hereford on 23 August.[3] On their arrival at Pontefract the envoys are said to have found no reason why a settlement should not be made, and they reported this to the King on their return, recommending him to make peace. However, for reasons which the *Continuation of Trivet* fails to make clear, these promising negotiations came to nothing,[4] and it remains for the *Vita* to supply the crucial background details. According to this source, the magnates who mediated with Lancaster arranged for him to meet the King in person, so that they could in this way reach a rapid solution to their differences. Before the meeting could take place Lancaster was told that the King had threatened to kill or imprison him if he came alone,[5] and the negotiations ended amid further recriminations and accusations.

None the less the Pontefract mission is still of considerable interest. The presence on the embassy of the two archbishops and five of the bishops of the Canterbury province argues a very strong clerical interest in the making of a settlement, an impression which is strongly reinforced during the negotiations of 1318. It is possible that the prelates, whom the Nottingham meeting in July had conveniently brought together, had taken a major part in persuading the King to negotiate with Lancaster. The participation of Pembroke and Hereford, who had probably taken a hand in urging peace on the King, also shows a concern for a settlement which, as in the case of the clergy, later events confirm. It is also very likely that the failure of this initiative once again owed much to the activities of Lancaster's enemies at court.

---

[1] *Trivet (Cont.)*, p. 23. This mission appears previously to have been overlooked.
[2] For the King's movements see *C. Ch. Warr.* and *C.P.R., 1317–21, passim.*
[3] Soc. of Antiqs. MS. 121, f. 48; C. 53/104, mm. 12, 13.
[4] *Trivet (Cont.)*, p. 23. The failure is expressed only in these words: 'versis faciebus incassum est laboratum'.   [5] *Vita*, p. 81.

Immediately following the abortive mission to Pontefract the King continued towards York with his army. He reached the city on about 4 September,[1] after travelling from Lincoln via Comeringham, Castlethorpe, and Barton-on-Humber,[2] a route which took him as far as possible to the east of the direct road passing through Pontefract, which Lancaster could easily block if he wished. This is in fact exactly what Lancaster did after the King had arrived in York, when he placed guards on the bridges to the south of the city and prevented armed reinforcements from reaching the King, justifying his actions on the grounds that because he was Steward of England the King ought to consult him first before taking up arms against any enemy.[3] Despite Lancaster's precautions the King probably already had a considerable force with him. John Giffard and his thirty men joined the King at York on 5 September, while John Crombwell and John de Somery with sixty men between them were still with the King, apart from the retainers gathered for the Scottish campaign by Pembroke, Hereford, Badlesmere, and others.[4] Other reinforcements which reached the King at York during September from Nottingham and from regions north of the city, where Lancaster's blockade was less effective, totalled six squires, 90 hobelars, 88 cross-bowmen, 638 foot archers, and 558 foot soldiers, of whom 30 hobelars and 384 foot came from Wakefield and Sandal, the Yorkshire lands of Lancaster's opponent, Warenne. Since Lancaster was at the same time busy gathering his own forces at Pontefract the position was explosive.[5]

This situation was made even more dangerous after Gilbert de Middleton captured Henry de Beaumont and his brother Louis, the Bishop-elect of Durham, on 1 September near Darlington. The two papal envoys, Cardinals Gaucelin and Luke, who were accompanying them to Durham for Beaumont's consecration, were robbed at the same time. They appear to have been

---

[1] *Trivet (Cont.)*, p. 23; *C.P.R., 1317–21*, p. 21.

[2] *C. Ch. Warr.*, p. 477; *C.P.R., 1317–21*, pp. 15, 18.

[3] *Trivet (Cont.)*, p. 23; *Vita*, p. 81. The *Vita* on its own does not make it clear that Lancaster closed the bridges only after the King reached York and not before. Cf. M. McKisack, *The Fourteenth Century, 1307–1399* (Oxford, 1959), p. 51.

[4] Soc. of Antiqs. MS. 121, ff. 19*v*., 29*v*., 31. Badlesmere, for example, had thirty-two men with him: C. 71/10, m. 17.

[5] Soc. of Antiqs. MS. 121, f. 43; *Vita*, p. 81.

caught up in this attack by accident and were afterwards permitted to make their way to Durham, while the Beaumonts,
who were the objects of the attack, were taken to Mitford
castle in Northumberland and held prisoner there by Middleton.[1] There can be little doubt that Lancaster was at least the
indirect author of this incident and gave encouragement to
Middleton, since he had ample reason for hating the Beaumonts.
Henry was one of those whose removal from court the Ordainers
had demanded in 1311, while Louis had been the successful
royal nominee for the see of Durham against Lancaster's
candidate in 1316.[2]

Apart from its serious effect on the political situation, the
incident has a special interest in that Pembroke was indirectly
involved in it, through the use by Gilbert de Middleton of his
Northumberland castle of Mitford as a base for the attack and
afterwards as a prison for the Beaumonts. Middleton himself
was not the constable of Mitford, as one local chronicler asserts,
and it appears certain that he had seized the castle from Pembroke for his own use.[3] At the same time there is some reason to
think that Pembroke's constable at Mitford, John d'Eure, a local
man whose home was within the Mitford lordship, and who
had been appointed by Pembroke as constable on 15 November
1316,[4] was a sympathizer of Middleton and may therefore have
been willing to surrender the castle for his use. On 25 April
1317 Eure had made an indenture at Durham with John de
Sapy, the Keeper of the temporalities of Durham, by which he
recognized a debt of 100 marks to Sapy, which was to be payable only if Louis de Beaumont were consecrated as Bishop of
Durham or received the temporalities of the diocese before 29
September 1317. The indenture was meanwhile to be kept by
the Prior of Durham.[5] Since the prior cannot have welcomed

---

[1] *Reg. Palat. Dunelm.*, vol. 4, p. 394; *Hist. Dunelm. Scriptores Tres*, p. 100; *Melsa*,
vol. 2, p. 334.

[2] In 1318 some of Lancaster's men were pardoned for their part in the attack
on the cardinals: *C.P.R., 1317–21*, pp. 233–5.

[3] *Hist. Dunelm. Scriptores Tres*, p. 100; *Melsa*, vol. 2, p. 334; A. E. Middleton,
Sir Gilbert de Middleton (Newcastle, 1918), p. 57 (quoting transcript of Middleton's
trial in 1318 printed in *Placitorum Abbrevatio* (London, 1811), p. 329).

[4] E. 101/68/2/36. Tout, *Place of the Reign of Edward II* (1936), p. 322, n. 4, wrongly
says he came from Iver, Bucks.

[5] A. E. Middleton, op. cit., p. 25, quoting Durham Treasury, Misc. Charters
4238.

the prospect of Beaumont's intrusion as bishop, both he and Eure had an interest in preventing Beaumont's consecration, and it can hardly be a coincidence that Middleton's attack on the Beaumonts on 1 September came only three days before the consecration was due to take place.[1] Eure's implication in the affair seems to be sealed by the fact that on 29 December 1317 he entered Lancaster's service as a banneret.[2] Pembroke was very unfortunate in his choice of constables at Mitford since Eure's predecessor, John de Lilburne, who was probably Pembroke's first constable there after his purchase of the castle from John de Stuteville in February 1315, was apparently also concerned in the attack upon the Beaumonts and the cardinals and was responsible for the seizure of the royal castle of Knaresborough on behalf of Lancaster in October 1317.[3]

While it is fairly certain that some of Pembroke's present and past servants were involved in the attack of 1 September 1317, this should not be taken to imply that Pembroke himself was also concerned in it. The explanation seems to be that in matters affecting the north of England Pembroke was an outsider who could have no direct influence on events there. The men of the region naturally gravitated towards the greatest source of power in the north, Thomas of Lancaster, who was at this time trying to extend his influence beyond his own lands in Lancashire and Yorkshire into the border counties of Durham and Northumberland.[4] Lancaster may not actually have ordered the seizure of Mitford from Pembroke and its use to imprison the Beaumonts, but it must certainly have suited him to see his old rival embarrassed in this way. It is also significant that both of Pembroke's attempts to provide himself with local bases of influence in areas in which Lancaster had an interest, at Thorpe Waterville in 1313 and 1314 and at Mitford in 1315, failed through movements in which Lancaster was either the prime or the indirect cause. It proved impossible

---

[1] *Reg. Palat. Dunelm.*, vol. 4, p. 394. H. de Stanford had been the monks' unsuccessful candidate for the see in 1316: *Hist. Dunelm. Scriptores Tres*, pp. 97–9.

[2] Bodleian, Dugdale MS. 18, f. 39*v*.

[3] *C.P.R., 1313–17*, p. 396; ibid., *1317–21*, p. 123; *C. Cl. R., 1318–23*, p. 270. He was also one of Lancaster's retainers: D.L. 41/1/37.

[4] Hence his efforts in 1316 to secure the see of Durham for his nominee. Lancaster was also building an important new castle at Dunstanburgh in Northumberland: J. K. St. Joseph, 'The Castles of Northumberland from the Air', *Archaeologia Aeliana*, 4th series, vol. 28 (1950).

for any rival to survive in an area where Lancaster could exert his influence, as Warenne also found to his cost in his Yorkshire and Welsh lordships in 1317 and 1318. In the case of Mitford, the castle was for all practical purposes lost to Pembroke after 1317. Although Middleton surrendered it to royal besiegers in January 1318, the castle was taken by the Scots soon after with the aid of one of Middleton's adherents, Walter de Selby. Mitford was finally recaptured by the Earl of Angus in 1321 and restored to Pembroke[1] but by that time the castle was a ruin and of no further use.[2]

Lancaster himself took a direct part in resolving the offence caused to the two papal envoys by Middleton's attack. On 7 September he joined the cardinals at Durham and had a meeting there with Gilbert de Middleton, at which he arranged for their property to be restored to them. Afterwards he escorted them south as far as Boroughbridge in Yorkshire, where they were met by Pembroke and Hereford and conducted to the King at York, where they probably arrived on about 8 September.[3]

The appearance of the cardinals at York proved to be the start of yet another attempt to make an agreement between the King and Lancaster, in which the two papal envoys took the lead by offering their services as mediators.[4] The details of these negotiations are not known but a summary of the agreements reached is given in the *Continuation of Trivet* and is probably to be accepted. This shows that the King promised not to take any action against Lancaster or his supporters, while Lancaster agreed to come to Parliament whenever and wherever it was summoned and to accept what was done there.[5] As an immediate consequence a Parliament was summoned on 24 September to meet at Lincoln on 27 January 1318.[6]

In addition to the contribution made by the two cardinals,

[1] Soc. of Antiqs. MS. 121, f. 19; *Lanercost*, p. 220; *C.P.R., 1321–4*, p. 37.

[2] By 1324 its value had declined from £29. 7s. 2d. to £4. 0s. 10d.: C. 134/84/74. See also C. H. Hunter-Blair, 'Mitford Castle', *Arch. Aeliana*, 4th series, vol. 14 (1937).

[3] *Hist. Dunelm. Scriptores Tres*, p. 100; *Melsa*, vol. 2, p. 334; Soc. of Antiqs. MS. 121, f. 7. Lancaster went back to Pontefract: *Trivet (Cont.)*, p. 23.

[4] Ibid.; *Flores*, vol. 3, p. 180; *Vita*, p. 82.

[5] *Trivet (Cont.)*, p. 23.

[6] *P.W.*, vol. 2, part 2, p. 171: this records only the intention to hold a Parliament on 27 Jan. The formal summons went out on 20 Nov.: ibid., p. 175.

Pembroke is also said to have played an important part in mediating between the King and Lancaster.[1] It may have been a desire to have Pembroke's advice on the cardinals' own offer of mediation that prompted the King to write on 13 September summoning him to come 'pur grosses e chargeauntes busoignes dount nous voloms avoir conseil e avisement de vous'. If so, it is likely that Pembroke's first action was to persuade the King to accept the offer. On 24 September Pembroke and Hereford successfully asked the King to give a safe conduct to Lancaster and his adherents, and were given powers to free any of Lancaster's men who should be arrested contrary to it. On 26 September Pembroke and Hereford were also commissioned by the King at their own instance to look after and safeguard the interests of Lancaster's men until the opening of the coming Parliament at Lincoln.[2] There can be no doubt that Pembroke and Hereford wanted to achieve a settlement, but at the same time it should be remembered that both of them were important members of the royal Council, so that, unlike the two cardinals, they could not be wholly neutral parties.

The agreement produced a reduction in the immediate tension which was reflected by the King's dismissal of many of the forces he had gathered around him during September. Lancaster did the same, returning to Pontefract with only a few men and giving up control of the bridges which he had held since the King's arrival in York.[3] In itself the agreement did no more than postpone consideration of the real problems outstanding between the King and Lancaster, and for there to be any genuine progress towards a final solution it would have to be observed sincerely by both sides. This, however, was not to be the case.

On 1 October the King left York to return to London,[4] taking the direct route to the south via Pontefract which was no longer held by Lancaster's men. The King still had a considerable force with him and as he approached Pontefract, which was weakly defended, he drew up his men and threatened to attack.[5] But for Pembroke's prompt action a full-scale attack

---

[1] *Vita*, p. 82.   [2] S.C. 1/49/43; *C.P.R., 1317–21*, pp. 27, 29; E. 163/4/7/1.
[3] Soc. of Antiqs. MS. 121, f. 43; *Trivet (Cont.)*, p. 23; *Flores*, vol. 3, pp. 180–1. The Scottish campaign was finally abandoned on 24 Sept.: C. 71/10, m. 16.
[4] Soc. of Antiqs. MS. 121, f. 19.
[5] *Vita*, p. 82; *Flores*, vol. 3, p. 181; *Trivet (Cont.)*, p. 24.

K

on the castle might have developed. Pembroke reminded the King that all disputes between him and Lancaster had been suspended until the coming Parliament under the agreement which the King himself had confirmed. If Lancaster were planning to attack the King, he would be risking the loss of all he possessed, so that his treachery was out of the question. Fortunately Pembroke succeeded in winning over the King by these arguments and Edward II and his followers restarted their journey to London.[1]

This incident is very revealing, since it demonstrates the limits of Pembroke's influence over the King. He was able in the end to persuade Edward II to draw back from the brink, but only after the damage had been done. Although the royal favourites are not specifically mentioned in connection with the King's threat against Lancaster, it is very likely that they had some share in urging him in his direction, since they had equally good reasons for wanting to see an end of Lancaster. Pembroke was, therefore, too late to prevent the hopes raised by the York agreement only a week before from being shattered, and the mutual suspicion and hatred of the King and Lancaster from being renewed in an even more serious form.[2] Any fresh attempt to mediate between the two would have to begin from scratch, and for it to succeed something would first have to be done to curb the royal favourites. For the moment, however, Pembroke could only continue on the road south with the King and hope to be able to prevent further trouble.[3]

Up to this point the history of the year 1317 had been that of successive attempts by members of the royal Council to re-establish contact and to negotiate with Lancaster and so remove the major internal source of danger. Each of these efforts had been frustrated in turn by a combination of the King's bad faith and of the hostility towards Lancaster of certain royal favourites, who also encouraged the King's own enmity towards him. Those principally and most actively involved in trying to mediate between the King and Lancaster were first of all the Earl of Pembroke, aided by the Earl of Hereford and by

---

[1] *Vita*, p. 82. The speech ascribed to Pembroke is of course invented but in view of the inside knowledge of events possessed by the author of the *Vita*, the impression given of Pembroke's opinions may be accepted as essentially true.

[2] *Trivet (Cont.)*, p. 24.

[3] On 4 Oct. he was asked to join the King at Retford: S.C. 1/49/44.

Bartholomew de Badlesmere; the Archbishops of Canterbury and Dublin and several of the prelates of the province of Canterbury, such as the Bishops of Winchester and Norwich; and the two papal envoys to England, Cardinals Gaucelin d'Eauze and Luke Fieschi. What has not yet been clarified is the identity of the royal favourites who were Lancaster's opponents.

Three of these can quickly be identified as William de Montacute, the Steward of the royal Household, Hugh Audley the Younger, and Roger Damory. These were the courtiers who had described Lancaster as a traitor at the Clarendon Council in February 1317, and they were themselves described by the pro-Lancastrian author of the *Flores Historiarum* as even worse than Gaveston had been.[1] It is hardly surprising that Lancaster should have bitterly distrusted them and demanded their removal from court. In July 1318, during the negotiations before the Treaty of Leake, Lancaster accused Damory and Montacute of having conspired to kill him.[2] It is also significant that Damory, Audley, and Montacute were forced to recognize debts of nearly £1,700 to Lancaster at the York Parliament of 1318 which followed the Leake settlement, evidently as damages for their real or attempted injuries to Lancaster.[3]

All three men began their careers as knights of the royal Household. Audley had been a royal knight since November 1311, Montacute since 1312 or 1313, and Damory since about January 1315, having come to royal attention at Bannockburn in June 1314.[4] They all came from families closely associated with royal service[5] and probably owed their initial positions in

---

[1] *Trivet (Cont.)*, p. 20; *Flores*, vol. 3, p. 178: 'fautores mendacii ipso Petro nequiores'; *Vita*, p. 87; *Hist. Anglicana*, vol. 1, pp. 148, 150.

[2] *Hist. MSS. Commn., Various Collections*, vol. 1, p. 267. This may have some connection with the royal letters inviting the Scots to help in killing Lancaster which were allegedly intercepted at Pontefract in the autumn of 1317: *Trivet (Cont.)*, pp. 23–4.

[3] Sums of 906 marks 7s. 4d., 1,299 marks 6s. 6d., 413 marks 4s. 0d. respectively: *C. Cl. R., 1318–23*, pp. 109–10.

[4] E. 101/373/26, f. 23v.; E. 101/375/8, f. 35v.; C. 81/90/3241; *C.P.R., 1313–17*, p. 666.

[5] The Damorys were an Oxfordshire family. Roger Damory's elder brother Richard Damory survived Roger's downfall in 1322 and was Steward of the Household from July 1322 to 1325. Audley also had Oxfordshire connections but the family was particularly associated with areas close to the Welsh March. Montacute was from the West Country and father of the future Earl of Somerset under Edward III. For further details see *G.E.C.* and C. Moor, *Knights of Edward I*.

the Household to this fact, but once there their rise was due entirely to royal favour. Just how they gained royal favour is not clear, but Damory at least had made sufficient impression on Edward II by early 1315 for him to order specifically that Damory was to stay at court.[1] By the beginning of 1317 they were already sufficiently conspicuous for the author of the *Flores* to note their activities[2] and they began to occupy a position which in many ways resembled that of Gaveston. In consequence they were acquiring influence over the King out of proportion to their rank and the nominal responsibilities which each held. The absence of Pembroke and other experienced councillors from England at precisely this time no doubt helped them in their rise. Late in 1316 Montacute was appointed Steward of the Household and on 15 January 1317 he and Damory both contracted to serve the King for life in return for 200 marks a year.[3] Audley and Damory also became potentially more important for good or ill as a result of the marriages which the King arranged for them. Audley married Gaveston's widow Margaret de Clare on 28 April 1317 and Damory married Elizabeth de Clare at about the same time.[4] Their wives were both heiresses to the lands of the vast Gloucester earldom and their marriages followed rapidly on the decision of 17 April to proceed with the long delayed partition of the Gloucester inheritance.[5] The hostility of the three favourites to Lancaster is perfectly understandable, since if Lancaster succeeded in his demands they would be removed from court. It was therefore in their interests to poison relations between the King and Lancaster as much as possible and to oppose any attempts to produce a settlement between them. The events of 1317 show that they had succeeded only too well.

Lancaster's opponents also included the two Despensers, of whom Hugh Despenser the Elder had been an antagonist of Lancaster since before the appointment of the Ordainers in

[1] C. 81/90/3241.

[2] *Flores*, vol. 3, p. 178.

[3] E. 403/180, m. 3.

[4] Audley married in the King's presence at Windsor: Soc. of Antiqs. MS. 120, f. 10. Damory married between 10 Apr. and 3 May: *C.P.R., 1317–21*, pp. 641, 644. A draft of a royal letter of 12 Sept. 1316 shows that considerable pressure was brought upon Elizabeth de Clare to marry Damory: S.C. 1/63/150.

[5] *Rot. Parl.*, vol. 1, p. 355. Formal orders for the partition were given on 12 May: C. 81/100/4231.

1310. His son Hugh the Younger had married the eldest of the Gloucester heiresses, Eleanor de Clare, in 1306 and would become a powerful figure in his own right as soon as he received his share of the earldom. From 1318 onwards the Younger Despenser developed into a royal favourite on an even bigger scale than either Gaveston or Damory and his two colleagues, but at this stage in 1317 he was apparently overshadowed both by Damory and company and by his own father. He had, for example, been pressing without success since 1315 for the partition of the Gloucester lands,[1] and it was in a sense accidental that the division which was now made for the benefit of Damory and Audley also benefited him. With these reservations about the position of the Younger Despenser, it is possible to agree with the statement by the author of the *Vita Edwardi Secundi* that Lancaster regarded the Despensers, Audley, Damory, and Montacute as his chief enemies.[2] These five men were apparently conscious of the fact that they were in danger of hanging together if Lancaster ever won, since on 1 June 1317 all five made a series of mutual recognizances for £6,000 each.[3] The purpose of the bonds was not stated, but it is very likely that they were taking out an insurance policy against the success of the attempts that had already been made to improve relations between the King and Lancaster.[4]

To these five opponents of Lancaster should be added the Earl of Surrey, whose abduction of Lancaster's wife gave him good reason to fear any political settlement. In the end he was abandoned by the King and his Council to make his peace with Lancaster as best he could, so that he had little influence either one way or the other on the settlement that finally was made in 1318.

Lancaster's natural reaction after the breakdown of the York agreement was to strike out at his opponents. In October he attacked Warenne's Yorkshire castles of Sandal, Wakefield, and

---

[1] For an account of his manœuvres see J. C. Davis, 'The Despenser War in Glamorgan', *T.R.H.S.*, 3rd series, vol. 9 (1915); and M. Altschul, *A Baronial Family in Medieval England: The Clares*, pp. 165–70.

[2] *Vita*, p. 87 (referring to 1318).

[3] *C. Cl. R., 1313–18*, p. 477; E. 163/3/6, m. 1. The bonds were payable on 29 Sept. following. Each bound himself to all the others, except for the Despensers who did not bind one another.

[4] Davies, *Baronial Opposition*, p. 435, saw the bonds as marking the formation of a court party which later became absorbed in Pembroke's 'middle party'.

Conisborough and quickly seized them, despite royal protests.[1] On 5 October he took the royal castle of Knaresborough in Yorkshire and by 3 November had also occupied Alton castle in Staffordshire. These last two exploits suggest that Lancaster regarded Roger Damory as his chief enemy among the royal favourites, since both Knaresborough and Alton were then in Damory's custody.[2] This apparent concentration upon Damory is confirmed by the measures which the King then took to preserve him from further loss. On 18 October Damory's lands in Yorkshire, Hereford, and Lincoln were taken into royal hands, in the hope that this would restrain Lancaster, and on 1 November, as an additional precaution, the custody of Gloucester castle, which Damory had received only on 24 October, was given to one of the Earl of Pembroke's retainers, Richard de la Ryvere, the Sheriff of Gloucester.[3]

In view of the importance that Damory had in Lancaster's calculations and of the imminent danger of civil war if events got even further out of control, it is very interesting to discover that on 24 November in London the Earl of Pembroke and Bartholomew de Badlesmere made an agreement with Damory in the form of an indenture.[4] Under its terms Damory promised to do his best to persuade the King to allow himself to be guided by Pembroke and Badlesmere and to trust their advice above that of anyone else, provided that they gave him counsel that was to his own profit and that of his crown and kingdom. Damory himself would also follow their advice and not oppose it in any way. He also promised not to procure or consent to the King's granting more than £20 of land without the knowledge and agreement of Pembroke and Badlesmere; nor would he connive at or consent to any action by the King which might

[1] *C. Cl. R., 1313–18*, p. 575. There is no evidence that Lancaster had attacked Warenne immediately after his wife's abduction in May as is usually thought. Cf. M. McKisack, op. cit., p. 51.

[2] *C. Cl. R., 1313–18*, p. 575; ibid., *1318–23*, p. 270; *C.F.R., 1307–19*, pp. 225, 316. Alton had belonged to Elizabeth de Clare's previous husband Theobald de Verdon.

[3] *C.P.R., 1317–21*, pp. 34, 38, 46. Damory's lands were restored on 2 Dec.: ibid., p. 58. There is no evidence that either Audley's or Montacute's lands were attacked at this time.

[4] The original is E. 163/4/6. The text is printed in *P.W.*, vol. 2, part 2, Appendix, p. 120, and in J. C. Davies, *Baronial Opposition*, Appendix 42. See also text in Appendix 4 of this book.

be prejudicial to himself or to his crown. If the King wished, in the absence of Pembroke and Badlesmere, to make any grant of more than £20 or to do anything prejudicial to himself, his crown, or realm, Damory would try to dissuade him and, if he failed, would inform the other two before the King's decision took effect, so that all three of them together could try to persuade the King to change his mind. Damory would also warn Pembroke and Badlesmere against anyone he discovered attempting to lessen the King's opinion of them and would act against such a person to the best of his ability. Lastly, Damory bound himself to keep the agreement by oath and by a pledge of £10,000. In their turn Pembroke and Badlesmere promised to defend and maintain Damory against all men, saving only their loyalty to the King, provided that Damory kept his part of the agreement.[1] As a further guarantee of their good faith, Pembroke and Badlesmere also bound themselves, their heirs, executors, and all their movable and immovable goods to the will of Damory. One part of the indenture was sealed by Pembroke and Badlesmere and the other by Damory.

This is an extremely important document for the study of the career of the Earl of Pembroke, since it was interpreted by W. Stubbs, and then by T. F. Tout and J. C. Davies, as proof that in the autumn of 1317 Pembroke and Badlesmere were attempting to form a political alliance which has been termed the 'middle party'.[2] On the interpretation of this one document rests the interpretation of the negotiations which preceded the Treaty of Leake in August 1318. It is also crucial to a final understanding of the significance of the events earlier in 1317 which have already been fully described. The next chapter is therefore a discussion of the origins of the 'middle party' interpretation and a critical examination of it. With this problem resolved it will be possible to draw wider conclusions about the events both of 1317 and 1318.

---

[1] Davies, *Baronial Opposition*, p. 434, mistranslated this last clause to read that Pembroke and Badlesmere promised that 'they like Damory would hold and observe the agreement fully'.

[2] W. Stubbs, *Constitutional History of England* (Oxford, 1875), vol. 2, p. 342; W. Stubbs (ed.), *Chronicles of the Reigns of Edward I and Edward II*, R.S. (London, 1882), vol. 1, pp. cxiii–cxiv; T. F. Tout, *The Political History of England, 1216–1377* (London, 1905), pp. 272–4; T F. Tout, *The Place of the Reign of Edward II* (Manchester, 1st edition, 1914), pp. 111–18, 144–5: J. C. Davies, *The Baronial Opposition to Edward II* (Cambridge, 1918), pp. 35–6, 433–4.

V

The 'Middle Party' and the
Negotiating of the Treaty of Leake
August 1318

As with many other ideas, the origins of the 'middle party' interpretation can be traced back to the pioneer work of Bishop William Stubbs. The indenture of 24 November 1317 had been in print since 1830,[1] but Stubbs in his *Constitutional History of England*, published in 1875, was the first historian to make any use of it. In his view the indenture was the basis of an alliance between Pembroke and Badlesmere on the one hand, whom he saw as enemies of Lancaster, and Roger Damory on the other, whom he regarded as an aspirant through his wife to the lands of the earldom of Gloucester. The purpose of this alliance was to form 'a middle party between Lancaster as the head of the old baronial faction, and the king sustained by the Despensers and the personal adherents of the royal house' and so gain 'supreme influence in the royal council'.[2] Both the name 'middle party' and the outlines of the later interpretation can therefore be discerned nearly a century ago.

Stubbs developed his ideas further in 1882 in his historical introduction to the *Chronicles of the Reigns of Edward I and Edward II*. He now thought that throughout the reign of Edward II there were three basic political groupings: 'a royal party comprising a few powerful bishops and barons . . .'; 'a party under the headship of the earl of Lancaster which was hereditarily opposed to royal aggression'; and a third 'mediating party . . . of politiques without any affection for the king or any aspirations for freedom, which was simply anxious to gain and hold power'. At one stage this mediating party was led by Pembroke, Badlesmere, and Damory whose indenture of November 1317 was the instrument of their party's formal

[1] *P.W.*, vol. 2, part 2, Appendix, p. 120.
[2] Stubbs, *Constitutional History of England* (1875 edition), vol. 2, p. 342.

creation. Referring specifically to Pembroke, Stubbs commented that he 'was personally faithful to the king' and that his influence over the King was 'more friendly but scarcely less irksome' than that of Lancaster.[1] These last two points are important and will be mentioned again.

However, it was left to T. F. Tout to adopt the 'middle party' idea and to develop it to a point where it appeared to be an interpretation that other historians might reliably follow. Tout used the term 'middle party' as early as 1889 in his *Dictionary of National Biography* article on Edward II, in which he said that it was led by Pembroke, Badlesmere, and Damory, with whom 'hatred of Lancaster was stronger than dislike of the royal policy'.[2] He repeated his views in his *Political History of England, 1216–1399*, published in 1905, in which he considered that Pembroke was the enemy both of Lancaster and of the King's personal following and consequently strove 'to form a middle party between the faction of the king and the faction of Lancaster' in order to exclude Lancaster from political power. At first he had the co-operation of Warenne, the abductor of Lancaster's wife, but later adopted Badlesmere and Damory as more trustworthy allies. Edward II then 'formed a coalition between his friends and the followers of Pembroke', after which Pembroke's 'middle party' proceeded to confirm itself in power by negotiating the Treaty of Leake between the King and Lancaster in August 1318. From then until the summer of 1321 he believed that it was in full control of the machinery of royal government.[3]

Tout's views reached their definitive form when he gave the Ford Lectures at Oxford in 1913. Here he argued that the 'middle party' began to develop late in 1316 after Lancaster's failure to provide stable government during his period as head of the royal Council, that it then negotiated the Treaty of Leake in 1318, and finally governed until 1321, when the crisis over the Despensers blew the whole structure apart.[4] Reversing

---

[1] Stubbs (ed.), *Chronicles of Edward I and Edward II*, vol. 1, pp. cxiii–cxiv.

[2] *D.N.B.* (London, 1885–1900), vol. 17, p. 43.

[3] Tout, *Political History of England, 1216–1377* (1st edn., London, 1905), pp. 272–4. These opinions are repeated in the 1920 edition.

[4] Tout, *The Place of the Reign of Edward II* (1st edn., Manchester, 1914), pp. 111–12, 144–5. Unless stated otherwise, references in this chapter are to the 1914 edition. References elsewhere are to the 1936 edition.

his opinion of 1905 that Badlesmere had been an opponent of Lancaster,[1] Tout now considered that until 1316 Badlesmere was closely associated with Lancaster but then broke with him because of his failure in that year. At about this same time Pembroke was re-emerging at the forefront of politics, and Tout supposed that when he and Badlesmere went on the royal embassy to Avignon early in 1317 the two men discussed the situation in England and began to reach some common viewpoint. But the formation of any closer alliance was then delayed by the accident of Pembroke's capture and imprisonment by Jean de Lamouilly while returning from Avignon. In the meantime Badlesmere, who had made one last abortive effort to co-operate with Lancaster, was ready to act with Pembroke when the latter finally came home, and 'before the end of the summer of 1317, Pembroke and Badlesmere had come to a perfect understanding'. In Tout's opinion 'their aim must now have been to establish a political party, which, while accepting the constitutional standpoint of the ordainers, would save the king and the kingdom from Lancaster, and restore Edward to dignity and some measure of power, on the condition that he amended his ways and ruled by their advice'. In November 1317 they began to create a political following among the baronage by their indenture with Roger Damory which, Tout said, 'affords clear evidence of the formal and legal character it was sought to give the new party'. As to the indenture's purpose, Tout claimed that 'though Lancaster is nowhere mentioned in the bond, the compact has no meaning unless it be regarded as an organised attempt to replace earl Thomas by earl Aymer as the king's chief counsellor'.[2] The party is then said to have gained in strength through the adhesion of members of the royal Household, such as the Chamberlain John Charlton, the Steward William de Montacute, the Keeper Roger Northburgh, and the Keeper of the Privy Seal Thomas Charlton. To these were added prelates, such as the Bishop of Chichester and Pembroke's companions at Avignon, the Bishops of Ely and Norwich, together with magnates, such as

---

[1] Tout, *Political History of England, 1216–1377*, p. 273. In this Tout was following Stubbs's opinion: *Constitutional History*, vol. 2, p. 342.

[2] Tout, *The Place of the Reign of Edward II* (1914), pp. 115–18. Tout also added that Stubbs had placed Badlesmere's hostility to Lancaster too early: ibid. (1914), p. 111.

the Earls of Surrey, Arundel, and Hereford, Roger Mortimer of Chirk, and his nephew Roger Mortimer of Wigmore. The result was that 'by the spring of 1318 the king was entirely in the hands of Pembroke and his allies'. The King was once again in tutelage, 'but his tutelage was now to be of a milder and more respectful character'.[1] This, briefly, is what Tout understood by the 'middle party'. At first glance his interpretation is an attractive one, based as it is upon the apparent simplicity of an alliance between two erstwhile political opponents, Pembroke and Badlesmere, and the completion of this union by their indenture with Roger Damory in November 1317.

The last major statement of the 'middle party' theory was made by J. Conway Davies in *The Baronial Opposition to Edward II*, published in 1918.[2] Davies made considerable use of Tout's arguments of five years before, but his work is a far more detailed study of the reign of Edward II, and the 'middle party' theory may therefore be said to have become a joint Tout–Davies interpretation. Davies accepted Tout's view that a 'middle party' began to develop during the Avignon mission of 1317; and once again he saw the indenture with Damory as the formal starting-point of the new party, after which it consolidated itself in power in 1318 and controlled the royal government until 1321.[3] Davies's views differed in some details from those of Tout. He considered, for example, that Tout had overstressed Badlesmere's previous connections with Lancaster and also included the Earl of Hereford as a founder member of the party. But the only significant difference is that he placed more importance on Pembroke's major part in the royal government between 1312 and 1314, his personal moderation

---

[1] Ibid. (1914), pp. 111–18. The editor of the 1936 edition of *The Place of the Reign of Edward II* considered that Tout's argument that Pembroke intended to supplant Lancaster on the Council was proved by a document of June 1318 which formed a part of the Leake negotiations: ibid. (1936), p. 104, n. 3. Tout himself cited the document in *Chapters in Medieval Administrative History* (Manchester, 1923–35), vol. 2, p. 205, n. 1. The document, which is discussed later in this chapter as part of the Leake negotiations, was published by E. Salisbury as 'A Political Agreement of June 1318' in *E.H.R.*, vol. 33 (1918).

[2] This is a very important work of pioneer scholarship, which was the first to make substantial use of the Public Record Office materials for the period.

[3] Davies, *Baronial Opposition*, pp. 429, 433–4, 437. His view of the 1317 indenture is brought out in the heading given to the text in Appendix 42, where it is described as an 'indenture to restrain the king'.

and friendship towards the King, and the latter's consequent willingness to co-operate with him.[1]

Since Tout and Davies published their conclusions the 'middle party' has been a regular part of writings on this period, although a careful study of later publications does reveal slight variations and developments on points of detail.[2] But, useful as the theory has been in bringing coherence to a particularly confused period of history, it would be surprising if historians had not had some reservations about it. In the first place the notion of an organized political group seems an anachronism in an era when politics were intensely personal in their nature. Secondly, it is not at all clear how the 'middle party' actually came together after the initial indenture with Roger Damory. The argument is apparently based on the assumption that the indenture really was the foundation of a party and, once this is accepted, the rest follows without much further discussion. Even supposing that Pembroke and Badlesmere had made indentures with other magnates besides Damory,[3] the idea of a party of the middle becomes strained when practically every prelate and magnate of any importance, except for Lancaster, appears to have been a member. A third and more important difficulty is that there is an unresolved tension between the views of Tout on the one hand and of Stubbs and Davies on the other. Stubbs's comment that Pembroke 'was personally faithful to the king' is in partial conflict with his own notion that there was a 'mediating party . . . of politiques, without any affection for the king'.[4] Similarly Davies's opinion that Pembroke was on close personal terms with the King seems, if correct, to

---

[1] Davies, *Baronial Opposition*, pp. 110–12, 428–9, 430, 440–2.

[2] See, for example, J. G. Edwards 'The Negotiating of the Treaty of Leake, 1318', in *Essays in History Presented to R. L. Poole*, ed. H. W. C. Davis (Oxford, 1927), p. 377, where he divides the 'middle party' into right and left wings in 1318; B. Wilkinson, 'The Negotiations Preceding the "Treaty" of Leake, August 1318', in *Studies in Medieval History Presented to F. M. Powicke*, eds. R. W. Hunt, W. A. Pantin, and R. W. Southern (Oxford, 1948), pp. 338–9, where the author says 'the outlook of the "middle party" was substantially the same as that of its clerical members'; N. Denholm-Young in the introduction to the *Vita Edwardi Secundi* (London, 1957), p. xii, saw the 'middle party' as the creation of Pembroke and Hereford.

[3] Davies, *Baronial Opposition*, p. 435, suggests there may have been other indentures.

[4] Stubbs (ed.), *Chronicles of the Reigns of Edward I and Edward II*, vol. 1, pp. cxiii–cxiv.

imply the need for some interpretation of Pembroke's activities other than the 'middle party' framework provided by Tout.[1]

There are therefore good general grounds for taking a closer look at the 'middle party' interpretation, and the natural place to start is with the famous indenture of 24 November 1317. This at once raises the wider issues of the relations of the alleged founders of the 'middle party', Pembroke and Badlesmere, with the King, with Lancaster, and with each other; and of course there is the question of just where Roger Damory fits into the picture. Most of these questions have already been partly answered by implication in the previous chapter, but there is some further evidence to be considered which will make it possible finally to pull together the various strands in the argument and decide whether or not there was a 'middle party'.

The nature of Pembroke's relations with the King is easily decided. Both Stubbs and Davies regarded him as on good personal terms with the King, but what has never been fully appreciated and what this study has so far attempted to emphasize is the full extent of Pembroke's loyalty to the Crown. From his very earliest experience of royal service in Flanders in 1297 up to 1317 Pembroke had, like his father before him, been loyal both to the person of the King and to what he regarded as the interests of the Crown. This loyalty had remained basically unaffected even by Pembroke's hostility to Gaveston in the early years of the reign and by his apparent breach with the King during his period as an Ordainer between 1310 and 1312. For Pembroke his normal place was to be with the King and in his service, more than ever perhaps when the weak character of the King meant that he needed the aid of responsible and trustworthy men. Pembroke should therefore always be numbered among the most consistent of the King's supporters. Pembroke was not a favourite in the sense that Gaveston had been, but nor was he so powerful in his own right that he was able to control the King, even had he wished to do so. The result was that the political power which Pembroke derived from his support of the King depended not so much on his possession of

---

[1] Davies's view of Pembroke is especially at variance with Tout's statement that Pembroke had joined in the royal government after Gaveston's execution in 1312 only because he and Warenne 'hated Lancaster and Warwick more bitterly than they despised the king': Tout, *Place of the Reign* (1914), p. 99.

royal favour, which indeed he never lost, as on the influence that could be brought to bear by the King's opponents outside the court or by any royal favourites who happened to be within it. Pembroke's real authority, therefore, varied in cyclical fashion as circumstances changed. None the less in the autumn of 1317, at the time of his indenture with Badlesmere and Roger Damory, Pembroke was a very prominent and highly respected member of the royal Council.

At the same time there is ample evidence of the trust which the King in his turn placed in Pembroke, another point which the preceding chapters have been intended to demonstrate. Edward II's attempts in 1310 to detach Pembroke from the Ordainers and bring him back into the day-to-day work of government, the obvious eagerness with which he welcomed him back into his circle after the execution of Gaveston, his request in May 1316 for Pembroke to fill the place left vacant on the Council by Lancaster's abandonment of his duties, his willing acceptance of Pembroke's advice for his future conduct before Pembroke left for Avignon in 1317, and his serious concern over Pembroke's capture in May 1317 all testify to the need which the King felt for his counsel. At another level Edward II's gifts to Pembroke at various times and his highly unusual offer in December 1316 to act as Pembroke's attorney show the personal regard which he had for the Earl. The same story could be repeated on many other occasions after 1317.

There is therefore ample reason to doubt whether a royal supporter of such prominence and consistency, who was so closely tied to the King, would feel the desire to form an independent political group in order to force himself upon the King. Nor would there be much point in his doing so in 1317, when he already held a very important position in the royal circle. What is known of Pembroke's character also suggests that he was not a man of great political ambition and that, even if he had harboured such desires, he would have lacked the ability to achieve them. These doubts about Pembroke's role as the leader of a 'middle party' rise almost to a certainty with the discovery that on 1 November 1317, only three weeks before the famous indenture which allegedly formed the party, Pembroke bound himself even more closely and specifically to the King in another indenture in which he promised to serve the King for life in peace and war in return for 500 marks of land and an annual peacetime fee of over 1,000 marks. In wartime he was to receive a fee of 2,000 marks and follow the King with a retinue of 200 men-at-arms.[1]

So far as his relations with the King were concerned, Pembroke may therefore be safely ruled out of any scheme to form a 'middle party'. Nor is there any good reason to believe that he wished to exclude Lancaster from the Council. This was indeed hardly necessary, since Lancaster had effectively excluded himself since the spring of 1316. If Pembroke had wished, he could have found ample grounds for wishing to see Lancaster humiliated or destroyed because of the humiliation that he had himself suffered at Lancaster's hands over the execution of Gaveston in 1312, the Thorpe Waterville dispute in 1314, and the recent seizure of his castle at Mitford in Northumberland. However, all the evidence that has been found points to the opposite conclusion that Pembroke was in reality actively concerned in trying to mend the breach between the King and Lancaster, so that on this count too Pembroke cannot be regarded as the likely founder of a 'middle party'.

A corrective also needs to be applied in the case of Badlesmere. There is no evidence that Badlesmere was at any time an associate of Lancaster. Tout's belief that this was so was based upon the contents of Lancaster's letter to Edward II on 21 July 1317, in which he justified his refusal to attend the assembly summoned at Nottingham. The Latin version of the letter given by the Bridlington chronicler, of which Tout made use, speaks of a reform commission whose members were the Archbishop of Canterbury and other bishops and earls 'una nobiscum [i.e. Lancaster] et domino Bartholomaeo de Badlesmere', and whose conclusions were taken to the King by Badlesmere and William Inge.[2] From these references to Badlesmere's name in conjunction with that of Lancaster and from the date of Lancaster's letter Tout concluded that Badlesmere

---

[1] E. 101/68/2/42D.: this is the original indenture but it has suffered damage. See text in Appendix 3. Pembroke's 500 marks of land were given to him in the form of a grant in tail on 4 Nov. of Haverfordwest and Hertford, both of which he already held for life: *C.P.R., 1317–21*, p. 47. The bad condition of the document makes it difficult to say what his peacetime fee was, but it was certainly very substantial and probably exceeded 1,000 marks.

[2] *Bridlington*, p. 51.

had been associated with Lancaster in an attempt at reform as late as the summer of 1317.[1] There is, however, a complete copy of the French original of Lancaster's letter attached to the chronicle of Adam Murimuth, which identifies the full membership of the reform commission as the Archbishop, the Bishops of Llandaff, Chichester, Norwich, and Salisbury, the Earls of Pembroke, Hereford, Arundel, Richmond, and Lancaster, and Badlesmere.[2] Badlesmere's name therefore appeared in association with other men, none of whom was a Lancastrian sympathizer, and was listed after that of Lancaster simply because he was next in rank after all the earls had been named. It is also clear from the contents of the letter that the commission was one set up at the Lincoln Parliament early in 1316, since Lancaster says in the letter that the commission had met in London, which he had not visited after his departure from the Council in April 1316. Lancaster's comments thus had nothing to do with the immediate events of 1317.

Badlesmere's earliest associations had in fact been as the leading retainer of the staunchly royalist Earl of Gloucester, and as early as 1311 he had been deputed as a member of the Council to assist Gloucester as Keeper of the Realm. In August 1313 he and Gloucester had to be dissuaded from laying siege to Bristol to settle Badlesmere's dispute with the town, and in March 1314 they both accompanied the Queen on a diplomatic mission to Paris.[3] After Gloucester's death at Bannockburn, Badlesmere remained prominent in royal service, probably as a result of his earlier Gloucester connections as well as of natural ability, despite his place in the second rank of the magnates. After Bannockburn he left some of his retainers to defend Berwick for the King[4] and in September 1314 was given custody of the former Gloucester lands in Glamorgan and Morgannwg. While in royal service Badlesmere's closest colleague was probably Pembroke, on whose information he had

---

[1] Tout, *Place of the Reign* (1914), pp. 106, 111.

[2] *Murimuth*, pp. 271–4. The Bridlington chronicler, p. 50, says the original was in French.

[3] C. 47/22/10/8; *C. Cl. R., 1313–18*, p. 69; *C.P.R., 1313–17*, pp. 85–6; *C. Treaty Rolls*, p. 207. For fuller details on Badlesmere's career see Davies, op. cit., pp. 427–8.

[4] E. 404/482/37/2, 3. According to a Canterbury chronicle, Badlesmere had abandoned the Earl of Gloucester at the battle: Trinity College Cambridge MS. R. 5. 41, f. 113*v*. I owe this reference to Miss E. A. Danbury.

been made constable of Bristol in 1312.[1] From July to November 1315 he had been in Pembroke's company and under his command in the Scottish March; in July 1316 he and Pembroke had gone to Bristol to resolve Badlesmere's dispute with the townspeople; and in January 1317 he and Pembroke had gone on the Avignon mission together. Badlesmere was thus associated both with the King and with Pembroke long before the Avignon mission at which he and Pembroke are said to have become allies. Like Pembroke, he was also by the end of 1316 an important member of the royal Council. Badlesmere's career also ran close to that of Pembroke in another way. On 29 September 1316 he too put his relations with the King on a clearly defined footing by an indenture to stay in the King's service in peacetime at an annual fee of 600 marks and in war with a retinue of 100 men. This was supplemented before 3 August 1317 by an annual fee of 1,000 marks, by which the King retained him for the value of his counsel.[2]

Examination of the careers and behaviour of Pembroke and Badlesmere thus shows that neither of them fits the traditional picture as founders of a 'middle party'. They were in reality close and valued associates of the King and not unscrupulous magnates who wished to force themselves upon him. In the case of Pembroke it is certain that he was playing a highly responsible role in trying to improve relations between the King and Lancaster, and it is very likely that Badlesmere was following a similar course of action before the autumn of 1317. The true nature of the career of Roger Damory, the third alleged founder of the 'middle party', has already been made clear in the previous chapter. Like Pembroke and Badlesmere, he too was closely associated with the King, but his role had been that of an ambitious and irresponsible royal favourite, who had done much to wreck the attempts during 1317 to make an accommodation between the King and Lancaster, because of such an agreement's implied threat to his position at court. It is scarcely probable then that Pembroke's and Badlesmere's indenture with Damory in November 1317 could have been the foundation of a 'middle party'. What in that case

---

[1] *C.P.R., 1313–17*, p. 194; ibid., *1307–13*, p. 483.
[2] Soc. of Antiqs. MS. 120, f. 45; ibid., MS. 121, f. 20*v.*; C. 81/101/4339; *C.P.R., 1317–21*, p. 14.

was the purpose of the indenture? The evidence already produced should have begun to suggest the answer.

It has been shown that Lancaster was well aware of the malignant character and activities of Roger Damory, and there is no reason to doubt that Pembroke and Badlesmere were equally aware that he was a dangerous man to be so close to the weak and easily influenced Edward II. In October 1317 Damory had almost involved the King in open conflict with Lancaster, and on top of this he had just become even more powerful with the livery on 15 November 1317 of his wife's share of the Gloucester inheritance.[1] It was therefore natural that Pembroke and Badlesmere should look for some way of preventing Damory from causing even greater trouble in the future, and their solution was an indenture between themselves and Damory. Their indenture with Damory on 24 November was not therefore intended to restrain the King and begin the formation of a 'middle party'; on the contrary, it was meant to restrain Roger Damory and act as a guarantee of his future good conduct. If one looks at the terms of the indenture, this conclusion becomes even clearer, since nearly the whole of it is taken up by promises on the part of Damory. When he promised, for example, not to urge the King to do anything unwise or to grant land worth more than £20, he was in effect restricting his own conduct, since no one was more likely to persuade the King to act in this way than Damory himself. There is no reason either to agree with the view that the King did not know of and approve Pembroke's and Badlesmere's action.[2] Damory had little choice but to accept the terms presented to him, since he knew the alternative would be his banishment from court if Lancaster ever succeeded in enforcing his demands. There is no evidence that Pembroke and Badlesmere made similar indentures with the other leading royal favourites, Audley and Montacute,[3] but even if they had done so the resulting agreements would be explicable in exactly the same way.

---

[1] C.F.R., 1307–19, p. 350.

[2] Davies, Baronial Opposition, p. 434, believed the indenture was kept secret from the King on the grounds of the King's pardon to Badlesmere in Aug. 1321 for his breach of a 'writing': C.P.R., 1321–4, p. 21. The term 'writing' referred in fact to Badlesmere's two contracts with the King in 1316 and 1317, which he broke by rebelling against the Despensers in 1321.

[3] This cannot be ruled out as the survival of Damory's indenture may be accidental.

The primary aim of the indenture was therefore to ensure Damory's good behaviour. It also followed that, once Damory had given a guarantee for the future, one of the major barriers to a settlement between Edward II and Lancaster would be at least reduced, if not wholly eliminated. Damory's promise not to seek grants from the King of more than £20 would also help to meet another of Lancaster's major complaints. The indenture had, however, the third purpose of helping to guarantee the political influence of Pembroke and Badlesmere. This might at first sight appear to be close to the traditional arguments that they were creating a 'middle party' to control the royal Council, but there is a major distinction to be made. Pembroke and Badlesmere were not trying to force themselves upon an unwilling King but were rather attempting to preserve the influence which they already possessed as leading members of the Council. Ironically the very existence and necessity of their indenture with Damory is really a mark of the weakness of their position rather than of their domination, and this was a direct consequence of the character of the King whom they both served. As Edward II's letters to Pembroke show, he was prepared to listen to and to follow sound advice when it was given by men whom he trusted. But Edward II was also very much the sort of man who agrees with the person to whom he has spoken last, and this meant that he might just as easily be influenced by the persuasion of irresponsible favourites without discriminating as to the quality of their advice. Edward II was as heavy a cross to his friends as he was to his enemies.

The traditional 'middle party' interpretation may therefore be discarded. The examination which has already been made of the events which preceded the indenture with Damory suggests a new general interpretation for this period of the reign of Edward II. The essential factor in this analysis is the already demonstrated division of the King's close associates into a group of capable and experienced councillors like Pembroke, Badlesmere, and others, and a second group of favourites whose position depended on the King's passing infatuation with them. The basis of the division between these two groups lay in their respective attitudes hitherto towards negotiations between Edward II and Lancaster, the one wanting a settlement while the other did its best to destroy all hope of one. At the same time there was a third most important group which has not so far been mentioned specifically. This was composed of the Archbishop and prelates of the province of Canterbury, the Archbishop of Dublin, and the two papal envoys, who had acted as mediators between the King and Lancaster both at Pontefract in August 1317 and again at York in the following month. The prelates were well placed to mediate collectively, because they could not be suspected of seeking power for themselves as a group, while the presence of several prelates on the royal Council acted as a useful link between the remaining prelates and the King and his other advisers.

There is, however, one further element in the 1317 situation to be taken into account, namely the part played by the magnates. The traditional view, which is stated either specifically or by implication, is that Edward II was opposed by a substantial proportion of the leading magnates, whose chief spokesman was the Earl of Lancaster and who aimed to control and to reform the royal government. In other words the King and barons were inherently divided by differing views on how government ought to be conducted. This 'constitutional' view of the reign is conveniently symbolized by the baronial declaration of 1308, which has been regarded as forming part of a magnate theory of constitutional opposition.[1] There is of course no doubt that Edward II's reign was politically a very disturbed one and that such a situation would tend to force any opposition movement to try to justify itself on occasion. On the other hand a close examination of the evidence reveals a more complex situation than has traditionally been understood.

In 1317, the point of immediate concern, it is evident that, far from being openly hostile to the King or sullenly neutral, most of the leading magnates were co-operating loyally with him. This was happening at the very moment when many of them are supposed to have been joining a 'middle party'. The attitude of the magnates is clearly shown by the fact that in late 1316 and during 1317 many of them were making contracts with the King. Few of the original contracts have survived, but

---

[1] *Ann. Lond.*, pp. 153–4. For comment see B. Wilkinson, *Constitutional History of Medieval England*, vol. 2, pp. 11–12. See also K. Schnith, 'Staatsordnung und Politik in England zu Anfang des 14 Jahrhunderts', *Historisches Jahrbuch*, vol. 88 (1968).

it is possible to reconstruct the terms of the remainder from scattered references. Where sufficient evidence is available the contracts are for life service, at an annual peacetime fee which was far greater than the usual fee of a Household knight or banneret, and which in the case of the most important men was very substantial indeed.[1] The number of men-at-arms to be brought for service in wartime was also specified. It is probably safe to say that the same kind of terms applied in the case of other contracts, about which their mere existence is known.

The contracts made with the King by Pembroke and Badlesmere have already been mentioned. Pembroke's wartime fee of 2,000 marks a year and his contingent of 200 men-at-arms were both the largest for any of the magnates involved, while Badlesmere was to provide 100 men in return originally for 600 marks and later 1,000 marks. Roger Damory had also made a contract on 15 January 1317 in return for 200 marks a year, but the size of his contingent is not known. His two co-favourites of 1317, Hugh Audley the Younger and William de Montacute, followed suit, but little is known about the details of their agreements. Of the other important magnates, the Earl of Hereford agreed to serve on similar terms to Badlesmere for 1,000 marks a year and with 100 men-at-arms; the Younger Despenser first contracted for two years with 30 men at 400 marks a year but later was given an additional 600-mark fee for staying with the King. There is also evidence of contracts made by John de Mowbray, John Giffard, John de Somery, John de Segrave senior, Henry FitzHugh, William de Ros of Helmsley (alias Hamelak), John Crombwell, John Botetourt, John de Wysham, Giles de Beauchamp, William de la Zouche of Ashby, and John de St. John for smaller fees and contingents.[2] Other magnates indicated their co-operation with the King by accepting important military and administrative posts. On 19 November 1316 the Earl of Arundel became Warden of the Scottish March and on 23 November 1316 Roger Mortimer of Wigmore and his uncle Roger Mortimer of Chirk were appointed respectively as Justices of Ireland and of North Wales.[3]

---

[1] The usual fee was 10 marks per year for a knight and 20 marks for a banneret.

[2] For full details of the indentures and some qualifications of the summary presented here see Appendix 3. Most of the figures quoted above, with the exception of those for Pembroke, are peacetime fees.

[3] E. 101/68/2/37; *C.P.R., 1313–17*, p. 563; *C.F.R., 1307–19*, p. 312. Mortimer of

In the light of earlier research into the period, this evidence of magnate behaviour is a wholly unexpected fact and requires some explanation. One possible conclusion might be that the King was consciously trying to form a royal party in order to buy off his opponents. But to create such a rigid framework of interpretation would be to repeat some of the mistakes of the 'middle party' theory, and would also demand a far greater degree of initiative and political skill than Edward II possessed. The contents of the contracts made by some of the leading magnates, such as Pembroke, Hereford, and Badlesmere, show that in their cases, at least, peacetime counsel and advice were to be a major part of their service to the King. An important clue to the purpose of the contracts as a whole is to be found in the element of military service which they all included. It is possible that the indentures reflect a debate among the members of the royal Council about how to provide the King with a reliable and permanent element of military strength. This was of particular urgency at the end of 1316, when the contracts first start to appear, since there was then a grave and continuing threat of Scottish invasion, and the traditional form of royal campaign was being nullified because of the political difficulties arising from the King's worsening relations with Lancaster. The Scottish threat may therefore have been one major reason for the willingness of the magnates to rally around the King.

However, a further probable cause was a growing irritation among the magnates with Lancaster himself. There is evidence that in the summer of 1318 the majority of the leading magnates had lost patience with Lancaster, because they regarded his unwillingness to co-operate with the King as a major reason for the Scottish ability to invade and devastate the north of England.[1] This attitude may already have begun to appear at the end of 1316 and have been reinforced by a feeling that Lancaster's demands for reform really cloaked a demand for supreme political power for himself which the other magnates were not prepared to concede. These two reasons, combined with Lancaster's proved incapacity when he had been given

Chirk was reappointed for life as Justice of North and South Wales on 7 Oct. 1317: *C.F.R., 1307-19*, p. 342.
   [1] C. 49/4/26, 27.

authority early in 1316, would have made the magnates even more ready to assist the King.[1]

For the moment then Edward II was receiving the active assistance of a majority of the leading magnates at both a political and military level and of many lesser magnates in a purely military role. However, one important result of the contractual obligations to the King which had been entered into by the magnates was that, if political circumstances changed and they found themselves in opposition, the King would then have excellent grounds for attacking and perhaps destroying them. Several of the magnates found themselves in just this position when they opposed the Despensers in 1321 and 1322, when both Badlesmere and Hugh Audley the Younger, for example, suffered because of their breach of contracts made in 1316 and 1317.[2] This was certainly, however, an unintended result, since none of the magnates who contracted to serve the King at this time could then be regarded as of doubtful loyalty, nor is there any evidence to suggest that they were acting under duress. The whole episode is indeed yet another object lesson in the speed with which the political situation could change in the reign of Edward II, turning the loyal allies of one year into the bitter opponents of the next.

This new interpretation of the indenture of 24 November 1317 between Pembroke, Badlesmere, and Damory offers an adequate explanation of the events of 1317. It now remains to be seen if it will also explain the negotiations which finally produced the Treaty of Leake in August 1318.

By the end of October 1317 there was a state of near civil war, following the King's threats against Lancaster and Lancaster's own retaliation against Warenne and Damory. Under these conditions it was natural that the royal government should give high priority to precautions against any further outbreak of violence. The King began by putting several of his castles into the hands of reliable supporters. On 1 November Pembroke was given custody of Berkhamsted, but was then reappointed instead as constable of Rockingham, which he had held for the King since 1314, while one of his retainers, Richard

---

[1] The problem of the relations between the King and magnates in the reign as a whole is developed in the Conclusion to this book.

[2] *C.P.R.*, *1317–21*, p. 572; ibid., *1321–4*, p. 21; ibid., *1327–30*, p. 30.

de la Ryvere, received charge of Gloucester. Badlesmere was put in command of Leeds in Kent, the Younger Despenser of Odiham in Hampshire, and the constables of sixteen other royal castles in the Midlands and elsewhere were ordered to prepare them for defence.[1] It was also on 1 November that Pembroke made his contract to serve the King with 200 men-at-arms; and on 25 November, at his manor of Hertfording-bury, he made the first of a probable series of indentures with other knights to enlarge his retinue.[2] On 24 November Pembroke and Badlesmere had also made their own personal contribution towards stabilizing the situation by their indenture to ensure the good behaviour of Damory. On 7 November, Pembroke, Hereford, Badlesmere, the Archbishop of Canterbury, and the Bishops of Ely and Winchester helped to provide the King with a supply of ready cash when they guaranteed a loan of 10,000 marks to Edward II by the Bardi.[3] Lancaster meanwhile remained securely at his castle of Pontefract.[4]

Under these conditions the chances of any fresh negotiations with Lancaster, no matter who initiated them, might appear very remote, and yet only nine months later a settlement was made at Leake. The reasons for this desirable result accordingly require close examination. The very seriousness of the situation probably provided the initial stimulus. If the crisis were not to be resolved by civil war, then the only way to reduce tension was to try once again for an accommodation with Lancaster, however slight its chances were. This would also be an opportunity to test the value of Pembroke's agreement with Damory.

There is evidence that this latter answer was the one adopted by the royal Council. An attempt to mollify Lancaster was made as early as 25 October, when Adam de Swynburn, a Northumberland man who had been in royal service in defence of the Scottish March in 1317, and whose arrest on 9 August for criticizing the King's defensive measures in the March was said to have been a cause of the activities of Gilbert de Middleton, was handed over to the protection of Lancaster at Nottingham.[5] A more positive step in breaking the deadlock was the

---

[1] *C.P.R., 1317–21*, p. 46; *C.F.R., 1307–19*, p. 344; *C. Cl. R., 1313–18*, pp. 504–5.
[2] E. 101/68/2/42D.; E. 101/68/2/41. The knight was a certain Sir John, whose full name is missing from the document. See text in Appendix 2.
[3] E. 368/88, m. 112.   [4] D.L. 25/2059: 26 Nov.
[5] Soc. of Antiqs. MS. 120, f. 45; ibid. MS. 121, f. 12*v*.; *Scalacronica*, p. 144. See

mission in November of the Archbishop of Dublin, who was
sent from London to visit Lancaster at Pontefract and explain
certain matters orally on the King's behalf.[1] The results of this
mission are unknown but it appears to have produced some
hope of progress in placating Lancaster, which is probably
reflected in the formal summons issued on 20 November for
Parliament to meet at Lincoln on 27 January 1318[2] as had
been agreed with Lancaster at York in September. This attempt
to contact Lancaster is specifically described as being made by
the Council, and responsibility for it may be safely assigned to
Pembroke and the others, whose presence with the Council is
revealed in the agreement with the Bardi on 7 November.

The part played by the Archbishop of Dublin, who had
already been involved in mediating with Lancaster at Pontefract in August and York in September, the presence of several
prelates on the Council, and the proximity to London of the
two papal envoys in November[3] once again suggest the possibility of a strong clerical initiative in getting negotiations restarted. As in earlier negotiations, the clergy could be regarded
as a neutral group for the purposes of mediation between the
King and Lancaster, and hence an approach from them was
likely to be more acceptable to Lancaster than a direct approach
from the Council, which Lancaster would probably reject out-
right. This situation therefore gave an opportunity for fruitful
co-operation between the lay members of the Council, such as
Pembroke, Hereford, and Badlesmere, who wanted a political
settlement, and the clergy, who would be able to act as mediators. This policy would be aided by the close liaison between
the two bodies provided by the membership of the Council of
prelates, such as the Archbishop and the Bishops of Ely and
Winchester.

Discussion of such a joint policy in dealing with Lancaster
may well have been held among the bishops of the Canterbury
province when they assembled at St. Paul's on 27 and 28
November to hear the papal envoys read out bulls directed

also C. H. Hunter-Blair, 'Members of Parliament for Northumberland, 1258–
1327', *Arch. Aeliana*, 4th series, vol. 10 (1933), p. 167.
    [1] Soc. of Antiqs. MS. 121, f. 30: he was away for fifteen days.
    [2] *C. Cl. R., 1313–18*, p. 585.
    [3] Cardinal Luke was at Sempringham on 2 Nov.: *Chroniques de Sempringham:
Le Livere de Reis de Britannie*, R.S. (London, 1865), p. 334.

against the Scots.[1] Whether this was so or not, an opportunity
for such discussions was given by the imminence of the coming
Parliament. This was the occasion of a summons to a meeting
with the royal Council at Westminster on 30 December which
was sent on 16 December to the Chancellor the Bishop of Winchester, the Treasurer the Bishop of Ely, and the Bishops of
Coventry and Lichfield, Bath and Wells, St. Davids, Worcester,
and Lincoln.[2] When the time came for the meeting there were
therefore, including the Archbishop and Bishops of Norwich and
Chichester, ten prelates of the Canterbury province assembled
together with the magnate members of the Council, who on
this occasion included Pembroke himself, as well as Hereford
and Badlesmere.[3]

That Lancaster was a prime topic of discussion is confirmed
by a valuable account of the assembly given by the author of
the *Vita*, who said that those present agreed that it would be
unwise to hold a Parliament immediately, because of the danger
of a clash between the large bodies of retainers whom the King
and Lancaster would certainly have with them. They decided
that it would be wiser first of all to restore harmony and confidence between the two by means of mediation, after which
a date could be fixed for Parliament to meet. The success of
this view is proved by the postponement on 4 January of the
Lincoln Parliament from 27 January to 12 March, and by the
King's renewal of Pembroke's and Hereford's powers to grant
protection to Lancaster and his followers.[4]

The next step was to regain contact with Lancaster and try
to arrange for mediation with him. It is very likely that in
November and December 1317 the prelates were looking for
ways of mediating with Lancaster, but from January 1318 it is
certain that they were doing so and that they agreed at their
meeting with the Council to take full responsibility for a new
initiative. One immediate result was a mission by the Bishop of
Norwich to visit Lancaster at Pontefract, presumably to find
out if he was willing to negotiate.[5] Another was the calling on
15 January of a council of the province of Canterbury to meet

---

[1] *Ann. Paul.*, p. 281.   [2] *C. Cl. R., 1313–18*, p. 586.
[3] C. 53/104, m. 9.
[4] *Vita*, p. 84; *C. Cl. R., 1313–18*, p. 590; *C.P.R., 1317–21*, p. 69.
[5] The bishop was at Pontefract on 22 Jan.: Norfolk and Norwich Record
Office, Register of John Salmon, f. 72.

at St. Paul's on 23 February to discuss the affairs of the Church and realm.¹ As a result of this council an assembly of clergy and magnates was arranged to meet the Earl of Lancaster at Leicester in April. The further postponement on 3 March of Parliament from 12 March to 19 June and the renewal on 4 March of the authority of Pembroke and Hereford to give safe conducts to Lancaster and his men were therefore performed in the knowledge that a meeting with Lancaster was in prospect.²

Previous accounts of the 1318 negotiations with Lancaster have all begun with the assembly that was now held at Leicester, and have therefore not indicated either that the prelates had a vital part in it or that the meeting was yet another stage in a long process of attempted negotiation extending back to the beginning of 1317. The negotiations have also been studied on the assumption that they were conducted by a 'middle party' led by Pembroke, so that it is all the more important to attempt to find out what was happening and why.³

Considerable difficulties have been caused in describing the events at Leicester and their significance by the varying ways in which the chronicle sources refer to the meeting.⁴ According to the Bridlington writer, the only source which dates the meeting, a 'parliament' was held at Leicester on 12 April, attended by the Archbishop of Canterbury, the Bishops of Norwich, Chichester, Winchester, Llandaff, and Hereford, the Earls of Lancaster, Pembroke, and Hereford, twenty-eight unnamed barons, William de Bereford, and Walter de Norwich. All those present swore on the Gospels to see that the Ordinances were observed, that evil and unsuitable royal councillors were removed, and that grants of land by the King contrary to the

¹ Cambridge Univ. MS. Ee. v. 31, f. 188*v*. (register of H. of Eastry, Prior of Canterbury); Hist. MSS. Comm., *Wells*, vol. 1, p. 179; *Trivet (Cont.)*, p. 26. On 16 Feb. the clergy were advised to do nothing prejudicial to royal authority: *C.P.R., 1317–21*, p. 104.

² *P.W.*, vol. 2, part 2, p. 178; *C.P.R., 1317–21*, p. 113.

³ The Leake negotiations are discussed in Tout, *Place of the Reign*, and in Davies, *Baronial Opposition*. The most detailed accounts are those of Sir Goronwy Edwards, 'The Negotiating of the Treaty of Leake, 1318', and of Professor Bertie Wilkinson, 'The Negotiations Preceding the "Treaty" of Leake, August 1318'. These are both very important contributions to the history of the reign of Edward II.

⁴ See Wilkinson's discussion, 'The Negotiations preceding the "Treaty" of Leake, pp. 333–6.

Ordinances should be rescinded and their holders made to come to Parliament for a decision on their possession of the lands. Lancaster's offences against the King in his search for better government of the realm, and his seizures of castles and property, should be pardoned, and all his men who had been arrested by the King should be freed.[1] According to the *Flores*, the magnates, papal envoys, and prelates met Lancaster at Leicester and agreed on oath to the observation of the Ordinances and the keeping of the peace.[2] The Leicester chronicle of Henry Knighton speaks of certain articles which were agreed at Leicester between Lancaster and the prelates and which were afterwards confirmed at London by the cardinals, Archbishops of Canterbury and Dublin, and the other prelates of the Canterbury province.[3] The *Vita* says that the archbishops, earls, and barons, acting on the King's behalf, met with Lancaster's councillors at Leicester, where they put to Lancaster, on behalf of the King, a number of points, to all of which he refused to give his assent unless the Ordinances were observed. Because of Lancaster's firm stand the Archbishop and certain earls promised on behalf of themselves and the King that the Ordinances should be observed and that a document embodying their oath and sealed by each of them should be drawn up. For his part Lancaster promised his due fealty and security to the King and his men, saving only his quarrel with Warenne over the latter's abduction of his wife.[4] A fifth source, *Trokelowe*, refers only to an apparently intended meeting at Leicester on 24 June, which has led Professor Wilkinson to suggest that there were two Leicester meetings, in April and in June.[5] It is most likely, however, that, as J. C. Davies and Sir Goronwy Edwards both suggest, all these references concern a single meeting at Leicester in April,[6] the variations in the accounts being explained by their concentration on different aspects and stages of the Leicester negotiations, and by their writers' opportunities to know what took place.

[1] *Bridlington*, pp. 54–5. Lancaster's seizure of Knaresborough had already been pardoned on 19 Mar.: *C.P.R., 1317–21*, p. 123.

[2] *Flores*, vol. 3, pp. 183–4.

[3] *Knighton*, vol. 1, p. 413.   [4] *Vita*, pp. 84–5.

[5] *Trokelowe*, p. 102; Wilkinson, 'The Negotiations preceding the "Treaty" of Leake', pp. 334–6.

[6] Davies, *Baronial Opposition*, p. 445; J. G. Edwards, 'The Negotiating of the Treaty of Leake', pp. 360–3.

Further light is thrown on the problem by a document from the Dodsworth manuscripts in the Bodleian, which is headed: 'Une accorde entre ercevesques e evesques dune parte e le conte de Lancastre daltre parte de dicto comite veniendo ad parliamentum.'[1] This agreement contains promises by Lancaster that he would not in future commit armed breaches of the peace, that he would come to Parliament when duly summoned and do reverence to the King, and would remit his quarrel with Warenne until the next Parliament. In return the prelates promised on behalf of themselves and the other prelates of the Canterbury province that Lancaster and his men should be given surety for when they came to Parliament, and that the agreement would be executed by the authority of the Church. At the same time Lancaster took an oath that he had never wished to deprive the King of his royal power, and that he wished to maintain the Ordinances and see that all alienations of land made contrary to them were restored to the Crown. The document is undated but the reference in it to Warenne proves that it belongs to some date after May 1317. The reference in Lancaster's oath to the Ordinances and the revocation of grants is in accord with other evidence about his demands at Leicester, so that the agreement seems most likely to belong to that time. It is very probable in fact that this document is the text of the articles which Knighton says were agreed at Leicester between Lancaster and the clergy.[2] The prelates are mentioned in the agreement as being those of Canterbury and presumably therefore include the five named in the Bridlington account, while the archbishops mentioned in the document's heading would be those of Canterbury and probably also of Dublin. This identification of the document with the Knighton articles is strengthened by the implication in the agreement that it was made on behalf of the prelates of Canterbury by part of their number and that, as in Knighton's account, it would need the confirmation of the remainder of the province.[3]

---

[1] Bodleian, Dodsworth MS. 8, p. 262. The Latin words in the title were probably added by the transcriber. For text and other details see Appendix 4.

[2] *Knighton*, vol. 1, p. 413.

[3] *Bridlington*, p. 54; *Knighton*, vol. 1, p. 413. A case could also be made for dating the document to the York negotiations of Sept. 1317. However, so far as is known from chronicle sources, those negotiations were restricted to the simple question

If the dating of this agreement is correct, it adds further valuable evidence on the details of the Leicester meeting and confirms the impression given by Knighton, a writer who, in respect of the 1318 negotiations, appears to have had access to documents unused by or unknown to other writers,[1] that the clergy played a prominent role at Leicester. This is fully in line with their importance earlier in mediating with Lancaster in order to arrange the Leicester meeting.

Having surveyed the main evidence, we may now attempt a reconstruction of the course of the Leicester meeting. It has already been suggested that the meeting was arranged by the prelates with the active encouragement and agreement of the royal Council. This impression of full government co-operation in what took place at Leicester is confirmed by the evidence of the *Vita* that those present were there on behalf of the King and put to Lancaster certain proposals in the King's name.[2] These points had presumably been carefully considered by the Council beforehand and had received the King's approval. The King's representatives at the meeting, or those who can readily be identified as such, were at least four in number. On 29 March the Chancellor the Bishop of Winchester was sent from London to Leicester by the King. On 3 April Badlesmere arrived at Northampton with 100 men-at-arms, at the King's orders, and on 5 April went on from there to Leicester with the Earl of Pembroke and the Archbishop of Canterbury.[3] It was probably with the arrival in Leicester of these four men that the conference began in earnest. The King and his envoys kept in close touch during the meeting. On 7 April a clerk of William de Montacute, the Steward, was sent to Leicester with private royal letters, and at some stage in the negotiations Pembroke, Badlesmere, and the Archbishop each sent

---

of Lancaster's attendance at Parliament and did not refer to the Ordinances or to gifts made by the King. The document also implies by Lancaster's promise not to commit armed attacks that he had already been doing so. In Sept. 1317 he had not yet attacked Damory or Warenne but had taken up arms by Apr. 1318.

[1] Although writing well after 1318, Knighton came from a religious house at Leicester which may have preserved evidence of the 1318 negotiations. This was probably also the source of the Tutbury articles of June 1318: *Knighton*, vol. 1, pp. 413–21.

[2] *Vita*, pp. 84–5.

[3] *C. Cl. R., 1313–18*, p. 603; Soc. of Antiqs. MS. 121, f. 20*v*. Pembroke, Badlesmere, and the Archbishop rejoined the King on about 20 Apr.: ibid.

messengers to the King at Windsor to report on their work at Leicester.[1]

The proceedings probably opened with further mediation between the prelates and Lancaster and his councillors in order to discover Lancaster's terms.[2] It is likely that the King's proposals were put forward at this stage, perhaps by the Archbishop and the Bishop of Winchester, who were present at Leicester both as mediating prelates and formally as royal envoys. During these conversations it would have become clear, as the *Vita* points out, that Lancaster intended to make acceptance of the Ordinances a pre-condition of any further negotiations with the King.[3] The Dodsworth agreement would fit naturally into this stage of the proceedings as a full statement of the terms on which Lancaster was prepared to negotiate.

With this initial process of sounding opinion and mediation by the prelates completed, it would then be possible for the conference to continue on a broader basis with the full participation of all the King's envoys, including Pembroke and Badlesmere, and of the other magnates present. From this point onwards the conference would have been virtually a meeting between the respective councils of the King and of Lancaster, with the prelates mediating between them.

The meeting of 12 April which is described in the Bridlington account was the culmination of the discussions which had taken place earlier, and was presumably the date on which a final formal agreement was made. There seems no reason to doubt the essential accuracy of the Bridlington statement that all the participants on both Lancaster's and the King's sides swore to the observance of the Ordinances, the removal of unsuitable and evil royal councillors, and the resumption of royal gifts.[4] Acceptance of the principle of the Ordinances is confirmed by the *Vita*, a source which can never be lightly discarded.[5] Since this point had been granted by the King on many other occasions, notably in 1315 and 1316, he could well allow it

[1] Soc. of Antiqs. MS. 121, ff. 12*v.*, 20*v.*

[2] Lancaster was certainly present in person on 7, 12, 13 Apr.: D.L. 42/11, f. 9*v.*; *Bridlington*, pp. 54–5; D.L. 42/2, f. 221.

[3] *Vita*, p. 84–5.

[4] *Bridlington*, pp. 54–5. Some of the twenty-eight barons present on 12 Apr. were almost certainly retainers of Lancaster and other important magnates.

[5] *Vita*, pp. 84–5.

now, and there is no reason to suppose that Pembroke and the other royal envoys were exceeding their powers in doing so. It is equally possible that the envoys did accept the specific demands as to evil councillors and gifts since, as will be seen when the Tutbury articles of June are examined, there were major differences in the ways in which the King and his Council and Lancaster interpreted the application of these points in practice.[1] Lastly it is also clear, from the *Vita* and the Dodsworth agreement, that each side promised the other security, and that the question of Lancaster's dispute with Warenne was shelved.[2]

In itself the Leicester agreement was no more than a first step towards a final settlement, and many details remained to be solved before any meeting could take place between Lancaster and the King. Much too would depend on how both sides interpreted the agreements and on whether the barrier of mutual distrust could be broken down. If the royal favourites, Damory and his like, tried to influence the King against accepting the statements of principle, which was what the Leicester agreement amounted to, they might again succeed in preventing a settlement. Limited as it was, the Leicester agreement was important and a triumph principally of clerical mediation. So far as can be seen, Pembroke as an individual had not been the dominant force in bringing about the meeting or in its course, but was instead one element, though perhaps an important one, in the group of clergy and royal councillors present there, all of whom desired the meeting's success.

Little is known in detail of what happened immediately after the Leicester conference, but it is apparent that the centre of events now moved back to Westminster. We may suppose that one of the first developments there was the formal confirmation by the rest of the Canterbury prelates of the articles of agreement between Lancaster and the clergy.[3] The next step for which there is clear evidence was a series of very important discussions held at Westminster in the early part of June to consider how the second round of negotiations with Lancaster ought to

[1] *Knighton*, vol. I pp. 413–15, 419–20.
[2] *Vita*, pp. 84–5; Bodleian, Dodsworth MS. 8, p. 262.
[3] *Knighton*, vol. I, p. 413. The Bishop of Norwich was at Leicester from 4 to 12 Apr. and returned to London by 19 May: Reg. John Salmon, ff. 74–5. The Bishop of Winchester was back in London by 20 Apr.: *Reg. Sandale*, p. lx.

be approached and what concessions would be necessary to his demands.

These fresh talks are first of all revealed in two documents, one dated at Westminster on 2 June and not previously known, the other also of early June and printed in 1918.[1] The exact chronological relation of the two documents, which differ in detail though not in substance, is uncertain, but both are drafts and probably resulted in a final version which has not survived. The document of 2 June lists the names of those present as the Archbishops of Canterbury and Dublin, etc., and the Earl of Pembroke, etc., and is also endorsed with the names of the Bishops of Norwich, Coventry and Lichfield, Chichester, London, Salisbury, Winchester, Ely, Hereford, and Worcester, the Earl of Hereford, the Elder and Younger Despensers, Badlesmere, Damory, and William Montacute. As well as being exactly dated, this document adds considerably to previous information in giving this list of names, the participants being named in the other version only as the Archbishops, Pembroke, Hereford, Despenser, 'e autres grandz du roiaume'. The agreement of 2 June is also very significant in showing that once again the prelates were acting as mediators[2] and that on this occasion they were meeting with members of the King's Council.[3]

Both documents are in bad condition, but by using each to supply gaps in the other it is possible to discover their contents. The texts reveal that the discussions had been given an added urgency by the Scottish invasion of Yorkshire in May, following their capture of Berwick in April,[4] and that the prelates and magnates of the Council had met to advise the King on the defence of his kingdom from the Scots and to give him prompt counsel and aid on the good government of the realm.[5] They

[1] C. 49/4/27 (see text in Appendix 4); *E.H.R.*, vol. 33 (1918) (C. 49/4/26). J. G. Edwards, 'The Negotiating of the Treaty of Leake', p. 367, argued that this document contains the articles between Lancaster and the clergy mentioned by Knighton.

[2] Wilkinson, 'The Negotiations preceding the "Treaty" of Leake', p. 340, n. 3, thought the prelates were not present.

[3] This is clear from the names of those present. It is also stated specifically on 2 June that they were all meeting *au conseil*, filling a gap in the printed text which its editor completed as *ovesque le conseil*, no doubt believing that Pembroke was there as the head of a 'middle party': *E.H.R.*, vol. 33, p. 81.

[4] *Chroniques de Sempringham*, p. 334; *Vita*, p. 85.

[5] C. 49/4/27 (fills gap in ibid. /26).

had also agreed that 'touz oiontement e chescun de euz li a son poer ben e loialment conseilleront nostre seigneur le Roi'.[1] Both texts also agree in seeing Lancaster's behaviour as a major barrier to the conduct of the King's administration and government 'des queux il se est esloigne ia une piece pur grosseur e malevolence de ceux qi sont pres du Roi, a ceo que home entente'.[2] This statement in the 2 June document does in passing recognize that Lancaster may have had cause to fear some of the King's associates, but its implied rebuke of Lancaster is made much more explicit in the other text, which says that he 'ne se est done a conseiller ne aider a nostre seigneur le Roi en ses busoignes come li appent', and that he had gathered men-at-arms at Parliaments and other royal assemblies 'en effroi du people, par quoi commune fame e voiz del people . . . est que par les dites enchesons les ditz maux sont avenuz'.[3] Lancaster's peers therefore saw his failure to co-operate with the King and his use of armed force as chief causes of the present troubles.

Following this general statement of the causes of the crisis, those present agreed on the terms of a possible solution. Both texts say, in slightly differing words, that Lancaster should not be allowed to gather armed forces under colour of the Ordinances to which the prelates and magnates as well as Lancaster had pledged themselves, and that he should not employ force 'e noun covenable manere (plus que un autre grant du Roiaume)',[4] except with the consent of the magnates and prelates named above or the greater part of them. Lancaster should also in future come to Parliament as a peer of the realm 'sanz sovereinete a li accrocher vers les autres',[5] a remark which implies that Lancaster's peers had taken strong exception to his previous attempts to acquire a dominant position for himself. It was also agreed that Lancaster should be offered a guarantee by trustworthy men against those whom he suspected of abducting his wife, but that any of the suspects who

[1] C. 49/4/26 (fills gap in ibid. /27).   [2] Ibid. /27.   [3] Ibid. /26.

[4] Ibid. (fills gap in ibid. /27). The text in parentheses was finally erased in the 2 June version.

[5] Ibid. /27. Lancaster had already promised not to use force and to attend Parliament when summoned in his agreement with the prelates at Leicester: Bodleian, Dodsworth MS. 8, p. 262. The point of repeating the promise as a future demand in June was probably to ensure that it had a formal place in a final settlement.

did not wish to do this should instead make amends, and that because of the urgency of the situation all this should be done without legal process.[1] All those present at Westminster finally agreed that they should all be bound by the agreement and should see that it was upheld.[2]

It has previously been concluded, on the basis of the printed version of the Westminster agreement which was the only one then known, that the discussions held in June 1318 are proof positive of the activity of a 'middle party' led by Pembroke and designed to oust Lancaster.[3] For the moment nothing need be said as to Pembroke's role in the 1318 negotiations, other than to repeat the earlier conclusion that he was not the leader of a 'middle party', that he was in reality an influential member of the royal Council, and that he wanted an accommodation with Lancaster. However, it has also been argued that the absence from the June agreement of any reference to the terms agreed with Lancaster at Leicester in April indicates a deliberate betrayal of Lancaster.[4] On this second point, it should first of all be appreciated that the Leicester agreement was not in itself a settlement, but was a means of discovering Lancaster's demands and so preparing the way for further negotiations. The discussions held at Westminster in June concentrated on the other side of the argument, namely the concessions that Lancaster would have to make if he really wanted a settlement.

There is, however, evidence that the June discussions went much further than this and also considered what concessions the King was ready to make to Lancaster. There can be little doubt that the biggest problem that the prelates, the Earl of Pembroke, and other moderates had to face, was to persuade the King to overcome his hostility to Lancaster and begin serious negotiations for a permanent settlement. The royal favourites, Roger Damory and the rest, would also have had to be persuaded that their safety could be guaranteed in any future agreement with Lancaster. By 8 June the initial barrier of the King's reluctance had been overcome when the Bishop of Norwich announced to an assembly of magnates and prelates at St. Paul's that the King was ready to follow the advice of his

[1] C. 49/4/26. This point is not in ibid. /27.   [2] Ibid.
[3] Tout, *Place of the Reign*, p. 104, n. 3 (editor's note, 1936 edition).
[4] Wilkinson, 'The Negotiations preceding the "Treaty" of Leake', p. 340.

earls and barons. On the following day the Archbishop of Canterbury also noted in a letter that the King was willing to embrace the way of peace discussed at Leicester.[1] On 9 June another important step was taken towards answering one of Lancaster's major demands by an order revoking all gifts made contrary to the Ordinances.[2]

A third stage in preparing the ground for negotiations was reached on 11 June in a very important document which has recently come to light at the Public Record Office. This takes the form of a promise by Hugh Despenser the Elder, Roger Damory, Hugh Audley the Younger, William de Montacute, and John Charlton that they would in no way impede or threaten Lancaster or any of his men when Lancaster came to make his peace with the King. In its initial draft the document contained a clause in which Damory and the others admitted that Lancaster had previously failed to come before the King 'par encheson de nous a ce qe home dit', but this was later crossed out, perhaps because it was too pointed a condemnation of them. All five men named were close associates of the King and particular enemies of Lancaster, and the document thus confirms very clearly the arguments put forward earlier that the royal favourites were a major hindrance to agreement between Lancaster and the King. The document also confirms particularly neatly the argument that the prelates and papal envoys were playing a very valuable mediating role, since it states that Damory and company had given their guarantee to Lancaster with the permission of the King and at the request of Cardinals Gaucelin and Luke, the Archbishops of Canterbury and Dublin, and the Bishops of London, Winchester, Coventry and Lichfield, Norwich, Chichester, Salisbury, Ely, Worcester, and Hereford, all of whom promised to see that the guarantee was upheld.[3]

---

[1] *Ann. Paul.*, p. 282; Hist. MSS. Comm., *Various Collections*, vol. 1, p. 267.

[2] E. 159/91, m. 64d. Grants to at least three men, Hugh Audley the Younger, J. Giffard, and Jakinettus de Marigny, were revoked on 9 June: *C.F.R., 1307–19*, p. 374; *C. Cl. R., 1318–23*, pp. 51, 64.

[3] S.C. 1/63/183 (added from unsorted miscellanea in Dec. 1967). See text in Appendix 4. The Younger Despenser was probably included in the guarantee by implication under his father's name, but his absence may again suggest that he was not as yet seen as a real threat in his own right. John Charlton, the Chamberlain of the Household, was included because of his dispute with Lancaster's knight, Gruffydd de la Pole, over Welshpool.

The determination of the King's advisers that a settlement should be reached was also shown in the Council's reply to a letter from Warenne on 14 June asking for royal assistance to expel Lancaster's men from his Welsh lands in Bromfield and Yale. The Council had no intention of being side-tracked by this issue and told Warenne to settle the matter himself, contenting itself with requesting Lancaster to desist from his attacks.[1]

Before a direct meeting could take place between the King and Lancaster it was necessary to settle definitively the detailed points in dispute between them. The first stage in this process was the sending of the Bishops of Norwich and Ely to visit Lancaster at his castle of Tutbury, and the start of this mission can be dated by the departure on royal business of the newly appointed Chancellor the Bishop of Ely on 13 June.[2] Details of what followed at Tutbury have fortunately been preserved in a long document included in Knighton's chronicle.[3] The date on which the Tutbury negotiations were held or, more likely, finished, can also be positively fixed by a document which shows that the Bishops of Norwich and Ely were accompanied to Tutbury by the Archbishop of Dublin, and that the negotiations there took place on the basis of a series of points drawn up at London by the Archbishops of Canterbury and Dublin and presented to Lancaster by the Bishop of Norwich on behalf of the Archbishop and province of Canterbury. Once again therefore the Canterbury province took the lead in mediating with Lancaster. The document, made in the form of a notarial instrument, records that on 23 June 1318 at Horninglow, between Burton-on-Trent and Tutbury, Stephen Segrave read the text of Lancaster's replies to the proposals brought by the Bishop of Norwich and his colleagues. The instrument quoted the first and final lines of this document, which proves to be almost identical with the one contained in Knighton's chronicle as the Tutbury articles.[4]

As the details given in the 23 June instrument and an

[1] S.C. 8/177/8829–31; *C. Cl. R., 1313–18*, p. 554.

[2] *Knighton*, vol. 1, p. 413; *C. Cl. R., 1313–18*, p. 619. Lancaster was already at Tutbury on 9 June: D.L. 34/14.   [3] *Knighton*, vol. 1, pp. 413–21.

[4] Foljambe Charters, Appendix 4, Osberton Hall, Worksop. I have to thank Dr. J. R. Maddicott for allowing me to see this document when on deposit at the Bodleian library.

examination of the articles themselves suggest, the Tutbury articles are in form a composite document and not a record of an impromptu conversation.[1] The articles are made up of a series of statements by the prelates, each of which had clearly been agreed in content by the other prelates, presumably in consultation with the Council, before the envoys left London, and to which Lancaster's replies are attached. The articles also give further proof that the points which had been agreed with Lancaster in April had in fact been discussed by the prelates and Council in London in early June. In April tentative agreement had been given to Lancaster's demands on the revocation of grants and the removal of the favourites or 'evil councillors' and both these points now reappear in the articles.

As already noticed, the recall of grants contrary to the Ordinances had been ordered on 9 June. The articles show that this acceptance of Lancaster's demand was combined with the suggestion that the recipients of such grants should restore them to the King, without punishment for breaking the Ordinances, and that a Parliament should decide whether or not to make the recall permanent. Lancaster refused to accept this compromise, and in reply quoted the clause of the Ordinances dealing with grants.[2] With regard to the royal favourites, it was suggested to Lancaster in the articles that they should come to Parliament and be judged there by their peers for any breach of the Ordinances they might have committed; that, instead of being removed altogether from the King's presence, these councillors should absent themselves when the King and Lancaster made peace together, so that Lancaster need have no fear of them; and that such councillors should make amends to Lancaster for their injuries to him. Once again Lancaster rejected such a compromise and insisted that they should be permanently removed under the terms of the Ordinances, of which he again quoted the appropriate clause.[3] On the question of a surety for his

---

[1] *Knighton*, vol. 1, pp. 413–21. The printed text has been checked against both the manuscript copies, B.M., Cotton Claudius MS. E. III, ff. 233–4, and ibid., Tiberius C. VII, ff. 121*v*.–3, and is correct apart from minor misreadings. Davies, *Baronial Opposition*, p. 445, thought the articles were those agreed at Leicester in April.

[2] *Knighton*, vol. 1, pp. 413–15. The reference is to Ordinance 7 of 1311, headed by 'Articuli ordinati sunt isti'.

[3] Ibid., pp. 418–21, referring to Ordinance 13, headed by 'Les poyntez des ordinances sont tiels'.

coming to the King, Lancaster said he did not trust the King's safe conducts, since when he had done so in the past he had been imperilled by the King's favourites; nor was he certain of the value of the surety promised by the magnates at Leicester, since he had heard that some of them had since agreed to protect the King's evil councillors; nor indeed did he consider the guarantee of safety given by the prelates and the papal envoys to be a sufficient safeguard.[1] At the conclusion of the Tutbury negotiations therefore there still remained a wide area of division on the questions of grants and favourites to prevent a settlement.

Before the results of the Tutbury negotiations were known it seems to have been hoped optimistically that a meeting between the King and Lancaster would not long be delayed. As early as 9 June Lancaster himself made mention of a planned meeting to be held at Northampton, though whether in the King's presence is unknown. On 12 June Lancaster and his men were given safe conducts to come to the King on 29 June at an unspecified place, the Parliament due on 19 June having been abandoned on 8 June, probably to allow for such a meeting in its stead.[2] On 22 June the two papal envoys were also given conducts to go to Northampton,[3] which appears to confirm it as the intended meeting-place.

But with the return of the envoys from Tutbury it became clear that much hard negotiation remained before a final settlement became possible, and there followed a period of about six weeks' concentrated negotiations with Lancaster, which were undertaken by several of the prelates, who were now joined by some of the magnate members of the Council. Details of the first stage of these negotiations are given in two letters.[4] On 4 July an embassy consisting of the Archbishop of Dublin, the Bishops of Ely and Norwich, the Earl of Pembroke, Badlesmere, and the Younger Despenser left Northampton to visit Lancaster at an unnamed place.[5] On 11 July the Archbishop of Canterbury wrote from Northampton saying that these envoys had

[1] Ibid., pp. 415–17. Lancaster was presumably referring to the guarantee of 11 June.
[2] D.L. 34/14; *C.P.R., 1317–21*, p. 162; *P.W.*, vol. 2, part 2, p. 178.
[3] *F.*, vol. 2, p. 366. Wrongly given as Norham in *C.P.R., 1317–21*, p. 166.
[4] Hist. MSS. Comm., *Various Collections*, vol. 1, p. 220.
[5] Ibid. The start of the mission can be dated by the Bishop of Ely's departure

met Lancaster and found him willing to reach a final settlement on a number of points which had earlier seemed likely to destroy any chance of peace, and which may be guessed to be connected with the vexed matters of gifts and the favourites. Lancaster had further agreed to come to the King at Northampton by 21 July to make a firm peace agreement.[1] Optimism was still high on 18 July, two days after the envoys' return from Lancaster, when the Archbishop again wrote from Northampton saying that he was now certain that, with the mediation of himself and others, peace between Lancaster, the King, and the magnates would be confirmed in a few days.[2]

However, a further letter from the Archbishop on 21 July shows that a settlement had not in fact taken place by that date, that the outcome of the negotiations was again uncertain, and that a further embassy, consisting of the Archbishop of Dublin, the Bishops of Chichester and Ely, the Earls of Pembroke and Arundel, Roger Mortimer of Wigmore, and Badlesmere, had been sent to Lancaster on 20 July.[3] Another letter of probably the same date, written by someone in the Archbishop's company, explains the Archbishop's optimism for an approaching settlement on 11 July and the reasons for the near breakdown of negotiations after that date. At their first meeting with Lancaster in early July the royal envoys had agreed to Lancaster's two main demands that gifts made contrary to the Ordinances should be revoked and that the favourites should be removed, with the reservation that the latter would still be allowed to answer parliamentary and military summonses. In return Lancaster promised to remit all offences against him, except for those committed by Roger Damory and William Montacute, whom he accused of plotting to kill him and who would have to make amends to him. A further proposal by Lancaster, which with modifications was finally included in the Leake treaty in August, was that eight bishops, four earls, and four barons should remain with the King in each year, of whom two

on 4 July: *C. Cl. R., 1313–18*, p. 620. The location of these and later negotiations is not stated but was probably again Tutbury. On 6 July the Bishop of Norwich was near there at Burton-on-Trent: Reg. John Salmon, f. 76.

[1] Hist. MSS. Comm., *Various Collections*, vol. 1, p. 220.
[2] Ibid.; *C. Cl. R., 1313–18*, p. 620.
[3] Hist. MSS. Comm., *Various Collections*, vol. 1, pp. 267–8; *C. Cl. R., 1313–18*, p. 620.

bishops, one earl, and one baron should stay with the King in each quarter.[1] This idea, we are told, was accepted by the envoys, although the prominence of the prelates in the working of such an arrangement suggests that the idea may have been partly inspired by them to ensure a permanent neutral group on the Council. Lancaster also promised to come to the King whenever the latter wished and join in a Scottish campaign. The envoys then returned to Northampton and reported to the King, who agreed with what they had done.[2] Lancaster's sudden change of face had probably been achieved at this point as much by the concessions made to him as by the knowledge that the prelates and magnates were tired of his continued intransigence.

The author of the letter goes on to say that the hopes of peace were shattered by the behaviour of some of the envoys who had just been to see Lancaster, and who now went back on their word and persuaded the King not to confirm the agreement.[3] However, it is possible that on this point the writer gives only part of the answer, since of the envoys who went to Lancaster on 4 July only the Younger Despenser might be described as personally hostile to him. Despenser may have been one of those concerned in advising the King against acceptance, but it is very probable that the King was far more swayed by the persuasion of those others who would lose their influence at court if a settlement were made, namely Damory and Montacute, whom Lancaster had attacked by name during the talks, and perhaps also by Audley. The writer then adds that there were differing views among those with the King at Northampton, but that Pembroke and the prelates insisted that the agreement should be performed, and that because of their determination the second embassy was sent to Lancaster on 20 July.[4]

Professor Wilkinson suggested that this division of opinion was caused by Lancaster's proposal for a standing council,

---

[1] This seems intended as a permanent arrangement, although Wilkinson in 'The Negotiations preceding the "Treaty" of Leake', p. 350, suggests it was to last for one year only.

[2] Hist. MSS. Comm., *Various Collections*, vol. 1, p. 268.

[3] Ibid.

[4] Ibid. The author, although relying on first-hand information, was not actually present at Northampton.

and Sir Goronwy Edwards argued that the episode showed the existence in the 'middle party' of a right and a left wing, consisting respectively of Arundel, Mortimer, and Badlesmere, and Pembroke and the prelates.[1] A far simpler and more plausible explanation is that Damory and his cronies were making a last-ditch attempt to prevent a settlement, as they had done before in October 1317.

It was therefore in these circumstances that the second mission left on 20 July to 'mitigate' Lancaster,[2] the replacement of the Younger Despenser as a member of the embassy being perhaps a part of the 'mitigation'. The second mission returned to Northampton on 29 July, and on 1 August a third and final embassy was sent from Northampton to Lancaster, consisting of the Archbishop of Dublin, the Bishops of Norwich, Chichester, and Ely, the Earls of Pembroke and Arundel, Roger Mortimer of Wigmore, John de Somery, Badlesmere, Ralph Bassett, and John Botetourt.[3] Some progress had evidently been made during the second mission, ending on 29 July, since on 31 July Lancaster's adherents were pardoned all offences committed before 25 July.[4] No more is known until a letter from the Archbishop of Canterbury on 8 August, which says that on 7 August the King and Lancaster had met between Loughborough and Leicester and exchanged the kiss of peace in the presence of the Cardinals, prelates, all the earls except Warenne, and many of the barons. The King was to meet Lancaster again on 8 or 9 August near Nottingham, to discuss steps to protect the north against the Scots until the King could go there in person after a Parliament which was to be held on 13 October at Lincoln.[5] The Treaty of Leake embodying the final settlement was drawn up at this second meeting on 9 August.[6]

As it stands the Treaty of Leake seems to differ considerably from the terms accepted from Lancaster by the royal envoys on

[1] Wilkinson, 'The Negotiations preceding the "Treaty" of Leake', pp. 350–1; Edwards, 'The Negotiating of the Treaty of Leake', p. 377.
[2] Hist. MSS. Comm., *Various Collections*, vol. 1, p. 269; *C. Cl. R., 1313–18*, p. 620.
[3] Hist. MSS. Comm., *Various Collections*, vol. 1, p. 268; *C. Cl. R., 1313–18*, p. 620; ibid., *1318–23*, p. 112. The Bishop of Ely dropped out at Leicester because of illness: ibid., *1313–18*, p. 620.
[4] *C.P.R., 1317–21*, p. 199. Some partial agreement had probably therefore been made on 25 July.
[5] Hist. MSS. Comm., *Various Collections*, vol. 1, p. 269.
[6] Enrolled in *C. Cl. R., 1318–23*, pp. 112–14 and E. 368/89, m. 84. The counter-

their first mission in early July. The recall of all gifts made contrary to the Ordinances and the removal of royal favourites were not mentioned directly, although the promise contained in the treaty to confirm the Ordinances might be taken to imply acceptance of both points. Another omission from the treaty was any reference to Lancaster's dispute with Warenne. As already seen in June, the Council regarded this matter as a private one between the two earls, which should not be allowed to impede the making of a public settlement. The omission of Warenne on 9 August was therefore deliberate and the exchange of lands which Lancaster forced him to make in a series of agreements made at Doncaster in November 1318 and Pontefract in March 1319 was unconnected with Lancaster's settlement with the King.[1]

However, the Treaty of Leake was in itself only a preliminary agreement made after the outlines of a settlement had been sufficiently established to permit the King and Lancaster to meet and make their personal peace with one another. The details of the settlement remained to be filled in at the York Parliament, which was called on 25 August to meet on 20 October.[2] To discover the true nature of the 1318 settlement it is therefore necessary to examine the Treaty and the Parliament together.

The most important point which immediately arises and the one with potentially the biggest impact on the future political situation was the form of standing royal Council set up by the treaty and confirmed at York.[3] Tout saw it as 'an expedient so drastic that Lancaster had shrunk from suggesting it', which 'was now brought into play by Pembroke and his friends at the moment of Lancaster's humiliation' in order that Pembroke and his 'middle party' might secure themselves in office.[4] As Sir Goronwy Edwards has already shown, the principle of the standing Council was mainly Lancaster's idea, although he

part of the indenture containing the treaty is E. 163/4/7/2. Lancaster's copy was found among his muniments in 1322: D.L. 41/1/37, m. 7.

[1] The relevant documents are: E. 42/A.S. 101; D.L. 25/3575; D.L. 42/11, f. 61; D.L. 42/2, f. 25*v.*; S.C. 8/174/8702B; E. 159/95, m. 29*d*.

[2] *C. Cl. R., 1318–23*, p. 99.

[3] Ibid., pp. 112–14.

[4] Tout, *Place of the Reign* (1936), p. 110. See also Davies, *Baronial Opposition* p. 463.

accepts Tout's view of its revolutionary nature.[1] At first sight it does indeed appear to be the case that the device would rob the King of any effective power, but an examination of those who were proposed to take part in the system's working suggests a different conclusion. Of the magnates who witnessed the Treaty of Leake on 9 August practically all were either bound to the King by indenture, that is to say Pembroke himself, Hereford, Badlesmere, the Younger Despenser, Segrave, and Somery; or were linked to the King by ties of blood or of service, these latter two groups including the King's brothers, Thomas and Edmund, and the Earls of Richmond, Ulster, and Arundel, Roger Mortimer of Wigmore, Henry de Beaumont, and Walter de Norwich. The bishops present had all either been involved in the royal administration or taken part in the mediation prior to the Leake agreement. Not a single recognizable supporter of Lancaster was named. The same pattern is visible among the intended members of the Council. There was no element hostile to the King among the clergy, and the Earls of Pembroke, Richmond, Arundel, and Hereford were all royal supporters, as were Courtenay and Grey the two barons named.[2] This picture was not changed by the addition at York to the Council's personnel of the Bishops of Coventry and Lichfield and Winchester, the Younger Despenser, Badlesmere, John de Somery, John Giffard, John Botetourt, Roger Mortimer of Chirk, and William Martin, the first five of the magnates all having earlier made contracts with the King.[3]

As to the banneret who was to represent Lancaster on the Council, there can be little doubt that his future influence would be slight, and that the Council system as a whole was in reality a serious defeat for Lancaster. Lancaster's relation to the royal government, which had been in effect the chief problem around which all the negotiations of 1317 and 1318 had centred, was thus defined in a way that would in practice largely exclude him from any direct influence over royal policy. Ironically, this solution may have suited Lancaster, since the

[1] Edwards, 'The Negotiating of the Treaty of Leake', pp. 377–8; Hist. MSS. Comm., *Various Collections*, vol. 1, p. 268.
[2] Courtenay's son had married Hereford's daughter in 1315; Grey was a royal knight.
[3] *Documents Illustrative of English History in the Thirteenth and Fourteenth Centuries*, ed. H. Cole (London, 1844), p. 12.

failure of his appointment as chief councillor in 1316 had been due in part to the excessive administrative burden which it had placed upon him and to the removal of his freedom to criticize the King from a safe distance which membership of the Council implied. To have his views represented on the Council by a banneret without the obligation to take an active part himself would therefore be a convenient arrangement. Equally this answer would be agreeable to the other members of the Council who did not wish to see Lancaster 'sovereinete a li accrocher vers les autres'.[1] But such a system, while it saved Lancaster's dignity, could not conceal his real weakness, which was also shown in the simultaneous shelving of his claim to appoint the Steward of the Household.[2]

In the scheme adopted at York for the reform of the royal Household the appointment of Hereford, Badlesmere, Roger Mortimer of Chirk, John de Somery, Walter de Norwich, the Archbishop of York, and the Bishops of Norwich and Ely as a commission to perform this task reveals that Lancaster would be likely to have no more influence over the reform of the Household than he had in the workings of the Council.[3]

Following the confirmation of the Ordinances at Leake a review was undertaken of the grants which the King had made contrary to them and which had been revoked the previous June. Part at least of this review was probably made in the course of some further negotiations with Lancaster after the making of the Leake agreement, since on 10 September the restoration of grants made to Hugh Audley the Younger was ordered with the consent of Pembroke and other magnates who are said to have recently been at Tutbury.[4] This review continued during the York Parliament itself, when formal approval was given to grants which had been made to Hereford, Badlesmere, Montacute, the Younger Despenser, and Damory, but with some reductions and modifications in their substance.[5] Lancaster's demands for the complete recall of all such grants had therefore been effectively side-stepped without serious loss to the royal supporters to whom the grants had been made.

[1] C. 49/4/26.   [2] *Documents Illustrative of English History*, pp. 4, 8.
[3] Ibid., p. 12.
[4] *C.F.R.*, *1307–19*, p. 374. This could however refer to the negotiations before 9 Aug.
[5] *Documents Illustrative of English History*, pp. 9–10.

All the major offices under the Crown were also reviewed during the Parliament. The Bishop of Ely was confirmed as Chancellor and his predecessor as Chancellor, the Bishop of Winchester, was appointed Treasurer, both being royal associates of very long standing; Badlesmere was advanced to Steward; and the Younger Despenser was confirmed as Chamberlain.[1] All these appointments could only be of the greatest personal satisfaction to the King. As to the favourites whose removal Lancaster had been so persistently demanding, a compromise was achieved. Montacute was removed from office as Steward and conveniently taken away from court by his promotion to be Seneschal of Gascony. Damory and Audley apparently did leave court as well after they and Montacute had made their peace with Lancaster on 23 November by agreeing to pay him compensation for their past hostility towards him.[2]

The pattern that has emerged from a detailed examination of the Leake negotiations confirms the general accuracy of the interpretation that has already been put forward for the events of 1317 in place of the 'middle party' theory. The most striking conclusion is to reinforce the impression gained from studying the events of 1317 that the prelates of the Canterbury province and the two papal envoys were a powerful mediating force in the negotiations. They organized the first serious negotiations at Leicester in April 1318 and once at Leicester gave Lancaster a guarantee of his safety and helped to ascertain his terms, so that the conference could then be broadened to take in the royal envoys and other magnates who were present; they then mediated with the King and his Council at Westminster in June and tried to reassure Lancaster by persuading the royal favourites to promise him a safe conduct; they were responsible for conducting the very important Tutbury negotiations later in June; they were also concerned in every stage of the final negotiations in July and early August and were included as a further guarantee of moderation in the scheme for a standing royal Council adopted at Leake. It is safe to say that, without the prelates as a neutral body which could be trusted by both

---

[1] *Documents Illustrative of English History*, pp. 3, 4.

[2] *F.*, vol. 2, p. 377; *Vita*, pp. 90–1; *C. Cl. R.*, *1318–23*, pp. 109–10. Their removal would have been very strange if they had really belonged to a 'middle party' which had just gained power.

sides, negotiations would probably never have started in 1318 and would not have succeeded as far as they did.

There is also ample confirmation of the view that the King's favourites, Roger Damory, Hugh Audley, and William de Montacute, and Lancaster's old enemy, the Elder Despenser, were a major barrier to any agreement. Their guarantee to Lancaster · on 11 June is sufficient to emphasize their importance, and even this did not wholly prove their good faith, as Lancaster's replies to the Bishops of Norwich and Ely at Tutbury demonstrate.

It is also apparent, as in 1317, that some of the other royal associates were equally active in trying for a settlement, and that the early initiatives by the prelates received the full consent and encouragement of the royal Council. The most prominent of this group were Pembroke, Badlesmere, and Hereford, of whom Pembroke in particular was perhaps the most important because he was so fully trusted by the King. The action that Pembroke and Badlesmere took to curb Damory in November 1317 did not in itself bring peace much nearer, but it may none the less have persuaded the prelates that their own intervention would be worth attempting. Pembroke's biggest known contribution to the Leake negotiations themselves was his insistence together with the prelates in July 1318 that Lancaster's terms should be accepted. Throughout the negotiations of 1318 Pembroke took part as a member of the Council and not as the leader of any 'middle party' of his own. His share in the negotiations is likely in general to have been the exercise of persuasion on the King to grasp the nettle and negotiate seriously, even if this meant making concessions which might harm his favourites. Pembroke was not, however, the architect of the Leake settlement. It was his fortune that in 1318 the tide was running generally in favour of an agreement and there was therefore much that he could do to assist it. If on the other hand those who wanted to destroy Lancaster by civil war had gained control, Pembroke could have done little to prevent it. The view that Pembroke supported, however, prevailed and at the conclusion of the negotiations Pembroke remained, as he had been earlier, an influential member of the Council.

The only modification that is necessary to the new interpretation advanced to replace the 'middle party' is to give greater emphasis to the role of the magnates as a body. It is already apparent that in 1317 they were co-operating with the King in the defence of England against the Scots, and that they were probably then growing increasingly irritated by Lancaster's behaviour. Their annoyance with Lancaster is very clearly shown in the discussions at Westminster in early June 1318, and this probably made Lancaster realize that he would get little sympathy from his fellow magnates if he dragged out the negotiations indefinitely. However, the pressure of magnate opinion probably also had its effect on the King's willingness to negotiate. While the magnates remained loyal to the King, they were determined that one way or another a settlement would be reached. In this way the magnates had an important influence on both Lancaster and Edward II. Their behaviour was not, however, that of a political party under the leadership of Pembroke or anyone else, but was rather that of a community of like minds. This element of moderate magnate opinion has been appreciated in the past, but its true nature and importance have been obscured by the belief that the magnates belonged to a 'middle party'.

The settlement that was reached in the Treaty of Leake and at the York Parliament of 1318 exhibits some of the forms of a political revolution, while almost totally lacking in its substance. For Lancaster the settlement amounted to a major defeat. The Ordinances had been accepted by the King as he had demanded, but this concession was in practice partly nullified by his failure to secure the permanent recall of all royal grants. Similarly the composition of the new standing Council and the reform commission out of long-established royal councillors and sympathizers deprived him of any real power in those directions. Lancaster had, however, succeeded in gaining the removal of his particular enemies, Damory, Audley, and Montacute, but it is ironical that it may in the end have been the King rather than Lancaster, the prelates, or the magnates who solved this particular problem. Just as the King's infatuation with his favourites in 1317 had created a major political crisis, so it is possible that in 1318 he began to get tired of them and contributed in this way to ending the crisis.

It is reasonable therefore to reject Tout's view that the 1318 settlement was a humiliation for the King, and to incline partially at least to that of Davies who realized that the members of the standing Council were 'nearly all personally acceptable to the King'. But he also saw the settlement as the triumph of Pembroke and a 'middle party' instead of the triumph of the King's moderate supporters and the prelates, which it was in reality.[1] In this sense the settlement of 1318 changed little, but in future the emphasis that was to be placed upon the consent of the magnates and prelates to the King's actions in Parliament and the existence of the standing Council would give a chance for the moderates like Pembroke to make themselves heard.

On the surface there were grounds for optimism at the end of 1318.[2] The big test of the new-found stability would come on the first occasion requiring personal co-operation between the King and Lancaster, and by its decision to summon a campaign against the Scots for June 1319 the York Parliament itself ensured that such an occasion would not be long delayed.[3] A new crisis would also be certain if another royal favourite appeared to replace Damory and company. Such a favourite very soon did appear in the form of Hugh Despenser the Younger, the son of Lancaster's old enemy, who had been appointed as Chamberlain of the Household at some point between early June and the beginning of the York Parliament. Despenser's appointment had initially been a royal concession to Lancaster, since he replaced John Charlton, one of the five opponents of Lancaster who had given him a guarantee of safe conduct on 11 June. Hitherto Despenser had been over-shadowed by his father and apparently had little importance on his own. He may indeed have shared his father's hostility towards Lancaster, but it is also arguable that Lancaster did not at this stage in the reign see him as a dangerous or even as one of the most important of his adversaries. However, Despenser's recent acquisition of a share of the Gloucester inherit-ance and the eclipse of Damory and his friends now gave him his opportunity. By a final irony the magnates who approved Despenser's promotion to Chamberlain had, without realizing it, allowed the entry of a new and even more dangerous favourite whose activities were to prove fatal to many of themselves and ultimately fatal to the King himself.

---

[1] Tout, op. cit. (1936), p. 118; Davies, *Baronial Opposition*, pp. 463, 468.
[2] See *Vita*, p. 90.   [3] *Documents Illustrative of English History*, p. 4.

VI

The Breakdown of the 1318 Settlement and the Despenser War of 1321

THE traditional view of the three years after the settlement of 1318 is that they were the time when the Earl of Pembroke and his 'middle party' were the dominant force in English politics. T. F. Tout's opinion was that Pembroke played 'the chief part in bringing about comparative peace and prosperity and the large measure of reform which mark this period', and he was convinced that Pembroke 'was the chief directive agent in the prevailing policy'.[1] J. C. Davies described Pembroke's role in more guarded terms and said that between 1318 and 1321 'Pembroke did not cease to take an active part in the administration but under pressure of circumstances he found it necessary to adapt his methods.' It was 'no longer necessary for him to take such a part as in the years 1312–13', since 'he could now work through his friends in office'.[2] This note of caution suggests that Davies did not discover in Pembroke's activities during this period the obvious dominance which was required by the 'middle party' theory.

The great virtue of the 'middle party' idea was that it did provide a framework within which to describe the events after 1318. With the removal of this framework it is necessary to re-examine the period to discover the main themes. The result of such an examination shows that in some ways the years 1318 to 1321 were a repeat performance of 1317 and 1318. Once again there can be found the rise of a new royal favourite and once again this leads to a deterioration in the relations between the King and Lancaster. But this time there is no eleventh-hour avoidance of civil war. By 1321 Lancaster was again bitterly hostile to the King and, even more sinister than this, a large number of the magnates who had rallied to Edward II in 1317

---

[1] Tout, *Place of the Reign* (1936), p. 18.
[2] Davies, *Baronial Opposition*, pp. 330, 439.

and who had helped to make peace in 1318 were now openly ranged against him. Once this point was reached only violence could resolve the situation.

At first sight the natural place to begin an examination of the post-1318 period is to try to discover how the political settlement of 1318 worked in practice. This can conveniently be approached through the operation of the standing royal Council of magnates and prelates which was the main feature of the scheme agreed at Leake and at York in 1318. A clear description of the working of this Council is, however, very difficult because of the lack of evidence and the ambiguity of much of what is available.[1] It is not always possible, for example, to say whether a given prelate or magnate was present in the vicinity of the court because it was his turn to serve on the Council or whether he happened to be there for entirely different reasons. Important royal officials such as the Chancellor the Bishop of Ely, the Treasurer the Bishop of Winchester, the Steward Badlesmere, or the Chamberlain the Younger Despenser were always likely to be at court because of their offices. Nor apparently was there any rule that Pembroke or any other magnate would be required to leave court as soon as his term was over.

None the less there are a few pointers to the possible functioning of the scheme in the period up to at least the late spring of 1319. The only piece of certain information is that in the period between the making of the Leake agreement and the holding of the York Parliament the four councillors deputed to stay with the King were Pembroke himself, the Bishops of Ely and Worcester, and John de Segrave.[2] It is probable that one of the first two prelates to serve in this capacity after the Parliament was the Bishop of Norwich, who wrote on 25 November 1318 that he expected to stay with the King at least until the start of Lent.[3] This period fits roughly into the pattern laid down that each councillor in turn should stay for three months. Moreover his witnessing of charters and details given in his register appear to confirm that he did stay as intended.[4]

---

[1] The main source is the witnessing of charters which are a good guide, if used with care, to those who were at court.

[2] *Documents Illustrative of English History*, p. 13.

[3] Hist. MSS. Comm., *1st Report, Documents of Dean and Chapter of Norwich*, p. 88.

[4] He last witnessed a charter on 4 Feb.: C. 53/105, m. 9. His register shows he

His colleague may have been the Bishop of Salisbury, whose presence can also be traced until early February. Their two successors may have been the Bishops of Chichester and Carlisle, who both appear as witnesses to royal charters from late February until May.[1] The Earl of Richmond may have been the first earl to serve after the Parliament, as he was a regular witness in the early part of 1319; and he was perhaps succeeded by Hereford, who starts to appear in early April.[2] The baronial representative on the Council is much harder to identify. There is evidence of the Younger Despenser's presence in February and March, but Roger Mortimer of Wigmore and John Botetourt also appear in mid-March, while Badlesmere seems usually to have been present through his office as Steward. The most intriguing question, however, is the identity of Lancaster's banneret representative. The only person with recognizable Lancastrian links to appear in early 1319 was his brother, Henry. But his name appears only on 4 February[3] and the evidence is therefore inconclusive. Otherwise there is no indication of the presence of a Lancastrian representative on the Council in 1319 or in 1320, but the evidence is much too slight to conclude that one never took part.

The standing Council may therefore have been functioning on the lines established in 1318 until about mid-1319. After this point the influx of magnates and prelates into the court produced by the Parliaments of May 1319 and January and October 1320 makes any attempt at identifying the members of the Council too hazardous to be worth while. Any formal examination of the effects of the 1318 settlement is not therefore very illuminating.

A more helpful approach is to try to trace the activities of the Earl of Pembroke and fit these into the wider political developments of the period as shown from chronicle and record evidence. After Pembroke had served his term on the Council in 1318 he spent the early months of 1319 away from the court,

was at York or Beverley between 15 Nov. 1318 and 21 Jan. 1319 and was back at Norwich on 22 Feb.: Norfolk and Norwich Record Office, Reg. John Salmon, ff. 77*v*., 78.

[1] C. 53/105, mm. 9–5. Carlisle was with the King by 4 Feb.: E. 101/377/3, m. 6.

[2] C. 53/105, m. 6. Hereford had been in Hainault from Jan. to Mar.: E. 404/484/2/1.

[3] C. 53/105, mm. 9–6.

but there is no doubt that he was still very active in royal affairs and that he retained the trust of the King. The real problem is to determine the quality of his work at this time rather than its mere quantity.

For Pembroke the beginning of 1319 was marked by a royal letter written from Beverley in Yorkshire on 3 January, in which the King said he had heard that Pembroke was planning to attend a tournament at Dunstable, contrary to a ban on all feats of arms unconnected with the Scots war. The King expressed surprise at Pembroke's intention, saying that the tournament would in the present state of royal affairs be dangerous if it took place, and forbade Pembroke on the loyalty he owed him to take part.[1] The reason for Pembroke's apparently strange behaviour is unknown, but he and the others may have thought that, following the 1318 settlement, it was again safe to indulge in such pastimes, perhaps also with the intention of preparing themselves for the coming Scottish campaign.

This incident was probably only a trivial matter and, as another event in January shows, Pembroke remained in royal favour. On 16 January the King wrote to the Pope saying he had heard that the royal financier and late Seneschal of Gascony, Anthony Pessagno, had while at the papal Curia accused Pembroke of committing various *falsitates* against the King and of obtaining certain letters from the Chancery for his own use. Edward said he was gravely perturbed by these false charges and that he trusted Pembroke implicitly.[2] Somewhere about this time Pembroke himself had written to the King from London complaining about Pessagno's slanders and asking Edward to take action against him.[3] It was probably in reply to this that on 26 January the King wrote to Pembroke informing him that he had told the Chancellor to order the Seneschal of Gascony to send Pessagno back to England by attachment and if necessary by force. These orders were accordingly sent to the Seneschal on the following day.[4] This

---

[1] S.C. 1/49/45. This is a private letter to Pembroke. No other magnates are mentioned.

[2] C. 70/4, m. 9: 'in omnibus et singulis nos tangentibus'. This is the original of the undated letter on p. 107 of the *Liber Epistolaris* of Richard of Bury.

[3] B.M., Cotton Charter II, 26, no. 8. This is an undated fragment in a file of miscellaneous letters addressed to Edward II.

[4] S.C. 1/49/46; C. 61/32, m. 3*d*.

strange affair is even more surprising in view of the King's earlier favours to Pessagno and his former relations with Pembroke. In November 1315, for example, the King had given Pessagno £3,000 in aid of his knighting and a further £3,000 in October 1317.[1] In November 1317 Pessagno had been made Seneschal of Gascony, with powers to raise a loan of 20,000 marks and to arrange the final liquidation of Clement V's loan of 1314.[2] He and Pembroke had been together on the 1317 Avignon mission and had probably worked together on many other occasions. Pessagno's motives in attacking Pembroke at the Curia are obscure, but one reason may perhaps have been connected with Pessagno's treatment of a Gascon magnate, Jordan de l'Isle, on whose behalf the Pope had asked Pembroke to intercede in 1318.[3] It also appears that while in Gascony Pessagno had retained more of the Duchy's revenues than he was owed by the King and had not accounted for what he had received there.[4] This may explain Pessagno's replacement as Seneschal on 20 November 1318 and his summons to England, without having been informed of his supercession, for a conference on Gascon affairs.[5] Pessagno may have seen Pembroke as responsible for this and proceeded to get his own back at the Curia. Whatever the true causes, this incident throws an interesting and unexpected light on the personal relations between two royal associates at this time.

While the King was complaining to the Pope about Pessagno, Pembroke remained in the south of England. Shortly before 14 January 1319 he and Hereford had together persuaded the Archbishop of Canterbury reluctantly to consecrate the new Bishop of London, Stephen Gravesend, at Canterbury.[6] Pembroke is next caught sight of on 6 March, when he wrote from his manor of Gooderstone in Norfolk asking the Chancellor not to issue a writ of warranty to the Abbot of Viterbo, who was trying to deprive him of his rights over the advowson of the

---

[1] C. 81/93/3556; ibid. /102/4481.
[2] Ibid. /4491, 4495; *F.*, vol. 2, pp. 346–7; C. 61/32, m. 16.
[3] *Cal. Papal Letters, 1305–42*, p. 421.
[4] *Liber Epistolaris*, p. 106.
[5] C. 61/32, m. 5. Pessagno did however return to England and appeared at the Exchequer on 26 Apr. 1319: E. 159/92/Recorda, Easter 12 Ed. II.
[6] *Documents Illustrating the History of St. Paul's*, Camden Society (London, 1880), p. 49.

church of Holkham, another of his Norfolk manors.[1] Pembroke's private affairs are again in evidence on 23 March, when the King wrote to tell him that he had asked the Treasurer and Walter de Norwich to see that money owed by a London burgess, John de Borford, and others was paid to the Bardi so that the latter might more rapidly pay Pembroke sums which the King owed him, as Pembroke had requested. The King also expressed his willingness to perform any other requests that Pembroke might have.[2]

Pembroke had moved from Norfolk to London by 24 March, when he appeared at the chapter-house of St. Paul's with the Earl of Norfolk and Bishop of Winchester to hear the complaints of the citizens of London against their mayor, John de Wengrave, and about the elections of the mayor, sheriffs, and aldermen. After a threat by Norfolk to summon all concerned to appear at Westminster on 25 March the mayor gave way and acceded to the citizens' demands.[3] By 2 April Pembroke had gone to Great Yarmouth with the Bishop of Norwich and Walter de Norwich to make preparations for ships to be sent to Scotland, probably to carry supplies for the summer campaign there.[4] Soon after this Pembroke returned to London, and just before 24 April he appeared with the Earl of Norfolk and Badlesmere at the Canterbury provincial council then being held at St. Paul's to ask the clergy to give the King a subsidy in aid of the Scots war.[5]

From London Pembroke went north to York to attend the Parliament which began there on 6 May. This Parliament added little to what had been settled in 1318, except to postpone still further the examination of Lancaster's claim to appoint the Household Steward and to confirm some of the details of the settlement made between Lancaster and Warenne.[6]

---

[1] S.C. 1/35/203. Pembroke received seisin of the advowson in June 1319 because of the abbot's default and execution of the judgement on Pembroke's behalf was ordered in Oct. 1321: C. 47/70/1/27; ibid. /70/1/4.

[2] S.C. 1/49/47.

[3] *Ann. Paul.*, p. 285. See G. A. Williams, *Medieval London*, pp. 281–2.

[4] Hist. MSS. Comm., *9th Report*, p. 302, Pyx Roll of Great Yarmouth: Pembroke and his colleagues received £6. 3s. 10d. from the town authorities for their retainers.

[5] *Reg. R.: Baldock, etc.*, Canterbury and York Series (London, 1911), pp. 207–8.

[6] *Documents Illustrative of English History*, p. 48; *C. Cl. R., 1318–23*, p. 68. Lancaster and his retainers were there in force: E. 368/93, m. 12.

More important, the Parliament was able, now that a full settlement had been made between the King and Lancaster, to turn to consideration of the problem which was second only to that of the King's relations with Lancaster and which had indirectly done much to ensure the making of a settlement in 1318: the Scottish threat to the north of England. A Scottish campaign had already been summoned in November 1318 to start on 10 June 1319. On 22 May 1319 the date was postponed until 22 July, the objective of the campaign being the recapture of Berwick, which the Scots had taken in April 1318.[1]

The mounting of this campaign, the first major royal offensive since 1314, was the great preoccupation of the royal government in the summer and autumn of 1319 and care was taken to ensure that it would be a full-scale military effort. A twelfth and an eighteenth had been granted at the York Parliament for this purpose, together with a clerical tenth. Measures were ordered for the distraint of knighthood and for the levying of fines of £20 on those who did not serve.[2] Purveyance of victuals on a large scale was organized in twenty-six English counties and included the collection of grain supplies, which the magnates had agreed at York to loan to the King for the war. Pembroke's share in this loan amounted to approximately 370 quarters of various grains, for part of which the King later repaid him at specially advantageous rates,[3] and he also sold nearly 980 quarters more to the King, for which he was paid £242. 4s. 2½d. in November 1320.[4]

When finally assembled the army was, in theory at least, a formidable force of about 14,000 men, including about 11,500 footmen and archers and over 1,000 hobelars, while the heavy cavalry force of knights and men-at-arms was in the region of 1,400 strong.[5] All the leading magnates took part, including Lancaster with at least 28 men,[6] Arundel with 61, Hereford

---

[1] *C. Cl. R., 1318–23*, p. 141.

[2] Ibid., pp. 79, 202–3.

[3] B.M., Add. MS. 17362, f. 14; E. 101/378, ff. 4, 6, 8, 10. Thirty quarters, for example, were paid for as 31 quarters 4 bushels: ibid., f. 6. This arrangement was not peculiar to Pembroke.

[4] Ibid., f. 9v. This may include part repayment of the loan of grain. In Apr. 1320 the Treasurer was told to repay Pembroke with all haste: E. 159/93, m. 29.

[5] E. 101/378/4, ff. 19–37v.

[6] C. 71/10, m. 4. This was its size at the start of the campaign. More men may have joined later.

with 121, Badlesmere with 96, the Younger Despenser with 98, Damory with 82, and Audley with 74.[1] Pembroke's contingent for whom protections were issued at York on 16 July and at Gosforth on 8 August totalled at least 78 knights and men-at-arms as well as 60 archers.[2] The opening of the campaign was marked by royal favours to Pembroke, including the grant to him of the hundreds of Bosemere and Cleydon in Suffolk, and permission in the event of Pembroke's death for his executors to have free administration of his movable property. The King also promised that repayment of his debts would be sought from his heirs.[3]

The siege of Berwick commenced on 7 September and was pressed forward without conspicuous success, despite a second attack on 13 September.[4] The siege then had to be broken off, because of the outflanking move by a Scottish force under Sir James Douglas which penetrated deep into Yorkshire and threatened York itself. The city's defence was hastily organized by the Archbishop of York, the Bishop of Ely, and others, but their men were defeated by the Scots at Myton-on-Swale on 12 September. Among the many prisoners taken at this rout was a certain Sir John de Pabenham,[5] who was probably the Pembroke retainer of that name. As a direct consequence of this battle the siege of Berwick had to be abandoned and the King left there on 17 September.[6]

The siege thus ended in a humiliating failure after only ten days, despite the great effort put into it. This defeat was bad enough in itself, but of far greater significance were the symptoms of disunity which appeared during the siege, reopening all the old suspicions between the King and Lancaster and producing the first ominous break in the political stability which

---

[1] E. 101/378/4, ff. 20, 19v., 20v., 29v. These are all maximum sizes reached during the campaign.

[2] C. 71/10, mm. 5, 2; C. 81/1736/60; E. 101/378/4, f. 36v. These are figures for the start of the campaign only. There is no information on men who joined him later.

[3] *C.F.R., 1319–27*, p. 3; *C.P.R., 1317–21*, p. 388. Pembroke probably therefore made his will at this time.

[4] *The Bruce*, vol. 2, pp. 418–30. The date of the start of the siege is confirmed by E. 101/378/3, m. 3.

[5] *Vita*, pp. 96–7; *Flores*, vol. 3, pp. 189–90; *Ann. Paul.*, p. 287; *Bridlington*, p. 58; *Melsa*, vol. 2, pp. 336–7. *Trokelowe*, p. 104, gives the date as 20 Sept.

[6] E. 101/378/3, m. 3.

the 1318 settlement had achieved. The best account of what happened or was rumoured to have occurred to produce this fresh outburst of hostility between the King and Lancaster is given by the writer of the *Vita* who, as so often elsewhere, gives the impression that he might have said a lot more than he did. The *Vita*, at earlier times unsparing in its strictures on the King's behaviour, now bewailed Lancaster's loss of his reputation through his betrayal of the King at Berwick, saying that it was strongly rumoured that Lancaster had impeded the siege, had allowed the Scots to penetrate into Yorkshire, had permitted Douglas to withdraw through his lines to Scotland on his return from York, and had been paid £40,000 by the Scots for his secret assistance. In mitigation of Lancaster's conduct, the *Vita* also hints that had the King succeeded in taking Berwick he would then have turned against Lancaster, whose execution of Gaveston he had still not forgiven.[1] Several other writers also speak of signs of division at Berwick. One speaks vaguely of suspicion between Lancaster and the King, while another says that some of the King's associates accused the magnates of treachery.[2] Another is more specific, saying that Lancaster withdrew from the siege in disgust because he heard that the King had promised custody of the town to the Younger Despenser and Damory after its capture. A chronicle from Canterbury says that during the siege trouble broke out between Lancaster and the King's Council and that he withdrew for this reason.[3]

General confirmation of the existence of such suspicions, and a hint that the Younger Despenser may have had something to do with fostering them, is given by a letter written by Despenser on 21 September to his Sheriff in Glamorgan, in which he said that the siege had been abandoned at Lancaster's instigation.[4] There can be little doubt that the failure of the Berwick siege was a political turning-point in the period between 1318 and 1321 and that the renewed estrangement of Lancaster from the King began to pave the way for the events

[1] *Vita*, pp. 97–104.
[2] *Melsa*, vol. 2, p. 336; *Bridlington*, p. 57.
[3] *Hist. Anglicana of Thomas Walsingham*, vol. 1, pp. 155–6; Trinity College Cambridge MS. R. 5. 41, ff. 113*v.*–114.
[4] B.M., Cotton MS. Vespasian F. VII, f. 6 (printed in *Cartae de Glamorgan*, ed. G. L. Clark (Cardiff, 1910), vol. 3, p. 1064).

of 1321 and 1322. It may also have indicated the developing importance of the Younger Despenser, whose later conduct was to turn most of the leading magnates against him and the King.

The final abandonment of the campaign was marked by the King's departure on 28 September from Newcastle for York, where he arrived on 5 October, having left Badlesmere behind at Newcastle to supervise the munitioning of the castles of the Scottish March.[1]

Pembroke himself does not appear to have lost by the failure. On 9 September the King granted him in return for his services the English lands of an Irish rebel, Maurice de Caunton; on 16 October one of his retainers, Constantine de Mortimer, was given licence to crenellate his house at Sculton in Norfolk; and on 5 November another retainer, John Darcy, was made sheriff of Nottingham and Derby.[2] The details of Pembroke's personal share in the Berwick campaign are unknown, but if he or any other royal councillor had tried to patch up relations between Lancaster and the King, it is clear that they did not succeed.

More successful, however, was Pembroke's part in the negotiations with the Scots with which he was occupied for the rest of 1319. Negotiations were under consideration as early as 24 October, when twelve Scots envoys were given safe conducts to come to Newcastle to discuss a truce or peace, and on 11 November Robert Baldock left London to go with other royal envoys to Berwick for the same purpose.[3] On 1 December full powers to negotiate a truce were given to Pembroke, together with the Chancellor the Bishop of Ely, the Younger Despenser, Badlesmere, Henry le Scrop, Robert Baldock, William Airmyn, William Herle, and Geoffrey le Scrop. The Scottish and English versions variously date the making of the truce that was eventually made to 22 and 24 December.[4] The truce was to last for two years from 29 December 1319, during which time the Scots were to build no new castles in the sheriffdoms of Berwick, Roxburgh, and Dumfries, while the English were to garrison Harbottle in Northumberland and later either deliver it to the Scots or destroy it.[5] On 24 January the Chancellor,

[1] B.M., Add. MS. 17362, ff. 9, 9*v*., 14*v*., 15.
[2] *C.P.R., 1317–21*, pp. 395, 397; *C.F.R., 1319–27*, p. 6.
[3] *F.*, vol. 2, p. 404; B.M., Add. MS. 17362, f. 9*v*.
[4] C. 47/22/12/29, 30, 45; *C.P.R., 1317–21*, p. 414; Bain, vol. 3, p. 681.
[5] Bain, vol. 3, p. 681; *C.P.R., 1317–21*, p. 416.

Pembroke, Badlesmere, and Despenser were appointed to perform the terms relating to Harbottle, which they had already put in the custody of Badlesmere's retainer, John de Penrith, on 28 December, and keepers of the truce were nominated on the same day.[1]

These last arrangements were made during the Parliament which met at York on 20 January, and which, through Lancaster's failure to attend because of his distrust of the King and his supporters, served to confirm the breach opened during the Berwick siege.[2] At this time it was decided that the King should go to France to do homage to Philip V for Aquitaine, the King's brother Edmund being sent to Paris in February in order to arrange safe conducts for the King.[3] It was also decided to send the Elder Despenser and Badlesmere to Gascony to consider reforms there and to visit the papal Curia, and that the Exchequer and Bench should return from York to London.[4]

Pembroke was very active during the proceedings of this Parliament. On 23 January the outgoing Chancellor the Bishop of Ely delivered up the Great Seal in the King's Chamber at the house of the Friars Minor in the presence of Pembroke, Badlesmere, and the Younger Despenser and it was handed to his successor, the Bishop of Norwich, on 26 January. On 28 January the Earl of Angus, Henry de Beaumont, John Mowbray, John Clavering, and Andrew Harcla made a bond for £6,000 with Pembroke, Badlesmere, and Despenser. The purpose of the bond was not stated, but it was probably intended as a guarantee of their observance of the truce. Pembroke and the two others were again in company on 29 January, when they acted at the Exchequer as mainpernors for the debts of John Sandal, the late Bishop of Winchester.[5] These three instances, and their participation in the Scots negotiations in December 1319, suggest that at this point Pembroke, Despenser, and Badlesmere were among the most prominent of the King's associates.

---

[1] *C.P.R., 1317–21*, p. 416; E. 101/378/4, f. 21v.

[2] *P.W.*, vol. 2, part 1, p. 237; *Vita*, p. 103. Lancaster was nearby at Pontefract on 3 and 18 Feb.: *C.P.R., 1317–21*, p. 431; D.L. 42/12, f. 22v.; E. 368/93, m. 12.

[3] B.M., Add. MS. 17362, f. 13. The King's visit was already under consideration in Nov. 1319: ibid.

[4] *F.*, vol. 2, p. 418; S.C. 1/32/78–82; *C. Cl. R., 1318–23*, p. 175.

[5] *C. Cl. R., 1318–23*, pp. 219–20; E. 159/93, m. 109.

After the end of the York Parliament the King left for the south, being greeted by cries of abuse from Lancaster's retainers as he passed by Pontefract, and on 16 February 1320 reached London, where he was met at Kilburn by the mayor and other officials.[1]

On 24 February Pembroke was appointed by the Council to be Keeper of the Realm when the King went to France to do homage.[2] On 27 February the King left Westminster for the coast at the start of his journey to France, but after reaching Canterbury it became necessary, for some reason, for the visit to be postponed. Having spent the rest of the month journeying around Kent, the King returned to Westminster on 7 April.[3] Despite the delay in his departure for France, the King probably still expected to cross over some time during March and it is for this reason that, although he was still in the country, Pembroke was consulted as Keeper of the Realm on at least two occasions during this time. On 1 March the King sent a copy of a letter from the Justice of Ireland from Rochester to Walter de Norwich, with instructions that when Pembroke, the Chancellor, and others of the Council had assembled they should read the letter and decide what action was needed.[4] On 7 March the King wrote to the Chancellor from Canterbury saying that he had charged Pembroke to inform him about certain unspecified matters which required quick action, and ordering the Chancellor to follow Pembroke's advice.[5] Pembroke left the King soon after this letter was sent, and on 11 March he was at Stratford in London, from where he wrote asking the Chancellor to appoint Thomas le Rotour as one of the viewers of the works at Windsor.[6]

On 13 April, shortly after the King's return from Kent, representatives of the Bardi and other foreign merchants appeared in the green chamber of the palace of Westminster before the King and the Council, which consisted of the Archbishop, the Chancellor and Treasurer, Pembroke, the Elder

---

[1] Trinity College Cambridge MS. R. 5. 41, ff. 113*v*.–114; *Ann. Paul.*, p. 288.

[2] *C.P.R., 1317–21*, p. 425.

[3] *Ann. Paul.*, p. 288; E. 101/378/3, mm. 7, 8. He was probably waiting for a safe conduct from Philip V, which was not issued till 24 Mar.: E. 159/93, m. 84.

[4] E. 159/93, m. 31.

[5] C. 81/110/5521.

[6] S.C. 1/36/18; *C.P.R., 1317–21*, p. 480.

and Younger Despensers, Badlesmere, the royal justices, and the barons of the Exchequer, to request that they be exempted from the provisions of the Ordinance of the Staple of 1313. In this the aliens were opposed by John Charlton, the Mayor of the Merchants of the Staple, and by other English merchants who succeeded in persuading the Council in their favour.[1] On 20 April Pembroke was a witness at Lambeth Palace, with the Bishops of Norwich, Exeter, and London, the Younger Despenser, his nephew John Hastings, and others, to the King's formal instrument of protestation on the admission of Rigaud d'Assier as the new Bishop of Winchester.[2]

Pembroke's continued good relations with the King are shown clearly by the contents of two letters which the King wrote to him in May and August 1320. The first of these, dated 8 May, related to an assize of novel disseisin brought by Pembroke's nephew John Hastings against the Earl of Arundel over the possession of some tenements in Surrey. The case had evidently aroused strong feelings, since on 10 April both Hastings and Arundel had been forbidden to bring armed retainers to a hearing of the case at Southwark on 14 April.[3] In his letter the King told Pembroke that, having heard about the case, he had sent for the Constable of Windsor on 6 May and discussed the matter with him. The King added that he had been told that Pembroke intended to be present at the next hearing of the case and asked him to join him at Reading on 17 May, presumably to discuss it further. He concluded by saying that if Pembroke wished him to attend the hearing, he would do so 'pur la graunt amistez qe nous avoms a vous . . . car nous tenoms toutes voz quereles les noz'.[4] The King's second letter was addressed to Pembroke from Langley on 16 August. Edward said that his brother, the Earl of Norfolk, had come to Langley to seek his advice on plans for his marriage, but he had told him to come later when Pembroke would be at Clarendon

---

[1] *C. Cl. R., 1318–23*, pp. 234–5. See Tout, *Place of the Reign* (1936), pp. 217–40. On 22 Feb. the Bardi had appeared before members of the Council at the Exchequer to restore two gold crowns pledged to them by the King in return for a loan of 5,000 marks the previous August. Pembroke and the Bishops of Exeter and Hereford were present on this occasion: E. 159/93, m. 77.

[2] E. 159/93, m. 83.

[3] *C. Cl. R., 1318–23*, p. 227. There is no trace of any record of the case.

[4] S.C. 1/49/48.

and able to give an opinion, 'pur ce qe en cele chose ne en autre qe porte charge nous ne voloms ouir ne rien faire saunz vostre conseil'.[1] Neither of these letters deals with a matter of any great political substance, but they do show how far Pembroke still held the King's trust at this point in the reign. The King gave further evidence of his regard for Pembroke a few weeks later on 14 September, when he had five silk cloths placed on the body of Pembroke's recently deceased wife, Beatrice, at the Convent Church at Stratford in London, where on 8 February 1321 he also attended a mass said in her memory.[2]

The spring and summer of 1320 may be said to be the high point of Pembroke's activity in the years immediately after the 1318 settlement. On 18 May he was appointed Keeper of the Forest South of the Trent, in succession to Ralph de Monthermer, until the next Parliament should confirm the appointment.[3] More important than this, however, was Pembroke's reappointment on 4 June as Keeper of the Realm in preparation for the King's departure for France to do homage, the King's absence lasting from 19 June to 22 July.[4] On the face of it this office would put Pembroke in a position of very great authority, and it is therefore worth considering how great it was in practice.

On the day of his appointment Pembroke appeared in the King's green chamber at Westminster with the Archbishop, Chancellor, Treasurer, the Bishop of London, Earl of Hereford, the Younger Despenser, and others. Two small seals were brought before the King, one of which had been used in England during Edward I's absence in Flanders in 1297 and the other when Edward II had previously been away in France. The first was broken and given to the Chancellor as his fee while the second was put in a bag under the Chancellor's seal for Pembroke's use while the King was in France. On 9 June the Chancellor, who was going to join the King, who had left for France on 5 June, closed up the Great Seal to take to the King and delivered the small seal to Pembroke, with instructions that

---

[1] Ibid. /49. Norfolk married Alice, the daughter of Roger de Hales of Norfolk, in about 1320.

[2] B.M., Add. MS. 9951, ff. 2v., 45v.

[3] *C.F.R., 1319–27*, p. 23. The need for Parliamentary confirmation of Pembroke's appointment suggests that some lip service was still being given to the settlement of 1318. [4] *C.P.R., 1317–21*, p. 454; E. 159/93, m. 92.

writs sealed by it should be given under the King's witness while he remained in England and under Pembroke's testimony after the King had crossed to France.[1] This clear distinction of Pembroke's authority from that of the King, by giving him a special small seal, would appear to give him little more than the power to issue routine orders. This impression is fully confirmed by an examination of the commands sent out under his authority in the King's absence, none of them being of more than minor importance.[2] It is also interesting to note that on 18 June, the day before the King crossed to France, a series of important orders was issued concerning the application of justice, the banning of tournaments, the enforcement of the provisions of the Staple, and counterfeit money.[3] All these decisions were made by the King and his advisers at Dover. Pembroke was not among those present, since on the same day the King wrote to him, enclosing two letters from Juliana de Leybourne, and ordered him to assemble the members of the Council who remained in London to take the necessary decisions.[4] All the decisions of any importance had therefore been made before Pembroke's authority became fully operative.

It is also apparent that very few magnates or prelates of any importance remained behind in London with Pembroke. The Younger Despenser and Roger Damory, and the Treasurer and Chancellor, the Bishops of Exeter and Norwich, all accompanied the King to Amiens. In addition, the Elder Despenser, Badlesmere, the Bishop of Hereford, the Earl of Richmond, and the King's brother, Edmund, had all been abroad on royal business since March and rejoined him during his stay at Amiens. Pembroke's wife, Beatrice de Valence, and his nephew, John Hastings, also went to France, in the company of the Queen.[5] The focus of political attention and of any major decisions that might be required had therefore moved in effect from London to Amiens.

Too much should not be made of Pembroke's lack of any power of initiative, since his position was the same as that of other Keepers of the Realm before him, such as the Earl of

[1] *C. Cl. R., 1318–23*, pp. 237–8.
[2] See *C.P.R., 1317–21* and *C. Cl. R., 1318–23*, 19 June–22 July, *passim*.
[3] *C. Cl. R., 1318–23*, pp. 198, 242–4.
[4] S.C. 1/45/193–5.
[5] B.M., Add. MS. 17362, ff. 11, 17*v*.

Gloucester in 1311. The fact that the King chose to confer the dignity of Keeper upon Pembroke was a quite sufficient means of showing his faith in him. Pembroke's period of office ended promptly with the King's return to Dover on 22 July, when he was told to stop using the small seal, which he restored to the Chancellor in the presence of the Council at the Exchequer on 29 July.[1]

This evidence of Pembroke's public activities and of the King's attitude to him shows that in 1320 Pembroke held a position of dignity and trust in the royal circle which was almost that of an elder statesman. But how far did this position bring Pembroke real power and authority? Already some evidence has been produced to show that the political situation was again starting to deteriorate and that the Younger Despenser was beginning to acquire a sinister prominence. This naturally was bound to have some effect upon Pembroke's own influence. These external developments can, however, be left on one side for the moment, since there were also two personal factors which showed the weakness of Pembroke's position and which suggest that he had nothing like the dominance in English politics after 1318 which has been assumed in the past.

The first of these weak points was shown by the attack made upon Pembroke's manor of Painswick in Gloucestershire on 31 July 1318 by one of his former close associates and retainers, Maurice de Berkeley, and by followers of the Berkeleys.[2] The fact that this happened while Pembroke was busy helping to negotiate the Treaty of Leake was humiliating enough, but worse was to follow. Despite the appointment of a royal commission of oyer and terminer to investigate the attack, it proved impossible to bring the attackers to justice. It was not until early 1320 that a series of private bargains between Pembroke and the attackers gave him some compensation for his losses. If Pembroke had really been a powerful political figure in the way that the Despensers were to become after 1322, he would not have had to wait so long for satisfaction. The whole episode is also a good illustration of the weakness of the royal

---

[1] *C. Cl. R., 1318–23*, p. 317; *P.W.*, vol. 2, part 1, pp. 246–7. The King reached London on 2 Aug.: E. 101/378/10, m. 1.

[2] J.I. 1/299/2, m. 2; S.C. 1/35/204. A full discussion of this episode is given in Chapter IX.

government at this time, since it shows how a family like the Berkeleys with great local influence could successfully defy the royal judicial and administrative machinery. The Painswick attack and its aftermath have the same kind of significance as the nefarious activities of the Folvilles of Ashby-Folville, which have been used to demonstrate local disorder in the reign of Edward III.[1] It is worth noting that the Folvilles began their career of crime in 1326, while Edward II was still King and conditions were ripe for this kind of banditry. A disturbed and disorderly reign such as that of Edward II might be expected to produce such a result but, as Dr. R. L. Storey has pointed out, even in the best ordered of reigns the forces of authority were barely adequate and 'the internal peace of the kingdom was poised on a razor's edge'.[2]

Pembroke's other weakness after 1318 was caused by the payment of the ransom of £10,400 which he had promised to Jean de Lamouilly in 1317. This put Pembroke into debt both to the King and to Italian bankers, and also placed him under a heavy obligation to several of his fellow magnates, which would certainly have restricted his freedom of action. To secure his release in 1317 Pembroke had managed by unknown means to pay £2,500. This amount was repaid to him by the King in July 1317,[3] but the remaining £7,900 Pembroke had to raise himself. Since he had been forced to leave hostages behind in Jean de Lamouilly's hands there was no way of evading payment.

Part at least of what remained was raised by Pembroke from the resources of his own lands, perhaps in the form of the traditional aid for the ransoming of a lord. A document of 17 December 1317 records that on this date the community of Haverfordwest in Pembrokeshire paid a sum of £20 to Pembroke's Steward, Hugh de Panton, to assist in the delivery of his hostages.[4] This was equivalent to about one seventh of the extended value of the lordship.[5] It is unlikely that Pembroke

---

[1] E. L. G. Stones, 'The Folvilles of Ashby-Folville and their Associates in Crime, 1326–47', *T.R.H.S.*, 5th series, vol. 7 (1957). See also J. G. Bellamy, 'The Coterel Gang', *E.H.R.*, vol. 79 (1964).
[2] R. L. Storey, *The End of the House of Lancaster* (London, 1966), p. 21.
[3] *C.P.R., 1317–21*, pp. 6, 9.
[4] N.L.W., Haverfordwest Deeds, no. 878.
[5] In 1324 it was extended at £133. 19s. 0d.: C. 134/85/77–8.

was able to collect a very significant sum in this way, since even if it were assumed that the remainder of his tenants contributed on a similar scale, and there is no evidence that they did, all of his English, Irish, and Welsh lands, which at this date were worth in the region of £2,500, would have yielded only about £350.

A further contribution to Pembroke's needs was made on 31 October 1317, when the Earl of Surrey was authorized to give him the towns of Grantham and Stamford. Pembroke was to hold them until he had recovered a sum of £4,000, which he had paid on Surrey's behalf while overseas,[1] and which may have been Edward of Bar's way of punishing Surrey for the treatment of his wife. This sum may be included in the £10,400 total of Pembroke's ransom and, if so, had probably been promised by Pembroke rather than actually paid in cash. The actual revenue of about £200 which Pembroke would receive from these two towns would take many years to total £4,000, and, like the contribution made by his tenants, would do little to solve his immediate financial needs.[2]

There is evidence that in 1319 Pembroke was being paid and was borrowing large sums of money, which it is reasonable to assume reflect a major effort on his part to liquidate what was left of his ransom. On 27 April Pembroke made a recognizance to the Bardi at the Exchequer for a loan of £3,000, repayable in £1,000 instalments on 1 November, 2 February, and 16 February following. Because Pembroke alone did not possess the resources to guarantee the repayment of such a large sum at such short notice the names of the Bishop of Winchester, Badlesmere, Walter de Norwich, Gilbert Pecche, Robert Baynard, and two of Pembroke's retainers, John Hastings and Constantine de Mortimer, were added to the obligation after Pembroke's name to act as guarantors.[3] These arrangements were taken a stage further on 28 May during the York Parliament, when the names of the Bishop of Ely, the Younger Despenser, and another of Pembroke's retainers, William de Cleydon, were also added to the list of guarantors of 27 April.[4]

[1] *C.P.R., 1317–21*, pp. 40, 48.
[2] C 135/86/4. (Warenne's *I.P.M.* in 1347.) The exact value is uncertain because of the state of the document. The Exchequer version of the inquest (E. 149/10/2) is in an even worse condition.   [3] E. 159/92, m. 73; E. 368/89, m. 136.
[4] E. 368/89, m. 141*d*.; *C. Cl. R., 1318–23*, pp. 79–80.

On 17 July Pembroke made a further transaction when he brorowed £1,000 from a Florentine merchant, Manent Francisci, whom he promised to repay on 11 November next.[1] Soon afterwards Pembroke raised another very large sum by persuading the King to pay him an advance of 2,000 marks on the wages which he would receive for future service against the Scots, of which he received 1,000 marks on 17 August and the rest between then and 10 April 1320.[2] Even this was not enough, and on 19 October 1319 Pembroke borrowed from the King a sum of £2,000 which the Bardi had paid into the Exchequer for this purpose on the same date.[3] On paper therefore Pembroke had received during 1319 in loans and advances a total of £7,333. 6s. 8d., but, as will be seen, the proportion of this amount which was directly available to be sent overseas to help pay his ransom was in fact some £3,000 less than this figure.

Both the loans made to Pembroke by Italian bankers were repaid promptly. The Bardi received two instalments of £1,000 on 19 October 1319 and 5 February 1320, and Manent Francisci's £1,000 was restored to him on 25 November 1319.[4] However, the repayment to the Bardi in October coincided in date with the King's loan of £2,000 to Pembroke and therefore at once absorbed half this amount, while the payment to Manent Francisci accounted for the rest of this sum. It is also revealed in February 1320 at the time of Pembroke's second payment to the Bardi that the Bardi's loan to Pembroke in the previous April was in fact for £2,000 and not for £3,000,[5] the extra £1,000 being presumably a penalty in the event of any delay in repayment. Pembroke's indebtedness was not ended by these repayments. By using the advance on his wages for service in Scotland to help pay his ransom Pembroke may have left the wages of some of his retainers in arrears. There was also the matter of the King's £2,000 loan. This may not have been

[1] E. 368/89, m. 148.
[2] E. 403/187, m. 8; ibid. /189, mm. 3, 4; ibid. /191, m. 1; E. 159/93, m. 146; C. 62/95, m. 1.
[3] E. 403/189, m. 1; E. 401/229, m. 2; E. 368/90, m. 4; F. Palgrave (ed.), *Antient Kalendars and Inventories of His Majesty's Exchequer* (London, 1836), vol. 1, p. 76, no. 10.
[4] E. 159/92, mm. 73, 86.
[5] Ibid., m. 73.

repaid in Pembroke's lifetime since no definite date for repayment was set, but his executors would certainly have been forced to pay it out of his estate. It seems likely that Pembroke was financially ruined by the effects of paying off his ransom and was dogged by financial troubles for the rest of his life, all the more so since he probably did not succeed in paying the whole of the ransom.[1]

The exact amount of his ransom that Pembroke managed to pay is unknown, but the bulk of it seems to have been paid by arrangements made by Pembroke himself. Of the total of £10,400 only £2,500 can be said with certainty to have been paid by the King, the remainder of the King's payments to Pembroke being either loans or advances on money which he would have received in any case. In view of Pembroke's services to the King in the past, his treatment was not particularly generous. Edward II was very eager to get Pembroke back when he was imprisoned in 1317, but once the Earl had returned other preoccupations and the usual shortage of cash probably made the King lose interest. Nor was Warenne's grant to Pembroke of Stamford and Grantham sufficient compensation for the £4,000 which Pembroke had pledged on his behalf.

Once again, as in 1312 when he had promised to protect Gaveston, Pembroke had got into a position where his honour was at stake, and it is hard to resist concluding that Pembroke would not have suffered this kind of humiliation if he had possessed a more developed and ruthless political sense. In 1320, then, he seems to have occupied a place of greater dignity than real political power.

Up to the time of the King's return from France at the end of July 1320 there were few overt signs, apart from the King's bad relations with Lancaster, of the political crisis that was to follow in the spring of 1321.[2] It was under these conditions that the Parliament summoned on 5 August met at Westminster on 6 October.[3] However, this Parliament proved to be a critical moment in the events after 1318, since for the first

---

[1] In 1324 Pembroke successfully petitioned the Pope to be relieved of the rest of his obligation and secured the release of one of his retainers who was still held hostage: *Cal. Papal Letters, 1305–42*, p. 240.

[2] The *Vita*, p. 108, emphasizes that trouble between the Younger Despenser and the other magnates did not begin until after the King's return.

[3] *P.W.*, vol. 2, part 1, p. 247.

time there are obvious signs of disturbance and of possible moves to avert trouble.

Pembroke was present at the opening of Parliament and with other magnates was appointed to hear petitions. On 13 October his tenure of office as Keeper of the Forest was confirmed,[1] and on 3 November one of his knights, Aymer la Zouche, was made Sheriff of Cambridge and Huntingdon. The appointments of the Younger Despenser as Constable of Bristol and of Badlesmere as Constable of Dover also tend to confirm an initial impression of normal routine and of unity among the associates of the King.[2]

However, the absence of Lancaster, who on 5 October was still at Pontefract, was a reminder of his continued hostility to the King, although he did send Nicholas de Segrave and others to represent him at Westminster.[3] Those attending Parliament were apparently aware of the dangers that might be created if Lancaster were not placated in some way and persuaded to resume his co-operation with the King. It may have been with the intention of reassuring Lancaster that on 14 November the King ordered the careful observation of the Ordinances.[4] The Bishops of London and Winchester were also sent to visit Lancaster, and by 16 November these two had reached St. Albans, where they met with the Bishops of Ely and Rochester. Although delayed at Northampton by the Bishop of London's illness, the mission continued and the Bishop of London finally returned to Westminster on 6 February.[5] This mission may have represented a further attempt at mediation on the part of the prelates (like that of 1318), but it is clear that it achieved nothing, and by the time the Bishop of London returned from Lancaster events were moving too fast for such intervention to have much hope of success. Against these conciliatory moves in Lancaster's direction during the Parliament it is possible to set the order of 5 November requiring Lancaster to answer for the relief for the lands he had inherited from the Earl of Lincoln in 1311. This move can only be regarded as provocative,

---

[1] *P.W.*, vol. 2, part 1, p. 247.
[2] *C.F.R., 1319–27*, pp. 37–8; *C.P.R., 1317–21*, p. 514.
[3] E. 159/94, m. 125; *Ann. Paul.*, p. 290.
[4] E. 159/94, m. 22.
[5] *Ann. Paul.*, p. 290; *Trokelowe*, p. 106. The nominal reason for their visit to Lancaster was to deliver a papal bull.

especially since on 20 December the Younger Despenser was respited the relief for his share of the Gloucester lands.[1]

Mention of Despenser brings attention to the most disturbing developments during the Westminster Parliament. Relations between Despenser and Audley and Damory had already begun to become strained at the end of 1317, when Despenser unsuccessfully tried to take control of Audley's lands at Gwynllwg, an act which culminated in Despenser's acquisition of the lands in May 1320.[2] Despenser's expansion of his hold on South Wales had also included the displacement in March 1319 as Sheriff of Carmarthen of one of Pembroke's men, John Paynel, by one of his own knights, John Iweyn.[3] Although, as the *Vita* points out, many of the leading magnates, including John Mowbray, Audley, Hereford, Roger Clifford, Damory, and the Mortimers, each had his own personal reason for disaffection towards the Younger Despenser, the crisis in Despenser's relations with his fellow magnates was not reached until the seizure by the King on 26 October 1320 of the lordship of Gower on the grounds that John Mowbray had taken possession of it from his father-in-law William de Braose without royal licence.[4] Whatever the precise legal position might be, the seizure of Gower could only be regarded as a threat to the magnates of the Welsh March, and the incident served to crystallize their grievances against Despenser and unite them in action.

Some attempt was, however, made to reassure some of the magnates who might feel most threatened by the decision over Gower. On 20 September and 26 December Damory's debts to the King were respited and on 14 November he was pardoned the whole of a fine of 2,300 marks which he had made for the regrant of certain wardships resumed under the Ordinances.[5] On 5 November the King confirmed at the request of Despenser, Damory, and Audley, the husbands of the three Gloucester

---

[1] E. 368/91, m. 127; E. 159/94, m. 27.

[2] *C.P.R.*, *1317–21*, pp. 60, 456; *Vita*, p. 108.

[3] *C.F.R.*, *1307–19*, p. 394. Iweyn was also appointed as Despenser's constable at Newport castle in Sept. 1320: E. 163/4/9.

[4] *Vita*, pp. 108–9; *C. Cl. R.*, *1318–23*, p. 268. For the background to the Gower problem and details of the 1321 revolt see J. C. Davies, 'The Despenser War in Glamorgan', *T.R.H.S.*, 3rd series, vol. 9 (1915), and also the *Glamorgan County History*, vol. 3, ed. T. B. Pugh (Cardiff, 1971).

[5] E. 159/94, mm. 7, 39*d*.; C. 81/113/5509. The enrolment of the second order says he was pardoned only 1,000 marks of this debt: *C.P.R.*, *1317–21*, p. 519.

heiresses, Edward I's regrant of 1290 of the Gloucester lands to Gilbert de Clare and his heirs by his second marriage.[1] This was probably a guarantee to Damory and Audley that Despenser would not usurp any of their rights in their respective shares of the Gloucester inheritance or claim the entire earldom. That measures such as these were necessary is an indication that in November 1320 the political situation was very delicate. Lancaster was already hostile to the King and also to Despenser, whom he regarded as responsible for the disgrace he had suffered at the time of the siege of Berwick,[2] and the enmity of Damory, Hereford, the Mortimers, and others towards Despenser was now in process of taking shape, with disastrous consequences for him and the King in 1321.

It is significant to discover that at this very point, when the internal political situation was beginning to deteriorate, Pembroke left the country to go to France, with the result that between then and his final return to England in August 1321 he took little direct part in English affairs. There is no doubt that in 1321 he shared the hostility of the Marchers, of whom he was himself one, towards the Despensers and that his absence from the country would be a suitable way of avoiding the choice between deserting the King, in whose service he had made his career and to whom he was legally bound by indenture, and formally joining the Marchers in opposition and in their open attack on the Despensers. But this is probably not a valid explanation of his departure from England in 1320, since the situation, though threatening, had not yet reached a stage where such a clash of loyalties was likely. Pembroke had in fact perfectly sufficient personal business reasons for leaving England when he did. His first wife had died in September and, since he badly needed a legitimate male heir, he went to France in order to arrange for his remarriage, a matter which would naturally take some time. He was also at this time conducting a legal action before the Paris Parlement with the family of his late wife. On the other hand, as the crisis in England developed, Pembroke probably found it very convenient to have a good reason for remaining abroad. When he did return briefly at the end of March 1321, this also allowed him to go back to France at the end of May and stay there while the crisis

---

[1] *C.P.R., 1317–21*, p. 531.   [2] *Vita*, p. 109.

reached its peak. On 9 November 1320 Pembroke was given a protection to last until 2 February and left England soon after 20 November.[1]

The political situation began to worsen rapidly at the beginning of 1321. Lancaster continued to keep to himself and on 6 January the King announced to the Chancellor that, allegedly because of illness, Lancaster would not be attending the eyre at London on 14 January.[2] Hereford's breach with the King was already apparent on 30 January, when he and twenty-eight others were ordered not to join armed assemblies or make secret treaties; by 6 March he was gathering troops in Brecon ready to invade Despenser's lands, and his hostility was recognized on 16 March, when the castle of Builth was taken back into royal hands following a last-minute effort by the Earl of Norfolk to parley with him.[3] Roger Mortimer had retired to his stronghold at Wigmore by 11 February, having been replaced on 1 February as Justice of Ireland by one of Despenser's men, Ralph de Gorges.[4] The opposition to the Despensers had begun to take a formal shape by 27 February, when the King was sent news from Newcastle that on 22 February Lancaster and other unnamed magnates had met at Pontefract and decided to attack the Younger Despenser in Wales. There is no positive evidence that any of the Marchers were present, but the area of the planned attack makes it likely that either they or their representatives were there.[5] Lancaster's efforts to stage-manage the events of 1321, while staying at Pontefract well clear of any danger, are thus apparent from the very beginning.[6]

Following this news from the north the King and Despenser took action on 6 March to ensure the safety of Despenser's Welsh lands and of Wales as a whole, and on 8 March the Justice of Wales, Roger Mortimer of Chirk, was told to inspect the royal castles in Wales.[7] On 1 March the King and Despenser had themselves left London for the danger area; they arrived

[1] *C.P.R., 1317–21*, p. 518; C. 53/107, m. 5.
[2] C. 81/113/5551. Lancaster had made a similar excuse in Nov. 1311: S.C. 1/45/221.
[3] *C. Cl. R., 1318–23*, p. 355; S.C. 1/58/10; *C. Ch. Warr.*, p. 519; B.M., Cotton MS. Nero C. III, f. 181.
[4] *C. Cl. R., 1318–23*, p. 360; *C.P.R., 1317–21*, p. 558.
[5] S.C. 1/35/8; C. 81/114/5602.
[6] See *Knighton*, vol. 1, p. 422.
[7] S.C. 1/58/10; *C. Ch. Warr.*, pp. 518–19; *C. Cl. R., 1318–23*, p. 290.

at Cirencester on 20 March.[1] The transition from threats of force by the Marchers to their open defiance of the King came soon after 28 March, when the King summoned Hereford and his allies to Gloucester on 5 April to discuss the situation with the Council.[2]

At this point in the proceedings Pembroke reappeared on the scene after an absence of four months. Following his departure from London in November, Pembroke had probably reached the French court by 7 December, when Edward wrote both to him and to the French King.[3] The King was again in contact with him on 15 December, 12 and 23 February, and finally on 6 March, when he was still in France.[4] The contract for Pembroke's marriage to Marie de Saint-Pol, the daughter of the late Count of Saint-Pol, was concluded in Paris in February 1321 and enclosed in letters patent of Philip V,[5] in which Pembroke promised to assign 2,000 *livres* dower to his future wife. On 29 March 1321, after Pembroke's return, the King wrote from Gloucester asking for a papal dispensation for the marriage because Pembroke and Marie de Saint-Pol were related in the fourth degree, giving as grounds for his request the hope that the marriage would strengthen peace and friendship between England and France. Papal permission was duly granted on 22 April, and the King confirmed Pembroke's marriage treaty and his assignment of dower on 12 April.[6] Despite the King's reference in his letter to the Pope to the diplomatic importance of Pembroke's marriage, which would indeed be real enough, it is clear, and is confirmed from royal correspondence of early 1321, that Pembroke's marriage negotiations were a purely private matter and not a part of royal policy.[7] The affair serves to underline once again the very close social links which Pembroke had with France.

[1] E. 101/378/10, mm. 6, 7.

[2] *C. Cl. R., 1318–23*, pp. 364–5.

[3] B.M., Add. MS. 9951, f. 34.

[4] Ibid., ff. 34, 34*v*., 35.

[5] A. Du Chesne, *Histoire de la maison de Chastillon sur Marne* (Paris, 1621), Preuves, p. 168. Du Chesne's source was a catalogue of the *Tiltres de la Fère* now in the *Archives Nationales*, Paris (KK. 909, f. 75; PP. 19 bis, f. 38*v*.). The original contract and full details of its contents are not extant.

[6] *C.P.R., 1317–21*, pp. 575–6; *F.*, vol. 2, p. 446; *Lettres communes de Jean XXII*, vol. 3, p. 271.

[7] S.C. 1/32/87; ibid. /45/197.

Apart from keeping him out of the political developments of early 1321, Pembroke's absence had also had the effect of delaying the start of a further series of truce negotiations with the Scots. These had originated in August 1320, when John Darcy, one of Pembroke's retainers and Sheriff of Nottingham, Andrew Harcla, and six squires, who included another Pembroke retainer, Percival Simeon, were sent to visit Robert Bruce. They carried letters of credence from Pembroke, Despenser, and Badlesmere asking for the postponement of the truce negotiations due to take place at Carlisle, to which the latter had earlier agreed.[1] After further contacts with the Scots at Carlisle in September and October these moves resulted on 19 January 1321 in the appointment of the Archbishop of York, the Bishops of Carlisle, Worcester, and Winchester, the Earls of Pembroke and Hereford, Badlesmere, and six others either to make a final peace treaty or to prolong the existing truce made by Pembroke and his colleagues in December 1319.[2] The composition of the embassy, and the intended participation of both French and papal envoys as well, indicate the importance placed upon these negotiations by the royal administration. The timing of the negotiations may also have been influenced by knowledge that Lancaster was intriguing with the Scots, who might therefore intervene in England in the event of further trouble between the King and Lancaster.

These plans did not, however, work out as intended. On 17 February the King wrote to Badlesmere and his colleagues telling them to delay their meeting with the Scots for two or three weeks, as he hoped that Pembroke would soon be back in England. When Pembroke did return he would be sent north with all speed.[3] Despite Pembroke's continued absence, the other envoys issued safe conducts for the Scottish envoys at Roxburgh on 19 February in his name and in that of Hereford, who had also failed to appear.[4] On 23 February the King wrote again to say that, because Pembroke was still engaged in private business in France and the date of his return was unknown, and because Hereford had not appeared 'for certain reasons', he

---

[1] B.M., Add. MS. 9951, f. 10.
[2] Ibid., f. 6*v*.; *C.P.R., 1317–21*, pp. 504, 554.
[3] S.C. 1/45/197.
[4] C. 47/22/12/31.

had appointed the Earl of Richmond in their place.[1] The King still had no idea of when to expect Pembroke when he wrote to the envoys on 1 March.[2] Pembroke's presence in the negotiations was evidently felt by the King to be important, and it was only with reluctance that he ordered the talks to proceed without him.

Pembroke's reappearance with the King at Gloucester on about 28 March[3] coincided with the final developments which preceded the Marchers' attack on the Despensers. The Earl of Hereford failed to answer the King's summons to come to Gloucester on 6 April and informed the King via two royal knights, John de Somery and Robert de Kendale, that he would not come while the Younger Despenser remained in the King's company. Hereford then sent the Abbot of Dore to the King with proposals that Despenser should be put in Lancaster's custody and permitted to answer the charges against him in Parliament.[4] The King sent a cleverly argued reply, which no doubt reflects suggestions made by Despenser himself, in which he refused to do as Hereford asked because Despenser had never been charged with any crime, and took his stand upon Magna Carta, the Ordinances, the common law, and his Coronation Oath. The King ended by summoning Hereford and Roger Mortimer of Wigmore to Oxford on 10 May to discuss the date for a Parliament. On 1 May the King postponed the date of this proposed meeting to 17 May at Westminster.[5] It is reasonable to suppose that Pembroke took part in these last desperate attempts to arrange a meeting with the Marchers and so avoid an open clash. His motives would no doubt be partly governed by the moderation which marked his career, but at the same time he had personal reasons for avoiding a violent outcome to the crisis. It is certain that Pembroke had a great deal of sympathy with the Despenser's opponents, but he had not so far carried it to the lengths of openly joining the Marchers in their opposition to them.[6] None the less, if

[1] S.C. 1/32/87. See *C.P.R., 1317–21*, p. 367.

[2] S.C. 1/45/200. The truce negotiations ended in April without success.

[3] C. 53/107, m. 2.

[4] *C. Cl. R., 1318–23*, p. 367.

[5] Ibid., pp. 367–8.

[6] *Murimuth*, p. 33, says: 'Comes vero Lancastriae consensit eis expresse et comes de Pembroke occulte.' This opinion is quoted by several other chroniclers: *Le*

force were used, he would find it difficult to avoid a public choice between allying himself with the Marchers and remaining with the King and indirectly lending his approval to the Despensers. The Marchers certainly knew of his sympathies, and it is likely that the letter brought to Pembroke on 19 April from the Abbot of Dore contained an appeal for him to join them or at least to mediate with the King on their behalf.[1] There is, however, no sign that at this point Pembroke did anything to help the Marchers, nor did he or any of his men, with the possible exception of his nephew, John Hastings of Abergavenny, take part afterwards in the attacks on the Despensers' lands in England and Wales.

Events now began to move rapidly. On 4 May the war of Hereford and his allies against the Younger Despenser began with an attack on Newport, followed by the capture of Cardiff on 9 May and Swansea on about 13 May.[2] Meanwhile Roger Mortimer of Wigmore seized the lands of Despenser's ally, the Earl of Arundel, at Clun and elsewhere in Wales.[3] On 24 May a group of northern magnates met Lancaster at Pontefract and made a defensive pact with him, although not apparently agreeing to join an attack on the Despensers.[4] Earlier, on 15 May, the King had summoned Parliament to Westminster on 15 July, no doubt hoping in this way to save the Despensers from the wrath of the Marchers.[5]

Interesting light on the extent of the government's preoccupation with the affairs of the Despensers at this time is thrown by a long letter to the Seneschal of Gascony which was probably written by Richard de Burton, a Chancery clerk, between 15 May and the end of the month. The author says that when he and the Bishop of Hereford arrived in England from Gascony they found that the King was absent from London

---

Baker, p. 11; *Vita et Mors*, p. 302; Bodleian, Laud Misc. MS. 529, f. 106 (this source is related to Murimuth but has much local information on the Welsh March).

[1] B.M., Add. MS. 9951, f. 36. The letter itself has not survived.

[2] *Flores*, vol. 3, pp. 344–5; B.M., Add. MS. 9951, f. 7v.

[3] Bodleian, Laud Misc. MS. 529, f. 106; Univ. of Chicago MS. 224 f. 55v. (formerly Univ. of Chicago MS. CS. 439. f. M.82.W.6.) (this chronicle of Wigmore abbey is available on N.L.W. Microfilm 30). Arundel's son had married Despenser's daughter on 9 Feb.: B.M., Add. MS. 9951, f. 45v.

[4] *Bridlington*, p. 61. See B. Wilkinson, 'The Sherburn Indenture and the Attack on the Despensers', *E.H.R.*, vol. 63 (1948), pp. 6–7.

[5] *P.W.*, vol. 2, part 1, p. 260.

and that, although he later spent three weeks with the King, he was unable to see either the King, Pembroke, or Despenser to get replies to the questions sent by the Seneschal, because they were all too busy with other matters.[1]

At the end of May Pembroke was once again preparing to leave the country for the ceremonies of his marriage to Marie de Saint-Pol in France. On 25 and 26 May he and twenty of his retainers were given protections until 1 August, and by 2 June he had crossed to Boulogne.[2] By 22 June he had joined the members of Marie's family and on 5 July he and Marie de Saint-Pol were married in Paris.[3] A subsidiary aim of Pembroke's stay in France may have been to try and obtain help in mediating between Edward II and the Marchers, but if this were so it was the result of his continuing personal loyalty to the King and not of any desire to save the Despensers. His distaste for the Younger Despenser was in fact clearly displayed during his stay in Paris. Despenser is said by a Canterbury chronicler to have crossed for safety to France disguised in the habit of a monk of Langdon abbey and gone to Paris, but to have left soon after and returned to England for fear of Pembroke and the information that the latter was spreading about him at the French court.[4]

In Pembroke's absence, events in England were rapidly coming to a climax. On 28 June the Earl of Hereford and the other Marchers who had attacked the Despensers met with Lancaster and a group of other magnates from the north at Sherburn in Elmet, and an indenture was drawn up in which all those present approved the Marchers' actions against the Despensers and the justice of continuing such action in the future.[5] Both T. F. Tout and J. C. Davies interpreted this agreement as placing Lancaster at the head of a united coalition of Marcher and northern magnates.[6] Professor Wilkinson, however, argues that the indenture was the result of prolonged

---

[1] S.C. 1/54/139. The bishop arrived in England on 24 Apr.: B.M., Add. MS. 9951, f. 9*v*.
[2] *C.P.R., 1317–21*, pp. 589–91, 596; C. 81/1750/21; C. 66/154, m. 4.
[3] B.M., Add. MS. 9951, f. 37*v*.; *Ann. Paul.*, p. 291; *C.P.R., 1321–4*, pp. 12–13.
[4] Trinity College Cambridge MS. R. 5. 41, f. 114*v*. (*Collectanea of John Leland*, vol. 1, p. 272).
[5] See text of the indenture in Wilkinson, op. cit.
[6] Tout, *Place of the Reign* (1936), pp. 128–9; Davies, *Baronial Opposition*, pp. 478–9.

bargaining, that it was never sealed, and that Lancaster was unsuccessful in trying to unite the Marchers and the northerners.[1] On one point at least this latter interpretation is certainly incorrect, since a copy of the indenture found in Lancaster's muniments in 1322 bore the seals of twenty-five persons.[2] None the less these conclusions are still preferable to those of Tout and Davies. Although the indenture was sealed, it is still possible that other magnates present were not prepared to put their seals to it, since the two versions of the indenture respectively record the presence of forty-eight and thirty-four persons.[3] It is also noticeable that many of those present, such as Fulk Lestrange, Robert de Holand, and John d'Eure, were Lancaster's retainers and hence of no independent weight. As Wilkinson points out, the northern barons who had met with Lancaster at Pontefract in May had been distinctly reluctant to involve themselves in any offensive action, and it may well also have been true that at Sherburn many of those present were ready to approve the Marchers' continued action against the Despensers provided they themselves were not asked to participate. It certainly seems reasonable to accept the suggestions that Lancaster did not control the north politically and that the Marchers did not therefore gain from the Sherburn meeting the accretion of strength that has been supposed.[4]

There was, however, one other development at the Sherburn meeting which makes it of particular importance. This was the defection to the side of the opposition magnates of Bartholomew de Badlesmere, the Steward of the Household, who hitherto had been one of the most prominent and loyal of the King's supporters. The precise reasons for Badlesmere's change of side are not known, but he probably shared in the growing hatred of the Younger Despenser in late 1320 and early 1321. He was, however, still loyal on 17 May 1321 when he was given custody of Tonbridge castle which had belonged to Hugh Audley the Younger, one of Despenser's opponents.[5] He was still apparently

[1] Wilkinson, op. cit., pp. 4, 6.

[2] D.L. 41/1/37, m. 7. The names of those who sealed it are not given. I should like to thank Dr. E. B. Fryde for drawing my attention to this reference.

[3] Wilkinson, op. cit., p. 28.

[4] Ibid., p. 7. A detailed analysis of the names contained in the indenture is beyond the scope of this book but would certainly clarify the problem.

[5] *C.F.R.*, *1319–27*, p. 57.

acting as Steward on 18 June, but two days before this, on 16 June, he had been replaced as Constable of Dover by the King's half-brother, the Earl of Kent.[1] It is possible either that this happened because the King was already uncertain of Badlesmere's loyalty or that Badlesmere took his replacement as a personal insult and began to consider changing sides. Shortly after this, however, Badlesmere and the Archbishop of Canterbury were sent to Sherburn by the King to persuade the magnates to end their attacks on the Despensers and instead put their complaints before Parliament.[2] While at Sherburn Badlesmere went over to the King's opponents.[3] At first sight it seems surprising, in view of the known hostility of Lancaster to Badlesmere, that Badlesmere should change allegiance at an assembly at which Lancaster and many of his personal retainers were present. But the real nature of the magnate opposition to the King in 1321 was that it was led and dominated in practice not by Lancaster but rather by the lords of the Welsh March, notably the Earl of Hereford and Roger Mortimer of Wigmore. Since the marriage of Badlesmere's daughter Elizabeth to Mortimer's eldest son Edmund in June 1316 Badlesmere had possessed a strong social connection with this Marcher group, so that he had a natural affinity with them when both they and he found themselves united against Despenser in 1321.[4] The Marchers were of course also at Sherburn, and it is most likely that when Badlesmere broke with the King he was joining with them and not with Lancaster. His action, however explicable it may be in these terms, did not gain him any sympathy from Lancaster, who still distrusted him, and also won him the undying hatred of the King. These two facts were to prove fatal for Badlesmere in 1322 and were to weaken the Marcher opposition seriously at critical moments in October 1321 and in early 1322.

From Sherburn Hereford and the other Marchers, un-

---

[1] C. 53/107, m. 1; *C.F.R., 1319–27*, p. 62.

[2] Trinity College Cambridge MS. R. 5. 41, f. 114; B.M., Cotton MS. Nero D. X, f. 111 (this is a chronicle, attributed in the MS. to Nicholas Trivet, which provided much of the material for the account of 1321–2 in Holinshed's *Chronicles*. This MS. was probably also known to John Leland: *Collectanea*, vol. 3, p. 403.)

[3] Ibid.; *The Brut*, vol. 1, pp. 213–14.

[4] D.L. 27/L.S. 93; B.M., Egerton Roll 8724, m. 5; B.M., Harleian MS. 1240, f. 113v.

accompanied by Lancaster, came south in order to present their demands for the Despensers' exile at the Parliament which had begun at Westminster on 15 July.[1] They reached St. Albans on about 22 July and there is evidence that during the magnates' stay there and in the days that followed there were attempts by members of the Canterbury province to mediate between them and the King as they had done in 1318. The Bishops of London, Salisbury, Ely, Hereford, and Chichester came to St. Albans to try and make peace but had to return to London without any success.[2] Following this the magnates moved to Waltham, where they spent four days, and on 29 July reached London and established themselves at Holborn, the New Temple, and elsewhere outside the city, which refused to admit them. Further attempts at mediation now took place. On several occasions the Archbishop and the Bishops of London, Ely, Salisbury, Lincoln, Hereford, Exeter, Bath and Wells, Chichester, and Rochester, and others attending Parliament met the magnates at the New Temple and the house of the Carmelites to try to make a settlement. But the magnates continued to insist on the Despensers' exile, while the King resolutely refused to make any concessions or even to meet his opponents.[3]

At this moment of deadlock Pembroke returned from France. His return was evidently seen with relief by the King, who on 1 August wrote asking him to come to Westminster the next day, because he greatly wished to meet him and have his advice, requesting him to come via Lambeth so that a boat might be sent for him.[4]

Both the King and the Marchers probably now hoped that they could induce Pembroke to give them his support, and it is clear that Pembroke did indeed play a major part in ending the deadlock. According to one apparently well-informed source the magnates made contact with Pembroke and three other earls who had so far remained loyal to the King, Richmond, Arundel, and Warenne, and put pressure on them to join their

---

[1] *Flores*, vol. 3, p. 197; *Ann. Paul.*, p. 293.

[2] *Ann. Paul.*, p. 293; *Trokelowe*, p. 109; B.M., Cotton MS. Nero D. X, f. 111.

[3] *Ann. Paul.*, pp. 294–6; *Vita*, p. 112.

[4] S.C. 1/49/50; Pembroke had probably just come from Dover via his manors in Kent. His wife reached Westminster on 8 Aug.: *Ann. Paul.*, p. 292.

ranks.[1] On the evidence of the *Vita* it does seem certain that Pembroke at least took an oath to uphold their demand for the Despenser's exile.[2] In view of Pembroke's proven hostility to the Despensers it is very likely that he was prepared to make such a commitment. But it is also clear that at the same time Pembroke was trying to play the part of a mediator[3] and that he saw the exile of the Despensers as necessary for the King's best interests. In this way he could attempt the difficult task of accepting the magnates' demands and at the same time remaining basically loyal to the King as he had in the past.

After their meeting with the magnates Pembroke and the other mediators brought to the King the baronial ultimatum that unless the Despensers were removed the King would be deposed. Pembroke now played the major role in urging the King to accept the magnates' demands. He is said to have told the King to take note of the power of the magnates and not to risk losing his kingdom for the sake of his favourites. He added that the barons had attacked the Despensers for the sake of the common good, which the King had sworn to uphold at his coronation. Pembroke concluded with the ominous statement that if the King refused the magnates' demands, even his loyalty would be lost because of the oath he had taken to the magnates.[4] Faced with the prospects outlined by Pembroke, the King gave way, and on 14 August he came into Westminster Hall, flanked by Pembroke and Richmond, and agreed to exile the Despensers, who were to leave the country by 29 August.[5] On 20 August the magnates were formally pardoned for their attacks on the Despensers.[6]

---

[1] B.M., Cotton Nero D. X, f. 111: 'in partem suam licet involuntarie attraxerunt.' The MS. of the *Historia Roffensis* (quoted by J. R. Maddicott, *Thomas of Lancaster, 1307–1322* (Oxford, 1970), p. 280) also says that pressure was put upon these four earls to join the opposition and gives the occasion of this as a meeting at Clerkenwell. It implies, however, that their consent was willingly given, which seems improbable: B.M., Cotton MS. Faustina B. V, f. 35v. The date of this meeting was apparently 27 July, so Pembroke had already been back for some days by 1 Aug.   [2] *Vita*, p. 112.

[3] Ibid.; *Ann. Paul.*, p. 297. The *Vita*, p. 112, suggests that in mediating Pembroke was not wholly loyal to his oath to the magnates, and this may well reflect contemporary opinion of his actions.

[4] *Vita*, pp. 112–13.

[5] *Ann. Paul.*, p. 297; *Vita*, p. 113; *French Chronicle of London*, p. 42; *C. Cl. R.*, *1318–23*, p. 494.

[6] *C.P.R.*, *1321–4*, pp. 15–21. Badlesmere was included among those pardoned.

The exile of the Despensers was not, however, enough to guarantee the magnates' permanent success, since as soon as the Marchers had left Westminster there was the possibility that the King would be able to recall his favourites and plan revenge against their opponents. At the same time the Despensers' lands, although nominally put in charge of royal keepers on 16 August,[1] remained firmly under magnate control. The situation was therefore ripe for a further round of conflict.

In conclusion it is now possible to give a final assessment of the views of Tout and Davies on the importance of the Earl of Pembroke between 1318 and 1321. The evidence produced in this chapter is sufficient to show that at least until the time of the Parliament of October 1320 Pembroke was in one way or another deeply involved in royal business. It is also apparent that his personal relations with the King remained close. These facts are entirely consistent with his position as an important and highly regarded member of the royal Council, which he had held since the summer of 1316, and in this sense his place in the royal circle was unaltered after 1318.

The examination in an earlier chapter of Pembroke's career in 1312 and 1313 showed that for that period there was a close correlation between the sheer quantity of Pembroke's government activity and political leadership by him. This was not, however, also the case after 1318, which is a further indication that the 'middle party' interpretation is not a satisfactory explanation of the events of these years. For a time Pembroke probably was important in the formal processes of making and performing royal policy, but at the more significant level of political manipulation and influence he was sadly lacking. His inability to control the rise of the Younger Despenser and the growth of a new crisis situation, as well as his virtual abdication from English politics between November 1320 and August 1321, do not suggest either that he dominated the political scene or was capable of doing so. The prolonged humiliation which he suffered through Maurice de Berkeley's attack on Painswick and defiance of royal authority afterwards, and through the financial difficulties produced by payment of his ransom, suggest the same conclusion. Towards the end of the period even Pembroke's traditional loyalty to the King was

[1] *C.F.R., 1319–27*, p. 69.

being placed under great strain because of his growing hostility
to the Younger Despenser. In Badlesmere's case, which in many
ways is not unlike that of Pembroke, since both men had been
closely associated with the King, the strain proved too great
and Badlesmere broke openly with the King. For Pembroke
such a public and final breach would have been a rejection of
all that he had ever attempted in his career, and it seems likely
that as the crisis developed to the point of open revolt during
his absence in France in 1321 he was happy to have an excuse
for staying abroad and avoiding a choice of sides. When he
returned to England in August 1321 he was unable to put off
this choice any longer, and he was torn between loyalty to the
King and to the Marcher opponents of Despenser, with whom
he secretly sympathized. The result was that his attempts at
mediation were probably intended as much to resolve his own
personal dilemma as to bring an end to the crisis. Inevitably,
as the events of 1322 were to show, he could satisfy neither side.

It is therefore possible to give a reasonably coherent explanation of Pembroke's place in the years after 1318, but without
the crutch of the 'middle party' interpretation it is peculiarly
difficult to give a full and clear description of what was happening in those years. The main feature of the period was the rise
of the Younger Despenser, partly as a result of the removal of
Roger Damory and the earlier favourites from court in 1318.
Through his behaviour and influence over the King he contributed to the renewed estrangement between the King and
Lancaster, and, more importantly, he was the prime cause of
the breach in 1321 between the King and the lords of the
Welsh March, whose power he was challenging directly on
their home territories.

This much is clear in general terms, but it is very difficult
to go deeper into the situation. One reason for this is that before
1318 the major political crises had often taken a public form,
which has made it possible to determine the nature of the main
political trends and their development with some precision.
Between 1318 and 1320, however, there was to outward appearances a stable political order, and it is likely that the most
significant developments were taking place within the closed
circle of the King's associates. By their nature these personal
relationships were largely private, and it is only rarely that

there is evidence of what was going on beneath the surface of political life. Pembroke's quarrel with Anthony Pessagno is but one minor example of what was happening, just as in 1317 his indenture with Badlesmere and Roger Damory also allows a glimpse of activities behind the scenes. It is therefore easy to describe the public crisis with which the period ended in 1321 but hard to say in detail just how and why it came about. A careful study of the career of the Younger Despenser at this time and of the charges made against him in 1321 would probably supply some of the answers, but that must be left for another occasion. For the moment it is safest to say that the years after 1318 were not a period of rule by a 'middle party' led by Pembroke, but instead witnessed a complex battle for power among the immediate associates of the Crown, from whom the Younger Despenser and his father finally emerged as the most successful.

VII

The Epilogue to Pembroke's Career
Civil War and After, 1321 to 1324

WHEN the Despensers were forced into exile in August 1321 few people can have believed that this was the end of the affair. The King was certain to try to reverse the verdict of the Marchers, since this had been one of those occasions, like the exiles and murder of Gaveston, when his own personal feelings were deeply involved. Whereas normally Edward II's contribution to the policy performed in his name was probably limited to formal approval, on such an occasion as this he could dig his heels in very effectively. Pembroke had certainly met with this kind of reaction earlier, when trying to patch up a peace between the King and Lancaster in 1313 and in his attempts to curb Roger Damory and the other royal favourites in 1317 and 1318. Except in August 1321, when the whole force of the Marchers was at his back, Pembroke was no longer in a position to persuade or cajole Edward. Once the Despensers were in exile it would take more ability and force than Pembroke could command to stop the King from recalling them. To make matters worse, it soon became clear that the Younger Despenser was still in close contact with the King and was planning their joint revenge against his and Edward's enemies. The campaign that finally destroyed the Marchers and Lancaster in 1321 and 1322 bears all the marks of careful preparation and execution, and there is little doubt that Despenser had a major part in it, even though he did not participate directly. The result was total victory for the King, the ascendancy of the Despensers, a massacre of English magnates unsurpassed even in the fifteenth century, and the creation in England of a regime supported only on fear and military force. Most of the chief opponents of the King were eliminated in 1322, but by their elimination the King and the Despensers had stirred up such hatred and such an undercurrent of conspiracy that sooner or later they were almost bound to lose control and be destroyed in their turn.

In such a situation there was little that a moderate like Pembroke could do except allow himself to be swept along by events. Pembroke's active career continued until his death in June 1324 but after the summer of 1321 he had little real authority, so that this period forms merely an epilogue to his life.

After the end of Parliament in August 1321 Hereford and his followers withdrew only as far as Oxford, so that they could still bring pressure on the King if he tried to recall the Despensers.[1] With the removal of the Despensers, Pembroke probably now felt free to associate openly with their opponents and at some point between late August and the end of September attended a tournament at Witney near Oxford, in which he and his men took part against Hereford and Badlesmere.[2] Pembroke's activities probably alarmed the King and may have been the cause of the King's sending William de Cusaunce to him on 31 August.[3] There can be little doubt that Pembroke did not approve of the King's action in leaving the Younger Despenser in the protection of the Cinque Ports, of Despenser's subsequent acts of piracy in the Channel, or of his encouragement of the attack on Southampton on 30 September by the men of the Cinque Ports.[4] There might accordingly have been a danger that Pembroke would identify himself fully with the Marchers in any future conflict. That Pembroke did not do so was probably the result of his personal loyalty to the King, as well as of Lancaster's advice to the barons that Pembroke could not be trusted and that they should reject his help.[5] Pembroke therefore had little option but to rejoin the King, and had apparently done so by the end of September,[6] just before Badlesmere's defiance of the King caused the outbreak of the conflict which led to the magnates' destruction in 1322.

The clash between the King and the magnates which began in October 1321 has all the appearance of deliberate provocation by the King. One writer claimed that the King had made

[1] Trinity Coll. Cambridge MS. R. 5. 41, f. 115.
[2] Ibid. Pembroke's manor of Bampton was nearby.
[3] S.C. 1/49/51.
[4] *C. Cl. R., 1318–23*, p. 507; *Ann. Paul.*, p. 300; *Vita*, p. 116; S.C. 8/17/833.
[5] *Vita*, p. 117.
[6] He was witnessing royal charters from 19 Sept.: C. 53/108, m. 8.

plans with Despenser on how to revenge himself against the magnates, and the orders in September and November to Hereford, Audley, and Damory to give the Despensers' lands to royal keepers, orders which they inevitably ignored, seem designed to produce a *casus belli*.[1] It is likely that of his opponents the King chose to attack the former Steward, Badlesmere, first of all, both because he regarded Badlesmere's treachery in joining the Marchers as unpardonable and also because the fact of Lancaster's hostility to Badlesmere meant there was a good chance of destroying him without baronial intervention.[2] As part of his plans against Badlesmere the King ordered him on 26 September to give up custody of Tonbridge castle and also sent men to Dover to check any move by Badlesmere there.[3] When he heard of this Badlesmere crossed into Kent from Tilbury, put the castles of Leeds and Chilham in a state of defence, and then rejoined the Marchers at Oxford.[4] The King and Queen then went on pilgrimage to Canterbury, after which the King went to meet the Younger Despenser on Thanet and told the Queen to go to Leeds on her return journey to London, in the hope that Badlesmere's men would refuse to admit her and that Badlesmere could then be justifiably attacked.[5] When the Queen reached Leeds on 13 October she was duly refused admittance as had been hoped, Badlesmere having risen to the bait and ordered his men not to admit her if she came.[6]

The King reacted swiftly to this affront and on 16 October announced that he would start to besiege Leeds on 23 October, sending Pembroke, with the Earls of Norfolk and Richmond, as an advance guard on 17 October. Pembroke could not refuse to go against his old colleague, Badlesmere, and his part in the

---

[1] *Murimuth*, p. 33; *C. Cl. R., 1318–23*, pp. 402, 408.

[2] Trinity Coll. Cambridge MS. R. 5. 41, ff. 114, 114*v*.; *Vita*, p. 116; *C.P.R., 1321–24*, pp. 47–8.

[3] *C.F.R., 1319–27*, p. 71; Trinity Coll. Cambridge MS. R. 5. 41, f. 114*v*. Badlesmere had already been dismissed as Constable of Dover on 16 June, but he had presumably not given up control. On 16 July one of his retainers, William de Setvans, was replaced as Sheriff of Kent: *C.F.R., 1319–27*, pp. 62, 65.

[4] Trinity Coll. Cambridge MS. R. 5. 41, f. 115.

[5] Ibid.: 'ut negatus sit reginae introitus in castellum'; B.M., Cotton MS. Nero D. X, f. 111.

[6] *Ann. Paul.*, p. 298; Trinity Coll. Cambridge MS. R. 5. 41, f. 115. Badlesmere had heard of the King's intentions.

siege thus confirmed that in future he would be fighting for the King, even if this eventually led to the return of the Despensers.[1] After the siege had begun Badlesmere persuaded Hereford and the Mortimers to go to the relief of the castle,[2] but on 27 October the baronial army stopped at Kingston-on-Thames while its leaders entered into tentative negotiations, in which Pembroke took a prominent part. The Archbishop, Bishop of London, and Pembroke went to Kingston and offered that, if the barons retreated, they would try to mediate with the King, to which the magnates replied that if the King raised the siege they would surrender the castle after the next Parliament.[3] Any chance of success was ended by the intervention of Lancaster, who was still at this time in the north at Pontefract,[4] and who wrote persuading the magnates to do nothing to help Badlesmere, whom he was quite prepared to see destroyed.[5] The King's gamble thus succeeded. Hereford and his allies withdrew, accompanied by Badlesmere, and, deprived of any hope of relief, Leeds surrendered on 31 October.[6]

Following the capture of Leeds, there were signs that both sides were preparing for the inevitable next stage in the conflict. Before 11 November Warwick castle, for example, had been seized by royal opponents. Even as close to the King as London there were rumours that royal enemies were being harboured and shortly before 17 November Pembroke had been sent there by the King to try and ensure the city's loyalty.[7] In the north Lancaster was again stirring and on 18 October summoned a meeting of magnates at Doncaster on 29 November.[8] Contrary to usual opinion, it is certain that, despite the King's prohibition, a meeting between Lancaster and the Marchers

---

[1] *C. Cl. R., 1318–23*, p. 504; *C.P.R., 1321–4*, p. 29. Badlesmere had first received custody of the royal castle of Leeds in Nov. 1317 and had been granted it in tail in Mar. 1318: *C.P.R., 1317–21*, pp. 46, 128. The siege of Leeds also had the effect of forcing other magnates, such as Richmond, Warenne, and Arundel, to declare themselves finally in favour of the King.

[2] Trinity Coll. Cambridge MS. R. 5. 41, f. 115*v*.

[3] *Murimuth*, p. 34; *Melsa*, vol. 2, p. 339.

[4] See G. L. Haskins, 'The Doncaster Petition of 1321', *E.H.R.*, vol. 53 (1938).

[5] *Melsa*, vol. 2, p. 339; *Vita*, p. 116.

[6] Trinity Coll. Cambridge MS. R. 5. 41, f. 115*v*.; *Ann. Paul.*, p. 299; *French Chron. of London*, p. 43. Note that Leeds had not surrendered before help could be brought, as is suggested in Tout, op. cit. (1936), p. 133; McKisack, op. cit., p. 64.

[7] *C. Cl. R., 1318–23*, p. 503; *Cal. of the Letter-Books of the City of London: E* (London, 1903), p. 151.   [8] G. L. Haskins, op. cit., p. 483.

did take place as planned,[1] although it is possible that, for reasons of security, it was held at Pontefract rather than Doncaster.[2] On 2 December Lancaster wrote from Pontefract to the city of London saying that he had just met with the Earl of Hereford, Roger Mortimer of Wigmore, and other magnates. With the letter Lancaster enclosed a copy of the document which the magnates had already sent to the King and which has become known as the Doncaster petition.[3] In the petition Lancaster and his allies accused the Younger Despenser of urging the King to pursue peers of the realm and seize their lands, contrary to the Great Charter, and charged the King with maintaining Despenser, despite his sentence of exile, and of encouraging him in his career of piracy. Lancaster asked the King to remedy these complaints by 20 December.[4] The petition was clearly intended as a propaganda move to justify any actions the magnates might take against the King and the Despensers, but politically it also had the effect of a threat and a challenge, by which the King could also justify taking up arms against the contrariants.

The King had, however, already decided to use force by 15 November, when he announced that he was going to various parts of the realm to remedy the trespasses of malefactors, although he was careful to deny that he was going to make war. On 28 November Damory and Audley were again ordered to give up the Despensers' lands, and Roger Mortimer of Chirk, still officially the Justice of Wales, was told to join the King at Cirencester on 13 December to report on the state of Wales. On 30 November orders were sent for troops to gather at Cirencester on 13 December, a week before the deadline included in the Doncaster petition.[5]

November 1321 also saw the start of moves to bring back the Despensers, moves which throughout carefully followed legal forms and in which Pembroke was prominent. The first important step was taken on 14 November, when the Archbishop

---

[1] Cf. McKisack, op. cit., p. 64.

[2] This suggestion is borne out by *Chroniques de Sempringham: Le Livere de Reis de Britannie*, R.S. (London, 1865), p 338; B.M., Cotton MS. Nero D. X, f. 111v.

[3] Bodleian, Kent Rolls 6, f, g (documents from Tonbridge priory. The copy of the petition is damaged but is clearly recognizable).

[4] G. L. Haskins, op. cit., pp. 483–5.

[5] C. Cl. R., 1318–23, pp. 408, 506, 508; C.P.R., 1321–4, p. 38.

of Canterbury called a provincial council to meet at St. Paul's on 1 December, because, as he put it, the realm which had once rejoiced in the beauty of peace was now in danger of shipwreck through civil war.[1] The meeting may have been planned by the Archbishop to be a means of mediating between the King and the magnates, as his province had done in 1318, but in practice it was used to the full by the King for his own purposes. On 30 November, the day before the council met, the Younger Despenser delivered to the King a petition outlining the legal flaws in the process of his exile and appealing for its annulment, after which Despenser surrendered himself to the King's custody. Then or a little later the Elder Despenser followed the same course.[2] On the same day the King announced that he was sending Richmond, Arundel, and Robert Baldock to deliver a message to the council, and it was presumably they who placed the Younger Despenser's petition before the prelates.[3] The Council itself was not fully representative, since, apart from the Archbishop himself, only the Bishops of London, Ely, Salisbury, and Rochester were present. Ten members of the province did not appear,[4] some of them at least, like the Bishops of Hereford and Lincoln, because they sympathized with the magnate contrariants. Despenser's petition was read before the prelates, who gave their opinion that the sentence against him was invalid and should be annulled. The petition and this reply were then read again in the presence of the prelates and the Earls of Pembroke, Kent, Richmond, and Arundel, all of whom gave the same answer. Pembroke, Richmond, and Arundel added, with some truth, that they had consented to the award against Despenser through fear of the other magnates and begged pardon for doing so. Afterwards the royal justices and others of the King's Council gave their opinions to the same effect.[5] In this way the King secured the widest possible consent for Despenser's return. Pembroke, who had been the chief agent, with Richmond, in persuading the King to accept the

---

[1] D. Wilkins (ed.), *Concilia Magnae Britanniae et Hiberniae* (London, 1737), vol. 2, pp. 507–8; Cambridge Univ. MS. Ee. v. 31, f. 223v.

[2] *C. Cl. R., 1318–23*, pp. 541–5. The Despensers probably did not appear in person at this point.

[3] *C.P.R., 1321–4*, p. 37; *C. Cl. R., 1318–23*, pp. 410, 543.

[4] *Ann. Paul.*, p. 300; *C. Cl. R., 1318–23*, pp. 510–11.

[5] Ibid., pp. 510–11, 543.

Despensers' exile, had in effect been humiliated and bound even more closely to the King in the war with his fellow Marchers.[1] On 8 December the Younger Despenser was given a safe conduct, which was renewed, with a formal protection, on 9 January, while his father received a conduct on 25 December.[2]

With this business accomplished, the King set out on 8 December to join his army at Cirencester for the start of the campaign against Hereford and his allies, who at about this time had seized Gloucester.[3] Pembroke, however, was still in London on 10 December and may have remained for a few days in connection with the annulment of the process against the Despensers, which was not formally announced until 1 January.[4] Pembroke rejoined the King with his forces after the latter reached Cirencester. It was while the King was at Cirencester over Christmas that Pembroke's nephew, John Hastings of Abergavenny, came and made his peace with the King.[5] Hastings had almost certainly been swept into the movement against the Despensers earlier in 1321 and his offence was probably slight, since he was later sent to take control of Glamorgan for the King.[6] While at Cirencester Pembroke busied himself with preparing the defences of his castle of Goodrich in Herefordshire against any possible Marcher attack.[7]

On 27 December the royal army left Cirencester for Worcester, which was reached on 31 December.[8] Because the

[1] On 18 Nov. Pembroke was paid a sum of £500 by the King, repayable on demand, for which he gave the King letters of obligation: E. 403/196, m. 4; E. 101/332/13. This may have been some kind of bond for his future loyalty, but the evidence is too ambiguous to be sure of this.

[2] *C.P.R., 1321–4*, pp. 45, 47.

[3] Bodleian, Laud MS. Misc. 529, f. 106v. (This chronicle, which is related to that of Adam Murimuth, has much new material on the Welsh March in 1321–2. Extracts from it are included in Bodleian, Dugdale MS. 20.)

[4] Westminster Abbey Muniments, no. 5110; *Ann. Paul.*, p. 301.

[5] B.M., Cotton MS. Nero D. X, f. 111v.; Bodleian, Laud MS. Misc. 529, f. 106v.

[6] *C.F.R., 1319–27*, p. 115; B.M., Cotton MS. Nero D. X, f. 111v.

[7] *C. Cl. R., 1318–23*, p. 620.

[8] E. 101/378/13, m. 5. While the army had been gathering at Cirencester John Giffard had raided some of the supply wagons being sent there. This episode is mentioned in Trinity Coll. Cambridge MS. R. 5. 41, f. 116v., and was included by Leland in his *Collectanea*, vol. 1, p. 274, in which form it is referred to by Ruth Butler in her article, 'The Last of the Brimpsfield Giffards and the Rising of 1321–22', *Trans. Bristol and Gloucs. Arch. Soc.*, vol. 76 (1957).

crossing of the Severn there was held by the contrariants, a royal
advance guard of cavalry and infantry, led by Fulk fitz Warin,
Oliver Ingham, John Pecche, and Robert le Ewer, was sent to
seize and hold the bridge at Bridgnorth. However, on 5 January
Bridgnorth was attacked by the Earl of Hereford and the royal
garrison was driven out and forced to retire to Worcester.[1]

The royal army was therefore forced to take a more cir-
cuitous route from Worcester, which it left on 8 January,
arriving at Shrewsbury on 14 January.[2] It was at this point
that the first break came in the Marchers' ranks, partly through
the influence of Pembroke and the other earls accompanying
the King. On 13 January at Newport in Shropshire a safe conduct until the night of 17 January was issued, at the request of
Pembroke, Norfolk, Kent, Richmond, Arundel, and Warenne,
for Roger Mortimer of Wigmore and twenty of his companions
to come to Betton Lestrange near Shrewsbury to treat with
Pembroke, Richmond, Arundel, and Warenne. Badlesmere was
specifically excluded from this and all subsequent safe conducts,
a fact which underlines the King's hatred of him. At Shrewsbury on 17 January this conduct was renewed until 20 January
for further meetings with Pembroke and the others at Betton,
and was again extended on 21 January until 22 January,[3]
when both the Mortimers came to Shrewsbury and surrendered
to the King.[4] One contemporary considered that their surrender had been brought about by the *mediatio fraudulenta* of
Pembroke and the other earls in the King's company, perhaps
having in mind the fact that the Mortimers were later imprisoned instead of being pardoned as they had been promised.[5]
However, the initiative for surrender talks probably came from
the Mortimers themselves, since early in 1322 the Mortimer-
controlled castles of Welshpool, Chirk, and Clun had all been
captured for the King by a Welsh army led by Sir Gruffydd
Llwyd.[6] At the same time Lancaster failed to send help to the

[1] Bodleian, Laud. MS. Misc. 529, f. 107; Trinity Coll. Cambridge MS. R. 5.
41, ff. 116v., 117.
[2] E. 101/378/13, m. 5.
[3] *C.P.R., 1321–4*, pp. 47–51.
[4] E. 368/92, m. 49; *Cal. of Letter-Books of the City of London: E.*, p. 150.
[5] *Murimuth*, p. 35; *Melsa*, vol. 2, p. 340.
[6] B.M., Cotton MS. Nero D. X, f. 111v. The account in Holinshed's *Chronicles
of England, Scotland and Ireland* (London, 1807–8), vol. 2, p. 565, is derived from
this MS. This material in the form given by Holinshed was used by Sir Goronwy

Marchers as he had promised, his ostensible reason being the presence with the magnates of Badlesmere, whom he refused to aid in any way.[1] Some of the magnates were apparently prepared to attack the royal army at Shrewsbury, but the Mortimers refused to do so because their men were starting to desert.[2] The Mortimers therefore had ample reason for throwing themselves on the King's mercy, and with their departure many others were also ready to surrender.

Hereford himself was prepared to surrender, but was deterred by news of the Mortimers' imprisonment[3] and instead went to Gloucester, whose baronial defenders had captured Worcester on 14 January.[4] On 24 January the royal army left Shrewsbury in pursuit and moved south via Hereford to reach Gloucester on 6 February.[5] Here Maurice de Berkeley and Hugh Audley the Elder both surrendered, and, at the request of Pembroke and others, safe conducts were issued for others who might wish to do the same. Hereford and his few remaining Marcher followers, including Hugh Audley the Younger and Roger Damory, fled to join Lancaster in the north as their last hope of safety.[6]

By early February the King and his allies had therefore totally destroyed all opposition in the Welsh Marches, and the remaining magnates were reduced to a state of desperation. While at Gloucester careful plans were made for the campaign against Lancaster, Hereford, and the remaining contrariants, and also against the Scots, who had invaded the north in January on the expiry of the 1319 truce and might be coming to Lancaster's aid.[7] Orders were given on 14 February to raise troops to join the King at Coventry on 5 March. Now that it was safe to do so, the King also recalled the Despensers from their refuges and told them to raise troops on their way to join him.[8] At the same

---

Edwards in his article on Sir Gruffydd Llwyd in *E.H.R.*, vol. 30 (1915). A royal receiver was formally in control of Chirk from 25 Mar. 1322: N.L.W., Chirk Castle Documents, D. 1.

[1] Trinity Coll. Cambridge MS. R. 5. 41, f. 116*v*.
[2] *Vita*, pp. 118–19; *Melsa*, vol. 2, p. 340.
[3] Trinity Coll. Cambridge MS. R. 5. 41, f. 117.
[4] Bodleian, Laud. MS. Misc. 529, f. 107; B.M., Cotton MS. Nero D. X, f. 111*v*.
[5] E. 101/378/13, mm. 5, 6.
[6] Bodleian, Laud. MS. Misc. 529, f. 107; B.M., Cotton MS. Nero D. X, f. 111*v*.; *Vita*, p. 119; *C.P.R., 1321–4*, p. 70.   [7] *Lanercost*, p. 241; *Bridlington*, p. 73.
[8] *C.P.R., 1321–4*, pp. 73–4; Bodleian, Laud. MS. Misc. 529, f. 107.

time the King contacted his loyal supporter in the north, Andrew Harcla, the commander of Carlisle, to arrange for him to move against Lancaster from that direction and gave him authority to make a truce with the Scots to prevent them from aiding Lancaster. On 8 March Lancaster was given a last chance to avoid the penalties of rebellion when he was formally ordered not to aid the contrariants.[1]

After these plans had been set in motion, the King left Gloucester on 18 February for the muster of his army at Coventry. On 26 February the King accepted the surrender of Lancaster's castle of Kenilworth and arrived in Coventry on 27 February.[2] On 1 March the ground was further cut from under Lancaster by the publication of his treasonable correspondence with the Scots, which had perhaps been found at Kenilworth, and on 3 March the King arrived at Lichfield, where he was met by the Despensers with a large force of troops.[3] When Lancaster and Hereford had heard of the royal advance they left Pontefract. On 1 March they came to Tutbury and took up defensive positions at the river-crossing at Burton-on-Trent.[4] The armies were now confronting one another.

This was the crisis of the campaign. After three days' unsuccessful fighting around the bridge and fords at Burton[5] it was decided to outflank the rebel army. On 10 March Warenne was sent to cross the river by a bridge three miles lower down and Pembroke and Richmond with three hundred men crossed by a ford discovered at Walton, followed by the main body of the army, while Robert le Ewer kept the contrariants busy by an attack on the bridge at Burton itself.[6] At first the contrariants prepared for battle, but then fled to Pontefract, abandoning Lancaster's castle of Tutbury, which the King captured on the same day along with the mortally wounded Roger Damory.[7]

---

[1] *Vita*, p. 120; *C.P.R., 1321–4*, p. 71; *C. Cl. R., 1318–23*, pp. 515–16.

[2] E. 101/378/13, m. 6; Bodleian, Laud MS. Misc. 529, f. 107.

[3] *C. Cl. R., 1318–23*, pp. 525–6; Bodleian, Laud MS. Misc. 529, f. 107.

[4] *Chroniques de Sempringham*, p. 340; *Melsa*, vol. 2, p. 341; B.M., Cotton MS. Nero D. X, f. 112.   [5] *Bridlington*, p. 74; *Vita*, p. 122.

[6] B.M., Cotton MS. Nero D. X, f. 112; Bodleian, Laud MS. Misc. 529, f. 107v.; *Chron. de Sempringham*, p. 340; *Bridlington*, pp. 74–5; *Vita*, p. 122; *The Brut*, vol. 1, p. 216.

[7] *C. Cl. R., 1318–23*, p. 522; B.M., Cotton MS. Nero D. X, f. 112; Bodleian, Laud MS. Misc. 529, f. 107v.; *Vita*, pp. 122–3; *Chron. de Sempringham*, p. 340; *Melsa*, vol. 2, pp. 341–2; *The Brut*, vol. 1, p. 216.

Lancaster's situation was made even worse by the defection of his principal lieutenant, Robert de Holand, who had been negotiating with the King since about 4 March and who attacked in Ravensdale some of Lancaster's men fleeing from Burton before giving himself up to the King.[1] On 11 March the fate of Lancaster, Hereford, and the rest was sealed when, with the advice and consent of Pembroke and five other earls, Kent, Richmond, Arundel, Warenne, and Athol, the King pronounced the leading contrariants to be traitors and appointed Warenne and Kent to take Pontefract.[2]

Meanwhile the contrariants were meeting at Pontefract to decide their next move. Some wanted to go to Lancaster's stronghold at Dunstanburgh in Northumberland, but Lancaster claimed that if they did so it would appear they were seeking Scottish help and refused to leave Pontefract until, under threats from Roger Clifford, he agreed to go with the others to Dunstanburgh.[3] However, they got no further than Boroughbridge where on 16 March they were met by Andrew Harcla's army from Carlisle and were defeated, with the death of Hereford and others.[4] On 17 March Lancaster was captured and taken to York,[5] and on 18 or 19 March the King, accompanied by Pembroke and the Despensers, reached Pontefract itself and received its surrender.[6] All the leading fugitives from the battle were captured, including Badlesmere, whom Donald de Mar, accompanied by one of Pembroke's retainers, Robert fitz Walter, captured a few days later at Stow Park.[7]

On 21 March Lancaster was brought from York to Ponte-

[1] *C.P.R., 1321–4*, p. 77; *C. Cl. R., 1318–23*, p. 525; *The Brut*, vol. 1, p. 216; *Vita*, p. 122; B.M., Cotton MS. Nero D. X f. 112.

[2] *C. Cl. R., 1318–23*, p. 522; *C.P.R., 1321–4*, p. 81.

[3] *The Brut*, vol. 1, p. 302; B.M., Cotton MS. Nero D. X, f. 112.

[4] *Ann. Paul.*, p. 302; *Bridlington*, pp. 75–6; *Melsa*, vol. 2, p. 342; *Flores*, vol. 3, p. 205; *Vita*, pp. 123–4; *The Brut*, vol. 1, p. 218; B.M., Cotton MS. Nero D. X, ff. 112–112v. (this MS. includes the text of Harcla's report on the battle to the King). Hereford planned to go to Hainault if he had escaped from the battle: D.L. 34/25.

[5] *Bridlington*, p. 76; *Flores*, vol. 3, p. 347; G. L. Haskins, 'A Chronicle of the Civil Wars of Edward II', *Speculum*, vol. 14 (1939), p. 78.

[6] E. 101/378/13, m. 7; *Chron. de Sempringham*, p. 342; *The Brut*, vol. 1, p. 221.

[7] B.M., Cotton MS. Nero D. X, f. 112v.; B.M., Cotton MS. Cleopatra C. III, f. 296; *The Brut*, vol. 1, p. 221. Fitz Walter had earlier been retained by the Elder Despenser for six months from 1 Nov. 1317: E. 42/271 (quoted in G. A. Holmes, *The Estates of the Higher Nobility in XIV Century England* (Cambridge, 1957), p. 81, n. 8).

fract for trial in the presence of the King, the Despensers, and
the Earls of Pembroke, Kent, Richmond, Warenne, Arundel,
Athol, and Angus, was judged guilty of treason, and beheaded
on the same day.[1]

At first sight the rapid and total defeat of the large body of
Marcher contrariants and of Lancaster may appear puzzling.
However, as Tout pointed out, their collapse was basically due
to the existence in 1321 and 1322 of two distinct oppositions,
led by Hereford and Lancaster respectively,[2] which never combined fully and suffered the penalty of defeat in detail, Throughout this period Lancaster attempted to exercise over-all control
upon both groups, while at the same time remaining securely at
Pontefract and letting the Marchers do the fighting. Lancaster's
failure to aid the Marchers at the time of the siege of Leeds and
before the King's arrival at Shrewsbury had much to do with
their defeat. His superficial reason for acting in this way was
the presence of his enemy, Badlesmere, with the Marchers, but
his real reasons were probably a reluctance to commit himself,
especially when the Marchers were in danger of defeat, and
a failure to realize the life-and-death nature of the struggle
which began in the autumn of 1321. Lancaster's behaviour was
also influenced by his lack of widespread support in the north
other than by his own immediate retainers. It is very significant
that his final defeat was accomplished by a northern-led army,
and that William de Ros and twenty-five other northerners all
served in the royal army.[3] Even some of his closest retainers,
such as Robert de Holand, Fulk Lestrange, and John de Lilburne, deserted him.[4] The Marchers too suffered from an
infirmity of purpose. Their only chance of success, once the
King had decided to fight, was to risk a battle even if the odds
were high. A battle fought before Leeds or even Shrewsbury
might have brought them victory, but the further they retreated
the fewer their numbers became and the more time the King
had to rally his own forces. By the time they reached Boroughbridge they were both weak and disheartened.

[1] *Bridlington*, p. 76; *Flores*, vol. 3, p. 347; *F.*, vol. 2, pp. 478–9, 493. For a discussion of the legal basis of this trial see M. Keen, 'Treason Trials under the Law
of Arms', *T.R.H.S.*, 5th series, vol. 12 (1962).
[2] Tout, *Place of the Reign* (1936), p. 134.
[3] E. 101/15/37.
[4] C. 53/108, m. 8; B.M., Stowe MS. 553, f. 60 (Wardrobe accounts).

The King's victory was aided by the support of Pembroke and seven other earls, Richmond, Arundel, Warenne, Norfolk, Kent, Athol, and Angus. The presence of the first four of these eight earls is a reminder that even in 1322 opposition to the King and Despenser was by no means unanimous among the senior magnates, however conditional or reluctant their support of the King may have been in practice. The Earls of Norfolk and Kent were the King's half-brothers and were in any case still in their early twenties, while the Earls of Angus and Athol were both exiles from Scotland. These last four earls were therefore of little weight on their own. A far more important factor in the King's success was the vigour with which the campaign was pursued. The Younger Despenser's inspiration was certainly one reason for this, but it is also very likely that, for once, the King made his own contribution through his determination to pursue his enemies to the death without deviation. As has already been pointed out, the latter part of the campaign especially was well planned, and particular emphasis was given to undermining the position of the King's opponents by the judicious use of propaganda. The publication of Lancaster's correspondence with the Scots was a very shrewd move, as also was the Younger Despenser's advice to the King not to unfurl his banners, so as to prevent the King's opponents from claiming that he was waging open war against them.[1]

Pembroke played a leading part in the entire campaign from Leeds to the death of Lancaster and may have had much to do with the detailed planning of its course, although it is impossible to define his share with any precision. Pembroke appears to have been followed in his actions by all his leading retainers, of whom at least ten can be traced from the evidence given in the Boroughbridge Roll, while others such as Aymer la Zouche assisted in raising troops for the King.[2] Pembroke was well rewarded by the King for his part in defeating Lancaster and on 15 March, the day before Boroughbridge, was granted

[1] *Bridlington*, p. 75. See also M. Keen, op. cit., p. 102.
[2] *P.W.*, vol. 2, part 2, Appendix, pp. 196–200; *C.F.R., 1319–27*, p. 108. The men listed in the Roll were not all present at the battle nor were they all the King's opponents. This view is also held by V. Gibbs in 'The Battle of Boroughbridge and the Boroughbridge Roll', *Genealogist*, new series, vol. 21 (1905), but is disputed by N. Denholm-Young in *The Country Gentry in the Fourteenth Century* (Oxford, 1969), p. 76.

Lancaster's valuable honour of Higham Ferrers in Northants., while on 23 March he regained Thorpe Waterville in Northants. and the New Temple in London, which Lancaster had forced him to give up in 1314.[1] Pembroke gained far more than other loyal earls such as Richmond and Arundel, but his gains were insignificant beside the steady stream of grants made from March onwards to both the Despensers, who were undoubtedly the greatest beneficiaries by Lancaster's death in both a material and political sense.

There can be no doubt of the completeness of Pembroke's loyalty to the King in the Boroughbridge campaign or of the King's gratitude, expressed in grants of land, for the part he had played. But the death of Lancaster had also confirmed the power of the Despensers, and they now demanded that Pembroke should suffer humiliation and pay the penalty for his hostility to them in 1321. After the end of the York Parliament in May 1322 Pembroke was arrested by royal knights at the King's orders and taken back to York, but at the suit of some leading magnates he was pardoned, after making a pledge of loyalty on 22 June at Bishopsthorpe near York.[2] In this deed Pembroke witnessed that the King had been 'aggrieved against him for certain reasons that he was given to understand' and that, 'desiring to obtain the King's grace and good will' so that the King might assure himself of him 'as his faithful and loyal liegeman in all points', he had sworn upon the Gospels of his own free will to obey, aid, and counsel the King in all matters, to come to him whenever ordered, to aid him in peace and war, not to ally with anyone against the King or anyone maintained by him, and to repress all alliances against him. For security Pembroke pledged his body and all his lands and goods, and also found mainpernors.[3] This incident is clear proof of the dominance which the Despensers had now attained, and it explains why the last two years of Pembroke's life were little more than an epilogue to his career. Pembroke's personal loyalty to the King had the effect of helping to confirm the

---

[1] *C.P.R., 1321–4*, p. 87; *C. Ch. R., 1300–26*, p. 441.

[2] B.M., Cotton MS. Nero D. X, f. 112v; *C. Cl. R., 1318–23*, pp. 563–4.

[3] *C. Cl. R., 1318–23*, pp. 563–4. This was in effect a repetition by Pembroke and a reminder of the terms of his indenture with Edward II on 1 Nov. 1317. There is no positive evidence that Pembroke actually did pay a fine as stated in B.M., Cotton MS. Nero D. X, f. 112v.

power of the Despensers and from now on, regardless of any misgivings he may have had, he could only follow the King along the path marked out by them.

The period immediately after Boroughbridge saw the detailed completion of the victory of the King and the Despensers at the York Parliament, which began on 2 May, during which the Ordinances were formally revoked, the processes against the Despensers annulled, and that against Lancaster confirmed.[1]

After the York Parliament the King and his supporters were able to turn their attention to the King's remaining enemies, the Scots. As early as 25 March a muster had been ordered at Newcastle for 13 June, and shortly before 31 March the King had written to Pembroke asking for his advice on a Scottish campaign.[2] On 11 May the start of the campaign was finally set for 24 July. The English army contained contingents from all the leading magnates, the Earls of Pembroke, Arundel, Louth, Norfolk, Kent, Carlisle, Warenne, Richmond, Winchester, Athol, and Angus, the Younger Despenser, and also from Henry of Lancaster,[3] who had been abroad in France during the crisis of 1321 and 1322 and had taken no part in his brother's rebellion.[4] Pembroke's own contingent to the army amounted at its biggest to 108 men-at-arms, including three bannerets and twenty-five knights.[5]

Bruce had forestalled the English attack and had entered England on 17 June near Carlisle, advancing eighty miles before withdrawing into Scotland on 24 July.[6] This Scottish freedom of action bode ill for the English army which invaded Scotland on 12 August in the hope of bringing Bruce to battle. Instead Bruce withdrew northwards, taking with him or destroying all the food supplies that the English would be relying on

[1] *C. Cl. R., 1318–23*, pp. 544–6; *C.P.R., 1321–4*, p. 115. There is no space to go into a lengthy discussion of the arguments on the significance of the Statute of York which annulled the Ordinances in 1322. The view which takes greatest note of the political realities of the time is that of M. McKisack, op. cit., p. 72, n. 2, where the Statute is represented as being intended to turn the clock back politically to the time before the appointment of the Ordainers in 1310. See also D. Clementi, 'That the Statute of York is No Longer Ambiguous', *Album Helen Maud Cam* (Louvain and Paris, 1961), vol. 2.

[2] *C. Cl. R., 1318–23*, p. 532; *C. Ch. Warr.*, p. 528.

[3] *P.W.*, vol. 2, part 1, p. 296; B.M., Stowe MS. 553, ff. 56–62.

[4] *C.P.R., 1321–4*, p. 69.

[5] B.M., Stowe MS. 553, f. 56.

[6] *Lanercost*, p. 246.

to continue their attack, and after reaching Edinburgh the English were forced to retreat through lack of supplies and withdrew into England in early September via Melrose and Dryburgh. Bruce followed behind the retreating army and on about 30 September entered England, reaching Northallerton in Yorkshire on about 12 October, only fifteen miles from Ryvaulx where Edward II was staying.[1] On 13 October the King wrote to Pembroke from Ryvaulx to tell him of the proximity of the Scots and asked him to come to Byland on 14 October with all the men he could muster. At Byland he would find the Earl of Richmond and Henry de Beaumont, to whom the King had already explained his intentions, and he was to make all the necessary plans with them.[2] Pembroke and Richmond fully carried out their orders and on 14 October stationed their men on the summit of Blackhowmoor near Byland. In the rout which followed they were defeated and Richmond and a French knight, Henry de Sully, were captured.[3] There is no record of what happened to Pembroke, but he is likely to have been with John Darcy, one of his retainers, who was among those who fled from the battle to York.[4] Thus the year which had begun with a royal triumph ended in humiliation at the hands of the Scots, who were as dangerous as ever. On 27 November it was therefore decided that the King and the leading magnates should remain in the north through the winter, and on 2 December a fresh muster was ordered at York for 2 February 1323.[5]

The disarray into which royal policy had been put by the success of the Scots is clearly marked by the truce which Andrew Harcla, the Earl of Carlisle, concluded on his own initiative with Bruce at Lochmaben on 3 January 1323, probably in the hope that the King might be induced to approve it.[6] The King's reaction was to denounce the agreement as

---

[1] *Fordun*, vol. 1, pp. 349–50; *The Bruce*, vol. 2, p. 451; *Lanercost*, p. 247; Barrow, *Robert Bruce*, p. 345; S.C. 1/49/52.   [2] S.C. 1/49/52.

[3] *Melsa*, vol. 2, pp. 345–6; *Lanercost*, p. 247; *The Bruce*, vol. 2, pp. 455–60; *Flores*, vol. 3, p. 210; B.M., Stowe MS. 553, ff. 68v., 69. The news of the battle caused great alarm when it reached London on 28 Oct.: S.C. 1/63/169.

[4] *Chron. de Sempringham*, p. 345.

[5] *C. Cl. R., 1318–23*, pp. 687, 690.

[6] *Lanercost*, p. 248; *C. Cl. R., 1318–23*, p. 692. The text of the treaty is in E. 159/96, m. 70 and is printed by E. L. G. Stones in *Anglo-Scottish Relations, 1174–1328* (London, 1965). See also the discussion in Barrow, op. cit., pp. 351–3.

treason and on 25 February Harcla was captured at Carlisle by Anthony de Lucy. Pembroke's nephew, the Earl of Athol, and his retainer, John Darcy, were among those appointed to receive the surrender of Harcla's adherents and another nephew, John Hastings, was one of the justices who tried Harcla on 3 March.[1]

Pembroke himself appears to have been with the King early in 1323.[2] There are signs that the King was still seeking his advice, since on 12 February he sent him letters from the burgesses of Ravensrod with instructions to consult with others of the Council and answer their complaints.[3] Several of Pembroke's associates were the recipients of royal favours. On 23 January John Hastings was given custody of Kenilworth castle until Easter; on 10 February John Darcy was appointed to the important defensive post of Sheriff of Lancaster, with a force of forty men-at-arms and twenty hobelars, and in November was made Justice of Ireland; on 9 March Ralph de Lepingdon, who may have been one of Pembroke's clerks, was made a clerk of the Great Seal at his request.[4]

Pembroke's major duty in 1323 was to take part in the negotiations with the Scots, which were to remove their danger for the remainder of the reign. The first steps in dealing with the Scots had been taken early in February, even before Harcla's arrest and execution, when some of the retainers of Henry de Sully who had been captured with him at Byland came to the King as intermediaries. As a result a temporary truce until 22 May was made on 14 March, and on 1 April, following an appeal from Robert Bruce to Sully, three Scots envoys were given safe conducts until 5 May to come to Newcastle. On the same date Sully was asked to prolong the truce after 22 May and English envoys were appointed to meet the Scots, but soon after all the orders issued on 1 April were cancelled, perhaps to give more time to prepare for the talks. On 29 April the truce was prolonged to 2 June, and on 30 April the Younger Despenser's son Hugh, John Hastings, and two

[1] B.M., Stowe MS. 553, f. 18v.; *Lanercost*, pp. 250–1; *C.P.R., 1321–4*, pp. 240, 260; *F.*, vol. 2, p. 509.
[2] *Cat. Anc. Deeds*, vol. 1, p. 162 and vol. 3, p. 116; C. 53/109, mm. 4, 5.
[3] S.C. 1/45/207.
[4] *C.P.R., 1321–4*, pp. 240, 348; E. 101/68/2/42A; B.M., Stowe MS. 553, f. 56v.; *C.F.R., 1319–27*, p. 193; *C. Ch. Warr.*, p. 537.

others were sent from Newark to stay at Tweedmouth as hostages while the Scots envoys, the Bishop of St. Andrews and the Earl of Moray, came to Newcastle and York to discuss a longer truce.[1]

Pembroke himself probably took little direct part in these early moves, except perhaps as an adviser, and in early April he was probably at Westminster with the King, while on 24 April he was at his manor of Winfarthing in Norfolk with eleven of his retainers.[2] He was back at York by 1 May, when, with the Bishop of Exeter, the Younger Despenser, and Robert Baldock, he was given authority to make a final peace treaty with the Scots. Pembroke, his retainer John Darcy, and his other colleagues met the Scottish envoys at Newcastle early in May.[3] The negotiations may not have gone well at first, most probably because a final settlement proved impossible and only a long truce was feasible.[4] On 11 May the King wrote to Pembroke to say that the truce had been extended until 12 June, but at the same time told him to be ready to answer the military summons to Newcastle if the talks broke down and indulged in a tirade against the Scots.[5] However, at the end of May Pembroke and his colleagues reached agreement with the Scots on a thirteen-year truce, after which they and the Scots envoys came to Bishopsthorpe near York, where on 30 May the truce was confirmed by the King and the Council.[6]

There is little further trace of Pembroke's movements until near the end of the year. He spent some time in visiting his lands in Wales, for on 17 October he and his wife were at Tenby in Pembrokeshire.[7] By 10 December he was back in London,[8] perhaps in connection with the session of pleas of

---

[1] *C.P.R., 1321–4*, pp. 236, 268, 277–9, 281; *F.*, vol. 2, p. 511; B.M., Stowe MS. 553, f. 27.

[2] *Ann. Paul.*, p. 503; C. 53/109, m. 4; *C. Cl. R., 1318–23*, p. 705; *C.P.R., 1374–7*, pp. 114–15.

[3] *C.P.R., 1321–4*, p. 279; E. 159/96, m. 27d.; *Lanercost*, p. 252; *Bridlington*, p. 84.

[4] *C.P.R., 1321–4*, p. 279; *F.*, vol. 2, p. 521.

[5] S.C. 1/49/53. A summons to Newcastle had been issued on 23 Feb.: *P.W.*, vol. 2, part 1, p. 346.

[6] *C.P.R., 1321–4*, p. 292; *C. Cl. R., 1318–23*, p. 717; *Placitorum Abbrevatio*, p. 342. C. 49/45/13 is a list of those present and is printed in Davies, *Baronial Opposition*, Appendix 94.

[7] N.L.W., Haverfordwest Deeds, nos. 930, 1246. They were also at Lowel in Pembrokeshire on 20 Oct. 1323: Cardiff Central Public Library, Pembrokeshire Deeds, no. 13.   [8] N.L.W., Slebech Papers and Docs., no. 11438.

the Essex forest which were to be heard at Stratford-atte-Bow on 20 January 1324 before himself, William de Cleydon, his retainer and lieutenant as Justice of the Forest, and William la Zouche of Ashby. The pleas took place as planned on 20 January, and on 27 February the Queen nominated Pembroke and his colleagues, with her steward Henry Beaufuiz, to hear the pleas of her forest of Havering in Essex.[1]

The last months of Pembroke's life were taken up by the diplomatic moves resulting from the crisis with France caused by the destruction of the French bastide of Saint-Sardos.[2] This dangerous situation was further complicated by news of the activities in France of Roger Mortimer of Wigmore, who had escaped from the Tower of London in August 1323,[3] and during the Parliament held at Westminster in February it was decided to send envoys to try to settle the Saint-Sardos dispute and post-pone Charles IV's demand for homage for Aquitaine.[4] On 29 March the King sent to Pembroke copies of letters from John Count of Luxemburg and King of Bohemia, which may well have related to the Anglo-French disputes, and asked him to come and give his advice on the following day. Pembroke was accordingly present and concerned in the appointment on 30 March of the Archbishop of Dublin and Earl of Kent to make an inquiry into the affair of Saint-Sardos.[5] Pembroke was peculiarly well fitted by his earlier experience to advise on these diplomatic problems. The major role he played in them is emphasized in a letter to the Queen from an unknown person, in which the writer advised her on the instructions to be given to a French knight returning to Charles IV on business con-nected with Saint-Sardos, saying that first of all Pembroke and Despenser, 'les plus privetz le Roi', should assemble the Council to deal with the matter.[6]

---

[1] *C. Cl. R., 1323–7*, p. 146; *C.P.R., 1321–4*, pp. 351, 389; E. 403/202, m. 9; Hist. MSS. Comm., *7th Report*, p. 582; Cambridge Univ. MS. Ff. 2. 33, f. 88; S.C. 1/36/34.

[2] The Seneschal of Gascony informed the King of this on 4 Nov. 1323: B.M., Cotton Ch. XVI. 59.

[3] *C. Ch. Warr.*, p. 548; E. L. G. Stones, 'The Date of Roger Mortimer's Escape from the Tower', *E.H.R.*, vol. 61 (1951).

[4] *Blaneford*, p. 140; *F.*, vol. 2, pp. 545–6.

[5] S.C. 1/49/55; *F.*, vol. 2, pp. 547–8.

[6] S.C. 1/60/126. Printed in *The War of St. Sardos*, ed. P. Chaplais, Camden 3rd series, vol. 87 (London, 1954), p. 42.

On 19 April the King wrote to Pembroke asking him to come to London on 6 May to discuss royal business with others of the Council, relations with France being probably high on the agenda. On 9 May another Council was called to meet at Westminster on 27 May,[1] and it was presumably on this occasion that Pembroke was appointed to go to the French court to negotiate on the problems over Gascony and the question of homage.[2] Pembroke's departure for France was announced on 7 June, on 8 June protections were issued for seventeen of his men who were to accompany him, and he probably left London shortly before 13 June.[3]

Pembroke, however, did not reach his destination. We are told dramatically that on 23 June he got up after dining, collapsed in the doorway, and died unconfessed in the arms of his servants.[4] The cause of his death is unknown, but there is little doubt that it was both sudden and natural,[5] and the remark (of a writer hostile to him for his part in Lancaster's death) that he was 'mordred sodeynly on a privy sege'[6] must be treated figuratively. News of his death was already known on 26 June to the King at Tonbridge in Kent, and on 27 June the King sent his confessor, Robert de Duffeld, to the Countess of Pembroke at Hertford, perhaps in order to break the news to her.[7] Pembroke's body was brought back to London on 31 July and was buried in Westminster Abbey near the high altar on 1 August.[8] On 29 October his will was proved by his executors, his widow and William de Cleydon, before the Hustings court in the city of London.[9]

[1] S.C. 1/49/56; *C. Cl. R., 1323–7*, p. 184.

[2] His commission has not survived but a general idea of it is given in *Ann. Paul.*, p. 307; *Chron. de Sempringham*, p. 350; *Melsa*, vol. 2, p. 348; *Blaneford*, p. 150; *C.P.R., 1321–4*, pp. 440–2.

[3] *C.P.R., 1321–4*, p. 427; C. 81/1750/2; E. 101/379/19, f. 13*v*.

[4] *Flores*, vol. 3, p. 222; *Blaneford*, p. 150.

[5] *Ann. Paul.*, p. 307; *Chron. de Sempringham*, p. 350. The suggested cause of his death is apoplexy but this can only be a guess: H. Jenkinson, *Archaeologia*, vol. 66 (1915), p. 406; *G.E.C.*, vol. 10, p. 387.

[6] *The Brut*, vol. 1, p. 252. This is a translation of the French Brut which says he was 'moerdriz sodeynement': B.M., Royal MS. 20. A. III, f. 216*v*.

[7] *C.F.R., 1319–27*, p. 287; E. 101/379/19, f. 15*v*.

[8] *Ann. Paul.*, p. 307; C. 81/1329/6925. Pembroke's widow requested the Council to decide where he should be buried and they settled on Westminster.

[9] *Cal. of Wills Proved in the Court of Husting*, part 1, p. 310 (Hustings Roll 53, no. 29). This contains only the part of the will relating to property in London. The full text of the will has not been found.

The date of Pembroke's death is known with certainty, but it is much harder to determine the exact place of his death, since the sources all give different accounts, saying respectively that he died near Paris, at Boulogne, 'in quadam villula sua' near Saint-Riquier, and at Miville, 'dimidia villa', three leagues from Compiègne in Picardy.[1] It is unlikely that Pembroke had time to get near Paris, and the first location may therefore be ruled out. Superficially the last of these descriptions seems the most reliable, and Miville could be taken to refer to either Moyvillers or Moyenneville, both near Compiègne. But Compiègne was not on Pembroke's likely route to Paris, and the author could have added Miville's distance from the town on the basis of personal knowledge. If the reference to Compiègne is left out, it is possible to reconcile the rest of the accounts fairly closely. Saint-Riquier was on the normal route from the coast to Paris and is close to Boulogne, through which a traveller would also pass. In addition there is a Moyenneville near Saint-Riquier which might easily be rendered as Miville, and in the same district is Tours-en-Vimeu, which was one of the Countess of Pembroke's French lands and could be described in reference to Pembroke as 'quadam villula sua'. While no precise answer is possible, it does seem likely that Pembroke died somewhere close to Saint-Riquier, a location which also tallies with the short period of three days which elapsed before his death was known in England.

Pembroke's widow received her dower fairly rapidly after his death, assignments in England, Wales, and Ireland, being made on 24 November and 3 December 1324, and on 1 March 1325.[2] These assignments totalled about £750, or roughly one third of the extended value of his lands, but £70 of this was in Ireland, where the effects of war had probably reduced the value of Pembroke's lands, and another £70 took the form of reversions and was therefore not immediately available to her.[3]

However, Pembroke's widow and his coheirs[4] were to suffer a good deal of harassment both over his lands and goods and over his alleged debts to the King. The source of much of these

[1] *Ann. Paul.*, p. 307; *Melsa*, vol. 2, p. 348; *Blaneford*, p. 150; *Flores*, vol. 3, p. 222.
[2] *C. Cl. R., 1323–7*, pp. 244, 362–4, 371.
[3] Ibid., pp. 362–4; C. 134/85/135.
[4] His coheirs were John Hastings and Joan and Elizabeth Comyn, the children of his sisters Isabel and Joan.

troubles was the Younger Despenser, and it is likely that to some extent he was picking on Pembroke's family for such treatment because of Pembroke's encouragement of his exile in 1321. However, until a full study is made of Despenser's activities it is difficult to say whether he treated them any more harshly than he did others.

Some time after Pembroke's death his widow complained to the King that Despenser would not allow the escheator to return an inquest on his lands at Hertford and Haverford because he wanted them for himself, and that Robert Baldock would not let her have dower in either of these places or in Pembroke's lands in Monmouth unless she produced the original royal charters.[1] In the latter case Despenser got what he wanted, when in July 1325 the King granted him Little Monmouth and its dependencies.[2] In August 1324 Pembroke's nephew, John Hastings, made a recognizance of £4,000 to Despenser. The purpose is unknown, but the fact that in 1328 Hastings's executors complained that Despenser had stolen goods worth £773 while he had custody of the Hastings lands does not suggest that his purposes in 1324 were likely to be worthy ones.[3] Elizabeth Comyn, another of Pembroke's heirs, was imprisoned by the Despensers until on 8 March 1325 she made obligations of £10,000 to each of them and then released to them her rights to the former Pembroke lands at Goodrich and Painswick.[4] In similar fashion she was made to give them Swanscombe in Kent.[5] In 1325 Pembroke's widow was induced to give up her rights in Grantham and Stamford to the King, who then restored them to Warenne, their original holder. Early in Edward III's reign, partly perhaps as a penalty for her husband's close relations with the former King, she also

[1] S.C. 8/294/14690–2; ibid. /277/13819.

[2] *C. Ch. R., 1300–26*, p. 478.

[3] *C. Cl. R., 1323–7*, p. 309; E. 163/3/6, m. 1; S.C. 8/51/2507–8; E. 159/104, m. 129. Despenser also received custody of Laurence Hastings's share of Pembroke's lands, which included Pembroke in Wales and Wexford in Ireland: *C. Cl. R., 1323–7*, pp. 288, 395.

[4] *C. Cl. R., 1323–7*, p. 357; E. 163/3/6, mm. 1, 2; S.C. 8/163/8132; ibid. /310/ 15484; B.M., Harleian Ch. 48. G. 39; E. 101/332/2; *Cal. of Miscellaneous Inquisitions, 1219–1349* (London, 1916), vol. 2, no. 1024; *Cal. of Bodleian Charters and Rolls* (Oxford, 1878), p. 674.

[5] S.C. 8/160/7956; *Cat. Anc. Deeds*, vol. 3, p. 125; *C. Ch. R., 1300–26*, p. 478. For other similar cases see G. A. Holmes, 'A Protest against the Despensers, 1326', *Speculum*, vol. 30 (1955).

gave up to the Crown Hertford, Haverford, Higham Ferrers, and Little Monmouth, which together were worth over £400, for lands worth £200.[1]

The proceedings after Pembroke's death over his movable goods and debts to the King also show a picture of harassment, in which the Younger Despenser was again concerned. In October 1322 Pembroke had been ordered to appear at the Exchequer to account for all his debts to the King, and the following April the Treasurer was told to compile a record of all sums received by Pembroke from the King.[2] In July 1324 the Treasurer was informed that John Hastings and Pembroke's other heirs had offered to purchase the Earl's movable goods in royal hands as a means of settling his debts, but this method was not in fact employed, and on 29 August Pembroke's executors mainprised for his debts, promising to make a valuation of his goods, after which the King could keep the items he wanted and offset their value against the total debts.[3] This procedure was apparently followed, and on 18 March 1325 Pembroke's goods were ordered to be restored to his executors, except for the corn stores on his manors, which were to be sent to Gascony, and his horses and jewels, which his executors had granted to the King. On 20 August 1325 Pembroke's widow released to the King all his corn, horses, armour, silver vessels, jewels, and other goods in royal hands and pardoned the King all his own debts to Pembroke at his death. In return, on 30 August Pembroke's widow and executors were pardoned all his debts to the Exchequer and Wardrobe, except those for which he was bound to the King by surety, mainprise, and recognition.[4]

On the surface this might appear a reasonable, if rather crude, means of settling the outstanding debts between the King and Pembroke and vice versa. But closer examination shows that the King would be allowed to keep practically all of Pembroke's property and evade payment of his debts to Pembroke,

---

[1] *C. Cl. R.*, *1323–7*, pp. 412, 479; ibid., *1327–30*, p. 109; *C.P.R.*, *1327–30*, p. 37. Pembroke's lack of a direct heir would also provide an excuse for these lands to revert to the Crown.

[2] E. 368/93, m. 52; E. 159/96, m. 33. Such a detailed record, if compiled, would have been extremely valuable, but there is no trace of it.

[3] E. 159/97, m. 92d.; *C.F.R.*, *1319–27*, p. 298.

[4] *C. Cl. R.*, *1323–7*, pp. 271, 412, 505; *C.P.R.*, *1324–7*, p. 165.

the amount of which was not stated in the transaction, while Pembroke's heirs could still be held liable for certain alleged debts to the King. Some idea of the losses to Pembroke's estate and the pressure and deception that had been practised on his heirs and executors emerges from his widow's later petition to Edward III for compensation. In this she claimed that, at Despenser's instigation, Edward II had seized all Pembroke's goods and debts owing to him, totalling in all over £20,000, and retained them until Pembroke's executors had given them to the Crown in return for a pardon for the receipts from the Wardrobe, which Pembroke had spent on wars, embassies, royal debts, and other expenses in the service of both Edward I and II. She claimed that if Pembroke had accounted for all this money in his lifetime, the King would have been found to owe him far more than he had actually received. Even, she added, when the remainder of his goods had been restored to his executors, there was not enough left to pay Pembroke's private debts or to settle even one tenth of the sums demanded from him.[1]

Allowing for some exaggeration in the total sum involved, there is no reason to disbelieve this account. As early as July 1324, for example, Pembroke's widow had had to sell to the Younger Despenser all her husband's cattle and livestock for 1,000 marks, a sum probably far below their true value, to obtain money for her husband's funeral expenses. The grain taken from Pembroke's lands was valued at over £1,100,[2] and when his armour, jewels, etc., are added to these items, it is hard to see what was left for his executors. Again, there is little doubt that the King owed Pembroke considerable sums, despite many records of payments of wages and expenses to him during the reign. It was not, for instance, until 1319 that Pembroke accounted for nearly £2,000 expenses dating from 1307 and 1309 and another sum of over £2,000, dating from 1307, was not paid to him until 1321.[3] Even Pembroke's fee of only £100 a year as Justice of the Forest was often in arrears or was sometimes paid to him by unusual means.[4] In addition to these real

[1] S.C. 8/66/3265.
[2] E. 159/97, mm. 90, 91; C. 81/1329/6925; C. 47/88/4/87.
[3] E. 101/373/23; E. 404/1/8; E. 403/202, m. 6.
[4] S.C. 8/296/14771; E. 403/202, m. 9; *C. Cl. R., 1323–7*, p. 235.

or supposed debts to the King, there is little doubt that in the last years of his life Pembroke was in constant financial difficulties, largely as an aftermath of his ransom in 1317. This may partly explain why, for example, his widow was ready in 1329 to give up Thorpe Waterville to the widow of Robert de Holand, who had been claiming it since 1324, in return for £1,000. In spite of all the Countess's efforts, some of Pembroke's debts were still unpaid when she died in 1377.[1]

For the moment any general assessment of Pembroke and his career can be left for the conclusion to this book and comment need only be made about his activities between 1321 and his death in 1324. In the autumn of 1321 and early in 1322 Pembroke had played an important part in the campaign to destroy the opponents of the Despensers and had been rewarded for it by the King. In doing so Pembroke was in effect betraying his own sympathies with Hereford and the other Marchers in the spring and summer of 1321, and by helping to ensure the survival and success of a dangerous royal favourite, Hugh Despenser the Younger, he had abandoned the moderation on which he had based his career. Pembroke's actions were, however, those of a man without any choice, except perhaps that of voluntary exile on his French lands.

The irony of Pembroke's role in defeating the magnate contrariants in 1322 was that as soon as the Despensers had regained control they were likely to try to humiliate him, because of his earlier hostility to them and his share in securing their exile in 1321. This is what they finally did in 1322, when Pembroke had to pledge his loyalty to the King. After 1322 the strings of power lay entirely in the hands of the Younger Despenser, whose influence pervaded the whole of the royal administration and who was able to manipulate the King in whatever direction he wished him to go. Pembroke remained a member of the circle of close royal associates, as the description of him in 1324 as one of 'les plus privetz le Roi'[2] would suggest. But the Younger Despenser's treatment of Pembroke's widow and heirs after his death shows how easily Edward II could forget what he

---

[1] *C. Cl. R., 1323–7*, p. 206; ibid., *1327–30*, pp. 281, 581; *C.P.R., 1327–30*, p. 455; C. 47/71/8/364; S.C. 1/38/203; *Cal. of Wills Proved in the Court of Husting*, part 2, vol. 1, pp. 194–6 and H. Jenkinson, *Archaeologia*, vol. 66 (1915), pp. 432–5.
[2] S.C. 1/60/126.

owed Pembroke for his years of loyal service. It remained for Pembroke's widow to remind the King of her husband's loyalty and friendship and later to complain about the money and energy he had expended in his service.[1]

Between 1321 and 1324 Pembroke remained very active in royal affairs, notably in the diplomacy for which his experience best suited him. Some of his retainers, especially John Darcy and his nephew John Hastings, were also prominent, probably through their connection with him and perhaps also as replacements for the many rebels of 1321 and 1322. Pembroke's experience and personal loyalty to the King continued to make him a useful member of the royal Council, but he now possessed only responsibility and lacked either power or influence. It was entirely appropriate that he died in France on yet another diplomatic mission. He was also fortunate that he did not live to see the final disaster of 1326, which he could have done nothing to prevent and which would certainly have destroyed him as well as the Despensers, unless he too had already fled from the tyranny of the Despensers and a hopeless King.

[1] In 1324 the Countess of Pembroke wished to leave the decision about her husband's burial to the advice of Edward II 'a qi il [Pembroke] fust si procheyn et vous ad servi si cum vous savetz': C. 81/1329/6925 (letter to Edward II, 23–30 June 1324). Later in a petition to Edward III she complained that her husband had been owed large sums by Edward I and Edward II 'qar il despendi tut le soen en les services les Rois susditz': S.C. 8/66/3265–6.

VIII

The Lands of the Earldom of Pembroke

BECAUSE of the lack of material it is not possible to make any very detailed study of the lands held by the Earl of Pembroke, other than to indicate where they were located[1] and to give some general idea of their value. Most of the information that is available relates to his English and Welsh lands; little is known about his Irish lordship of Wexford,[2] and even less about his hereditary lands in France.

Between 1296 and 1307, the years of the widowhood of Joan de Valence the Countess of Pembroke, Aymer de Valence was in possession of only a part of the lands held by his parents during their lifetime. He inherited his father's lands in France on William de Valence's death in 1296 and was styled lord of Montignac from then on, continuing to use the title after he became Earl of Pembroke in 1307. However, many of the lands in England, Wales, and Ireland remained outside his control. The palatine lands of the earldom in Pembroke and Wexford and the other lands of Joan de Valence's own inheritance stayed in her hands until she died in 1307, and she also had possession of one third of her husband's lands as her dower.[3] The remaining two-thirds went to Aymer, together with lands worth £200 which he was assigned by his mother from her dower in 1297.[4] Aymer de Valence's only other territory at this period consisted of Bothwell and Selkirk in Scotland, granted to him by Edward

[1] See the outline maps at the end of this book. See also the lists of officials in Appendix 1.

[2] One of the few documents relating to Wexford is a petition of 1303 from Adam de la Roche, Steward of Wexford (printed as Waterford), to Joan de Valence: E. 101/505/29 (printed in H. G. Richardson and G. O. Sayles, *The Administration of Ireland, 1172–1377* (Dublin, 1963), pp. 233–6).

[3] Details of the nine manors which made up Joan's dower are given in *C. Cl. R., 1296–1302*, p. 3.

[4] *C.P.R., 1292–1301*, p. 289. Documents of 1297, 1299, and 1304 show that Aymer held the manors of Bampton in Oxfordshire, Beenham in Berkshire, Gainsborough in Lincolnshire, Kentwell in Suffolk, and Dunham in Nottinghamshire, which had all been part of his father's personal lands: S.C. 8/77/3817; ibid. /325/E. 709; S.C. 1/31/210; *Cal. I.P.M.*, vol. 3, no. 362.

I,[1] but his practical hold over these was probably very short-lived.

Study of the lands forming Aymer de Valence's earldom reveals that they bore little relation to those held by the Marshal Earls of Pembroke. The only lands held continuously by the Marshals and by William and Aymer de Valence were those forming Joan de Munchensy's purparty in 1247, that is: the lordship of Pembroke and its members, the county of Wexford in Ireland, Goodrich in Herefordshire, Inkberrow in Worcestershire, and Brabourne, Sutton, and Kemsing in Kent.[2] Apart from this basis, Aymer's lands were derived from lands acquired in his father's lifetime and from the inheritances of his sister, Agnes de Valence, and his cousin, Denise de Vere.

William de Valence's land acquisitions mainly represented a series of royal grants early in his English career made in fulfilment of Henry III's promise in 1247 to give him lands worth £500.[3] These grants were made as and when lands came into royal hands and consequently were scattered over a wide area of England and Wales. In this fashion William de Valence acquired the manors of Saxthorpe and Stiffkey in Norfolk,[4] Bampton in Oxfordshire,[5] Swindon in Wiltshire, Newton in Hampshire, Compton in Dorset, Moreton and Whaddon in Gloucestershire,[6] Gainsborough in Lincolnshire, Dunham in Nottinghamshire,[7] Collingbourne in Wiltshire,[8] Beenham in Berkshire, Kentwell,[9] Ridlington, and Exning in Suffolk,[10] Pollicott and Chearsley in Buckingham, Postwick, Filby, and Lexham in Norfolk, Reydon in Suffolk,[11] and the commote of Ystlwyf in Carmarthenshire.[12] In addition William also purchased from Roger Bertram the vills of Molesdon, Calverdon, and Little Eland in about 1262 and the manor of Great Eland

---

[1] Bain, vol. 2, p. 308; *C. Ch. R., 1300–26*, pp. 69–70.
[2] *C.P.R., 1364 7*, pp. 263 75 (enrolment of partition).
[3] Ibid., *1232–47*, p. 508.
[4] *C. Ch. R., 1226–57*, p. 329 (1248): late of Rob. de Wendevall.
[5] Ibid., p. 339 (1249).
[6] Ibid., pp. 339 (1249), 402 (1252): late of Rob. Pontdelarche.
[7] Ibid., *1257–1300*, pp. 1–2 (1257).
[8] Ibid., *1226–57*, p. 416 (1253): late of Avice de Columbariis.
[9] Ibid., pp. 352, 365 (1251).
[10] Ibid., *1257–1300*, p. 8 (1258). These manors had apparently been granted to him earlier than 1258.
[11] Ibid., p. 92 (1268): late of Steph. de Cressy.
[12] Ibid., p. 427 (1292).

in 1269,[1] which all formed part of the Mitford barony in Northumberland. Aymer de Valence had controlled part of his father's lands since the latter's death in 1296, and when his mother died in 1307 he inherited the portion of them that had formed her dower, together with her purparty of the Marshal lands and the title of Earl of Pembroke.[2]

The third component of Aymer's lands came when his sister Agnes died in 1309, leaving him Dagenham in Essex, Great Shelford in Cambridge, and Hertfordingbury in Hertfordshire.[3] The death of Denise de Vere in 1313 completed Pembroke's inheritance by bringing him Hanningfield, Stanford, Vange, Great Fordham, Thorrington, and Great Braxted in Essex, Great Anstey, Little Hormead, and Meesden in Hertford, Donnington in Buckingham, Nutfield in Surrey, Towcester in Northampton, Swanscombe, Hartley, Melton, Luddesdown, and Wickham in Kent, Painswick in Gloucestershire, and Gooderstone, Holkham, Hockham, Burgh, Kerbrook, Foxley, Sutton, and Winfarthing in Norfolk.[4]

These inherited lands were supplemented by Pembroke's acquisition during Edward II's reign of Haverford in 1308, Hertford in 1309, the New Temple in 1312,[5] Thorpe Waterville in 1313, Little Monmouth in 1314, Mitford in 1315,[6] Castle Acre in 1316, Stamford and Grantham in 1317, Higham Ferrers in 1322, and by the recovery, also in 1322, of the New Temple and Thorpe Waterville.[7]

The accompanying tables show how widely Pembroke's lands were distributed, there being scarcely a county in southern and eastern England where they were unrepresented. The tables also show that in terms of value the core of the earldom lay in eastern England, in the fourteen Norfolk manors and the four in Suffolk, and also in the counties around London, in Kent with eleven manors, Essex with ten, Hertfordshire with five, and in Buckinghamshire, Berkshire, and Oxfordshire. These were

---

[1] *Cat. Anc. Deeds*, vol. 4, p. 99, and vol. 3, p. 103.
[2] *Cal. I.P.M.*, vol. 5, no. 56.
[3] Ibid., no. 203.
[4] Ibid., no. 475.
[5] *C.P.R., 1307–13*, pp. 145, 153; *C. Ch. R., 1300–26*, p. 203.
[6] *C. Cl. R., 1313–18*, pp. 80–1; *C. Ch. R., 1300–26*, p. 242; *Cat. Anc. Deeds*, vol. 3, A. 4767.
[7] *C.P.R., 1313–17*, p. 607; ibid., *1317–21*, pp. 40, 48; ibid., *1321–4*, pp. 87–8; *C. Ch. R., 1300–26*, p. 441.

linked by his lands in Wiltshire, Hampshire, and Dorset to the important block of lands in Gloucestershire and in Hereford, where he had the border castle of Goodrich. In the north of England Pembroke possessed only insignificant holdings in Yorkshire and the outlying lordship of Mitford in Northumberland. In terms of value the English lands accounted for about two thirds of the extended value of the earldom in 1324, or £1,542. 15s. 7d. The palatine lands of the earldom, that is Pembroke and its immediate dependencies, accounted for only £239. 1s. 2d. or a little over ten per cent of the total, but, with the addition of Haverford and other lands, Wales made a useful contribution of £383. 9s. 4d. to the earldom's value.

The total extended value of the earldom in 1324 came to £2,263. 4s. 7d., but to this figure must be added the values of lands which Pembroke held at his death, but for which there are no extents, since in most cases they were not held as permanent parts of the earldom.[1] These lands can be valued only approximately, but their inclusion would probably bring the earldom's 1324 face value to over £3,000. Against these figures, however, allowance should be made for the effects of war damage, which had probably reduced the Irish lands, like those in Northumberland, to well below their extended valuation. At the same time it is likely that many of the other extents understate rather than exaggerate the lands' true value.[2] With these qualifications, and bearing in mind that no estimate can be made of the value of Pembroke's French lands, the figure of £3,000 does give us a general idea of the earldom's value. Pembroke could not compare in landed wealth with either Thomas of Lancaster, whose revenue in 1313–14 was £6,661. 17s. 11d., or Gilbert de Clare, whose lands were extended in 1317 at £6,532. 5s. 7¾d.,[3] but in comparison with the majority of magnates he would certainly have ranked very high, his likely peers in wealth being men like Hereford, Arundel, or Warenne.

---

[1] For an explanation of their loss to the earldom after 1324 see Chapter VII.

[2] For example, 11 manors and tenements extended at £179. 0s. 6d. in 1324 yielded an actual revenue of £205. 15s. 1½d. when in royal hands for the full year 1324–5: C. 47/88/7/150.

[3] J. F. Baldwin, *E.H.R.*, vol. 42 (1927), p. 198; J. C. Ward, *The Estates of the Clare Family, 1066–1317*, Ph.D. (London, 1962), p. 281. See also the figures cited in the Introduction to this book.

TABLE 3

The Lands of the Earldom of Pembroke

DISTRIBUTION OF LANDS BY EXTENDED VALUE
(1324 EXTENTS)

England

Norfolk	£285.	10s.	9d.
Kent	£204.	15s.	2d.
Gloucestershire	£161.	3s.	0d.
Suffolk	£119.	2s.	3d.
Essex	£116.	5s.	2d.
Buckinghamshire	£93.	15s.	4d.
Nottinghamshire	£70.	19s.	8d.
Berkshire	£66.	7s.	11d.
Oxfordshire	£65.	14s.	2d.
Lincolnshire	£63.	14s.	11d.
Northamptonshire	£63.	13s.	6d.
Hampshire	£52.	6s.	0d.
Hertfordshire	£47.	19s.	9d.
Wiltshire	£42.	13s.	2d.
Herefordshire	£41.	1s.	0d.
Yorkshire	£30.	0s.	0d.
Northumberland	£13.	9s.	4d.
	(£119.	4s.	0d. in peacetime)
London	£3.	16s.	0d.
Surrey	£0.	8s.	6d.
Total:	£1,542.	15s.	7d.

Wales

Pembroke and members	£239.	1s.	2d.
Haverford	£133.	19s.	0d.
Ystlwyf commote	£7.	13s.	4d.
Tregaer	£2.	15s.	10d.
Total:	£383.	9s.	4d.

Ireland

Wexford and members	£336.	19s.	8d.
Total:	£336.	19s.	8d.

Grand total:	£2,263.	4s.	7d.

(Figures from summary of *I.P.M.* in C. 134/84/74–80.)

LANDS HELD IN 1324 BUT NOT EXTENDED
(APPROXIMATE VALUES)

Northamptonshire

Higham Ferrers	£303 in 1313–14	D.L. 29/1/3, m. 23.
Thorpe Waterville	£221 in 1307–8	E. 358/13, mm. 11–12.
	£165 in 1308–9	Ibid., mm. 48–9.

Hertfordshire

Hertford castle and town	£92 in 1297	*C.P.R., 1292–1301,* p. 316.

Lincolnshire

Grantham and Stamford	*c.* £200 in 1347	C. 135/86/4.

Wales

Little Monmouth	£106. 10s. 8¾d. in 1310	*C.P.R., 1307–13,* p. 273.

Total: *c.* £900

Grand total: £3,000+

The complete absence of any of Pembroke's household or manorial accounts[1] prevents any study of the administration of his estates. It is, however, possible to describe briefly the administrative structure of the county of Pembroke where Pembroke exercised palatine rights, although little of the available material relates directly to Aymer's period as Earl.[2]

The first point to emerge is that Aymer de Valence controlled directly only a relatively small part of the county. In 1245 the last Marshal Earl had held the lordship of Pembroke itself and also the lordships of Haverford, Narberth, and Cilgerran, but after the partition William de Valence held only the lordship

[1] The account roll of 1320 which is ascribed to Pembroke in the P.R.O. list (E. 101/372/4) in fact belonged to Hugh Audley the Younger. However, the account rolls of Joan de Valence for 1295–7 (E. 101/505/25–7) and the scattering of private correspondence (S.C. 1) and of deeds relating to Pembroke in the P.R.O. may be the remnants of a much greater bulk of Pembroke records in the royal archives.

[2] Most of the surviving evidence is printed in the *Calendar of Public Records relating to Pembrokeshire*, ed. H. Owen, Cymmrodorion Record Series, no. 7 (London, 1911–18). It is unfortunate that there is not enough material for a satisfactory comparison between Pembroke and Wexford, which closely resembled it.

of Pembroke with its members, Tenby, St. Florence, Castle Martin, and Coytraeth.[1] Pembroke therefore remained the only base of the earldom in Wales until Aymer recovered Haverford. In 1246 Haverford had been assigned to Roger Mortimer, Humphrey de Bohun junior, and William de Cantilupe, the husbands of William de Braose's three coheiresses. By 1276 Cantilupe had exchanged his third of the lordship with Humphrey de Bohun and Bohun himself exchanged these two thirds with Queen Eleanor by May 1289.[2] The remaining third was still in Mortimer control as late as 1354.[3] After Queen Eleanor's death Haverford came into royal hands until it was given to Prince Edward in 1301. In 1308 the lordship was granted for life to the Earl of Pembroke and in 1317 in perpetuity. After Pembroke's death in 1324 it was retained in royal control and in 1327 Pembroke's widow gave up her rights there to Edward III.[4] During his lifetime Pembroke appears to have had complete control of the lordship and its steward's court, despite the residual Mortimer interest there.

The status of the remaining lordships within the county shows a number of variations. The commote of Ystlwyf, which was under Aymer's direct control, had originally been annexed to the county of Pembroke by Gilbert Marshal, but when granted to William de Valence in 1292 had been made dependent on the county of Carmarthen,[5] and is technically therefore beyond the scope of this survey. The barony of Walwyn's Castle, held in Aymer's time by Guy de Brian, was held from the earldom of Gloucester;[6] the lordship of Cilgerran was held in chief as a free barony of Wales by John Hastings, who also controlled the commote of Emlyn, which, like Ystlwyf was territory disputed between Pembroke and Carmarthen;[7]

[1] *C.P.R.*, *1364–7*, p. 275.

[2] K.B. 27/21, m. 28; *C.P.R.*, *1281–92*, pp. 330–1.

[3] *Cal. I.P.M.*, vol. 10, no. 188. The Mortimer portion is described here as being one third of the town of Haverford rather than of the lordship, but it is not clear exactly what financial rights or other jurisdiction this involved.

[4] *C. Ch. R.*, *1300–26*, p. 6; *C.P.R.*, *1307–13*, p. 145; ibid., *1317–21*, p. 47; *C. Cl. R.*, *1327–30*, p. 109.

[5] *Cal. Inquis. Misc.*, vol. 1, no. 1443 (1288); *C. Ch. R.*, *1257–1300*, p. 427. For the boundaries of the lordships see W. Rees, *Historical Map of South Wales and the Border in the Fourteenth Century* (London, 1933).

[6] *Cal. I.P.M.*, vol. 5, p. 33.

[7] Ibid., vol. 6, p. 388; *Cal. Inquis. Misc.*, vol. 1, nos. 1443, 1800.

William Martin's lordship of Cemaes was also held in chief.[1] All three lordships, however, owed suit at the Pembroke county court,[2] and Cilgerran's link with Pembroke was strengthened by the fact that Hastings was Aymer's nephew. Most of the remaining lordships were held directly from the earldom of Pembroke and in consequence automatically owed suit at the county court.[3] These were Carew held by John de Carew, Manorbier held by John de Barry, Roch held by William de Roch, and probably also Deugleddau.[4] There remained in addition a substantial area of land in the county, including the cantref of Pebidiog, which was held by the Bishops of St. Davids and for which they owed no services of any kind to the county.[5]

In its administration the county of Pembroke was much like any royal county—and probably nearer still to another marcher area like Glamorgan. The county was governed by a sheriff and a steward appointed by the Earl, the latter of whom presided over the sessions of the county court at Pembroke, which remained the administrative centre until after 1536. All executive and legal orders were issued from the county chancery under a special seal.[6] Haverford also had its own steward, who in Aymer's time was probably the same as the steward of Pembroke, and a seal for internal affairs,[7] but of the business performed in the stewards' courts of Haverford and Pembroke little trace has survived, apart from a few final concords and releases.[8]

[1] *Cal. I.P.M.*, vol. 6, p. 358.

[2] Ibid., vol. 5, p. 33; ibid., vol. 9, p. 128. Suit is not expressly mentioned in the case of Cilgerran but may reasonably be assumed.

[3] Ibid., vol. 9, pp. 128–9 (Carew and Manorbier); *C.P.R., 1281–92*, p. 331 (Roch).

[4] *Cal. I.P.M.*, vol. 6, p. 336. The lords of Deugleddau were probably Walter Wogan and Walter de Staunton, who held 2½ fees at Wiston within the lordship: ibid. The lordship of Narberth, held by Roger Mortimer of Wigmore, appears still to have been connected with Pembroke, as in 1246, but there is no clear information on this point.

[5] R. F. Walker, 'Richard Marshal and the Rising of 1233–4', M.A. (Wales, 1950), pp. 347–8; *Black Book of St. Davids* (1326), Cymmrodorion record series, no. 5 (London, 1902), pp. 4–7; *C. Ch. R.*, 1341–1417, pp. 289–90.

[6] *Rot. Parl.*, vol. 1, pp. 30–2; *Cal. of the Letters and Papers of the Reign of Henry VIII* (London, 1888), vol. 11, p. 570. For the organization of Glamorgan see J. C. Ward, op. cit., pp. 254–7, 350–1, and J. B. Smith, 'The Lordship of Glamorgan', *Morgannwg*, vol. 2 (1958), pp. 15–16.   [7] S.C. 1/30/103.

[8] There are many such documents in the National Library of Wales among the Haverfordwest Deeds and the Picton Castle MSS.

It is fortunately possible to describe in some detail the nature of the palatine rights held by the Earls of Pembroke and to give at least a general idea of the relations between the county and its component parts. The existence in theory of such rights seems never to have been disputed either by the Crown or by the tenants of the county. In the Parliament of 1290 it was declared that Walter Marshal had exercised all royal rights within the county, that is the county's free tenants, in obedience to writs from the county chancery, had been accustomed to plead in the county court all pleas of the Crown and all pleas that were pleadable before the sheriff and steward, while the Earl's bailiffs and ministers had made summonses and attachments anywhere within the county and had received the profits and amercements of pleas.[1] More precise evidence on the jurisdiction of the Earl within the county is given in the *I.P.M.* of Laurence Hastings, Earl of Pembroke, in 1348. This information applies to the lordships of Walwyn's Castle, Cemaes, Carew, and Manorbier, but is probably true of the other lordships also. In addition to suit of court the Earl held all pleas of free tenement and trespasses impleaded by writ, trespasses in which fines and ransoms were impleaded without writ, pleas of debt under letters of obligation with or without writ, and all pleas of the Crown except pleas with mainour at the suit of the party; the lords and their tenants were bound to assist the Earl or his ministers at the county court and at the court of the castle gate of Pembroke for pleas of obligation and fresh force; twice a year the sheriff of Pembroke held his tourn within the lordships, attached those indicted before him and took them to Pembroke castle for judgement according to law and custom, and acted as coroner when necessary.[2]

On occasions, however, these liberties of the earldom were not willingly recognized in practice by its tenants. In 1348, for example, Guy de Brian of Walwyn's Castle withdrew his suit and Nicholas Audley of Cemaes did the same in 1376.[3] In the case of Cemaes at least this reflected a good deal of past dispute

---

[1] *Rot. Parl.*, vol. 1, pp. 30–2; Geo. Owen of Henllys, *Description of Pembrokeshire*, Cymmrodorion record series, no. 1 (London, 1897), vol. 1, pp. 211–12, vol. 2, pp. 395–6. The palatine rights were again recognized by implication by Edward III in 1339: *C.P.R., 1338–40*, p. 395.

[2] *Cal. I.P.M.*, vol. 9, pp. 128–9.

[3] Ibid.; *C. Cl. R., 1374–7*, p. 386.

over the bounds of the Earls' jurisdiction. In an agreement with Nicholas Martin of Cemaes in 1277 William and Joan de Valence had allowed Nicholas and his heirs cognizance of pleas of wounding, of thieves caught with stolen goods, wreck, and of homicide provided the murderer was caught red-handed and tried promptly. In return William and Joan kept the right to hold inquests on outlaws who escaped into Cemaes from Pembroke, and all pleas of the Crown, that is homicide, arson in peacetime, rape, treasure trove, and all writs of course. This agreement was confirmed in 1290 between William de Valence and Nicholas's son William.[1]

Another dispute of a similar kind was resolved on 20 October 1323 in an agreement made between the Earl of Pembroke and William de Roch the lord of Roch. In this Pembroke allowed William de Roch to hold pleas of hue and cry, of bloodshed without mayhem, of debt, of conventions made without written agreement and according to the common law of the land, of trespasses committed without mayhem, of contracts made upon the bank of the Pool, and of burglaries committed within Pool and Steynton, provided that judgement was made according to the law of the land. The men of the lordship were to be allowed to capture thieves and homicides found on the bank of the Pool and those found elsewhere they could put in stocks or in irons. Such men were not to be held longer than three days, after which they should be delivered to the prison of the Earl of Pembroke. Pembroke also granted that, although William de Roch and his ancestors had been accustomed to do their suit at the county court at Pembroke, William could in future for his own convenience perform his suit at the foreign court of Haverford, provided that the Earl of Pembroke continued to hold a court there. In return William de Roch promised not to claim any further jurisdictions beyond those just given to him.[2]

[1] I. H. Jeayes (ed.), *Descriptive Catalogue of the Charters and Muniments at Berkeley Castle* (Bristol, 1892), pp. 142–6; *C. Cl. R., 1288–96*, p. 188.

[2] Cardiff Central Public Library, Pembrokeshire Deeds, no. 13. Some details of the document relating to other matters, such as the assize of bread, weights and measures, and the buying and selling of goods, have been omitted from the description just given. It is interesting to note that in 1323 Pembroke appears to have been paying particular attention to his affairs within the county of Pembroke, perhaps as a remedy for neglect of the county earlier. In addition to the agreement just mentioned, he confirmed a charter of his father to the town of Tenby on

However, Aymer de Valence's difficulties in enforcing his jurisdiction in Roch were small compared with the disputes in the thirteenth century between his father William de Valence and the lords and burgesses of Haverfordwest.

It had been agreed in the royal curia by the coheirs to the Marshal lands in Pembrokeshire that the assignment to William and Joan de Valence of the lordship of Pembroke included possession of the county court and the suit of its tenants, and the coheirs had informed their tenants of this in a series of letters between 1249 and 1256, two of these being addressed to Haverford.[1] This agreement did not, however, settle the matter, and in 1276 Humphrey de Bohun junior was summoned by the King to Kingston to answer Joan and William for impeding circulation of their writs for pleas within Haverford and for holding Haverford pleas before his own steward. Judgement was given in Joan's and William's favour that the pleas of the county belonged to them and this was accompanied by a recognition by Bohun that within Haverford there were two separate courts held on different days, that of the lordship and that of the sheriff of the county.[2] In 1285 a further case was heard at Haverford following complaints by the burgesses that Joan and William were forcing them, against custom, to answer pleas outside the borough and were imprisoning, outlawing, or amercing those who refused. At the same time Humphrey de Bohun and Roger Mortimer's widow, Maud, who between them then held the lordship, claimed that the 1246 partition had not assigned the pleas of Haverford to Joan and William as part of the pleas of the county.[3] The first part of the case ended with judgement by the royal justices that the burgesses did enjoy freedom from suit at Pembroke and that until the 1276 decision they had attended inquests or taken oaths only before the bailiff of Haverford and had been imprisoned there. The decision in the second part of the case is not recorded, but

24 Apr. 1323, received some money from Tenby on 17 Oct. when he visited the town (perhaps in payment for the confirmation of their charter), and on 10 Dec. granted a charter to the Knights Hospitaller at Slebech: *Cal. of the Public Records relating to Pembrokeshire*, vol. 3, pp. 220–4; N.L.W., Haverfordwest Deeds, nos. 930, 1246; N.L.W., Slebech Papers and Docs., 11438.

[1] S.C. 1/47/44. [2] K.B. 27/21, m. 28.
[3] J.I. 1/1148, m. 1; S.C. 8/61/3017; S.C. 8/219/10932; William's counter-complaint is contained in S.C. 1/10/111.

it is likely that William and Joan succeeded, since they based their counter-claim against Humphrey and Maud on the 1276 decision in their favour.[1]

The case has also a wider significance both as an example of an appeal to the King by the tenants of a palatine liberty against their lord and in what it reveals about the royal attitude to such liberties, even when held by a confirmed royal supporter like William de Valence. Following his tenants' appeal William visited the King at Llanbadarn Fawr to ask him not to send justices to Haverford, since it was within his palatine county of Pembroke. In reply the Council said that since William, Humphrey, and Maud held their lands in chief and did not hold from one another, they were incapable of judging one another. Furthermore since all lands in the kingdom were held in fee from the King, the latter was entitled to send his justices to hear pleas wherever he wished.[2] In consequence royal justices were sent to hear the case at Haverford. William, however, did his best to hinder their activity by rejecting all the 200 men proposed as members of an inquest jury to settle the facts of the case, so that the justices finally ordered the royal sheriffs of Cardigan and Carmarthen, who were present, to select the jury themselves.[3]

In later disputes William and Joan were themselves the injured parties and took the initiative in inviting royal justices to enter their lands. In 1289, after Bohun's exchange of his two-thirds of Haverford with the Queen, the latter tried to hold pleas at Haverford by writs from her own chancery in cases from the lordships of Walwyn's Castle and Roch which had previously done suit at Pembroke.[4] In 1290 it was revealed that the Queen had also tried to obtain the suit of the lordship of Cemaes and of the foreign jurisdiction of Haverford. At Parliament in 1290 the Queen received judgement by default,[5] but in 1295, after her death, William reopened the case and laid claim to jurisdiction over the foreign pleas of Haverford and of Roch and other places.[6] The issue was still alive in 1297 when Joan de Valence complained about the usurpation by the

[1] J.I. 1/1148, mm. 3d., 1.   [2] Ibid., m. 1.
[3] Ibid., m. 3d.   [4] *C.P.R., 1281–92*, pp. 330–1.
[5] Ibid., p. 398; *Rot. Parl.*, vol. 1, pp. 30–3.
[6] S.C. 8/152/7553; *Rot. Parl.*, vol. 1, pp. 138–9.

King's bailiffs in Haverford of her jurisdiction in the lordship of Walwyn's Castle.[1] So far as is known no formal solution of the problem was ever reached, but it ceased to matter once the Earl of Pembroke gained control of the lordship of Haverford in 1308.

It is not likely that there had been any deliberate royal attempt to undermine the palatine jurisdiction within the county of Pembroke, but the disputes between 1289 and 1297 and the King's intervention in Haverford in 1285 do show the potential weakness of even palatine rights if a concerted attack were ever to be made upon them. Edward I may not have been trying to do this with Pembroke, but, as has been pointed out, 'his lordship was exacting rather than "good" '.[2]

[1] S.C. 1/47/92.
[2] K. B. McFarlane, 'Had Edward I a "Policy" towards the Earls?', *History*, vol. 50 (1965), p. 159.

IX

The Earl of Pembroke and his Retainers

THE active career of the Earl of Pembroke, spanning nearly thirty years, gives an excellent opportunity to study the structure and development of an important magnate retinue in the late thirteenth and early fourteenth centuries. Although certainly smaller than that of the Earl of Lancaster, for example, Pembroke's retinue was probably typical of those of the leading magnates of the period.[1]

Much of the evidence for the composition and size of Pembroke's retinue survives in the form of protection lists for those retainers who accompanied him on campaigns, royal diplomatic missions, or private visits abroad. Although such lists are not necessarily exhaustive, it is possible by collating them to produce fairly comprehensive information as to the size of the retinue at any given date and a generally reliable guide to any particular individual's connection with it. In some cases exact figures for the size of the retinue, though not details of names, can be found from the records of the payment of wages in royal Household accounts. For ease of access and clarity the analysis of this material is presented in tabular form in Appendix 2. For the same reason detailed information on such matters as official posts held by Pembroke's retainers, contracts which he made with them, and grants of land to them has been relegated to the same appendix.[2] This treatment makes it unnecessary to supply detailed biographies of Pembroke's retainers, the more important of whom can in any case be found in such works as the *Complete Peerage* and C. Moor's *Knights of Edward I*.

[1] For earlier work on retinues, most of which relates to the period after the end of Pembroke's career, see A. E. Prince, 'The Indenture System under Edward III', *Historical Essays in Honour of James Tait*, ed. J. G. Edwards, V. H. Galbraith, E. F. Jacob (Manchester, 1933); N. B. Lewis, 'The Organisation of Indentured Retinues in Fourteenth-century England', *T.R.H.S.*, 4th series, vol. 27 (1945); K. B. McFarlane, 'Bastard Feudalism', *B.I.H.R.*, vol. 20, 1943–5 (London 1947); G. A. Holmes, *The Estates of the Higher Nobility in Fourteenth-century England* (Cambridge, 1957), chapter three, 'Retinue and Indenture'.

[2] See tables in Appendix 2.

As might be expected, Pembroke's retinue fluctuated in size during his career. There was in particular a marked contrast between its inflated numbers on campaigns and its size on diplomatic or personal missions, when Pembroke's companions represented the hard core of his permanent retainers. There were also considerable differences even between one campaign and another. Thus in the years 1297 to 1299 Pembroke's personal retinue comprised between 40 and 50 knights and men-at-arms, but had risen to 60 by 1307 when the next full figures are available. The Scottish campaigns of Edward II's reign saw an increase well beyond these levels to a total of 81 in 1314 and a peak figure for Pembroke's career of 124 in 1315. Pembroke's indenture with the King in 1317 in which he promised to serve with 200 men-at-arms in future campaigns[1] ought to have produced a further increase but the figures of 55 and 78 for 1318 and 1319, although admittedly incomplete, do not reflect this.[2] The nearest approach to the required total was 108 men in the Scottish campaign of 1322.[3] The reason for this apparent failure is unknown, but there may have been a scarcity of the necessary trained manpower, which would have been aggravated by the demands of the other magnates who made contracts with the King between 1316 and 1318.

One means of enlarging the retinue for a campaign was by the temporary enlistment of other smaller retinues, such as the 23 men of William Latimer in 1307.[4] In the same year Pembroke's retinue was increased from 60 to 90 by the attachment at royal orders of the retinues of Robert Clifford, John Hastings, and Robert FitzMarmaduke.[5] Similar accessions of strength were provided by the presence of the retinues of Thomas and Maurice de Berkeley from 1297 to 1299 and in 1314, of John Hastings in 1313 to 1315 and in 1319, and of John Mowbray in 1319. Another method was the recruitment for just one or two campaigns of individual knights and valets, a process which is particularly noticeable in 1314, 1315, 1318,

---

[1] E. 101/68/2/42D. See text in Appendix 3.
[2] The 1318 campaign was abandoned before it began. Both figures are those of protections issued before the beginning of the campaign and would have increased as the campaigns progressed.
[3] This is the maximum figure for the campaign.
[4] C. 67/16, m. 1; C. 81/1736/25.
[5] B.M., Add. MS. 35093, ff. 3, 3v.

and 1319. This sometimes involved the attachment for a single campaign of royal knights, such as John de Kingston and Nicholas de la Beche in 1314.

However, the permanent basis of Pembroke's retinue was composed of men who had made contracts with him for long-term service. He is known to have made indentures with Thomas and Maurice de Berkeley in 1297, with John Darcy in 1309 and 1310, and with an unidentified knight, known only as Sir John, in 1317, but it is reasonable to suppose that there were many more. Most, if not all, of the dozen or so life grants of land by Pembroke to his retainers were probably made as part of such contracts. As further evidence on the question of contractual military service comes to light, it is becoming apparent that Pembroke's use of indentures was quite normal and that this device was already a very common one by the reign of Edward II. Other surviving indentures between individual magnates are those made with the Earl of Hereford by Thomas de Mandeville in 1310, with Ralph FitzWilliam by Nicholas Hastings in 1311, with the Younger Despenser by Peter de Uvedale in 1316, with the Earl of Lancaster by Adam de Swilyngton, Hugh de Meignel, and John d'Eure in 1317, with the Elder Despenser by Robert Fitz Walter in 1317, with the Younger Despenser by the Earl of Louth in 1321, and those made with Bartholomew de Badlesmere by Robert de Waterville, Henry de Leybourne, John de Penrith, and Walter Colepeper on unknown dates.[1] These are chance survivals and represent a far greater bulk that certainly once existed. At a higher level, the very important series of indentures made between the King and Pembroke and other magnates between 1316 and 1318 has been discussed earlier.[2]

In addition to the formal contractual business relationship, which was the reason for the making of an indenture, there was a variety of other causes to explain the presence of individuals in Pembroke's retinue. A few retainers, such as Pembroke's natural son Henry de Valence,[3] his nephews John

---

[1] D.L. 25/1981; W. H. Dunham, *Lord Hastings' Indentured Retainers* (Yale, 1955), p. 134; *Cat. Anc. Deeds*, vol. 4, p. 252; Bodleian, Dodsworth MS. 94, f. 122*v*.; Bodleian, Dugdale MS. 18, f. 39*v*.; E. 42/271; B.M., Egerton Roll 8724, m. 6.

[2] See Chapter V and also Appendix 3.

[3] He died in 1322: *C.P.R., 1321–4*, p. 141.

Hastings[1] and John Comyn,[2] and William and Richard de Munchensy,[3] had family connections with him. Others, such as William de Wauton, Thomas de Gurney, William de Brom, and Thomas Murdach, served him because of their links with Thomas and Maurice de Berkeley or with John Hastings. In a few cases, those of Nicholas de Carew, Alan Plokenet, Roger Ingpen senior, John de la Ryvere, and the Berkeleys, there had been an earlier link with William de Valence which had survived his death.[4] In William de Cleydon's case there had been a previous connection with the elder John Hastings;[5] William de Huntingfield's first wife was Pembroke's niece Joan, the daughter of the elder Hastings;[6] Philip de Columbiers, the son of Pembroke's knight John de Columbiers, married Eleanor, the widow of William Hastings, John Hastings senior's eldest son.[7] Another retainer, Walter de Huntingfield, had some connections with Pembroke's sister Agnes.[8] A few retainers, such as John and Nicholas de Carew, served because of their inheritance of land held from the earldom.[9] It was also common for several members of one family to serve as retainers, either together or on separate occasions. This category includes the brothers John and Richard de la Ryvere, the brothers William and Walter de Huntingfield, William and Percival Simeon who were probably father and son, Roger Ingpen senior and his nephew Roger Ingpen junior,[10] John, Walter, and Edmund Gacelyn, William and John Paynel, Baldwin and Walter de Insula, and the brothers Aymer and Alan la Zouche.[11]

There is at least one striking example of a retainer serving two different lords. This was Richard de la Ryvere, who can be traced with Pembroke until 1300 and again in 1313, 1318, and 1322, but who is also recorded as Henry of Lancaster's

[1] His regular service with Pembroke began after his father's death in 1313.
[2] His mother was Pembroke's sister Joan.
[3] They were members of the family of Pembroke's mother.
[4] C. 67/10, mm. 6, 7; C. 81/1736/49; *C.P.R.*, *1292–1301*, pp. 177–9.
[5] C. 67/10, m. 2; *C.P.R.*, *1292–1301*, p. 36.
[6] *G.E.C.*, vol. 6, p. 667.
[7] *C.P.R.*, *1317–21*, p. 126.
[8] Ibid., *1307–13*, p. 528.
[9] *Cal. I.P.M.*, vol. 6, pp. 331, 336.
[10] A. R. Ingpen, *An Ancient Family: Genealogical Study of the Family of Ingpen* (London, 1916), p. 208.
[11] For the complex relationships of the Zouche family see *G.E.C.*, vol. 12, part 2, pp. 934–41.

steward at Kidwelly in 1308, 1319, and 1332 and as his knight in 1329.[1] After Pembroke's death in 1324 several of his retainers formed new associations. Aymer la Zouche and Thomas West entered royal service;[2] Constantine de Mortimer, William Lovel, and a clerk Thomas de Goodrichcastle joined the Younger Despenser;[3] and by 1327 John de Wollaston was with Earl Henry of Lancaster.[4] At an earlier period two successive constables of Pembroke's castle of Mitford between 1315 and 1317, John de Lilburne and John d'Eure, had both joined Thomas of Lancaster by the end of 1317.[5] The best-documented case of a retainer moving from one lord to another is that of the clerk Edmund of Martlesham, who began his career with John de Champvent. Shortly before 1307 he transferred to the service of Pembroke, assisted by a glowing reference from Champvent, which testified to his skill at writing letters in both French and Latin, his ability to keep accounts, the value of his counsel, and to his general clean living. By 1312 he had moved on again to become the Chamberlain of the Earl of Surrey.[6]

Over the whole of Pembroke's career about forty to fifty men could be regarded as regular retainers, of whom perhaps fifteen to twenty would be active at any one time. Analysis of their home districts shows that the great majority came from England and probably none at all from France or Ireland. The palatine lands in Pembrokeshire provided only about six, Nicholas and John de Carew, Philip and Thomas de Stackpole, and Ralph and John de Castle Martin, and even these were not active together. It is probable, however, that some Pembrokeshire retainers, such as Richard Simond, spent most of

---

[1] G. P. Bevan, 'Kidwelly Charters', *Archaeologia Cambrensis*, 3rd series, vol. 2 (1856), p. 277; N.L.W., Haverfordwest Deeds, no. 1142; N.L.W., Muddlescombe Deeds, no. 308; D.L. 25/2307.

[2] Soc. of Antiqs. MS. 122, f. 24v.; E. 101/381/6, f. 4; *Cal. of Memoranda Rolls, 1326–1327* (London, 1968), pp. 373, 377. John Darcy had already entered royal service in 1323: *C.P.R., 1321–4*, p. 348. By 1328 the Countess of Pembroke and two ladies of the Carew family were members of the Queen's household: *Cal. of Memoranda Rolls, 1326–1327*, p. 373.

[3] E. 101/127/17; E. 101/127/20/3, 4; S.C. 1/49/149 (all quoted in E. B. Fryde, 'The Deposits of the Younger Despenser with Italian Bankers', *Econ. Hist. R.*, 2nd series, vol. 3 (1950–1), Appendix.

[4] C. 71/11, m. 6.

[5] E. 101/68/2/36; *C.P.R., 1313–17*, p. 396; Bodleian, Dugdale MS. 18, f. 39v.; D.L. 41/1/37.

[6] S.C. 1/47/192; E. 403/150, m. 2; B.M., Cotton Ch. XXVII. 29.

their careers in Pembroke's service within the county and are hence rarely traceable.[1] John Hastings of Abergavenny was the only important retainer with Welsh connections, although a large part of his lands was in England. A number of the English retainers, such as John and Richard de la Ryvere, the Berkeleys, and their dependants, came from Gloucestershire, Wiltshire, and other western areas. Others like Roger Ingpen, Percival Simeon, and John Lovel were from Berkshire and Oxfordshire. John Hastings, John Lovel, and John Pabenham had important interests in Northamptonshire and Bedfordshire. A substantial number came from eastern England, John Darcy from Lincolnshire, William de Munchensy, William Lovel, Constantine de Mortimer, and Richard Plaiz from Norfolk, and William de Cleydon and William and Walter de Huntingfield from Suffolk. The only retainers with a northern background were John and Gilbert de Stapleton from Yorkshire.[2]

This wide distribution in the home areas of Pembroke's retainers, the large number of retainers who were connected with him for reasons of personal relationships or sentiment, and especially the absence of any substantial and coherent group of retainers from his palatine lands either in Wales or in Ireland are all very significant. These facts suggest that Pembroke lacked any firm and localized power base from which he could regularly draw support, and on which he could rest his political career at a national level. One likely reason for this is the fact that Pembroke spent most of his career in the service of the Crown and so spent very little time in his Welsh lands and perhaps none at all in those in Ireland. This would have prevented the creation of strong personal ties of loyalty to him in these areas. In this respect he probably differed from other Marcher lords, such as the Earl of Hereford and Roger Mortimer of Wigmore, who appear to have had important personal followings in the lands with which they were most closely associated. It is also probable, in the light of what is known of Pembroke's political behaviour, that he never systematically attempted to build up a following of retainers to

[1] This was probably also the case with retainers who served in Ireland and Poitou.

[2] Strictly speaking, John Lilburne and John d'Eure should be added as northern retainers because of their short terms of office as constable of Mitford.

support his political career. Here his conduct differed very markedly from that of the Earl of Lancaster, for example. Whatever the reasons for this situation, the result was that Pembroke was very dependent for the making of his career on his continued good relations with the King and on the patronage for himself and for his retainers which flowed from this connection.

The table listing official posts held by Pembroke's retainers which is included in Appendix 2 shows that his men did regularly share in the patronage that was available from the Crown. Pembroke's visit to the papal Curia at Avignon in 1317 also provides examples of patronage which were enjoyed from another source. For example, one of his knights, Constantine de Mortimer, was given permission for his chaplain to celebrate mass at certain manors which became cut off from their local parish church by winter floods; Pembroke's own chaplain, Henry de Stachesden, who was the receiver for his lands in Poitou and held the chapel of Saint Gemina in the diocese of Soissons, was provided to a canonry of Wells, and another chaplain, Walter Alexander, was made a canon of St. Davids. One of his clerks, John de Bruneshope, became a canon of Hereford and another clerk, Mr. James de Berkeley, the younger brother of another of his retainers, Maurice de Berkeley, and a future Bishop of Exeter, was given a canonry at Chichester.[1] However, the over-all impression is that the patronage obtained by Pembroke's men and the lands that he himself received at intervals from the Crown were no more than might be expected in the case of a prominent and loyal magnate of Pembroke's standing. There is no evidence that he ever deliberately exploited his position in the way followed by favourites such as Gaveston or the Younger Despenser.

Among the large number of men who served as Pembroke's retainers a few stand out as of especial importance. Aymer la Zouche was one of these, and for the last four years of Pembroke's life acted as his lieutenant as constable of Rockingham and keeper of the forest between Oxford and Stamford. John Hastings, Pembroke's nephew and executor[2] and father of

---

[1] *Cal. of Entries in the Papal Registers relating to Great Britain and Ireland: Papal Letters, 1305–42*, ed. W. H. Bliss *et al.* (London, 1895), pp. 141, 143, 145, 161.
[2] *C.F.R., 1319–27*, p. 298.

Laurence Hastings, Pembroke's eventual successor as Earl, was another, as was John Darcy, who was in Pembroke's service continuously from 1307 to 1323. The most important of Pembroke's retainers was probably William de Cleydon, who appears to have acted as a kind of general business manager for his English affairs.[1] In 1314 Cleydon acted as Pembroke's attorney in business arising from Pembroke's inheritance of Denise de Vere's lands; in 1315 he received payments of wages on Pembroke's behalf in London; and in 1319 he presented Pembroke's accounts for his unpaid wages for the 1307 Scots campaign and 1309 Avignon mission.[2] Later he acted as Pembroke's lieutenant as Justice of the Forest,[3] as one of his fellow justices of the forest pleas in 1324, and as a mainpernor for his debts after his death.[4] Cleydon's reputation was apparently, however, an unsavoury one, since there exist two letters, one from the Earl Marshal to Pembroke himself and the other to an unknown recipient, which warn of his malevolence.[5] There are also several petitions complaining of his conduct. In 1317 an action of novel disseisin was issued against him and Pembroke for dispossessing John de Freston of lands in Essex.[6] On another occasion he was accused of imprisoning certain of his tenants of Sandon in Essex at Pembroke's manor of Hanningfield until they surrendered their deeds and did fealty to him. Later the community of Essex alleged he had exceeded his authority as Justice of the Forest and his tenants at Sandon complained he had forced them to do unaccustomed services by distraining on their property. Cleydon's most spectacular known achievement in dishonesty was the occasion when he stole the goods and land of Thomas de Witnesham at Cleydon in Suffolk and then acted in conspiracy with the Sheriff's clerk, William Waffre, to delay the resulting assize of novel disseisin by three and a half years.[7]

[1] There is no record of his holding any defined position such as Steward.
[2] *C. Cl. R., 1313–18*, pp. 190–1; E. 404/485/20/10; E. 403/174, m. 2; E. 101/373/23.
[3] B.M., Add. MS. 15568, f. 23*v*. (Newent Priory Cartulary); *The Glastonbury Cartulary*, vol. I, Somerset Record Soc., vol. 59 (Frome, 1947), p. 182.
[4] *C.P.R., 1321–4*, p. 351; *C.F.R., 1319–27*, p. 298.
[5] S.C. 1/49/137; S.C. 1/48/159. Neither is readily datable.
[6] D.L. 10/227. Cleydon was the real offender: *C. Cl. R., 1313–18*, p. 610.
[7] S.C. 8/17/831; S.C. 8/14/676, 677; *Rot. Parl.*, vol. 2, pp. 380–1; S.C. 8/322/E. 523.

Membership of the retinue of a magnate like Pembroke was, at least for its most prominent members, more than just a formal contractual relationship, but was also personal and social. This was the case with Bartholomew de Badlesmere, for example, when he was in the service of the Earl of Gloucester, or with Robert de Holand and the Earl of Lancaster. John Hastings, John Darcy, and William de Cleydon occupied a similar place in Pembroke's retinue. However, the most interesting of Pembroke's associations of this kind was with the members of the Berkeley family of Gloucestershire, both because it was of long duration and because it finally broke down in spectacular circumstances in 1318.

Thomas de Berkeley senior and his eldest son Maurice de Berkeley senior had been retainers and family friends of William de Valence,[1] and in 1297 this connection was continued when they both became indentured retainers of Aymer de Valence.[2] They were in Aymer's retinue in 1297, 1298, 1299, and probably in 1308, and were again under his command in 1313 and 1314.[3] In January 1316 they witnessed a charter of Pembroke in London and in July 1316 Pembroke and Maurice de Berkeley took part in the knighting of Richard de Rodeney at Keynsham just before the siege of Bristol.[4] Maurice probably owed his appointments as Constable of Berwick in 1315 and as Justice of South Wales in 1316 to Pembroke's influence.[5]

However, soon after this something went seriously wrong with this long-established relationship. On 31 July 1318 a band of men broke into the park of Pembroke's manor at Painswick in Gloucestershire, killed 200 of his deer, and caused damage which Pembroke later valued, no doubt with considerable exaggeration, at £3,000.[6] After a complaint to the King by Pembroke four royal justices were ordered on 8 August to make an inquiry into the incident. No immediate action followed, and on 30 December 1318 Pembroke again complained to the

---

[1] *C.P.R., 1292–1301*, p. 177.

[2] E. 101/68/1/1. See summary of the indenture in Appendix 2.

[3] E. 101/6/28; ibid. /39; C. 67/14, m. 9; C. 71/6, m. 1; *C.P.R., 1307–13*, pp. 43, 581.

[4] *Cartulary of St. Peter's, Gloucester*, p. 272; R. Glover, *Nobilitas Politica*, p. 150; *Cal. of Hereford Cathedral Muniments*, vol. 2, p. 759.

[5] E. 101/68/2/35; *C.F.R., 1307–19*, p. 285.

[6] J.I. 1/299/2, m. 2. For the general significance of this episode in Pembroke's career and in national politics see Chapter VI.

Chancellor.¹ As a result on 11 January 1319 Pembroke was
granted the goods which would be forfeited to the King by
those responsible. On 14 January a commission of oyer and
terminer was issued, which named twenty-two men as having
been concerned in the attack and was supplanted on 18 April
by a fresh commission adding a further thirty names.²

The names of the alleged attackers are very interesting, since
they included Thomas and Maurice de Berkeley, the sons of
Maurice de Berkeley senior, and Thomas de Gurney, a former
Berkeley retainer and associate who had just become a royal
knight.³ These three had all in the past served in the Berkeley
retinue under Pembroke's command. Another of the attackers
was John Mautravers junior who was the son-in-law of Maurice
de Berkeley and also a Berkeley retainer.⁴ At least two more of
those involved, Thomas de Bradeston and Roger Mayel, also
had connections with the Berkeley family, as did Thomas de
Berkeley of Beoly and Robert de Berkeley of Arlingham.⁵ The
names of the other attackers suggest that most if not all came
from Gloucestershire within the area of the Berkeley family's
territorial influence. There are therefore good grounds for
believing that the Berkeleys made a deliberate attack upon
Painswick, their responsibility being openly acknowledged by
the family historian.⁶

The problem is why the Berkeleys should have taken such
dramatic action against Pembroke, with whom they had previously been on very good terms. There is no evidence that
they were acting with or at the instigation of any other greater
magnates, and they were in any case of sufficient local importance in Gloucestershire to be quite capable of committing
such an offence on their own initiative, given a motive. The
record of the judicial inquiry in 1319 does not throw any light
on the causes of the attack, but it is none the less possible to
suggest reasons which may help to explain the problem,
although it is unlikely that they provide the full answer.

¹ *C.P.R., 1317–21*, p. 276; S.C. 1/35/204.
² *C.P.R., 1317–21*, pp. 265, 307, 364.
³ C. 71/6, m. 1. Gurney became a royal knight in Apr. 1318, but his social
links were still with the Berkeleys: Soc. of Antiqs. MS. 121, f. 36.
⁴ He was a Berkeley retainer by 1316: *C. Cl. R., 1313–18*, pp. 77, 126, 352.
⁵ *C.P.R., 1317–21*, pp. 364, 432; J. Smyth, *Lives of the Berkeleys*, vol. 1, p. 297.
⁶ J. Smyth, op. cit., vol. 1, pp. 297–8.

The brief explanation is that in 1318 Maurice de Berkeley senior may have believed that he had some kind of claim to a share of the lands of the Gloucester earldom, in addition to the claims of the Younger Despenser, Hugh Audley the Younger, and Roger Damory, the husbands of the three Gloucester heiresses. This strange situation arose from Maurice's marriage to Isabel, the elder of the two daughters of Gilbert de Clare of Gloucester by his first wife, Alice de la Marche, whom Gilbert married in 1253 and parted from in 1271.[1] On Gilbert's marriage in 1290 with Edward I's daughter Joan he surrendered his lands to the King, receiving them back on condition that they were to descend to his heirs by this second marriage, and therefore disinheriting Isabel and Joan, his daughters by Alice de la Marche.[2] In 1297 Isabel married Guy de Beauchamp, the future Earl of Warwick, but had separated from him by 1302. She held £100 land in her own right at Bromsgrove and Norton in Worcestershire, the manor of Stanley in Gloucestershire, and by the gift in 1307 of her half-brother, the new Earl of Gloucester, the manors of Shipton and Burford in Oxfordshire, and rents at Speenhamland in Berkshire and Thornbury in Gloucestershire. All of these lands she continued to hold after Gilbert's death in 1314.[3]

Isabel herself was not a particularly wealthy woman, but her lands would still make her a useful match for some important local baron, such as Maurice de Berkeley. Maurice's first wife died in December 1314 and he married Isabel in 1316 or 1317.[4] His reason for remarrying was not to have further children, as he already had male heirs and his new wife was by now aged over fifty.[5] Isabel's own lands could have been reason enough, but Maurice may have had hopes of something more. Isabel had specifically been excluded from inheriting any part of the Gloucester earldom in 1290 and moreover contemporary legal opinion appears to have rejected the possibility of inheritance

[1] G. W. Watson, 'Alice de la Marche, Countess of Gloucester and Hertford', *Genealogist*, new series, vol. 38 (1922), p. 169.

[2] *C. Ch. R.*, *1257–1300*, pp. 350–1. See K. B. McFarlane, 'Had Edward I a "Policy" towards the Earls?', *History*, vol. 50 (1965), p. 154.

[3] G. W. Watson, 'Alice de la Marche', pp. 170–1.

[4] A date before the summer of 1316 is unlikely, as Maurice was at Berwick in 1315 to 1316.

[5] She was born in 1263: *Annals of Tewkesbury: Annales Monastici*, vol. 1, R.S. (London, 1864), p. 163.

through the half-blood.[1] But Maurice may have thought there was sufficient doubt about his wife's exclusion to make it worth his while to put in a claim in the hope that, if not a full share in the inheritance, then at least a few useful fragments of the earldom might come his way. The fact that some of the inquest returns wrongly named Isabel as an heiress might have given him encouragement.[2] If Maurice could find some source of influence close to the King to help press his claim, he might well stand to make gains.

Pembroke could have become involved in any such Berkeley ambitions on two counts. He was related to Maurice's new wife through Isabel's mother, Alice de la Marche, who was the daughter of Hugh XI, Count of La Marche and Angoulême, the elder brother of Pembroke's father William de Valence. Secondly, Berkeley was a retainer and close associate of Pembroke. For both reasons Maurice might have counted on Pembroke's assistance, especially since in 1317, when the Gloucester lands were being divided, Pembroke was well placed to use his influence at court in Maurice's favour had he wished to do so. Pembroke was, however, too much a follower of the letter of the law for him to use his authority in this way, and it is unlikely that he responded to any petitions from Maurice to help him. The delivery of the partitioned Gloucester lands in November 1317 would have ended any ambitions Maurice may have had. Maurice could also have been provided with a further cause of disaffection against Pembroke in October 1317, when Roger Mortimer of Chirk was appointed as Justice of South and West Wales, depriving Maurice of the office he had held since 1316.[3] An attack upon Pembroke's Gloucestershire lands at Painswick may accordingly have seemed to Maurice to be an appropriate way of showing his opinion of Pembroke's behaviour towards him. The timing of the attack, 31 July 1318, when Pembroke was well away from Painswick taking part in the final critical negotiations with Lancaster, would also have been especially convenient. This explanation of the attack on

---

[1] *Year Book of 4 Edward II, 1311*, Selden Society, vol. 42 (London, 1926), pp. xlv–xlvi, p. 42, appears to confirm this. However, Pollock and Maitland considered the doctrine was not fully formed in Edward II's reign: *History of English Law* (Cambridge, 1911), vol. 2, pp. 302–5.

[2] *Rot. Parl.*, vol. 1, p. 353.

[3] *C.F.R., 1307–19*, p. 342.

Painswick is necessarily speculative, but it probably does give at least part of the answer.

To add insult to injury it proved very difficult to bring the attackers to justice since they took every possible illegal action to delay a settlement. Although the justices held seven sessions on the case at Gloucester, Clifford, and Lechlade between 21 June and 3 July 1319, the Berkeleys and their followers failed to attend any of them to answer the complaint of Pembroke's attorney, John Amyot.[1] On orders from the justices, the sheriff of Gloucester summoned the offenders to four successive sessions of the county court between July and October and, because they again failed to appear, outlawed them at the session of 1 October. The county court of 5 November was unable to promulgate the sentence because of the absence of the county coroners, who had been arrested by Thomas and Maurice de Berkeley, John Mautravers, and Thomas de Gurney.[2] On 13 December the justices ordered the sheriff to summon the attackers to appear at Lechlade on 20 February, when they at last appeared and denied all Pembroke's charges. The sheriff was then told to empanel a jury from Painswick to establish the truth, but at least five attempts to do this between February and July 1320 failed because the jurors did not attend,[3] fear of the Berkeleys evidently being stronger than that of the law. The legal inquiry produced no satisfactory results, although the justices were still sitting on the case as late as August 1320.[4]

However, a series of recognizances, made to Pembroke between 24 February and 25 June 1320 by men involved in the attack, shows that he did eventually gain some compensation for his losses.[5] Each recognizance linked together two or three men, some of those who are included not being among the known attackers but perhaps appearing as guarantors for others who were. On 24 and 25 February Maurice and Thomas de Berkeley and John Mautravers recognized debts of £150 and 300 marks; on 26 February William de Whitefield, Thomas de Bradeston, and Mautravers recognized one for £40, and on

---

[1] J.I. 1/299/2, mm, 1–3*d*.
[2] Ibid., m. 3*d*.; *C.P.R., 1317–21*, pp. 451–2.
[3] J.I. 1/299/2, mm. 3*d*., 4.   [4] Ibid., mm. 4, 4*d*.
[5] These appear to be the result of private bargains rather than of legal action, but the offenders may have acted in the belief that the law was at last about to catch up with them.

6 March Matilda and Thomas de Rodborough one of £80. Other recognitions on 28 February, 9 April, and 25 June brought the total amount pledged to Pembroke to £613 6s. 8d., most of which seems to have been paid.[1] Pembroke did therefore gain some satisfaction from the invaders of Painswick, but only at the cost of long delay, defiance of the law, and considerable personal humiliation.

The Painswick attack also had a significant effect on the personal allegiances of some of the men in the Gloucestershire area, which is worth pointing out. Even before the attack on Painswick the connection between Pembroke and Maurice de Berkeley and his two sons had probably ended, and after it had taken place there was no possibility of a reconciliation. In 1318 the Berkeleys appeared in the retinue of Roger Mortimer of Wigmore and in May 1319 the link was cemented by the marriage of Maurice de Berkeley's son Thomas to Mortimer's daughter Margaret.[2] This switch had important consequences, since it meant that in 1321 and 1322 Maurice de Berkeley senior, his sons Thomas and Maurice, and John Mautravers junior all took part with Mortimer in the war against the King and the Despensers.[3] After 1322 both Mortimer and Berkeley were imprisoned, the one in the Tower of London and the other at Wallingford, but this was not the end of their relationship or of its importance. The seizure of Wallingford in January 1323 by Berkeley and others was apparently intended as part of a *coup d'état* to capture the three major castles of Windsor, the Tower of London, and Wallingford and so release Mortimer.[4] Berkeley did not benefit by Mortimer's escape from England in August 1323 and did not live to see his triumph in 1326, but the link between Mortimer and the Berkeleys had one further dramatic turn to take. In 1327 Mortimer imprisoned the deposed Edward II at Berkeley castle in the custody of Maurice de Berkeley's son Thomas and two other associates of the Berkeleys, Thomas de Gurney and John de

[1] *C. Cl. R., 1318–23*, pp. 222–4, 227, 241.

[2] C. 71/10, m. 12; G. W. Watson, 'Marriage Settlements', *Genealogist*, new series, vol. 35 (1919), p. 96.

[3] *C.P.R., 1321–4*, pp. 15–18; *C.F.R., 1319–27*, p. 84.

[4] *Chroniques de Sempringham*, p. 346; *Vita*, pp. 129–30; *C.P.R., 1321–4*, p. 257; E. 159/97, m. 187d. See also *P.W.*, vol. 2, part 1, p. 374; G. O. Sayles, ' he Formal Judgements on the Traitors of 1322', *Speculum*, vol. 16 (1941).

Mautravers. These three men had earlier been connected through the Berkeley retinue with the Earl of Pembroke, who had been conspicuous in his loyalty to Edward II, and had taken part in the attack on Pembroke's manor at Painswick in 1318. By a final irony they were now also concerned in the murder of the King at the instigation of their new master, Roger Mortimer of Wigmore.

Pembroke's breach with the Berkeleys was not, however, typical of his relations with his retainers. Normally he took his responsibilities towards his retainers seriously and was concerned about their welfare. The best example of this is his reaction in 1317, when he was forced to leave five of his knights, Aymer la Zouche, William Lovel, Constantine de Mortimer, John de Stapleton, and his natural son Henry de Valence, and one of his valets, John Merlyn, as hostages in the County of Bar for the payment of his ransom to Jean de Lamouilly.[1] This undoubtedly added to the urgency with which Pembroke tried to pay off the ransom. The six hostages were all given formal protections on 20 June 1317 to cover them during their absence abroad[2] and these were renewed on 2 November for all the hostages except John de Stapleton and John Merlyn, which suggests that these two had been released or were soon expected back in England.[3] The four remaining hostages were still held prisoner on 18 April 1318, when their protections were again renewed. There is evidence at the same time that Pembroke was appealing to the King to see that the affairs of one of his hostages, Aymer la Zouche, did not suffer while he was held prisoner.[4] By 25 September 1318 Henry de Valence and Constantine de Mortimer had apparently been freed, since the protections were then renewed for the last time in the names of Aymer la Zouche and William Lovel alone. These last two had also returned to England by July 1319.[5] This unfortunately was not the end of the affair, since Pembroke's attempts to raise

[1] *C.P.R., 1313–17*, p. 672. The existence of hostages is proved by *Cal. Papal Letters, 1305–42*, p. 240; C. 81/1706/16.

[2] *C.P.R., 1313–17*, p. 672.

[3] Ibid., *1317–21*, p. 45. They had rejoined Pembroke by Oct. 1318: C. 71/10, m. 12.

[4] *C.P.R., 1317–21*, p. 133; C. 81/1706/16.

[5] *C.P.R., 1317–21*, p. 217; C. 71/10, m. 5. Henry de Valence had returned by 24 Sept. 1318: C. 71/10, m. 13. Constantine de Mortimer was back in England by 28 Apr. 1319: E. 368/89, m. 136.

money for his ransom in 1319[1] probably exhausted his credit without paying the complete sum. It is likely that Constantine de Mortimer junior, who had not gone to Avignon with Pembroke in 1317, was sent to Bar either to take his father's place or to act as a fresh hostage until payment was made in full. Payment was apparently not possible, since Constantine was still a prisoner in June 1324, when Pembroke finally broke out of the impasse by persuading the Pope to relieve him of his oath to pay the remaining part of his ransom, and it was not until the autumn of that year, after Pembroke's death, that Constantine returned home.[2]

This was a tragic episode, which was not wholly under Pembroke's control, but there can be no doubt that Pembroke was very concerned about the fate of his men. It seems that some of them at least responded to him with loyalty and affection. The last word may be left to John Darcy, one of the longest serving of Pembroke's retainers, whose reaction on being appointed to the important office of Justice of Ireland in 1323 was one of regret at having to leave the service of Pembroke, 'son bon maistre e seigneur'.[3]

[1] For details of this see Chapter VI.
[2] *C.P.R., 1324–7*, p. 39; *Cal. Papal Letters, 1305–42*, p. 240.
[3] S.C. 8/239/11949.

Conclusion

CONTEMPORARY or near-contemporary comments upon the character of the Earl of Pembroke ran the gamut from extravagant adulation to execration. Of those favourable to him the most balanced, surprisingly, is that of the Scottish author of *The Bruce*, who, in describing the English disaster at Bannockburn in 1314, could nevertheless refer to Pembroke in respectful terms despite his earlier leadership of invading English armies in the reign of Edward I.[1] Less credence can be placed on the contents of the roll of the besiegers of Caerlaverock in 1300, in which Pembroke is mentioned as 'Aymer li vaillans' in an obvious pun upon his family name.[2] Least of all can we rely on the eulogy written about him in 1363 by James Nicholas of Dacia, a scholar of Pembroke College in Cambridge, which had been founded by Pembroke's widow Marie de Saint-Pol, who was still alive when the poem was composed.[3] But to counterbalance the excessive praise of James Nicholas there is the equally excessive hostility reflected in other writers, which arose out of the enmity between Pembroke and Lancaster in the latter's lifetime and especially from the part played by Pembroke in Lancaster's judgement and execution in 1322. The *Vita Edwardi Secundi*, for instance, while not itself hostile to Pembroke, quotes in its account of the events of 1321 Lancaster's alleged remark that Pembroke was both faithless and fickle and not to be trusted by his fellow magnates.[4] In referring to Pembroke's death in 1324 the author of the *Flores Historiarum* described him as a man who was always ready to commit any kind of evil and whose death was a divine vengeance for his share in shedding the blood of Thomas of Lancaster.[5] This was

---

[1] Aymer 'that wes worthy': *The Bruce*, vol. 1, p. 264.

[2] N. H. Nicholas, *The Siege of Caerlaverock* (London, 1828), p. 11.

[3] B.M., Cotton MS. Claudius A. XIV. See extracts published by H. Jenkinson in 'Mary de Sancto Paulo, Foundress of Pembroke College, Cambridge', *Archaeologia*, vol. 66 (1915), pp. 443–6.

[4] *Vita*, p. 117.

[5] *Flores*, vol. 3, pp. 222–3. This writer also described Pembroke and Richmond as 'trahentibus genus a Gwemlone': ibid., vol. 3, p. 205.

a view that was shared by the author of the *Brut*.[1] Thomas Walsingham and John Capgrave, two chroniclers who wrote well after Pembroke's death, both considered that the death of John Hastings, Earl of Pembroke, in a tournament in 1389 was no accident but the result of his family relationship with Aymer de Valence, and added for good measure that since the time of Aymer's judgement on Thomas of Lancaster no Earl of Pembroke had ever known his father.[2] Taken on their own, such literary sources are therefore of little direct help in making a final assessment of Pembroke.

The opinions of modern writers on the other hand, especially those of T. F. Tout and J. C. Davies, have been much more favourable to Pembroke. They regarded him as the one attractive figure in an otherwise disastrous reign, as a man of moderation with 'the ability of the moderate', and as 'a leader of consummate ability' who in consequence was often able to take a predominant and constructive role in political affairs. In particular he has been credited with the formation and leadership in 1317 of a 'middle party' of magnates, prelates, and royal administrators, which took the reins of power from the unsuitable hands of the King and exercised a benevolent and reforming regime until the King and his new favourite, Hugh Despenser the Younger, effectively destroyed the party in 1321. It has also been suggested that, had Pembroke lived, there would have been no political crisis and royal deposition in 1327.[3] These are wide claims to make on behalf of any man, and in order to assess them properly it has been necessary to treat Pembroke's career in as much detail as possible, to re-examine existing accounts of the politics of the reign, and to try to reconstruct those periods of the reign which have not been adequately studied before. As will already be apparent, the conclusions reached in this book have often differed from those put forward in the past.

The main conclusion has been to give full weight to Pembroke's loyalty to the monarchy and to its interests. This loyalty was in part the result of allegiance to the monarchy as

[1] *The Brut*, vol. 1, p. 232.

[2] *Hist. Anglicana of Thomas Walsingham*, vol. 2, p. 195; *Chronicle of England of John Capgrave*, R.S. (London, 1858), p. 253.

[3] Davies, *Baronial Opposition*, pp. 354, 441; Tout, *Place of the Reign* (1936), pp. 17–18, 135.

an institution, but it is also essential to recognize his devotion to the person of the King himself. If Pembroke ever gave assent to the doctrine of capacities put forward by the magnates to justify their attack on Gaveston in 1308, then he would seem to have interpreted it in an opposite sense to them.[1] Far from Edward II's deficiencies turning Pembroke into an opponent they may in reality have strengthened his support of Edward, because of the King's evident need of someone he could trust. One of the probable reasons for Pembroke's behaviour was, as has been suggested earlier, the close relationship which had existed between his father William de Valence and William's half-brother Henry III and nephew Edward I.[2] As a result the attitudes of Aymer de Valence towards the monarchy were to some extent predetermined. There was, however, another factor involved, which one can recognize but without being able to give it a precise definition. It is noticeable that Pembroke did not possess a strong power base in the lands of his earldom, nor is there any evidence that he tried to create one by the systematic recruitment of retainers or by the leadership of other magnates. This meant that Pembroke was very dependent upon his connection with the monarchy and its patronage both for the establishment and for the continuation of his career. Just why this was so is difficult to explain, but it is possible that in some way Pembroke remained an outsider in English society, despite the fact that the King himself and many other magnates also retained close links with the Continent.[3] This may be the reason why, for example, both his marriages were to the daughters of prominent French magnates instead of being used to forge alliances within England itself. Pembroke's position may therefore have been not unlike that of the Earl of Richmond, whose family origins lay in Brittany and who was also very closely associated with the monarchy during his English career.

Whatever the precise causes were of Pembroke's attachment to the King, the consequence was that he was never very far from the centre of power, even when circumstances prevented him from exercising it himself. This meant that when other rivals for authority, such as the opposition Earls of Lancaster

---

[1] *Ann. Lond.*, pp. 153–4. [2] See Chapter I.
[3] See details in the Introduction.

and Warwick, were unable to force themselves into the King's counsels, or when royal favourites such as Gaveston or Roger Damory lost their influence, Pembroke very soon regained prominence, a fact which might easily be misunderstood as the result of a deliberate bid for power by Pembroke. Pembroke's place in the royal circle was that of a trusted and reliable elder statesman, rarely absent from the public view, who might or might not also be in a position of real authority.

Pembroke's loyalty to the King was not, however, unlimited or unconditional. It suffered severe strain during the period of Gaveston's influence over Edward II early in the reign and there can be little doubt that it was primarily Gaveston rather than any hostility to the King that forced Pembroke into the ranks of the Ordainers in 1310 and helped to keep him there. When Gaveston was removed in 1312 Pembroke returned to his old allegiance and remained in it until the magnate movement against the Despensers in 1321 again brought his loyalty into question. On that occasion Pembroke succeeded by the barest of margins in preventing his own enmity towards the royal favourites turning into an open breach with the King. One can only speculate on what would have happened if Pembroke had not died in 1324 before the opposition to the Despensers had once again reached fruition, but it is likely that he would have been forced to declare himself against them. Failing that, he would probably have met the same fate as the Earl of Arundel and the Despensers in 1326.

For the greater part of Pembroke's career, however, his loyalty to the King was unquestioned, and in consequence Edward II respected and trusted him. The details given in the King's surviving correspondence with Pembroke have provided plenty of evidence of this and need not be repeated. Edward II's attitude towards Pembroke was not, however, the same as that towards his favourites and there is nothing to suggest that Pembroke was ever regarded in this light by his contemporaries. Pembroke was instead a man of experience and of some ability, upon whose support the King could rely and whose advice would be intended to further the best interests of the Crown. This did not mean that Pembroke's advice was necessarily always accepted or was followed without a struggle, since Edward II was equally capable of being swayed by the ill-qualified and irresponsible suggestions of favourites such as Gaveston or Roger Damory. The negotiations which lay behind the Treaty of Leake in 1318 are a particularly good example of this kind of situation, where the King was being subjected to pressures both to negotiate with Lancaster and to destroy him if opportunity arose. On this occasion the view represented by Pembroke and others of like mind finally prevailed, but in the much more dangerous situation created by the dominance of Edward II's last and most powerful favourite, Hugh Despenser the Younger, Pembroke's advice probably went largely unheard.

The first ten years of Pembroke's active career, from 1297, when he went to Flanders with Edward I, until Edward II's accession in 1307, have not been examined in any detail, as they lie outside the terms of the present study. It was, however, during this period that the future pattern of Pembroke's career was profoundly shaped, so that by 1307 he was a devoted servant of the monarchy with a long record of diplomatic activity in France and of military experience in Scotland. This helps to explain why the crises which quickly followed the death of Edward I did not have any immediate damaging effect upon Pembroke's loyalty to the new King. Nevertheless it was impossible for Pembroke to ignore the worsening political situation brought about by the behaviour of Gaveston and by the demands for the reform of administrative abuses, whose origins could be traced back to the previous reign. For this reason Pembroke and other magnates who were still sympathetic to the King participated in the agreement made at Boulogne on 31 January 1308 in the hope that reforms approved by the King himself would forestall the more radical demands that might be made by the King's opponents. This attempt was soon lost sight of amid the serious crisis in 1308, which resulted in the exile of Gaveston. Pembroke remained loyal to the King to the extent of going to Avignon in 1309 to urge the Pope to lift the ecclesiastical sanctions imposed against Gaveston's return to England. Gaveston's arrogant behaviour after his reappearance in England in 1309, combined with the failure of the reforms promised by the King at Stamford in August, provoked a new crisis, which finally left Pembroke no option but to join Lancaster, Warwick, and other magnates hostile to

Gaveston in the demands which led to the appointment of the
Ordainers in March 1310. Despite the King's attempts to lure
him away from the ranks of the Ordainers and persuade him
to resume his active part in royal affairs, Pembroke remained
adamant and apparently took a prominent share in the framing
of the Ordinances, which were published in 1311.

Pembroke remained with the Ordainers until 1312, when he
was appointed by the council of magnates and prelates which
met at St. Paul's in March to pursue and capture Gaveston,
who had once again returned from exile. This Pembroke duly
performed, and Gaveston surrendered to him at Scarborough
in May. There is no evidence that Pembroke exceeded the
powers given to him when he offered lenient terms to Gaveston
and had them approved by the King, but it is likely that some
of Gaveston's most bitter enemies believed that he might yet
again slip through their fingers and decided to settle their
account with him permanently. This explains why Warwick
seized Gaveston from Pembroke's custody in June and executed
him with the full approval of Lancaster and the cautious support of Hereford. Whatever the legal grounds for this action
might have been, its inevitable effect was to create an undying
hostility between Edward II and Gaveston's killers, which no
political settlement could ever remove. In the years that followed the King was constantly looking for an opportunity to
revenge himself and was not satisfied until Lancaster had been
executed in his turn in 1322. So far as Pembroke was concerned
his loyalty to the Ordainers was now at an end, because of
their treachery towards him, and he promptly rejoined the
King. It is very likely that he would have done so in any case,
if Gaveston's influence had been curbed by legal means, but
the circumstances of Gaveston's death ensured that in future
Pembroke would be one of the most loyal of the King's
supporters.

The King's earlier regard for Pembroke now came to the
latter's advantage. Far from being treated as an opponent who
had changed sides merely because he had fallen out with his
allies, Pembroke was welcomed back by the King and entered
on the greatest period of influence and authority of his career,
either before 1312 or later. Pembroke emerged for the first time
as an important political figure in his own right, and from June

1312 until June 1314 he was the most significant magnate supporter of the King, taking a leading and probably dominant part in the making of royal policy. Much of the detailed administrative work of the period shows signs of Pembroke's activity: he took a very large part in the negotiations between England and France in 1312 and 1313, and he was also a prominent royal adviser and envoy in the talks which produced the peace treaty between the King and his opponents in December 1312 and the more permanent settlement of October 1313. Ironically this settlement began to weaken the basis of Pembroke's authority, because it meant that some of the magnates, such as the Earl of Hereford, who were newly reconciled to the King reappeared at court. The months after the 1313 agreement also saw the growth of a bitter dispute between Pembroke and Lancaster over possession of territory in Northamptonshire.

However, a far more serious blow both to Pembroke and to the King was the defeat of the royal army by the Scots at Bannockburn in June 1314, in a campaign from which the Earls of Lancaster, Warwick, Surrey, and Arundel had deliberately abstained. Lancaster and Warwick, in particular, had only superficially made their peace with the King in 1313, and the King's humiliation in Scotland provided them with an opportunity to reassert their own influence. The York Parliament of September 1314 was the first stage in a long process by which the political consequences of Edward II's defeat worked themselves out. One of the immediate effects was that Pembroke was forced to give up to Lancaster the land at Thorpe Waterville in Northamptonshire which the latter had been claiming.

In the early part of 1315 it seemed for a time as if there was a balance of forces between magnates sympathetic to the King, such as Pembroke, and the King's opponents, but this really concealed the battle for power which was continuing. The King had been forced to confirm the Ordinances and the Earl of Warwick was present on the Council to represent himself and Lancaster, who remained aloof. Pembroke was not excluded from government activity but he was being pushed increasingly into the background. In the summer and autumn of 1315 Pembroke spent much of his time on a diplomatic mission to Paris and on the defence of the Scottish March. These activities took him away from the focus of events at an important time, although this was probably not their purpose.

The death of Warwick in August 1315 deprived Lancaster of his spokesman on the Council and meant that he had to take a more active part in national politics than hitherto. In the autumn of 1315 Lancaster's growing influence can be traced, as the King regularly consulted both him and the members of the Council who remained in London. During most of this period Pembroke was absent in the north of England, and his share in these new developments is uncertain. The final step was taken at the Lincoln Parliament in February 1316, when Lancaster was formally appointed as head of the King's Council. This apparently was a complete victory for Lancaster, but it was in fact illusory, since the remaining members of the Council were men like Pembroke who were sympathetic to the King. By the end of April 1316 Lancaster had left the Council, never to return.

There was now an entirely new political situation. Lancaster had withdrawn, and from then on his relations with the King became rapidly worse, as he criticized the King and his government from the security of his estates. By the end of 1316 there was again a political crisis, which had been made worse by a clash of policy between Edward II and Lancaster over the election of the new Bishop of Durham. Lancaster's departure from his office had created a political vacuum, which the King hastened to fill in May 1316 by recalling Pembroke, who had never been totally excluded from the Council and was readily available whenever needed. When the year ended Pembroke had thus recovered much of the authority he had lost between June 1314 and February 1316. While he was again a very prominent and trusted member of the Council he did not, however, possess the same degree of personal power as in the period between the summer of 1312 and 1314, since there were other important figures on the Council, such as the Archbishop of Canterbury Walter Reynolds, the Earl of Hereford, and Bartholomew de Badlesmere, who, like Pembroke, were all supporters of the King at this time. Another factor was the appearance at the end of 1316 of three new royal favourites from among the knights of the royal Household, Roger Damory, Hugh Audley the Younger, and William de Montacute.

Early in 1317 Pembroke, Badlesmere, and others went on a major royal embassy to the newly elected Pope John XXII at Avignon to seek his assistance against the Scots and to try to regain control for the King of the revenues of the Duchy of Gascony, which had been pledged to the Pope's predecessor Clement V in return for a loan in 1314. Pembroke's return from this mission was delayed until late in June 1317 by his capture by a former royal squire Jean de Lamouilly who held him prisoner in the County of Bar. In Pembroke's absence the situation in England grew markedly worse through the abduction of the Countess of Lancaster in May, an action for which Lancaster believed the King and his favourites responsible.

The main political problem in 1317 was, therefore, how to reconcile the King and Lancaster and restore internal peace so that the continuing external threat from the Scots could be met. From the early months of 1317 attempts were being made by certain members of the royal Council to regain contact with Lancaster, with a view either to making a formal settlement with him or at least ensuring his co-operation in future royal policy. These attempts had, however, been frustrated by Lancaster's own suspicions of the King and in particular by the events of May 1317. There is good reason to believe that Pembroke was one of those who desired a settlement, and that the initial moves in 1317 owed something to his inspiration. It is certain that once he came back to England in June 1317 he was very much concerned with this problem of relations between Edward II and Lancaster. Further attempts were made to deal with Lancaster during the late summer and autumn of 1317, but all failed because of Lancaster's distrust of the King and the latter's bad faith. It was at this point, in November 1317, that Pembroke and Badlesmere made an indenture with Roger Damory, which has previously been interpreted as an attempt by these three men to form a 'middle party' designed to win power for themselves from the King and to exclude Lancaster from any future share in government. However, a re-examination of the events of 1317 reveals a different pattern. It now appears that throughout that year a number of the most experienced and responsible members of the Council, notably Pembroke, Hereford, and Badlesmere, had been trying to lay the basis for a settlement with Lancaster.

Their efforts had, however, been frustrated partly by the King's own hatred of Lancaster but also by the actions of the King's new favourites, especially Roger Damory, whose removal from court was one of Lancaster's constant demands and who may even have hoped to see the earl destroyed so that his lands could be divided up between them. In October 1317 their behaviour had brought the country to the verge of civil war. Both Pembroke and Badlesmere realized that there was little hope of making peace with Lancaster unless the favourites were curbed, and it was for this reason that they made their contract with Damory, and not in order to create a political following.

The protracted negotiations which finally produced the Treaty of Leake between the King and Lancaster were, therefore, partly the result of this essential preparatory work by Pembroke and Badlesmere at the end of 1317. In the negotiations themselves Pembroke took an important part, but not so far as can be traced a commanding one. He was present as a negotiator on behalf of the King and not as the would-be leader of any political group of his own. The really vital role in the Leake talks was, however, played by the prelates of the province of Canterbury and by the two papal envoys, whose presence in England was one of the results of Pembroke's mission to Avignon in 1317. The contribution made to the 1318 settlement by this group has not hitherto been given the weight or the prominence which it deserves.[1] Without this clerical intervention, which was made with the full knowledge and agreement of the King and his Council, it is unlikely that peace talks would have begun at all and almost certain that once begun they would not have succeeded to the extent they did. In the crisis of 1321 the prelates were again to attempt to mediate between the King and his opponents, but this time with less success. Another important element in the making of the Leake agreement was the attitude of the leading magnates, who were irritated by Lancaster's continued unwillingness to co-operate with the King and unsympathetic to the attempts by the King's favourites to sabotage negotiations, and so were able to bring pressure on both sides to reach agreement.

---

[1] This is not, however, to underrate the important work of Miss Kathleen Edwards in her article, 'The Political Importance of the English Bishops in the Reign of Edward II', *E.H.R.*, vol. 59 (1944).

The 1318 settlement was a satisfactory face-saving formula for Lancaster, since the favourites were removed from court, grants that had been made by the King were examined in Parliament, and his suggestion of a standing royal council of prelates and magnates was adopted. But a closer study of these items shows that they brought Lancaster little real advantage. Nor was the settlement the victory of a Pembroke-led 'middle party'. At the end of it all Pembroke remained what he had been before, a respected and prominent member of the King's Council, who was loyal to the King and trusted by him.

Peace in 1318 had been brought about by the combination of ecclesiastical mediation and moderate opinion among the King's advisers and the magnates. This cleared the ground for a more fruitful royal policy in the future, but instead the years which followed turned out to be the setting for a new political battle, resulting in the rise of Hugh Despenser the Younger as a new and powerful royal favourite. Pembroke remained an influential figure for a time after 1318, but by the end of 1320 it was apparent that he occupied a position of greater dignity than real power. By this point the Younger Despenser, whose growth in royal favour had been assisted by the removal of the earlier favourites in 1318, was beginning to unite the leading magnates against him, many of whom had previously been sympathetic to the King and had been co-operating with him. Relations with Lancaster had already begun to deteriorate rapidly, following the abortive Berwick campaign of 1319 and the accusations of treachery that had then been made against him. When the enmity against Despenser finally broke out in 1321 Pembroke, who had been conveniently absent in France during much of the prelude to these events, sympathized with Despenser's opponents but managed to avoid being drawn into open alliance with them. Eventually he was able to resolve his clash of loyalties between the opposition magnates and the King, to whom he was also under a legal obligation because of his contract for life service in November 1317, by advising the King to consent to the exile of Despenser and his father in August 1321.

However, Pembroke's first loyalty was still to the King, and in addition he was distrusted by the magnate enemies of the

Despensers, especially by Lancaster. He had no option but to join the King in the campaign of 1321 and 1322, which resulted in the destruction of the magnate contrariants and the installation of the Younger Despenser in a position of almost supreme power. Pembroke continued to be a prominent member of the royal circle and to have the respect of the King, but his enforced behaviour meant that he had lost all independence of action and that his former moderation was now thoroughly compromised. In the last two years of his career, from 1322 until his death in 1324, Pembroke was a dignified cipher and little more. Luckily for him he died before the full consequences of the Despenser regime, which he had himself helped to create, produced the inevitable catastrophe. The revenge of the Despensers for his hostility to them in 1321 pursued him even beyond the grave in the shabby treatment which was meted out to his widow and heirs.

Any estimate of Pembroke's ability must therefore depart from that which has traditionally been made. There is no doubt that he possessed the trust of the King and that he was a very experienced and honest royal adviser. His French origins and social contacts at the French court also made him a very important figure in the frequent negotiations with France, and to a lesser degree with the Papacy now established at Avignon. The real extent of his military capacity is uncertain until a proper study is made of his activities in Scotland under Edward I, but it is unlikely that his ability in this direction was more than average. However, his experience and knowledge of Scotland did make him very useful as an adviser on Scottish affairs and made him a natural choice for any major truce or peace negotiations with the Scots.

He was by inclination and practice a moderate in politics, devoted to the service of the King and averse to any extreme solution to the political crises of the period. But unfortunately there is no logical connection between moderation and ability, as has been suggested.[1] In a reign that was stable, as that of Edward I was for the most part, Pembroke's talents would have appeared to best advantage, since he was essentially a fair-weather politician. The reign of Edward II required something more than this, and it is doubtful whether any of the leading

---

[1] Davies, *Baronial Opposition*, p. 441.

figures of the period, except for the Earl of Lincoln at the beginning of the reign, could have provided it. Far from being 'a leader of consummate ability',[1] Pembroke was deficient in precisely those qualities. It is very noticeable that the time of Pembroke's greatest authority, between 1312 and 1314, was the period when there was no royal favourite to dispute that authority and when the King's opponents, Lancaster and Warwick, were as yet not sufficiently strong to impose themselves upon the King. On the other hand he was quite unable to prevent the development of dangerous political situations or to control them once they had occurred. He was able to effect some restraint on the dangerous behaviour of the King's favourite, Roger Damory, in November 1317, but he had been incapable of doing anything to curb him earlier before his conduct had brought the country close to civil war; nor could he do anything to prevent the rise of the Younger Despenser after 1318, and he could only show his displeasure by in effect abdicating from English affairs between November 1320 and July 1321. He can also be accused of lacking the political sense which a less moderate and far more ruthless magnate like the Earl of Warwick possessed. In 1312 his failure to appreciate the treacherous nature of Warwick and Lancaster, his supposed colleagues and the enemies of Gaveston, cost him both his own honour and the life of Gaveston. The episodes of his capture by Jean de Lamouilly in 1317, with the attendant personal and financial difficulties which that produced, and of Maurice de Berkeley's attack on his manor of Painswick in 1318 also suggest that he was not the master of his situation. Perhaps most important of all for his political influence and future reputation, was his conduct in 1321 at the time of the magnate attack on the Despensers. His prime loyalty was still to the King, as it always had been, but he also sympathized with his fellow magnates. At earlier times he had managed to reconcile the two loyalties at times of crises, if sometimes rather uneasily: loyalty to the other magnates had probably been one reason for his joining the group which became the Ordainers in 1310 and for staying with them until 1312. But in 1321 this kind of balancing act was no longer possible, and he ended by being distrusted both by the King's magnate opponents and by the

[1] Ibid., p. 354.

King's favourites, the two Despensers. It is hardly surprising therefore that he was not the leader of a 'middle party' as has usually been supposed, since he lacked the capacity to be so even had he wished it.

This brings us to the important question of the nature of the King's relations with the magnates as a whole. It has already been shown that between 1316 and 1318, when the crisis over Lancaster was at its height, Pembroke and all the other important magnates had bound themselves in the service of the King by means of a series of contracts.[1] This was not in any sense the result of an effort by the King to create a kind of court following and so neutralize all future magnate opposition. There is no reason to believe that the actions of the magnates were other than voluntary, and their motives seem to have been the creation of a readily available military force to assist the King to defend the country against the Scots and also the result of a profound irritation with the Earl of Lancaster, whose actions had been disturbing the kingdom and laying it open to external attack. This situation alone would be enough to draw the whole idea of a united baronial opposition to the King seriously into question. But a closer examination of the rest of the reign shows that baronial co-operation with the King was by no means abnormal. Concentration in the body of this book on the close connection between the Earl of Pembroke and the King may have given the impression that his behaviour was exceptional, but this was not so. The significant point about Pembroke's loyalty to the King was its intensity and duration and not the mere fact of its existence.

The frequency and severity of the crises of the reign of Edward II are real enough, and no attempt has been made to minimize them or their importance. But the effect of past study of these periods of the reign has been to give the false impression that all the magnates of any importance were in opposition to the King. In fact, even at the times of greatest crisis there were always magnates who sided with the King, and among his declared opponents there was never unanimity of outlook. It is true for example that in 1310 eight of the earls became Ordainers, but that still left two, the Earls of Surrey and Oxford, who did not do so. The only remaining earl was Gaveston, who

---

[1] See discussion in Chapter V and details in Appendix 3.

for obvious reasons did not join them. On the other hand, of the earls who were Ordainers, the Earls of Gloucester, Richmond, and Lincoln still continued to co-operate actively with the King, and of the remainder Pembroke at least was basically sympathetic to him. The most aggressively hostile earls were Lancaster and Warwick, less definitely Hereford, and perhaps also Arundel. The only moment in this period when the earls could be said to have acted together was in their pursuit of Gaveston in 1312, but this was no more than a momentary unity and ended with the division of the magnates and the return of Pembroke and Surrey to the King, with whom they then remained.

During the negotiations with the King's opponents in 1312 and 1313 the Earls of Gloucester and Richmond were able to act as neutral mediators and, after the settlement was completed, were wholly aligned with the King. In 1312 the Earl of Hereford had given his approval of the execution of Gaveston only after firm guarantees of protection by Lancaster and Warwick. He was later a sufficiently moderate opposition member to act as negotiator with the King on behalf of the other two earls and after the 1313 settlement he returned to the King. The Earl of Arundel's links with Lancaster also appear to have been tenuous and did not last long after the 1314 Bannockburn campaign, from which he had abstained. Of the important second-rank magnates Roger Mortimer of Chirk and Roger Mortimer of Wigmore, for example, seem never to have been associated with Lancaster in 1312. By 1315 only Lancaster and Warwick remained as an identifiable opposition group, and once Warwick died in August that year Lancaster was left on his own. Long before the important magnates made their contracts with the King in 1316 and 1317 most of them had already rejoined the King. This remained the situation until the autumn of 1320, when magnate opposition once again began to grow against the King and the new favourite, the Younger Despenser. It is very noticeable, however, that the opposition at this time was basically composed of the lords of the Welsh March, notably the Mortimers and Hereford, with the addition of new men who had acquired importance since 1312, Roger Damory and Hugh Audley the Younger. Lancaster too was then in opposition, but his attempts to rally support for himself in the north and to put himself at the head of the Marchers to create a united opposition failed lamentably. In 1321 and 1322 there were therefore really two oppositions, with similar aims but drawn from different sources.

Once again, as in 1310 and 1312, the magnate opposition was far from total. In the civil war fought between October 1321 and March 1322 the Earls of Pembroke, Surrey, Richmond, and Arundel, the king's half-brothers the Earls of Norfolk and Kent, and two Scottish earls all fought for the King. For present purposes their individual motives for this are unimportant; the fact that they did so is enough in itself. The period from 1322 until the Queen's invasion in 1326 has not been treated in any detail in this book, but once more, despite the development of a new opposition group out of the ruins of the one destroyed in 1322, there were still for a time important magnates with the King in addition to the Despensers and their followers.

The pattern then is one of partial magnate opposition to the King at the times of greatest crisis, combined with substantial magnate co-operation at other times. This should not really be a very surprising conclusion, since there were powerful reasons why the magnates should have tended to act with the King. In the first place the traditional mystique of the monarchy itself was a factor that transcended the personal deficiencies of the monarch. It was to solve this difficulty that in 1308 the opposition to Gaveston was forced to put forward the doctrine of capacities, but even with such a doctrine opposition movements were likely in the long term to have a thin time so long as it seemed more natural to co-operate with the King than to oppose him. This implied that only a very strong motive would unite the magnates in opposition. Such a motive was supplied by the activities of royal favourites, especially Gaveston in 1312 and the Younger Despenser in 1321, but even these situations did not last, and once the immediate crisis was past magnates tended to return to their earlier allegiance.

There was, however, a further very strong reason for magnates to stay on good terms with the King. This was because of the King's position as the dispenser of patronage both to a magnate himself and through him to his retainers. To be a member of the immediate royal circle or even just to be in a state of normal good relations with the King would imply the receipt of patronage. Only a magnate of very great independent resources could cut himself off from the source of patronage, and there is no reason to believe that any of the magnates of the reign of Edward II, including even Lancaster, could afford to do so. At the same time co-operation with the King might bring with it a measure of political influence in the making of royal policy and at the very least provided the attraction of feeling on the inside and of being near the centre of power. No magnate with any sense of his social status or pretensions to taking part in public affairs would voluntarily withdraw from such a political state of grace, however intangible its rewards might be.

In the particular situation of Edward II's reign there was, however, another reason why the majority of the magnates were prepared to rally around the King. This arose basically from the behaviour of the Earl of Lancaster. Lancaster has always been depicted as the opposition magnate *par excellence*, the upholder of the Ordinances against the King's attempts to destroy them. Lancaster certainly did make repeated references to the Ordinances in his conflicts with the King and posed as their champion. It is also very likely that he saw himself as the appointed scourge of the King and of the misdeeds of his favourites. This was scarcely surprising since Lancaster was the inheritor of the earldom of Simon de Montfort, he was the most powerful magnate in the kingdom and the King's first cousin and held the dignified office of Steward of England. He was clearly cut out in these respects for a pre-eminent role. Whether he ever thought of deposing his cousin and establishing himself at the head of a Lancastrian regime we do not know, but he certainly aimed at exercising as much power as possible short of this.

However, the reality of Lancaster's part in the history of the reign did not match up to his pretensions. In the first place the importance of the Ordinances and of Lancaster's repeated declarations in their favour have probably both been exaggerated. This is not to say that when the Ordinances were first issued in 1311 there were no abuses of royal government that required reformation or that the majority of the leading magnates did not then give them their support as a reform programme.

But at the same time one of the principal reasons why the magnates had demanded the appointment of the Ordainers in 1310 was the personal one of hatred of Gaveston and his followers. Once Gaveston had gone in 1312 much of the original urgency and passion which lay behind the making of the Ordinances had gone too. The Ordinances as a whole were not immediately regarded as a dead letter, but with the passage of time they tended increasingly to become a routine programme, around which opposition could rally and whose confirmation would be demanded whenever the King's opponents were on top. The history of the Ordinances is in this sense not unlike that of Magna Carta in the thirteenth century.

Edward II still on the other hand had good reason to resist the application of the Ordinances, since if fully enforced they would have restricted his freedom of action, especially in such matters as his ability to reward his favourites with grants of land. But the Ordinances in their original form became increasingly unreal as the true issues dividing the King and his opponents changed. We have already seen how the death of Gaveston in 1312 removed the main cause of opposition to the King and enabled most of the Ordainers to return to their earlier allegiance. Gaveston's death had, however, at the same time created the basic cause of political disruption in the period between 1312 and 1322, since a degree of hatred now existed between Edward II and Thomas of Lancaster that no amount of negotiation or peace formulas could ever settle without the death or captivity of one or the other. In 1317 and 1318, for example, this reason, combined with the appearance of the new royal favourites, Roger Damory and the rest, and their enmity towards Lancaster, was the real cause of political tension rather than the King's alleged failure to observe the Ordinances. The same was true in the crisis of 1321, with the difference that this time the current royal favourite, Hugh Despenser the Younger, had also united many of the other leading magnates in opposition to himself and the King. For the most part it was personal matters such as these which joined the magnates together against the King, rather than questions of principle or the pursuit of the chimera of reform.

The second weakness in Lancaster's position stemmed from his own character and ambitions, since his conduct in practice was inconsistent with his lofty claims. As it began to appear that Lancaster's demands for the enforcement of the Ordinances were a cloak for increasing his own political power, so his former supporters began to fall away. Once Gaveston, the real stumbling block to magnate co-operation with the King, had been removed in 1312 there was in any case little reason for the magnates to continue to support Lancaster, if that would mean only the supplanting of the rule of the King and his favourite by that of Lancaster. This attitude towards Lancaster received its fullest expression in June 1318, when his fellow magnates complained that he had used force 'e noun covenable manere plus que un autre grant du Roiaume' and accused him of wishing 'sovereinete a li accrocher vers les autres'.[1] Magnate irritation with Lancaster was probably also increased by his spectacular failure when he was given the opportunity of showing what he could do at the time of his appointment as head of the Council in 1316. From then on, as Lancaster was seen more and more as a barrier to political peace within England and to be making defence against the Scots more difficult, there was little sympathy to be found for him. For this reason even Lancaster's genuine fears and distrust of the King and his favourites may have been given less attention than they warranted. After the death of Lancaster's one remaining ally, the Earl of Warwick, in 1315, he had become a one-man opposition to the King, supported only by his personal retainers. It is probably not altogether unfair to describe Lancaster as a muddler and a messer, who nursed his hatred of the King and concealed his own ambitions and lack of constructive ideas behind the façade of the Ordinances and his claim to exercise authority as Steward of England.

The conclusions that have just been outlined differ very considerably from the views expressed by Tout and Davies: that the reign of Edward II witnessed a struggle between the King and magnates on issues of constitutional principle, to which the King responded by trying to build up the power of his Household as an inner bastion free of baronial control. Their approach provided a framework of interpretation for a period whose workings would otherwise have been very difficult

---

[1] C. 49/4/26 and 27. See texts in E. Salisbury, 'A Political Agreement of 1318', *E.H.R.*, vol. 33 (1918) and in Appendix 4.

to follow, and this is an appropriate point to give due credit to their pioneer work. But at the same time their ideas have also created a barrier to understanding of the reign by omitting to give sufficient weight to the importance of personal factors in the relationships between King and magnates and between the magnates themselves. Whatever later generations may have read into the events of the reign of Edward II, it is hard when they are regarded in this personal light to see clear-cut constitutional issues being consciously perceived by the participants in the history of the time. For this reason an air of profound unreality hangs over much of the learned discussion of such problems as the Coronation Oath of 1308 or the Statute of York of 1322. This is equally true of the interpretation of the Treaty of Leake in 1318 and of the 'middle party' which allegedly produced the treaty. It is unrealistic to expect fourteenth-century politicians to fit themselves into party categories or to accuse them of betraying a particular principle if, for example, they deserted the Ordainers and rejoined the King. The same general comment may be made about much writing on medieval English constitutional history. This does not mean that there were no problems which might be described as constitutional, or that political conflicts never had effects on the framework of government and politics, but the greatest care is needed to avoid anachronism and reading too much into the evidence. As the reign of Edward II aptly demonstrates, there was no inherent and inevitable division between the monarchy and the baronage. Any given political situation was always the result of and complicated by a mass of purely personal factors which must be isolated and allowed for in any over-all interpretation. If, on the other hand, we must seek the unique constitutional significance of the reign of Edward II, it may be found in the ultimate catastrophe of the King's deposition and death.

However, when all these alterations have been made to the traditional notions of the baronial opposition to Edward II, to the role of Lancaster, and to the 'constitutional' interpretation of the reign, the fact remains that the reign consisted largely of a series of grave and recurring crises. What went wrong? In fairness to Edward II we should take into account the deterioration in the relations between the King and the magnates in the last ten years of the reign of Edward I,[1] the poor state of royal finances in 1307, and Edward II's inheritance of a war in Scotland which was steadily being lost but which no one could admit was being lost. To these we should add the continuation of financial difficulties throughout the reign and the consequences of the famine of 1315 to 1317, both of which made any consistent and rational policy of defence against the Scots almost impossible to sustain. The devastation caused by Scottish raids on the north of England in turn added to the general misery of that part of the country and further reduced the available resources with which these attacks might have been resisted. But the existence of these problems did not necessarily mean that there was bound to be a political crisis when Edward II became King, nor was there one in the first few months of the reign. The opposition of 1297 was dead and the other problems together with those that developed in the course of the reign might have been solved or at least mitigated by intelligent royal leadership.

The real source of the trouble lay in Edward II himself. When a medieval king proved himself incapable of ruling and was unable to discriminate between sound advice and bad, then the essential working partnership between king and magnates was likely to break down. When, as in Edward II's own case, the King was also ready to allow influence and authority to favourites of humble origin, when his personal tastes and interests were not those accepted in magnate society, and when the magnates themselves included individuals who were quick to take offence at the king's behaviour, the result was a political crisis of classic proportions. Edward II's personal failings made him the object of contempt to some and of pity to others, while his incapacity as a ruler created a vacuum which somehow or other had to be filled. Sometimes able and trustworthy men like Pembroke were willing to try to remedy this situation, but all too often power fell to irresponsible and dangerous men like Piers Gaveston, Roger Damory, or the Younger Despenser. It is certainly no accident that the worst troubles of the reign coincided with the influence of favourites and subsided when

---

[1] See H. Rothwell's important study, 'Edward I and the Struggle for the Charters, 1297–1307', in *Studies in Medieval History presented to F. M. Powicke* (Oxford, 1948).

they were removed or declined in favour. The real fault of the favourites was not, however, their relatively humble origin or even the homosexual attachment which some of them at least had with the King. Their relationship with the King was overclose rather in the sense that their presence and activities disrupted and diverted the normal flow of royal patronage, and also pushed aside the leading magnates from their place of dignity as the King's natural advisers. It is even possible that in the early years of the reign there were fears that Gaveston's hold over Edward II would mean an indefinite delay in the appearance of a male heir to the throne.

In the end it was the personal qualities of Edward II rather than the conduct of the royal administration or issues of constitutional principle that caused the initial crises of the reign and lay behind the final disaster. Much of the success of his father Edward I and his son Edward III can be traced to the fact that they behaved in the ways expected of kings and of the nobility, of which they were the greatest members. Edward II flouted these elementary rules of the game and suffered the consequences.[1]

---

[1] This point is brought out very clearly in Professor M. McKisack's article, 'Edward III and the Historians', *History*, vol. 45 (1960), p. 8: 'It needed no unusual insight to perceive the consequences to the monarchy of Edward's deliberate flouting of the social conventions of his age, of his indulgence in simple and economical pleasures, like swimming and boating and thatching and ditching. Such eccentricities not only offended the pride of the aristocracy; they outraged the nation.'

Appendix 1

Pembroke's Officials

(*Acting*)	*Steward*	
1320: Apr.	Herman de Brickendon (prob. Steward of only part of lands)	E. 101/371/8/96
1321: 23 Feb.	Walter de Nas (prob. Steward only in Glos.)	E. 368/91, m. 154
1323: 24 Apr.	J. de Neville	*C.P.R.*, *1374–7*, pp. 114–15

	Receiver	
1301: 19 Dec.	Ralph de Sutton (Joan de Valence's Receiver)	B.M., Harleian Ch. 57. B. 43
1302: 28 Sept.	Ralph de Sutton (Joan de Valence's Receiver)	B.M., Harleian Ch. 57. B. 47
1315: 3 July	W. de Lavenham	E. 403/174, m. 5
1319: 2 Sept.	W. de Lavenham	Gough, *Sepulchral Monuments*, pt. 2, p. 86, n. 1

	Chamberlain	
1306: 25 Apr.	J. Merlyn	*Cal. Letter-Books: B*, p. 171
1312: 29 Oct.	J. Merlyn	B.M., Cotton Ch. XXVII. 29

OFFICERS IN COUNTY OF PEMBROKE

(*Acting*)	*Steward*	*Sheriff*
1292: 12 Dec.	Th. de Anvers	
		B.R.C.S., vol. 13, p. 219
1299: 2 Feb.	J. de Neuborth	Rob. de Shirburn
		B.M., Sloane Ch. XXXII. 14
1301: 13 July	Philip Abbot	W. de Trylleg
		Cat. Anc. Deeds, vol. 3, p. 546
1323: 24 Apr.	Rich. Simond	W. Goodman
		C.P.R., *1374–7*, pp. 114–15
1325: 2 Mar. (date of appt.)	Rich. Simond	
		C.F.R., *1319–27*, p. 334; E. 357/1, m. 21

OFFICERS OF LORDSHIP OF HAVERFORD

(*Acting*)	*Steward*	
1309: 11 Mar.	Rich. Simond	N.L.W., H.[averfordwest Deeds] 852
1310: 11 Aug.	Rich. Simond	H. 957
1312: 22 Aug. until	Hugh de Panton	H. 1137
1321: 3 Nov.	Hugh de Panton	H. 1109
1322: 16 Nov.	Rich. Simond	H. 1158
1323: 28 June	Rich. Simond	H. 1170
1324: 3 Apr.	J. de Neyvile [Neville?]	H. 1081
1325: 2 Mar. (date of appt.)	Rich. Simond	*C.F.R., 1319–27*, p. 334

	Deputy Steward	
1310: 10 Feb.	Walter Seuer	H. 773
1315: 24 June	Walter Seuer	H. 994
1317: 13 Sept.	Walter Seuer	H. 1196

OFFICERS IN COUNTY OF WEXFORD

(*Acting*)	*Steward*	
1296: 15 Oct.	J. fitz Henry	*Cal. of Docs. relating to Ireland, 1293–1301*, p. 151
1297: 7 May	J. fitz Henry	Ibid., p. 181
1298: 6 Apr.	Rich. de Pevensey	Ibid., p. 233
1299: 5 June	Rich. de Pevensey	Ibid., p. 296
1299: 30 Sept.	Adam de la Roche	Ibid., p. 312
1301: 14 Oct.	Adam de la Roche	Ibid., p. 374
1302: 1 June	Adam de la Roche	*Cal. of Justiciary Rolls of Ireland, 1295–1303*, p. 398
1303	Adam de la Roche	E. 101/505/29
1304: 22 Nov.	Gilbert de Sutton	*Cal. of Docs. relating to Ireland, 1302–7*, p. 124
1305: 1 Mar.	Gilbert de Sutton	*Cal. of Justiciary Rolls, 1305–7*, p. 41
1306: 27 Jan.	Adam de la Roche	Ibid., p. 190
1306: 3 Apr.	Maurice de Rochefort	*Cal. of Docs. relating to Ireland, 1302–7*, p. 150
1306: 13 Oct.	Maurice de Rochefort	*Cal. of Justiciary Rolls, 1305–7*, p. 293
1309: 30 June	Walter Wogan	E. 163/1/31/8
1325: 7 Feb.	Maurice de Rochefort	*Rotulorum Patentium et Clausorum Cancellarie Hiberniae Calendarium*, vol. 1, p. 33

Sheriff

| 1299/1300 | Rich. Cadel | E. 101/505/29 |
| 1302: 1 June | Adam Hay | Cal. of Justiciary Rolls, 1295–1303, p. 395 |

Treasurer

| 1302 | Hamond Peris | E. 101/505/29 |

OFFICERS IN FRENCH LANDS

(Acting)   Seneschal (of Bellac, Rancon, Champagnac)

1320: 19 May	Girard Guyon	Titres de Bourbon, no. 1545
1325: 1 Apr.	Robert de Préaux	A. Thomas and Olivier-Martin, Revue historique de droit français, 4th series, vol. 14 (1935), p. 722
	Bertrand de la Vergne (Lieutenant)	Ibid.

Receiver

1296: 21 Feb.	Bertrand de Cigognes	Archives historiques du Poitou, 58, no. 374
1313: 3 July	H. de Stachesden	S.C. 1/50/58
1315: 6 Feb.	H. de Stachesden	E. 163/4/1/2

Auditors

| 1312: 20 July (date of appt.) | H. de Stachesden and Citard de Penna Varia | B.M., Add. Ch. 19835 |

Proctor-General for French Affairs

| 1318: 23 Nov. (date of appt.) | Citard de Penna Varia | E. 30/53 |
| 1324: 4 Oct. | Robert de Préaux | Archives départmentales de la Charente, G. 138/23 |

CONSTABLES OF PEMBROKE'S CASTLES

(Acting)   Bothwell

| 1302: Sept. | Nich. de Carew | Bain, vol. 2, no. 1324 |

Castle Acre

| 1319: 19 July | J. Paynel | E. 40/A. 3043 |

Goodrich

| 1320: 27 Feb. | J. de Sutton | Reg. Orleton, p. 122 |

Hertford

| 1322: 25 Mar. | J. Pabenham junior | C.F.R., 1319–27, p. 113 |

(*Acting*)	*Mitford*	
1316: 20 Feb.	J. de Lilburne	*C.P.R., 1313–17*, p. 396
1316: 15 Nov. (date of appt.)	J. d'Eure	E. 101/68/2/36

	Rockingham	
1316: 30 Dec.	Simon Sydrak	E. 368/91, m. 99
1320: 3 Nov.	J. Pabenham junior	Ibid., m. 55
1321: 25 May	Aymer la Zouche	*C. Cl. R., 1318–23*, p. 302

Appendix 2

The Retainers of the Earl of Pembroke

DURATION OF SERVICE

THE table which is given here is not an exhaustive list of every single person who can be shown to have served with Pembroke, but it does include all his regular retainers as well as the majority of those who accompanied him on only one or two occasions. The retainers who were certainly knights are marked as such, although in some cases they were not knights during the entire period of their service. The major sub-retinues, those of the Berkeleys and of John Hastings, are listed separately at the end of the table. It should be stressed that the service of many retainers, such as William de Cleydon and John Darcy, was certainly more continuous than is shown in the table, the gaps being the result of a lack of evidence rather than of breaks in service.

The main source of the information given is to be found in the lists of letters of protection for Pembroke and his retainers which were issued before campaigns and embassies. These are preserved on the Patent Rolls (C. 66), Supplementary Patent Rolls (C. 67), Scottish Rolls (C. 71), and among the Chancery Warrants (C. 81). Use has also been made of surviving lists of retainers and horse valuations preserved among the records of the Exchequer (E. 101). On a few occasions membership of Pembroke's retinue has also been deduced from miscellaneous sources, such as the witness lists of the Earl's charters. Full details of the material used may be found in the references attached to the table of retinue strengths which follows the present table.

N.B. The table showing dates of service in Pembroke's retinue should be used in the light of the interpretations given in Chapter IX. For example, it would be wrong to conclude from the appearance of John de Kingston and Nicholas de la Beche in 1314 that they were normally connected with Pembroke. Both men were in fact royal knights who were evidently attached to Pembroke for the purposes of the Bannockburn campaign.

The order of the table is basically chronological, starting with men who are known to have been with Pembroke in 1297, the first year of his career, and ending with those who accompanied him in

[*Cont. on p. 307*]

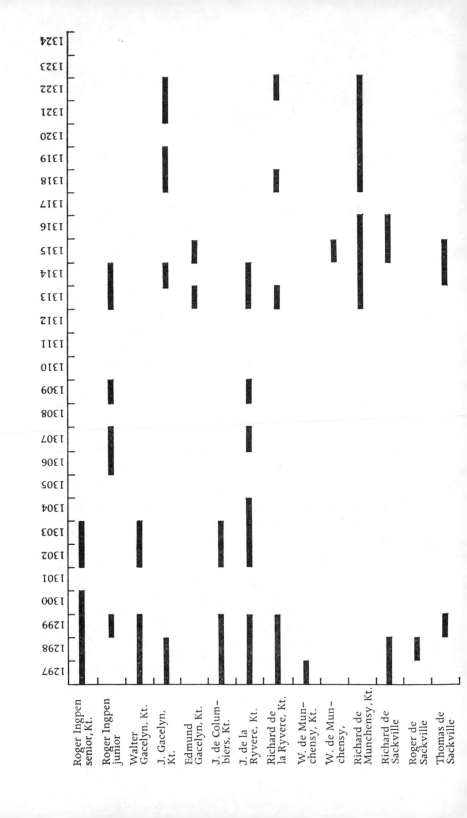

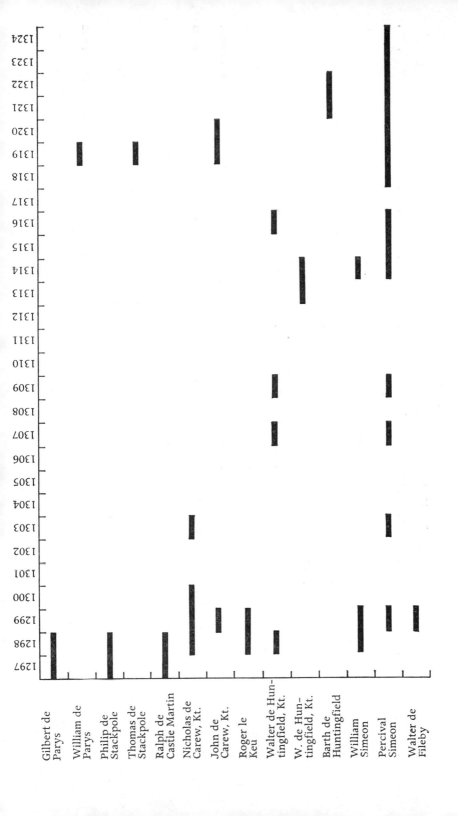

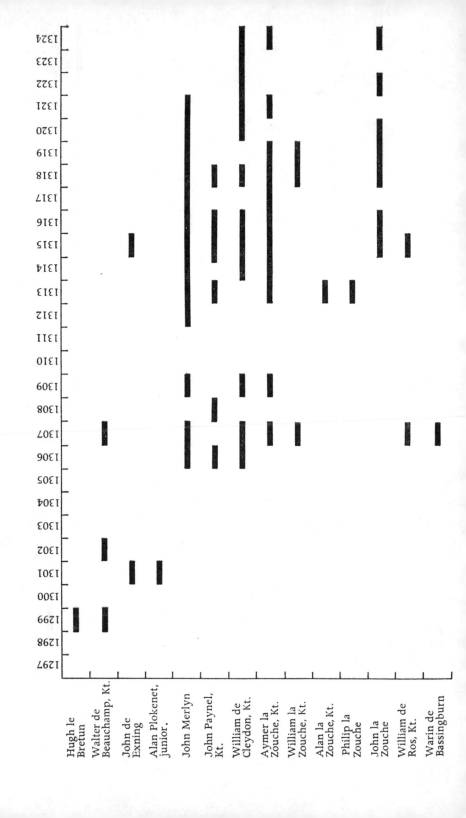

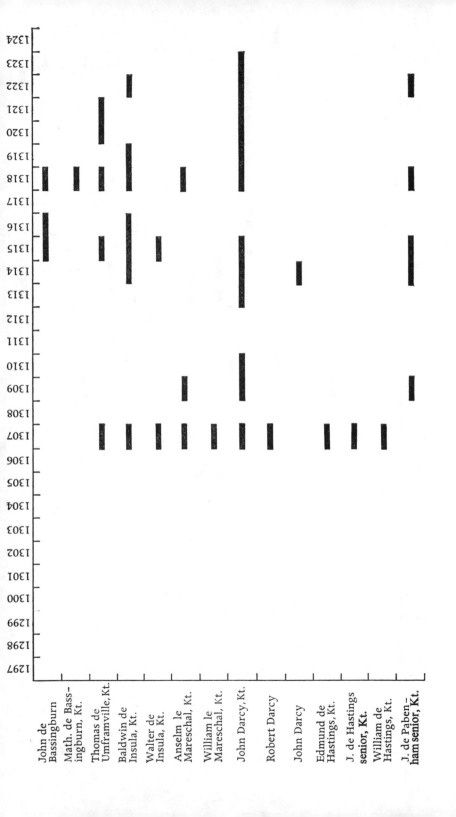

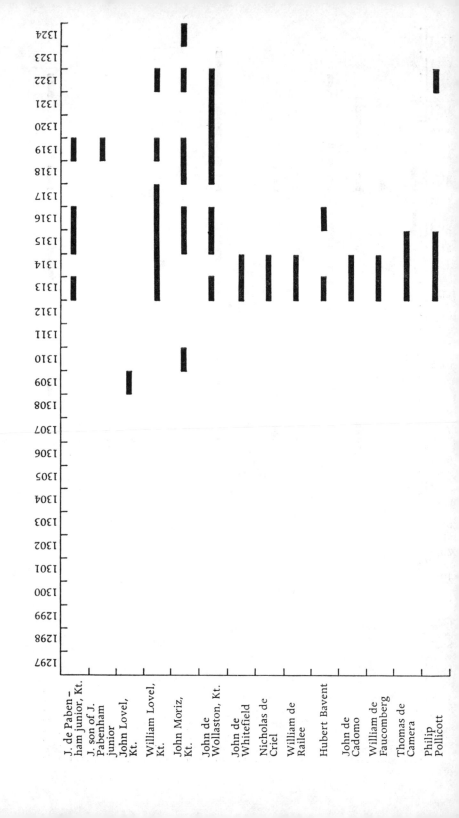

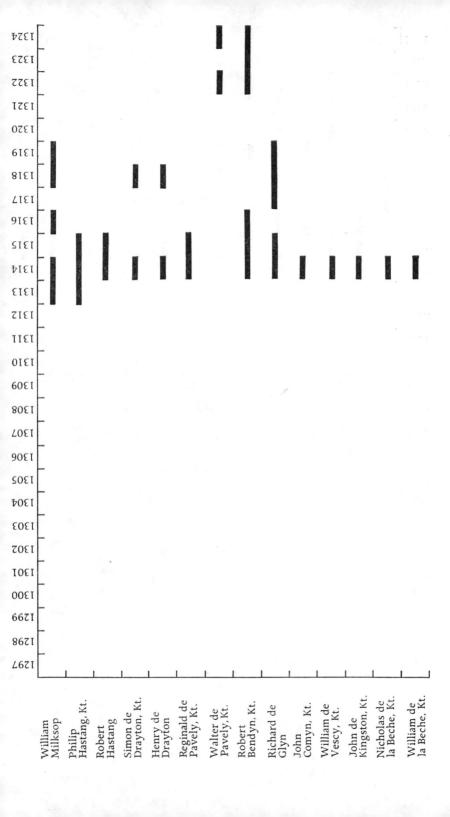

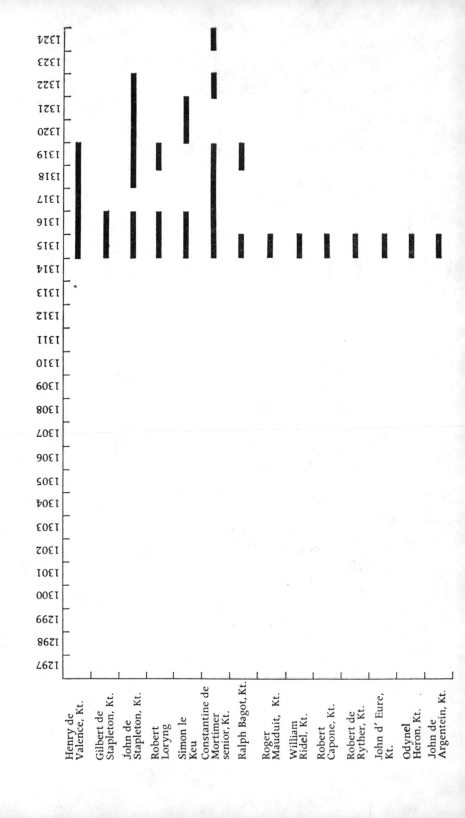

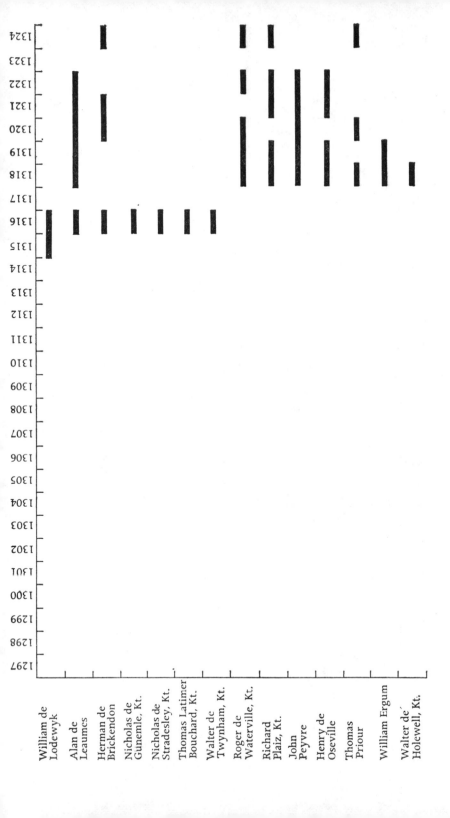

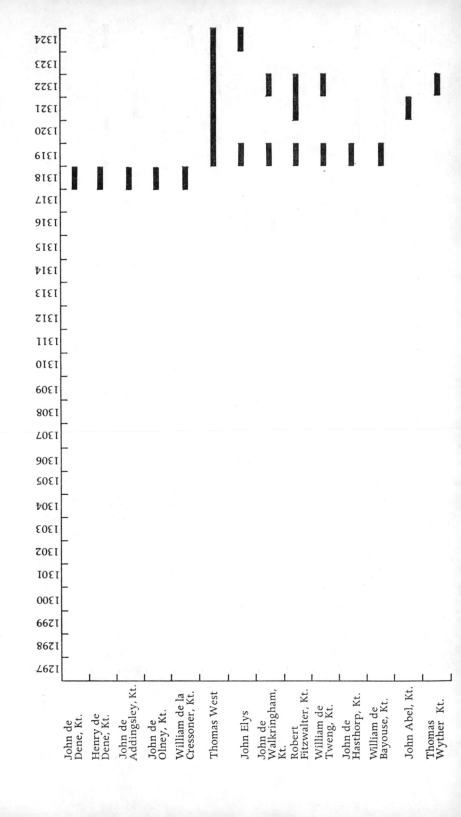

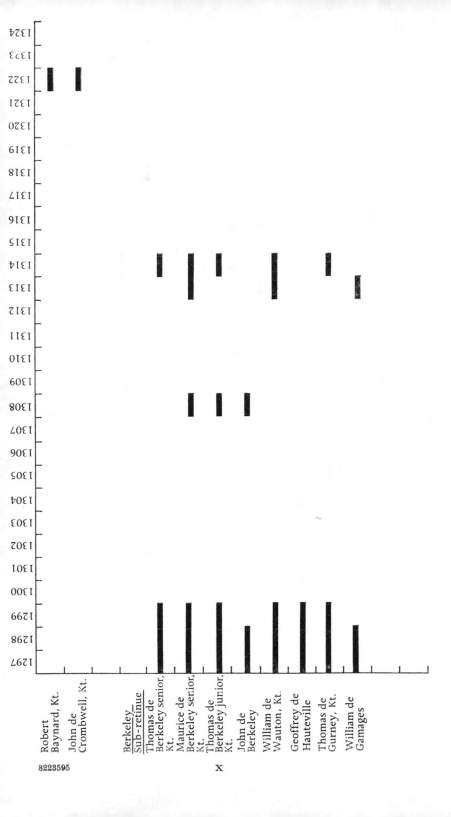

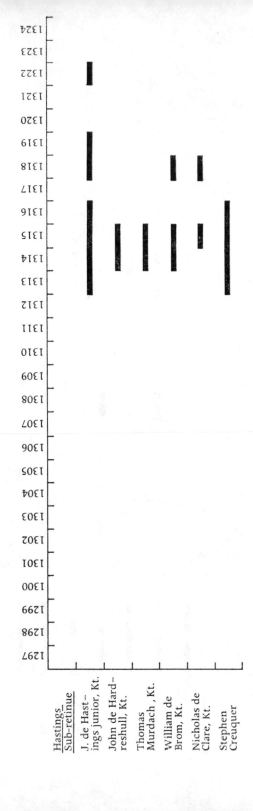

1324, the year of his death. However, in order to illustrate service by several members of a single family at different times, such entries are grouped together. For example, the first name in the table is that of Sir Roger Ingpen, who served at intervals between 1297 and 1303. He is followed by his nephew Roger Ingpen junior, who began his service in 1299 and can be traced at least as far as 1314. The third entry, Sir Walter Gacelyn, returns to the basic chronological order with someone whose service began in 1297, but, as in the previous instance, other members of his family who served in the retinue at other times are listed immediately after his name.

RETINUE STRENGTH

Date	Knights	Men-at-Arms	Total	Occasion	
1297	8	41	49	Campaign	E. 101/6/28; C. 67/12, mm. 8–2; Add. MS. 7965, ff. 68–68v.
	(5	27	32	Berkeley retinue)	
1298	8	41	49	Campaign	E. 101/6/29, mm. 2, 3; C. 67/13, mm. 6–4
	(at least 14 Berkeley retainers present)				
1299	11	33	44	Campaign	C. 67/14, mm. 11–9
1307 Apr.	9	52	61	Campaign	C. 67/16, m. 1; C. 81/1736/25
	(includes 23 Latimer retainers)				
Aug.	18	42	60	Campaign	Add. MS. 35093, ff. 3–3v. E. 101/373/23, m. 2
1313	14	20	34	Embassy	*C.P.R., 1307–13*, p. 581
1314	22	59	81	Campaign	C. 71/6, mm. 5–1; C. 81/1748/73; C. 81/1728/23; C. 81/1736/23, 24, 47 48, 54, 56, 59
	(includes 12 Hastings and 6 Berkeley retainers)				
1315	29	95	124	Campaign	E. 101/15/6; C. 81/1736/46, 51
	(includes some Hastings retainers)				
1316 Oct.	15	20	35	Campaign (not held)	C. 71/0, m. 0; C. 81/1736/22
Dec.	6	20	26	Embassy	*C.P.R., 1313–17*, p. 573; C. 81/1706/10; C. 81/1750/52
1318	22	33	55	Campaign (not held)	C. 71/10, m. 12; C. 81/1749/34
1319	23	55	78	Campaign	C. 71/10, mm. 5, 2; C. 81/1736/60
	(includes J. Mowbray with 7 men and some Hastings retainers)				

Date	Knights	Men-at-Arms	Total	Occasion	
1320	7	9	16	Private Mission	*C.P.R., 1317–21*, p. 521; C. 81/1750/14
1321 May	10	10	20	Private Mission	*C.P.R., 1317–21*, p. 590; C. 81/1750/21
1322 July	22	22	44	Campaign	*C.P.R., 1321–4*, pp. 185–6; C. 81/1736/20
Sept.	28	80	108	Campaign	B.M., Stowe MS. 553, f. 56
1324 June	6	11	17	Embassy	*C.P.R., 1321–4*, p. 427; C. 81/1750/2

INDENTURES BETWEEN PEMBROKE AND HIS RETAINERS

1297: 2 July: Thomas and Maurice de Berkeley

Thomas de Berkeley promises to serve in peace and war in England, Wales, and Scotland in return for £50 per year and robes for his knights. Thomas is to have in Pembroke's service a banner, 4 knights (excluding himself), 6 squires, and 3 valets, and is to bring a total of 24 men with barbed horses in war. His wages in wartime are to be a banneret's pay of 4s. a day for himself, 2s. for each knight and 1s. for each squire. If Thomas fights in Pembroke's service elsewhere than in England, Wales, or Scotland, he is to draw 100 marks per year for himself and wages and diet for himself and his men. If Maurice de Berkeley serves as a banneret, Thomas is to bring 4 knights (3 apart from himself), and to have a total of 15 men. Maurice is to have a banner of 3 knights (2 apart from himself), and to have a total of 11 men. Maurice and Thomas shall then draw £20 and £30 per year each in peace and war in England, Wales, or Scotland, and 40 marks and 60 marks elsewhere, besides wages as agreed above. (*Bain*, vol. 2, no. 905 (the original is E. 101/ 68/1/1). *Bain*, vol. 2, nos. 981, 1004, relate to the performance of the terms of the indenture.)

1303: 8 November: Robert fitz Payn

Robert promises to serve with 2 bachelors at a tournament at Christmas 1303, from then until Easter 1304, and for a year from that date. He is to have diet at the tournament for himself, 4 bachelors, 3 valets, and 2 squires. He is to receive £100 for his service during the agreed period. He is to accompany Pembroke to any other tournaments, to Parliaments, and elsewhere on his affairs during this term. (*Bain*, vol. 2, no. 1407.)

1309: 29 November: John Darcy

John promises to serve for life as Pembroke's valet in peace and war, receiving in peacetime his keep and robes, and in war his keep, mount, and armour. He is to attend Pembroke's person. He is free to choose his own lord at tournaments in peacetime when Pembroke does not attend. In return Pembroke grants him 100s. rent in tail at Gainsborough town. On his taking knighthood Pembroke will enfeoff him of 13½ marks of land and rent and he will serve Pembroke as one of his bachelors on both sides of the sea and in the Holy Land. (*Cat. Anc. Deeds*, vol. 5, A. 11547.)

1310: 10 April: John Darcy

Pembroke promises to enfeoff John in tail of the fords of the Trent at Gainsborough and Dunham until he shall enfeoff him of 20 marks of rent and land elsewhere. John is to take knighthood by the quinzaine of Easter next (3 May 1310) and will serve Pembroke for life in peace and war, at home and abroad, and in the Holy Land. (*Cat. Anc. Deeds*, vol. 4, A. 6404.)

1317: 25 November: John de . . .

John promises to stay with Pembroke in peace and war and to serve against all men, saving the King, as one of his bachelors. He is to receive £20 per year with diet and the replacement of horses lost in war. (E. 101/68/2/41 (damaged).)

GRANTS OF LAND BY PEMBROKE TO HIS RETAINERS

Grantee	*Extent of Grant*	*Terms of Grant*	
J. Hastings	Inkberrow manor, Worcs.	In tail, but regranted to Pembroke for life	*C. Cl. R., 1323–7*, p. 223 (grant made on 12 Aug. 1310)
J. Hastings	Compton manor, Dorset	In tail, but regranted to Pembroke for life	*C.P.R., 1324–7*, p. 49
Maurice de Berkeley	Half of Aure manor, Somerset	Unknown	*C.P.R., 1327–30*, p. 269
J. Darcy	Fords of the Trent at Gainsborough and Dunham	In tail	*Cat. Anc. Deeds*, vol. 4, p. 35
J. Pabenham	Ridlington manor, Suffolk	For life	*Cal. I.P.M.*, vol. 6, p. 317
J. Pabenham	£6. 13s. 4d. rent at Jenningsbury, Herts.	For life	Ibid.
W. de Cleydon	Sandon manor, Essex	Unknown	*Cal. I.P.M.*, vol. 6, p. 332; ibid., vol. 7, p. 206

Grantee	Extent of Grant	Terms of Grant	
J. de Wollaston	Icklington manor, Cambs.	For life	*Cal. I.P.M.*, vol. 6, pp. 320, 339; *C. Cl. R., 1337–9*, p. 422
Miles de Stapleton	Northmorton manor, Berks.	For life of Earl of Pembroke	*Cal. I.P.M.*, vol. 5, p. 279
Gilbert de Stapleton	Reversion of the above	For life of Earl of Pembroke	Ibid.
Thomas West	Sharnbrook manor, Beds.	For life	*C.P.R., 1321–4*, p. 223
Rich. Simond	£30 rent at Fileby, Norfolk, till given £20 land elsewhere	Unknown	*C.P.R., 1292–1301*, p. 602
Rich. Simond	Land at Fernham, Berks.	For life	*Cal. I.P.M.*, vol. 6, p. 339
Mr. Stephen de Cheshunt	La Walle manor, Essex	For life	*C.P.R., 1307–13*, p. 326
J. de Cadomo	Reversion of the above	In tail	Ibid.
Mr. Rich. de Winfarthing	Anestey manor, Herts.	Unknown	*C.P.R., 1324–7*, p. 108

OFFICIAL POSTS HELD BY PEMBROKE'S RETAINERS

Retainer	Post	Length of Tenure	
Maurice de Berkeley	Keeper of Gloucester Town	20 July 1312– date unknown	*C.P.R., 1307–13*, p. 480
J. Pabenham jun.	Sheriff of Beds. and Bucks.	24 Apr. 1313– 1 Nov. 1314	*C.F.R., 1307–19*, pp. 168, 220
W. de Cleydon	Keeper of Temporalities of Canterbury	13 May 1313– 3 Jan. 1314	*C.F.R., 1307–19*, p. 171; *C.P.R., 1313–17*, p. 77
Rich. de la Ryvere	Sheriff of Gloucester	16 Nov. 1314– 20 May 1318	*C.F.R., 1307–19*, pp. 221, 360
Maurice de Berkeley	Constable of Berwick	18 Apr. 1315– spring 1316	E. 101/68/2/35
W. de Cleydon	Constable of Orford	7 Oct. 1315– c. Nov. 1323	*C.F.R., 1307–19*, p. 262; *C.P.R., 1321–4*, p. 347
Maurice de Berkeley	Justice of S. and W. Wales	24 June 1316– 7 Oct. 1317	*C.F.R., 1307–19*, pp. 285, 342
J. Darcy	Constable of Norham	20 Jan. 1317– pre 13 May 1320	*C.P.R., 1313–17*, p. 616; ibid., *1317–21*, p. 571
Maurice de Berkeley	Justice of St. Davids	25 Jan. 1317– 7 Oct. 1317	*C.F.R., 1307–19*, pp. 316, 342

Retainer	Post	Length of Tenure	
Rich. de la Ryvere	Constable of Gloucester	1 Nov. 1317– 20 May 1318	C.P.R., 1317–21, p. 46; C.F.R., 1307–19, p. 360
Rich. de Glyn	Keeper of the Stannaries and Dartmouth	29 Nov. 1317– 26 May 1319	C.F.R., 1307–19, pp. 345, 399
J. Paynel	Sheriff of Carmarthen	27 Dec. 1317– 15 July 1318 and 29 July 1318– 23 Mar. 1319	C.F.R., 1307–19, pp. 349, 369, 371, 394
J. Darcy	Sheriff of Notts. and Derby	5 Nov. 1319– 26 Nov. 1322	C.F.R., 1319–2, , pp. 6, 183
Aymer la Zouche	Sheriff of Cambs. and Hunts. and Constable of Cambridge	3 Nov. 1320– 24 Apr. 1327	C.F.R., 1319–27, p. 37; ibid., 1327–37, p. 37
Aymer la Zouche	Pembroke's Lieutenant as Constable of Rockingham and Keeper of forest between Oxford and Stamford	Acting by 25 May 1321. Reappointed 28 June 1324– 12 Feb. 1325	C. Cl. R., 1318–23, p. 302; E. 368/94, m. 15; C.F.R., 1319–27, p. 329
J. Darcy	Sheriff of Lancaster	10 Feb.–15 July 1323	C.F.R., 1319–27, pp. 193, 222
J. Hastings	Constable of Kenilworth	27 Feb.–Easter 1323	C. 81/122/6423
W. de Cleydon	Pembroke's Lieutenant as Justice of forest S. of Trent	Acting at least from 9 June 1323– 23 June 1324	Add. MS. 15668, f. 23v.; S.C. 8/296/ 14771
J. Darcy	Justice of Ireland	18 Nov. 1323– 1327	C.P.R., 1321–4, p. 348; Powicke and Fryde (eds.), Handbook of British Chronology

Appendix 3

Indentures between the King and Leading Magnates

THE details of most of the contracts listed have been built up from a variety of sources, since only a few of the original indentures survive. One of those that does exist, however, is that made by the Earl of Pembroke on 1 November 1317 and this is given in full. For a discussion of the significance of these agreements see Chapter V.

Date	Magnate	Terms of Indenture	Reference
1314?	E. of Hereford	War service with 60 men-at-arms at fee of 400 marks/yr. (short-term agreement)	E. 101/68/2/34 (origina indenture but badly discoloured)
1316 10 Sept.	J. de Mowbray	Service for life at 150 marks/yr.	E. 101/378/4, f. 16
1316 29 Sept.	Barth. de Badlesmere	Service for life in peace and war with 100 men-at-arms. Fee of 600 marks/yr. Given land worth 400 marks for staying with King, 12 Nov. 1317 (but in Oct. 1318 his fee is given as 500 marks)	Soc. of Antiqs. MS. 120, f. 45; ibid., MS. 121, f. 20v.; C. 81/103/4514 (Cole, op. cit., p. 9)
1316 10 Oct.	Hugh le Despenser the Younger	Service in war with 30 men-at-arms for 2 years at 400 marks/yr.	E. 101/13/36/139 (original indenture)
1316 1 Nov.	E. of Hereford	Service in peace and war, at fee of 1,000 marks in peace and 2,000 marks in war, and with 100 men-at-arms. Wardrobe accounts for 1317–18, 1319–20 give fee as 600 marks for life in peacetime. On 20 Sept. 1317 he received Builth in return for past and future services	E. 404/1/7; Soc. of Antiqs. MS. 121, f. 38; E. 101/378/4, f. 16; C. Ch. R., 1300–26, p. 367
1316 30 Dec.	J. Giffard	Life service in peace and war at fee of 200	C.P.R., 1313–17, p. 620; Soc. of Antiqs. MS.

Date	Magnate	Terms of Indenture	Reference
1316 30 Dec. (*cont.*)	J. Giffard (*cont.*)	marks/yr. and with 30 men-at-arms	121, f. 28*v*.
1317 15 Jan.	Roger Damory	Granted 200 marks/yr. for life to maintain him in King's service	*C.P.R., 1313–17*, p. 609; E. 403/180, m. 3
1317 15 Jan.	W. de Montacute	Granted 200 marks/yr. for life to maintain him in King's service	*C.P.R., 1313–17*, p. 609; E. 403/180, m. 3
1317 18 May	W. la Zouche	Service for 1 year with 30 men-at-arms in time of war	E. 213/162 (original indenture); printed in *B.I.H.R.*, vol. 20 (1943–5), pp. 111–18
1317 10 June	J. de Somery	Service with 30 men-at-arms at fee of 200 marks/yr.	Soc. of Antiqs. MS. 121, ff. 31, 36*v*.
1317 pre 3 July	J. Crombwell	Service with 30 men-at-arms	Soc. of Antiqs. MS. 121, f. 29*v*.
1317 29 July	J. de Segrave senior	Life service at fee of 150 marks/yr.	Soc. of Antiqs. MS. 121, f. 36*v*.
1317 pre 3 Aug.	Barth. de Badlesmere	Granted fee of 1,000 marks/yr. by King for value of his counsel	C. 81/101/4339; *C.P.R., 1317–21*, p. 14
1317 3 Aug.	J. de Wysham	Grant of 200 marks/yr. for life because of his service to the late King	*C.P.R., 1317–21*, p. 10
1317 16 Aug.	Giles de Beauchamp	Grant of £40/yr. for life because of his good service and to enable him to continue better in King's service	*C.P.R., 1317–21*, p. 14
1317 6 Sept.	H. Fitzhugh	Service in peace and war at fee of 200 marks/yr.	Soc. of Antiqs. MS. 121, f. 21*v*.
1317 25 Sept.	W. de Ros of Helmsley (alias Hamelak)	Granted 400 marks/yr. in return for surrender to King of Wark castle, 100 marks being his fee for staying with King. Agreement terminated at his request, 22 Aug. 1322	*C.P.R., 1317–21*, pp. 29–32; ibid., *1321–4*, p. 212
1317 1 Nov.	E. of Pembroke	Life service in peace and war with 200 men-at-arms in return for 500 marks land and wartime fee of 2,000 marks. Peacetime fee	E. 101/68/2/24D (original indenture but badly damaged); B.M., Add. MS. 9951, f. 48; *C.P.R., 1317–21*, p. 47

Date	Magnate	Terms of Indenture	Reference
1317 1 Nov. (*cont.*)	E. of Pembroke (*cont.*)	uncertain because of condition of document but probably 1,000+ marks/yr. He received the 500 marks land on 4 Nov. in form of grant in tail of Hertford and Haverford previously held only for life	
1317 18 Nov.	Hugh le Despenser the Younger	Life grant of 500 marks land in Wales in satisfaction of his 600 mark fee for staying with King (clearly made to fulfil an indenture for life service)	*C.P.R.*, *1317–21*, p. 56
1318 2 Dec.	J. de St. John	Life service in peace and war at wages of a household banneret in peacetime (20 marks/yr.)	E. 101/68/2/42c (original indenture)
Date unknown	Hugh Audley the Younger	Life service of King in all matters, on pain of forfeiture if failed to perform terms	*C.P.R.*, *1317–21*, p. 572; ibid., *1327–30*, p. 30
Date unknown	J. Botetourt	Life service with 20 men-at-arms. Agreement terminated at his request, 13 Mar. 1323	*C.P.R.*, *1321–4*, p. 265

INDENTURE FOR LIFE SERVICE OF EDWARD II BY THE
EARL OF PEMBROKE, 1 NOVEMBER 1317
(BADLY DAMAGED)

1. . . . le iour de touz seintz lan du regne notre seigneur le Roi Edward unzisme acovint par entre notre seigneur le Roi *2*. . . . de Valence Counte de Pembrok dautre part, cest a savoir qe le dit Counte est demorez od le dit notre seigneur le Roi *3*. . . . outre . . . qe porront vivre e morir a terme de la vie le dit Counte, et si nul eit desobei ou desobeist *4*. . . . notre seigneur le Roi en sa roiaume le dit Counte de Pembrok mettra tote sa peine e son loial poair a faire *5*. . . . li desobeissant obeir sicome fair deivent lour lige seigneur. Et notre seigneur le Roi dorra au dit Counte *6*. . . . de terre a li e a ses heirs de son corps engendrez, et sil moerge sanz heir de son corps engendrez, adonqes les *7*. . . . (marc)-hees de terre doivent revertir a notre seigneur le Roi e a ses heirs. Et voet le Roi qe le dit Counte eit e *8*. . . . par an a Lescheker as termes de la Pasqe, de la Seint

John, de la Seint Michel, et du Noel par oweles *9.* . . . . tant qe notre seigneur le Roi li eit fait chartre de feffement e mys en seisine de certeines terres qe vaillent par an *10.* . . . . et outre ce le Roi doit donner cynk centz marchees de terre a avoir au dit Counte de Pembrok, a ses heirs *11.* . . . . ses assignez a touz iours et ce doit estre dedeinz lan apres la date de ceste endenture. Et en temps de guerre le dit *12.* Counte servira notre seigneur le Roi a deux centz hommes darmes en touz lieux la ou le corps notre seigneur le Roi irra et seront touz ses *13.* chevaux darmes prisez le primer iour qil serra venuz au mandement notre seigneur le Roi por la guerre et avera restor de ceux qe se *14.* . . . . en service le Roy, le quel restor li serra paiez dedeinz les quarrante iours apres qe nul des ditz chevaux soit mort en le service *15.* notre seigneur le Roi ou liverez en sa garderobe. Et prendra de notre seigneur le Roi por les avant-ditz deux centz hommes darmes *16.* deuz? mille marcs par an en temps de guerre, les queux li seront paiez de quarter en quarter en oweles portions. Cest a savoir le primer *17.* . . . . le lieu ou il serra venuz au mandement notre seigneur le Roi od chevaux e armes serra il paiez por un quarter *18.* . . . . partie des gentz darmes qil amerra, e issint de quarter en quarter si quil soit totes foitz paiez por un quarter devant *19.* . . . . Et si le dit Counte mesne plus de gentz darmes qe ne soit contenuz en ceste endenture, il prendra a lafferant pur tantz *20.* . . . . il amerra outre le noumbre des deux centz hommes darmes avantditz. Et a ces covenantes bien a loiaument *21.* . . . . acomplir en la forme dessusdite le dit Counte de Pembrok oblige lui ses heirs e ses executeurs e touz ses *22.* . . . . moebles e noun moebles a la volunte notre seigneur le Roi. Et si notre seigneur le Roi lui faille de nul des ditz covenantes *23.* . . . . le dit Counte deschargez vers notre seigneur le Roi e ses heirs de tout dont covenant ne li serra tenuz issint qe por *24.* . . . . ntes qe li seront tenuz il face au Roi ce qil devera selonc lafferant des paiementz qil avera receu de notre seigneur *25.* le Roi avantdit. En tesmoignance de queu chose la partie de ceste endenture demorante devers le dit Counte est sealee *26.* du prive seal notre seigneur le Roi e lautre en la garderobe meisme notre seigneur le Roi du seal le dit Counte de Pembrok. *27.* Donne a Westmoster le iour e lan dessusditz.

Later note added at foot of indenture: . . . CCL mars . . . e guerre MMD mars.

Endorsed: Com. Pem. . . . fac. mense Nov. . . . a terme de vie. (E. 101/68/2/42D.)

Appendix 4

Documents

1. *Boulogne Agreement of 31 January 1308*

A tous ceus, etc. Antoni par la grace de Deu Patriarche de Jerusalem et Evesque de Duresme, Henri de Lasci Counte de Nicole, Johan de Garenne Counte de Surreie et Sutsexe, Eymar de Valence Counte de Penebrok, Unfrai de Bohun Counte de Hereford et de Essex, Robert de Clyfford, Paen Tybetot, Henri de Grey, Johan Botetourt, Johan de Berewyk saluz en nostre seigneur. Come al honeur de Deu et de Seint Eglise et au profit de nostre seigneur le Roy d'engle-terre et de son Royame soions tenuz au dit nostre seigneur le Roy par la Foy que nous ly devons a garder son honeur et les dreits de sa Corounne, nous touz avantnomes d'une volente et de commun assent sumes acorde que de tout nostre leal pooir mettroms peine et eide en quant que nous porrons et saverons l'onour du dit nostre seigneur le Roy garder et meintenir, e les choses que sount feites avant ces houres countre soen honour et le droit de sa Coronne, et les oppressiouns que ount estre feit et uncore se fount de jour en jour a soen poeple de redrescer et mettre pur amendement al honour de Deu et de nostre seigneur le Roy et de tout son poeple avantdit. E a ceste chose bien et leaument faire (en touz poinz si come est desusdit, nous trestouz avantnomez et chescun de nouz avons jurez sur seinz et sumes souzmis et nous souzmetoins nous et chescun de nous a la jurisdiction del honourable pere Sire Antoni par la grace de Deu Patriarche de Jerusalem et Evesque de Duresme q'il puisse escuminger et mettre hors de communion de Seint Eglise cely ou ceux que vendreient countre les covenantes susdits, etc.) En tesmoigne de queu chose chescun de nous avant nomes ad mis son seal a ces lettres. Escrites a Boloigne le darrein jour de Janver l'an de grace MCCC et septisme. (Bodleian, Dugdale MS. 18, f. 80, transcribed by Dugdale from an autograph in the Cotton Library.)

Examination of early catalogues of the Cotton Charters (*Bodleian, Smith MS. 90* made *c.* 1680–1700 (now Bodleian MS. 15695) and *B.M. Harleian MS. 7647* made in 1703) shows that this document was originally known as Cotton Charters, Faustina 24. There is, however, no trace of it in cata-logues made since 1703, and it was probably destroyed in the Cotton Library fire of 1731 or lost in some other way. A further transcript of the document exists in Bodleian, Dugdale MS. 18, f. 1 and was copied by Dugdale from volume 5 of the 'Miscellanea' of Robert Glover, Somerset Herald. This version is identical with that in Bodleian, Dugdale MS. 18, f. 80, except for the omission of several lines which are indicated between brackets in the transcript above.

2. *Letter from Edward II to the Earl of Pembroke, 19 December 1316*

Edward par la grace de dieu Roy Dengleterre Seigneur Dirlaunde e Ducs Daquitaine a nostre cher cousin e foial monsieur Aymer de Valence Counte de Pembroke saluz. Trescher cousin nous avoms bien entenduz les lettres e la creaunce qe vous nous avez envoiez par noz chers e foiaux monsieur Johan de Sapy e Olyver de Burdeux et vous mercioms taunt cherement come nous pooms, et savoms molt bon gre de ce qe vous avez si tendrement a cuer noz busoignes, et vous faisoms savoir trescher cousin qe nous averoms especialment recommendez totes les busoignes qe vous touchent e serroms vostre attornez taunt come vous serrez es parties de dela, e voloms qe vous chargez voz gentz qi demorront par de cea, qe totes les foitz qil averont affaire pur busoignes qe vous toucheront qil veignont a nous meismes pur monstrer a nous lestat de voz dites busoignes e nous y mettroms tieu conseil si dieu plest qe vous tendrez a paiez a vostre retournir a nous. E sachez trescher cousin qe touz les pointz qe vous avez ordenez endroit de nostre estat, nous les garderoms taunt qe a vostre revenue saunz nule defaute. Par quoi vous prioms e chargeoms especialment qe noz busoignes qe vous avez si bien comencez, voillez aver tendrement a cuer e pursure a tote la diligence qe vous saverez e porrez, sicome nous nous fyoms especialment de vous. Et lesploit de noz dites busoignes nous facez savoir de temps en temps, od les nouvelles qe seront devers vous, si cher come vous nous amez. Donne souz nostre prive seal a Clipstone le XIX iour de Decembre lan de nostre regne disme. (S.C. 1/49/39.)

This is one of a block of fifty-three letters from Edward II to Pembroke contained in vol. 49 of the P.R.O. Ancient Correspondence. Many of them show evidence of the trust and confidence which the King had in Pembroke, but this letter, written just before Pembroke's departure for Avignon in January 1317, is a particularly good and important example.

3. *Indenture between the Earl of Pembroke, Bartholomew de Badlesmere, and Roger Damory to Guarantee Damory's Future Good Behaviour, 24 November 1317*

Fait a remembrer qe le jour de la date de ceste endenture monsieur Roger Damory chevaler promyst en boune foy come loyau chevaler aus nobles homes monsieur Aymar de Valence Counte de Pembroke e a monsieur Berthelmu de Badlesmere ce qui est apres contenuz. Cest assavoir quil mettra tote sa diligence e son loyau poair devers nostre seigneur le Roy parquoi il se laisse mener e gouverner par les conseaus des ditz Conte e monsieur Berthelmu e qe il croie les conseaus de eus deus sur totes autres genz terrienes tant come bien e loiaument le consailleront a honour e profyt de lui de sa corone e de son Roiaume et par meismes les conseaus se gouvernera le dit monsieur Roger e ne les trespassera en nul poynt. Et ne procurera par lui ne par autre, ne savera nassentera qe nostre seigneur le Roy doygne a home vivant sanz lassent des ditz Conte e monsieur Berthelmu terre ne avoir outre vynt liverees de terre ou la value en avoir, ne qe nostre seigneur le Roy face autre chose de grant chearge qui soit preiudiciale a lui na la corone en nul caas. Et se aensuite estoit qe nostre seigneur le Roy voudra terre ou avoir doner en absence des diz Conte e monsieur Berthelmu, a quiconqe ce fust, outre la value dessusdite ou autre besogne de grant chearge faire de lui meismes qui en preiudice fust de lui de sa corone ou de son Roiaume, le dit monsieur Roger mettra tote son loyau poair a ce destourber tout sus. Et se destourber nel pourra en nulle manere, il le fera savoir aus ditz Conte e monsieur Berthelmu devant qe effect sen preignes, si qe adonc eus toutz trois sefforcent dune accord a ostier le seigneur de cele volentie. Et si le dit monsieur Roger sentist qe nul deist ou feist chose devers nostre seigneur le Roy en preiudice deshonour ou damage des ditz Conte e monsieur Berthelmu dont leur estat puist estre de riens empirez devers nostre seigneur le Roy, il leur en guarnira sans nul delay e le destourbera a tout son loyau poair. Et a cestes couvenantes bien e loiaument tenir e accomplir sicome dessus est dyt e de non faire ne venir iamais alencontre, le dit monsieur Roger a iure sur le corps dieu et estre ceo se ad oblige en dys mille livres desterlyns a payer aus ditz Conte e monsieur Berthelmu a leur requeste quiele hore e quant il deist feist ou venist en nul poynt contre les couvenantes dessusdites. Et les ditz Conte et monsieur Berthelmu ont promys en bonne foy comes loyaus chevalers qe il defendront guaranteront e meyntendront le dit monsieur Roger contre totes gentz de quielle condicion qe il soient, sauve la ligeance quil doivent a nostre seigneur le Roy, tant come le dit monsieur Roger tendra e observera pleynement les couvenantes dessusdites. Et a ceo ont obliges eus leur heirs leur executeurs e touz lur biens moebles e nonmoebles presentz e avenir a la volentie le dit monsieur Roger. En tesmoignaunce des quieux choses lune part de ceste endenture est sealee des seaus les ditz Conte e monsieur Berthelmu e lautre du seal le dit monsieur Roger entrechainablement. Donne a Londres le vintisme quart jour de Novembre lan du regne nostre seigneur le Roy Edward unzisme. (E. 163/4/6.)

Transcripts of this indenture, which has been interpreted as the foundation of a 'middle party' by Pembroke and Badlesmere, can also be found in *P.W.*, vol. 2, Appendix, p. 120, and in Davies, op. cit., Appendix 42. For a discussion of the document and its significance see Chapter V.

4. *Agreement between the Archbishops and Bishops and the Earl of Lancaster regarding the Latter's Attendance at Parliament: April 1318?*

Une accorde entre Ercevesques et Evesques dun parte et le Conte de Lancastre daltre parte de dicto comite veniendo ad parliamentum.

Il est accorde entre les honurables peres en dieu les Ercevesques et Evesques dun parte et le Conte de Lancastre daltre parte qe le dit Counte ad graunte e lealment promise qe par ley ne par ses soens ne chivauchera as armes sur nuly en damage fesant encontre la pees, ne sur querra apertement ne privement par malice fors qe en forme de ley, si home ne ly surquerque ou les gens. Et en totez le foiz qil vendra au parlement il vendit duement et en peisible manere com pere de la terre, sicom son estat demande. Et aussi est accorde qe covenable surte seit fait pur ly et pur les soens en avaunt qil viegne au parlement, e qe le dit Count, quant il vendra, fet reverance a son seyneur le Rey, sicom il fere doit a son seigneur lige. Et fet a remembrer qe a tut la parlaunce le dit Count de Lancastre ad reserve devers ly totes les maners des actions et des querels qil ad devers le Count de Garenne tant qe au procheyn parlement. E les prelatz avantnomes ount grante au dit Count de Lancastre pur eus et pur lez autres prelatz de la province de Canterbery qe tant com le dit Cont veut les choses avantnomes tenir e continuer lez ditz prelates li tendrent le bon lieu qil purront en ben et en reson. Et si le dit Count voet lez chosez avantditz enfreyner, lez ditz prelates par autorite de Seint Eglise feround la execution qil purront ou deyvent par ley de Seint Eglise auxi com a cely qi serra destourbeur de la pees. Et si nul del realme vousit le dit Count ou les soens privement ou apertement surquer, les prelatz avantditz feround semblable execution encontre ceus. (Serement qe le dit Count de Lancastre fit as ditz prelatz) qe ie unqes ne pensei de ostir le real poer de la dignite nostre seyneur le Rey E. qi ore est en desheritaunce de ly ne de ses heires, si me eide deus et ses seyntes. Unqore le serment fit il, si me eide deus et ses seyntes, ieo voyle garder et meyntenir les ordinances fet par les prelatz, contez et barons e affermes de par le Rey, et les choses qe ne sont mie duement alienes du Rey e de la corounne encontre les avantditz ordinances voyle a mon poer qil seent reprises e retournes au Rei selonc le serement qe ie fesoi a la fesaunce des ditz ordinances, etc. (Bodleian, Dodsworth MS. 8, f. 262.)

This document comes from a volume of Dodsworth's transcripts of charters, etc., which is headed 'Monasticon Boriale Tomus Secundus: Cartas de Estriding praecipue continens'. The source of the document is not stated, but it is flanked by charters from Monk Bretton Priory near Pontefract and may well also have come from there. For discussion of the document's date and significance see Chapter V.

5. *Agreement of 2 June 1318 between the Royal Council and Prelates*

1. Fait a remembrer qe come les honurables pieres en dieu, Wauter par la grace de dieu Ercevesque de Caunterbir primat de tote *2.* Engleterre, Alisaundre Ercevesqe de Dyvelyn, etc., et les nobles hommes, monsieur Aymar de Valence Counte de Pembrok, etc., le secunde *3.* iour de Juin lan du regne nostre seigneur le Roi Edward fuiz le Roi Edward unzime feussent assembletz au conseil . . . . . *4.* pur conseiller sur les busoignes le Roi e lestat e la salvacion du roiaume contre la malice e mavoiste de ses enemis . . . . . *5.* adonk furent entretz la terre Dengleterre as grandz ostz iesqes en le Counte Deverwyk endestruantz . . . . . *6.* e terres du Roi e des autres occupantz e gastanz et grant tens devant estoient entretz sa terre Dirlaunde . . . . . *7.* et pur hastif conseil e avisement aver e aide mettre en le bon giement (*i.e.* gouvernement) du roiaume, se . . . . . *8.* fraude ou feintise a ceo qe chescun diseit endroit de sei sur les choses suthescrites en la forme qe . . . . . *9.* touz iointement e chescun de eus pur li a son poer ben e loialment conseilleront nostre seigneur . . . . *10.* . . . de . . mesmes bon giement de son poeple e commun profit sanz ~~esgarde de~~ (avoir regarde a) malevolences. . . . . *11.* profit e de ben e loialment a leur poer sanz feintise mettre adrescement en ses busoignes . . . . *12.* le ben qil porront qe choses noundues si nules seient al honur e profit du Roi seient adrescees e . . . . *13.* menees. Dautre part pur ceo qe les ditz prelatz e grantz ne veent pas qe si covenable e hastive remedie e aide . . . . *14.* estre mises es ditz perils e autres busoignes touchantes lestat du Roiaume come si le Counte de Lancastre . . . . *15.* busoignes du Roi e du Roiaume des queux il se est esloigne ia une piece par grosseur e malevolence . . . . *16.* qi sont pres du Roi, a ce qe homme entente, et qe entre li e eux sur mesmes la grosseur e . . . . *17.* les ditz prelatz e grandz se accordent en la manere qe sensuit. Cest assavoir qe apres les . . . . *18.* . . . . . ~~come del esloigner de sa femme hors de sa garde e dautres queux il vodra~~ (ou as aucuns de eux a ceo deputetz) . . . . *19.* peine qil porront qe le dit Counte resceive acquitance due de ceux qi acquit . . . . *20.* -bles amendes et si le dit Counte voille tailler laquitance ou les amendes . . . . *21.* acquitance due e amendes resonables (a leur avis)

enpriant, conseillant, e amovestant qil . . . . *22.* Counte ~~de Lancastre~~ les refuse e se tiegne a la lei adonk seit requis dassu
. . . . *23.* . . . . . . a . . . . issint moustre ses grevances par
serment ou en autre manere al avisement . . . . *24.* apertement ne les pursura ne mal fera ne procura estre fait si noun par
la lei e solom . . . . *25.* assurer, adonk les ditz prelatz (tesmoigneront sa dereson e eus e les dit) grandz uniement
emprendront les busoignes nostre seigneur . . . . *26.*
sainte eglise e du Roi e a la salvacion du poeple e de lestat le Roi
sanz attendre ou r. . . . . *27.* de Lancastre (~~si le seit desresonable~~)
et ne seoffrent tant come en eux est qe le dit Counte face as autres
choses e fois qe par . . . . *28.* A ceo les ditz prelatz e grandz
se accordent qe le dit Counte de Lancastre ~~par colour des ordenances nadgaires~~ . . . . *29.* des gentz darmes ne force use (e noun covenable manere) ~~plus qe un autre grant du Roiaume si noun par commun assent~~ . . . . *30.* de eux et qe es parlementz e aillours
au conseil le Roi le dit Counte ~~de Lancastre~~ sera (seloni sous est
dit sera) come . . . . *31.* sovereinete outre les (autres) piers du
roiaume. Estre ceci par aventure les ditz prelatz e grantz ou aucun
de eux. . . . . *32.* ou del dit Counte de Lancastre pur cestes
busoignes eux touz e chescun de eux a tout leur poer garder
. . . . *33.* sera encuru tieu maugre desicome il se
~~ioignent~~ (sont acordetz) en cestes choses pur le commun profit du
Roi e du roiaume . . . . *34.* encheson. Et volent les ditz prelatz e grantz qe cest acord ~~e ioindre se tiegnent~~ (se tiegne) vers
chescun de eux tant . . . . *35.* solonc les pointz susecritz
et qe si nul de eux venist lencontre qe dieu defende qe les autres
ne li . . . . *36.* en cest acord.

Endorsed with the names of the Bishops of Norwich, Coventry and Lichfield, Chichester, London, Salisbury, Winchester, Ely, Hereford, and Worcester; the Earl of Hereford; the Elder and Younger Despensers, Badlesmere, Roger Damory, William de Montacute (C. 49/4/27: added from unsorted Chancery Miscellanea on 19 Sept. 1922).

This document is badly damaged along its right-hand side. There are several erasures and alterations in its wording made during drafting, the latter being indicated by phrases in brackets. The document bears a close relation to that already printed as 'A Political Agreement of June 1318' (C. 49/4/26: E. Salisbury, *E.H.R.*, vol. 33 (1918), pp. 78–83), and both are clearly drafts of an unknown final agreement.

6. *Promise of Safe Conduct made to the Earl of Lancaster by the Elder Despenser and Others at the Request of the Prelates: 11 June 1318*

A touz ceux qi cestes presentes lettres verront ou orront Hugh le Despenser le piere, Roger Damory, Hugh Daudele le fuiz,

Willeam de Mountagu, e Johan de Cherleton, chivaliers, saluz en notre seigneur. Sache votre universite qe nous[1] a la requeste des honerables pieres en dieu, Gauselin par la grace de dieu du titre des seintz Piere e Marcellins chapelein, e Luk de seinte Marie en la voie lee, diakre cardenaux, messages del eglise de Rome, e des honorables pieres en dieu, Wauter par la grace de dieu Ercevesque de Canterburi, primat de tote Engleterre, Alisaundre Ercevesque de Divelyn, Richard de Loundres, Johan de Wyncestre, Wauter de Cestre, Johan de Norwiz, Johan de Cicestre, Roger de Salesbur', Johan de Ely, Thomas de Wyrecestre, e Adam de Hereford, Evesques, notre seigneur le Roi eit graunte e assentu qe monsieur Thomas Counte de Lancastre, [qi ia une piece sest sustret du dit notre seigneur le Roi e de son consail, par encheson de nous a ce qe homme dit],[2] deinz brief temps veigne (dits venir)[3] au Roi por li faire reverence e obeissaunce due, nous del assent e congie du dit notre seigneur le Roi, asseuroms le dit Counte e les seons tantqe en nous est e chescuns de nous, qil sauvement e seurement veigne au dit notre seigneur le Roi, par lencheson avantdite, e nous ne feroms privement ou apertement au dit Counte ne as seons en venant ne en alant a notre seigneur le Roi, ne illoeqes demorant, ne en retournant, mal oue damage, ne lor soeffreroms estre fait, si avant come nous le porroms desturber a notre poer, e avoms nous e chescuns de nous iurez devant les ditz prelatz en la presence des cardinaux avantditz, de loiaument tenir totes les choses desusdites, e a issint sumes seizmes a sentence descomenge des ditz prelatz, si nous venissons al en countre, qe dieux defende, et avoms grante cele submission seit confermee par les cardinaux avantditz. Et en tesmoignaunce des queux choses a cestes presentes lettres avoms mis noz sceaux. Donne a Westmoustier le XI iour de Juyn lan du regne notre dit seigneur le Roi unzisme. (S.C. 1/63/183.)

The volume of Ancient Correspondence in which this document is included was made up from unsorted miscellanea and added to the class in December 1967.

[1] 'Nous' is an anticipation of 'nous' in line 15 and should correctly be deleted. The true subject of the clause is 'notre seigneur le Roi' after the list of cardinals and prelates.

[2] Ultra-violet light shows that this clause was crossed out. It is possible that Despenser, etc., objected to its implication that they were to blame for the estrangement between Edward II and Lancaster. This may explain why the document which was prepared with slits for the suspension of five seals was apparently never sealed.

[3] Marked for addition to the document in place of 'veigne'.

Appendix 5

Pembroke's Itinerary, 1307–1324

SINCE there is no substantial surviving body of Pembroke's own charters, letters, or accounts to supply details of his itinerary, material has been collected from a variety of other sources, chiefly royal records. One important source is his witnessing of royal charters which, if used with care, may be used to give some indication of his movements. Only specific references to Pembroke at a particular place on a given day are included here. At other times his movements may sometimes be deduced but for information of this kind the text of this book should be consulted.

1307

6 Aug.	Dumfries	C. 53/94, m. 9
21 Aug.	Cumnock	Ibid., m. 10
3 Nov.	Berkhamsted	Ibid., m. 8
22 Nov.	Langley	Ibid.

1308

15 Jan.	Dover	E. 101/373/6, m. 2
19 Jan.	,,	C. 53/94, m. 8
31 Jan.	Boulogne	Bodleian, Dugdale MS. 18, ff. 1v., 80
25 Feb.	Westminster	C. 57/1, m. 3d.
1 Mar.	Chearsley (Bucks)	C. 115/Box LI/6689, ff. 82v.–83
15 Nov.	Westminster	C. 53/95, m. 14
21 Nov.	Byfleet	Ibid.
24 Nov.	London	Paris, *Archives Nationales*, J. 374, no. 4
20 Nov.	Westminster	C. 53/95, m. 13
1 Dec.	,,	Ibid., m. 12
3 Dec.	,,	Ibid., m. 11

1309

1 Jan.	Windsor	Ibid.
4 Jan.	,,	Ibid.
17 Feb.	Paris	Paris, *Archives Nationales*, J. 374, no. 6
4 Mar.	Westminster	C. 53/95, m. 10
7 Mar.	Langley	Ibid., m. 8

1309 *(cont.)*

8 Mar.	Langley	Ibid.
10 Mar.	,,	Ibid., m. 9
15 May	Avignon	*G.R., 1307–17*, no. 260
24 May	,,	S.C. 1/50/56
– June	Rancon (Poitou)	Ibid. /57
5 Aug.	Stamford	C. 53/96, m. 10
6 Aug.	,,	*Ann. Lond.*, pp. 161–5
27 Nov.	Norwich	Bodleian, Dugdale MS. 17, p. 100
29 Nov.	Exning (Suffolk)	*Cat. Anc. Deeds*, vol. 5, p. 162

1310

18 Jan.	Hertford	Ibid., vol. 3, p. 152
17 Mar.	London	*Ann. Lond.*, pp. 170–1
20 Mar.	,,	*P.W.*, vol. 2, part 1, p. 43
10 Apr.	Hertford	*Cat. Anc. Deeds*, vol. 4, p. 35

1311

12 July	St. Paul's	Powicke and Cheney, *Councils and Synods*, vol. 2, p. 1314
18 Oct.	Westminster	E. 368/82, m. 20, schedule

1312

13 Mar.	St. Paul's	*Reg. Gandavo*, pp. 418–19
25 Mar.	London	*Cat. Anc. Deeds*, vol. 5, p. 163
3 Apr.	Westminster	E. 368/82, m. 46*d.*
4 Apr.	,,	Ibid.
17 May	Scarborough	*C. Cl. R., 1307–13*, p. 460
19 May	,,	*Ann. Lond.*, pp. 204–6
26 May	York	C. 53/98, m. 2
28 May	,,	Ibid.
9 June	Deddington (Oxon.)	*Ann. Lond.*, p. 206
10 June	Bampton (Oxon.)	Ibid.
6 July	Friston (Lincs.)	C. 98, m. 2
13 July	Hertford	E. 101/375/8, f. 27
17 July	Westminster	C. 53/99, m. 26
20 July	London	B.M. Add. Ch. 19835
23 July	Westminster	E. 159/85, m. 70
24 July	London	C. 53/99, m. 26
28 July	,,	Ibid.
16 Aug.	Canterbury	Ibid.
17 Aug.	Faversham	S.C. 1/49/12
22 Aug.	Westminster	C. 53/99, m. 26
24 Aug.	,,	Ibid., m. 22
27 Aug.	,,	C. 53/99, m. 26
28 Aug.	,,	Ibid.
7 Sept.	,,	Ibid.
10 Sept.	,,	Ibid.

14 Sept.	Windsor?	Ibid., m. 23
16 Sept.	Westminster	Ibid., m. 22
20 Sept.	London	*Ann. Lond.*, p. 215
21 Sept.	Westminster	Ibid., p. 217
26 Sept.	Windsor	E. 101/375/2, m. 3
4 Oct.	,,	E. 368/95, m. 15*d*.
6 Oct.	Westminster	E. 403/168, m. 1
23 Oct.	Windsor?	C. 53/99, m. 23
29 Oct.	Kennington	B.M. Cotton Ch. XXVII, 29
1 Nov.	Windsor?	C. 53/99, m. 16
2 Nov.	Windsor?	Ibid., m. 24
3 Nov.	Westminster	E. 159/86, m. 52*d*.
7 Nov.	Windsor?	C. 53/99, m. 23
16 Nov.	Windsor	*F.*, vol. 2, p. 187
28 Nov.	,,	C. 53/99, m. 21
30 Nov.	Chertsey	E. 101/375/2, m. 5
15 Dec.	Westminster	C. 53/99, m. 20
16 Dec.	,,	*Cal. of Letter-Books, D*, p. 21
20 Dec.	London	*F.*, vol. 2, pp. 191–2
28 Dec.	Windsor?	C. 53/99, m. 9
30 Dec.	London	*Cal. of Letter-Books, D*, p. 305

1313

7 Jan.	Windsor	S.C. 1/49/19
10 Jan.	Windsor?	*Cal. of Letter-Books, D*, p. 306
15 Jan.	London	Camden 3rd series, vol. 41 (1929), p. 4
17 Jan.	Windsor	S.C. 1/49/20
19 Jan.	Westminster	E. 159/86, m. 76*d*.
24 Jan.	Windsor	C. 53/99, m. 14
29 Jan.	Sheen	S.C. 1/49/21
3 Feb.	Westminster	C. 53/99, m. 13
5 Feb.	Windsor	Ibid., m. 17
12 Feb.	Windsor?	Ibid., m. 14
2 Mar.	Paris	*G.R., 1307–17*, pp. 326–8
14 Mar.	Paris?	Paris, *Archives Nationales*, J.633, no. 35
28 Mar.	Westminster	C. 53/99, m. 7
3 Apr.	,,	Ibid., m. 9
29 Apr.	,,	Ibid., m. 5
1 May	,,	Ibid., m. 4
3 May	,,	Ibid.
16 May	,,	Ibid., m. 5
20 May	Canterbury	Ibid., m. 2
22 May	Dover	Ibid.
23 May	,,	Ibid., m. 3
28 May	Saint-Riquier	E. 101/375/8, f. 30
3 June	Paris	Ibid., f. 30*v*.
7 June	,,	Ibid., f. 3*v*.

1313 *(cont.)*

1 July	Pontoise	E. 163/4/1/1
3 July	Saint Germain-en-Laye	S.C. 1/50/58
22 July	Eltham	S.C. 1/49/22
26 July	Westminster	C. 53/100, m. 18
10 Sept.	Witney	Hist. MSS. Comm., *Various Collections*, vol. 1, p. 245
17 Sept.	Chertsey	S.C. 1/49/23
25 Sept.	Westminster	C. 53/100, m. 18
4 Oct.	Sheen	Ibid.
7 Oct.	Westminster	Ibid., m. 16
8 Oct.	,,	Ibid., m. 17
10 Oct.	,,	Ibid., m. 16
28 Oct.	,,	Ibid., m. 15
29 Oct.	,,	Ibid., m. 18
2 Nov.	,,	Ibid., m. 17
9 Nov.	,,	Ibid., m. 15
10 Nov.	,,	Ibid.
12 Nov.	,,	Ibid.
14 Nov.	,,	Ibid., m. 12
19 Nov.	,,	Ibid., m. 14
20 Nov.	,,	Ibid., m. 13
25 Nov.	,,	E. 30/1368
27 Nov.	,,	C. 53/100, m. 11
12 Dec.	Dover, Boulogne	*C. Cl. R., 1313–18*, p. 86
20 Dec.	Sandwich	Ibid.

1314

4 Jan.	London	*Reg. Sandale*, p. xxv, n. 4
8 Jan.	,,	E. 101/375/8, f. 30*v*.
20 Jan.	Westminster	*F.*, vol. 2, pp. 322–4
26 Jan.	Windsor Park	D.L. 25/338
8 Feb.	Fulham	E. 404/482/19/9
17 Feb.	Canterbury	C. 53/100, m. 7
10 Mar.	Westminster	Ibid.
11 Mar.	,,	Ibid., m. 6
13 Mar.	London	E. 101/375/8, f. 30*v*.
16 Mar.	Westminster	C. 53/100, m. 5
18 Mar.	,,	Ibid., m. 7
23 Mar.	,,	Ibid.
1 Apr.	St. Albans	*C.P.R., 1313–17*, p. 102
16 Apr.	Berwick	C. 81/1705/64
6 May	,,	B.M. Cotton MS. Nero C. VIII, f. 172
7 June	Newminster (Northumb.)	C. 53/100, m. 4
24 June	Bannockburn	*Ann. Lond.*, p. 231
17 July	York	C. 53/101, m. 22
19 July	,,	Ibid.

1 Aug.	York	Ibid.
15 Aug.	,,	Ibid.
9 Sept.	,,	*C.P.R., 1313–17*, p. 169
29 Sept.	,,	D.L. 25/2343
5 Oct.	,,	C. 53/101, m. 20
6 Oct.	,,	D.L. 42/2, f. 194
7 Oct.	,,	B.M. Harleian Ch. 43. C. 46
9 Oct.	,,	C. 53/101, m. 18
20 Nov.	Northampton	Ibid., m. 20
6 Dec.	King's Langley	Ibid.

1315

2 Jan.	Langley	B.M. Cotton MS. Cleopatra D. III, f. 56*v*.
20 Jan.	Westminster	E. 159/88, m. 145
24 Jan.	,,	C. 53/101, m. 15
30 Jan.	,,	Ibid.
2 Feb.	,,	Ibid., m. 17
6 Feb.	London	E. 163/4/1/2
10 Feb.	Westminster	C. 53/101, m. 16
20 Feb.	London	B.M. Harleian Ch. 56. F. 40
1 Mar.	Westminster	C. 53/101, m. 7
8 Mar.	,,	Ibid., m. 6
12 Mar.	,,	Ibid., m. 7
14 Mar.	,,	Ibid., m. 6
13 Apr.	,,	S.C. 1/49/29
17 Apr.	,,	C. 53/101, m. 6
18 Apr.	,,	E. 101/68/2/35
1 May	,,	C. 53/101, m. 8
3 May	,,	Ibid., m. 5
4 May	,,	Ibid.
6 May	,,	*C.P.R., 1313–17*, p. 279
7 May	,,	S.C. 1/45/186
8 June	Bois de Vincennes	C. 47/27/8/34
24 June	Sutton (Kent)	C. 81/1752/56
1 July	Westminster	E. 101/376/7, f. 60
3 July	,,	Cambridge Univ. MS. Dd. IX. 38, f. 77
4 July	,,	C. 53/101, m. 2
9 July	,,	Ibid., 102 m. 19
12 July	,,	Ibid.
21 July	York	E. 101/15/6
3 Aug.	Newcastle	Ibid.
8 Aug.	Barnard's Castle	Ibid.
16 Aug.	Lanercost	Ibid.
24 Aug.	Newcastle	Ibid.
7 Sept.	Alnwick	Ibid.
9 Sept.	Morpeth	S.C. 1/31/147

1315 *(cont.)*

14 Sept.	Chatton (Northumb.)	E. 101/15/6
26 Oct.	Dalby (Leics.)	C. 53/102, m. 15
16 Nov.	Clipstone	E. 101/376/26, m. 4

1316

18 Jan.	London	*Cal. of Hereford Cathedral Muniments*, vol. 2, no. 1658
6 Feb.	Lincoln	C. 53/102, m. 12
7 Feb.	,,	Ibid.
8 Feb.	,,	*P.W.*, vol. 2, part 1, p. 169
10 Feb.	,,	C. 53/102, m. 12
12 Feb.	,,	Ibid., m. 11
14 Feb.	,,	Ibid., m. 10
20 Feb.	,,	Ibid., m. 7
23 Feb.	,,	Ibid.
24 Feb.	,,	Ibid., m. 6
27 Feb.	,,	Ibid., m. 7
3 Mar.	London	*C. Ch. Warr.*, p. 436
20 Apr.	Westminster	C. 53/102, m. 6
21 Apr.	,,	Ibid., m. 5
1 May	,,	Ibid., m. 6
12 May	,,	Ibid., m. 5
25 May	,,	Ibid., m. 3
15 June	,,	Ibid., m. 2
20 June	,,	Ibid., m. 3
26 June	,,	Ibid.
1 July	,,	*Placitorum Abbrevatio*, p. 324
7 July	Keynsham (Somerset)	R. Glover, *Nobilitas Politica*, p. 150
11 July	Westminster	*Chartae Privilegia et Immunitates*, p. 46
14 July	,,	B.M. Cotton MS. Galba E. IV, f. 158
15 July	,,	C. 53/103, m. 24
4 Aug.	Lincoln	Ibid.
5 Aug.	,,	Ibid., m. 22
6 Aug.	,,	Ibid.
7 Aug.	,,	Ibid.
10 Oct.	York	*C.P.R., 1313–17*, p. 548
15 Oct.	Ripon	C. 81/1706/37
17 Oct.	Craike	S.C. 1/49/37
6 Nov.	Durham	*Hist. Dunelm. Scriptores Tres*, pp. 97–9
12 Nov.	York	C. 53/103, m. 15
18 Nov.	,,	*C. Cl. R., 1313–18*, p. 441
20 Nov.	,,	C. 53/103, m. 15
22 Nov.	,,	Ibid.
24 Nov.	,,	E. 404/1/6

4 Dec.	London	*C. Ch. Warr.*, p. 450
13 Dec.	Westminster	*Rot. Parl.*, vol. 1, p. 354
21 Dec.	London	S.C. 1/45/192

1317

1 Apr.	Avignon	*F.*, vol. 2, pp. 322–4
May–June	In captivity somewhere in the county of Bar	
23 June	London	Soc. of Antiqs. MS. 120, f. 24
4 July	Northampton	E. 368/89, m. 2
5 July	,,	E. 101/371/8/30
20 July	Nottingham	C. 53/104, m. 16
24 July	,,	Ibid.
25 July	Radcliffe-on-Trent	*Chartae Privilegia et Immunitates*, p. 47
27 July	Nottingham	C. 53/104, m. 16
28 July	,,	Ibid.
30 July	,,	Ibid., m. 15
2 Aug.	,,	Ibid.
7 Aug.	,,	Ibid.
29 Aug.	Lincoln	Ibid., m. 11
10 Sept.	York	Ibid., m. 13
20 Sept.	,,	Ibid., m. 11
25 Sept.	,,	Westminster Abbey Muniments, no. 1376
26 Sept.	,,	C. 53/104, m. 12
27 Sept.	,,	Ibid.
29 Sept.	,,	Ibid.
30 Sept.	,,	Ibid.
5 Oct.	Retford	S.C. 1/49/44
6 Oct.	Sutton-on-Trent	C. 53/104, m. 11
28 Oct.	Westminster	Ibid., m. 10
1 Nov.	,,	E. 101/68/2/42D.
2 Nov.	,,	C. 54/104, m. 11
4 Nov.	,,	Ibid.
7 Nov.	,,	E. 368/88, m. 112
8 Nov.	,,	*Cal. of Letter-Books*, *E.*, p. 98
20 Nov.	,,	C. 53/104, m. 10
22 Nov.	,,	Ibid.
24 Nov.	London	E. 163/4/6
25 Nov.	Hertfordingbury	E. 101/68/2/41
29 Nov.	,,	S.C. 1/36/82

1318

7 Jan.	Westminster	C. 53/104, m. 9
8 Jan.	,,	Ibid.
22 Jan.	Windsor	Ibid., m. 6
27 Jan.	Westminster	Ibid., m. 9
30 Jan.	,,	Ibid., m. 8

1318 *(cont.)*

2 Feb.	Windsor	Ibid., m. 9
7 Feb.	,,	Ibid., m. 8
10 Feb.	,,	Ibid.
11 Feb.	Hertfordingbury	C. 81/1706/16
18 Feb.	Sheen	C. 53/104, m. 8
21 Feb.	Windsor	Ibid., m. 5
23 Feb.	Kennington	Ibid.
28 Feb.	Westminster	Ibid., m. 8
1 Mar.	,,	Ibid.
3 Mar.	,,	Ibid.
5 Mar.	,,	Ibid., m. 5
6 Mar.	,,	Ibid.
18 Mar.	,,	Ibid.
20 Mar.	,,	Ibid.
30 Mar.	Thundersley	Ibid., m. 6
5 Apr.	Northampton	Soc. of Antiqs. MS. 121, f. 20*v*.
12 Apr.	Leicester	*Bridlington*, p. 54
9 May	Windsor	C. 53/104, m. 5
10 May	,,	Ibid., m. 4
16 May	Westminster	Ibid., m. 6
21 May	,,	Ibid., m. 3
22 May	,,	Ibid., m. 6
25 May	,,	Ibid.
27 May	,,	Ibid., m. 7
28 May	,,	Ibid.
2 June	,,	C. 49/4/27
3 June	,,	C. 53/104, m. 3
5 June	,,	Ibid.
10 June	,,	Ibid.
12 June	,,	Ibid.
25 June	Woodstock	Ibid., m. 1
19 July	Northampton	C. 53/105, m. 18
20 July	,,	*Chartae Privilegia et Immunitates*, pp. 49–50
30 July	,,	C. 53/105, m. 18
8 Aug.	Leake (Notts.)	Ibid.
9 Aug.	,,	*C. Cl. R. 1318–23*, pp. 112–14
24 Sept.	York	C. 53/105, m. 17
25 Sept.	,,	Ibid.
28 Sept.	,,	Ibid.
30 Sept.	,,	Ibid.
1 Oct.	,,	Ibid.
5 Oct.	,,	Ibid.
2 Nov.	,,	Ibid., m. 16
3 Nov.	,,	Ibid.
4 Nov.	,,	Ibid.
8 Nov.	,,	Ibid.

9 Nov.	York	Ibid.
10 Nov.	,,	Ibid.
12 Nov.	,,	Ibid.
13 Nov.	,,	Ibid., m. 15
14 Nov.	,,	Ibid., m. 16
20 Nov.	,,	Ibid., m. 15
21 Nov.	,,	Ibid., m. 14
22 Nov.	,,	Ibid., m. 16
23 Nov.	,,	Ibid., m. 14
25 Nov.	,,	Ibid., m. 15
30 Nov.	,,	Ibid., m. 14
1 Dec.	,,	Ibid., m. 13
3 Dec.	,,	Ibid., m. 10
7 Dec.	,,	Ibid., m. 14
8 Dec.	,,	Ibid., m. 10
10 Dec.	,,	Ibid.

1319

14 Jan.	Canterbury	*Documents Illustrating the History of St. Paul's*, p. 49
6 Mar.	Gooderstone (Norfolk)	S.C. 1/35/203
24 Mar.	London	*Ann. Paul.*, p. 285
2 Apr.	Great Yarmouth	Hist. MSS. Comm., 9th Report, p. 302
c. 24 Apr.	London	*Reg. R. de Baldock*, etc., p. 207
27 Apr.	Westminster	E. 159/92, m. 73
16 May	York	C. 53/105, m. 5
18 May	,,	Ibid., m. 3
28 May	,,	E. 368/89, m. 141d.
3 June	,,	C. 53/105, m. 3
4 June	,,	Ibid., m. 1
6 June	,,	Ibid., m. 3
8 June	,,	Ibid., m. 2
17 July	York?	E. 159/92, m. 10
5 Aug.	Newcastle	C. 53/106, m. 8
12 Aug.	Gosforth	Ibid.
21 Aug.	Fenham	Ibid.
7 Sept.	Berwick	E. 101/378/3, m. 3
16 Sept.	,,	C. 53/106, m. 8
25 Sept.	Newcastle	Ibid.
26 Sept.	,,	Ibid., m. 7
8 Oct.	York	Ibid.
9 Oct.	,,	Ibid.
12 Oct.	,,	Ibid.
19 Oct.	,,	E. 403/189, m. 1
23 Oct.	,,	C. 53/106, m. 7
5 Nov.	,,	Ibid., m. 6
6 Nov.	,,	Ibid.

1319 *(cont.)*

22 Dec.	Berwick	C. 47/22/12/29
24 Dec.	,,	Ibid. /30

1320

1 Jan.	York	B.M. Add. MS. 17362, f. 49
10 Jan.	,,	C. 53/106, m. 5
22 Jan.	,,	Ibid.
23 Jan.	,,	*C. Cl. R., 1318–23*, pp. 219–20
28 Jan.	,,	Ibid., p. 220
29 Jan.	,,	E. 159/93, m. 109
6 Feb.	Loughborough	C. 53/106, m. 1
11 Feb.	Thame	Ibid., m. 4
20 Feb.	Westminster	Ibid., m. 5
22 Feb.	,,	E. 159/93, m. 77
23 Feb.	,,	C. 53/106, m. 5
28 Feb.	,,	Ibid., m. 4
5 Mar.	Canterbury	Ibid., m. 5
11 Mar.	Stratford (London)	S.C. 1/36/18
13 Apr.	Westminster	*C. Cl. R., 1318–23*, pp. 234–5
16 Apr.	Lambeth	*F.*, vol. 2, p. 422
18 Apr.	,,	C. 53/106, m. 4
27 Apr.	Westminster	Ibid., m. 1
10 May	Fulmer (Wilts.)	Ibid.
13 May	Windsor	Ibid.
17 May	Reading	S.C. 1/49/48
28 May	Odiham	C. 53/106, m. 1
4 June	Westminster	E. 159/93, m. 92
9 June	,,	C. 53/106, m. 1
25 June	,,	*C.P.R., 1317–21*, p. 456
27 June	,,	*C.F.R., 1319–27*, p. 27
28 June	,,	Ibid.
2 July	,,	Ibid., p. 28
3 July	,,	Ibid.
5 July	,,	Ibid.
8 July	,,	*C.P.R., 1317–21*, p. 536
9 July	,,	Ibid., p. 490
10 July	Stratford (London)	Ibid., p. 536
11 July	Westminster	Ibid.
12 July	,,	Ibid., p. 490
13 July	,,	Ibid.
14 July	,,	*C.F.R., 1319–27*, p. 30
15 July	,,	*C.P.R., 1317–21*, p. 490
16 July	,,	*C.F.R., 1319–27*, p. 30
17 July	,,	Ibid.
20 July	Stratford (London)	S.C. 1/36/83
29 July	Westminster	*C. Cl. R., 1318–23*, p. 317
6 Oct.	,,	*P.W.*, vol. 2, part 1, p. 251

7 Oct.	Westminster	C. 53/107, m. 8
20 Oct.	,,	Ibid.
27 Oct.	,,	Ibid.
28 Oct.	,,	Ibid.
4 Nov.	,,	Ibid.
10 Nov.	,,	Ibid., m. 7
12 Nov.	,,	Ibid., m. 8
17 Nov.	,,	Ibid., m. 7
20 Nov.	,,	Ibid., m. 6

Nov. 1320 to Mar. 1321: Paris and perhaps elsewhere in France

1321

28 Mar.	Gloucester	C. 53/107, m. 2
13 Apr.	,,	Ibid.
10 May	Westminster	Ibid.
18 May	,,	Ibid.
20 May	,,	Ibid.
22 May	,,	Ibid., m. 1
23 May	,,	Ibid.
24 May	,,	Ibid., m. 2
2 June	Boulogne	C. 66/154, m. 4
5 July	Paris	*Ann. Paul.*, p. 291
27 July	Clerkenwell	B.M. Cotton MS. Faustina B. V, f. 35*v*.
2 Aug.	Westminster	S.C. 1/49/50
14 Aug.	,,	*Ann. Paul.*, p. 297
17 Aug.	,,	C. 53/108, m. 8
20 Aug.	,,	Ibid.
19 Sept.	Harwich	Ibid.
30 Sept.	Tower of London	Ibid.
23 Oct.	Leeds (Kent)	*C. Cl. R., 1318–23*, p. 504
27 Oct.	Kingston	*Vita et Mors*, p. 302
c. 17 Nov.	London	*Cal. of Letter-Books, E*, p. 151
18 Nov.	Westminster	E. 403/196, m. 4
10 Dec.	London	Westminster Abbey Muniments, no. 5110

1322

13 Jan.	Newport (Salop)	*C.P.R., 1321–4*, p. 47
14 Jan.	Shrewsbury	C. 53/108, m. 8
16 Jan.	,,	Ibid.
20 Jan.	,,	*C.P.R., 1321–4*, p. 51
22 Jan.	,,	C. 53/108, m. 7
23 Jan.	,,	Ibid.
14 Feb.	Gloucester	*C.P.R., 1321–4*, p. 70
10 Mar.	Burton-on-Trent and Tutbury	*The Brut*, vol. 1, p. 216
11 Mar.	Tutbury	*C. Cl. R., 1318–23*, p. 522
12 Mar.	,,	C. 53/108, m. 6

1322 *(cont.)*

21 Mar.	Pontefract	*F.*, vol. 2, pp. 478–9
23 Mar.	,,	C. 53/108, m. 6
24 Mar.	,,	Ibid.
25 Mar.	,,	Ibid., m. 5
30 Mar.	,,	Ibid.
4 Apr.	Altofts	Ibid.
11 Apr.	Pontefract	Ibid.
30 Apr.	York	Ibid.
1 May	,,	B.M. Stowe MS. 553, f. 85
8 May	,,	C. 53/108, m. 5
15 May	,,	Ibid., m. 4
22 June	Bishopsthorpe	*C. Cl. R.*, *1318–23*, p. 563
26 June	York	Ibid., p. 575
27 June	,,	Ibid.
30 June	,,	*C.P.R.*, *1321–4*, p. 142
5 July	,,	C. 53/108, m. 1
9 July	,,	*C. Cl. R.*, *1318–23*, p. 574
14 July	,,	C. 53/109, m. 7
15 July	,,	*C.P.R.*, *1321–4*, p. 194
16 July	,,	C. 53/109, m. 6
17 July	,,	*C. Cl. R.*, *1318–23*, pp. 574–5
20 July	,,	C. 53/109, m. 6
21 July	,,	*C.P.R.*, *1321–4*, p. 190
27 July	Barlings (Lincs.)	*Cat. Anc. Deeds*, vol. 1, A. 198
6 Aug.	Stannington-in-the-Street (Northumb.)	C. 53/109, m. 6
8 Sept.	Newbiggin (Northumb.)	Ibid.
4 Oct.	Barnard's Castle	Ibid.
14 Oct.	Byland	S.C. 1/49/52
6 Nov.	Conisborough	C. 53/109, m. 6
30 Nov.	York	B.M. Stowe MS. 553, f. 8
3 Dec.	,,	C. 53/109, m. 5

1323

3 Jan.	Newark	C. 53/109, m. 5
20 Jan.	Stowe Park	*Cat. Anc. Deeds*, vol. 3, p. 116
3 Feb.	Newark	Ibid., vol. 1, p. 162
12 Feb.	Pontefract	C. 53/109, m. 5
14 Feb.	York	B.M. Stowe MS. 553, f. 8*v*.
1 Mar.	Knaresborough	C. 53/109, m. 4
4 Mar.	,,	Ibid.
8 Mar.	,,	B.M. Stowe MS. 553, f. 113
13 Mar.	,,	Ibid., f. 14
3 Apr.	Westminster	C. 53/109, m. 4
16 Apr.	Tower of London	Ibid., m. 3
24 Apr.	Winfarthing (Norfolk)	*C.P.R.*, *1374–7*, pp. 114–15
1 May	York	*C.P.R.*, *1321–4*, p. 279

3 May	York	C. 53/109, m. 4
22 May	Rothwell	Ibid., m. 2
30 May	Bishopsthorpe	*C. Cl. R., 1318–23*, p. 717
4 June	,,	C. 53/109, m. 5
3 July	Westminster	Ibid.
17 Oct.	Tenby (Pembs.)	N.L.W., Haverfordwest Deeds, nos. 930, 1246
20 Oct.	Lowel (Pembs.)	Cardiff Public Library, Pembrokeshire Deeds, no. 13
12 Nov.	Nottingham	C. 53/110, m. 9
18 Nov.	,,	Ibid.
10 Dec.	London	N.L.W., Slebech Papers and Documents, no. 11438

1324

20 Jan.	Stratford (London)	*C. Cl. R., 1323–7*, p. 146
3 Mar.	Westminster	C. 53/110, m. 5
4 Mar.	,,	Ibid., m. 7
10 Mar.	,,	Ibid.
24 Mar.	,,	Ibid., m. 6
25 Mar.	,,	Ibid., m. 7
29 Mar.	,,	Ibid., m. 6
30 Mar.	,,	S.C. 1/49/55
1 Apr.	,,	C. 53/110, m. 5
6 May	London	S.C. 1/49/56
7 May	Westminster	C. 53/110, m. 5
10 May	,,	Ibid., m. 4
1 June	,,	Ibid., m. 2
10 June	,,	Ibid., m. 1
23 June	Vicinity of Saint-Riquier in France: Pembroke's death	*Blaneford*, p. 150
31 July	Body brought to London	*Ann. Paul.*, p. 307
1 Aug.	Pembroke buried in Westminster Abbey	Ibid.

Map 1. Lands of the Earl of Pembroke in England and Wales in 1324

Map 2. Lands of the Earl of Pembroke in Ireland in 1324

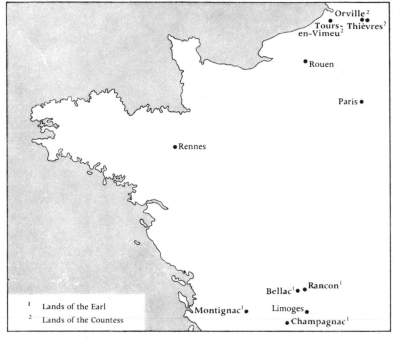

Orville [2]
Tours- Thièvres [2]
en-Vimeu [2]

● Rouen

Paris ●

● Rennes

Bellac [1] ● ● Rancon [1]

Montignac [1] ●   Limoges ●

● Champagnac [1]

[1]   Lands of the Earl
[2]   Lands of the Countess

Map 3. Lands of the Earl and Countess of Pembroke in France in 1324

Bibliography

1. UNPRINTED SOURCES

A. PUBLIC RECORD OFFICE

Chancery

C. 47: Chancery Miscellanea.
C. 49: Parliamentary and Council Proceedings.
C. 53: Charter Rolls.
C. 57: Coronation Roll.
C. 61: Gascon Rolls.
C. 62: Liberate Rolls.
C. 66: Patent Rolls.
C. 67: Supplementary Patent Rolls.
C. 70: Roman Rolls.
C. 71: Scottish Rolls.
C. 81: Chancery Warrants.
C. 115: Chancery Exhibits.
C. 134: Inquisitions *post mortem* (Edward II).
C. 135: Inquisitions *post mortem* (Edward III).

Common Pleas

C.P. 25(1): Feet of Fines.
C.P. 26(1): Notes of Fines.

Duchy of Lancaster

D.L. 10: Royal Charters.
D.L. 25: Ancient Deeds (Series L).
D.L. 27: Ancient Deeds (Series L.S.).
D.L. 29: Ministers' Accounts.
D.L. 34: Ancient Correspondence.
D.L. 36: Miscellaneous Charters.
D.L. 41: Miscellanea.
D.L. 42: Miscellaneous Books.

Exchequer

E. 13: Plea Rolls.
E. 30: Diplomatic Documents.
E. 36: Exchequer Books.
E. 40: Ancient Deeds (Series A).
E. 41: Ancient Deeds (Series A.A).
E. 42: Ancient Deeds (Series A.S.).
E. 101: Accounts Various.
E. 135: Ecclesiastical Documents.

E. 142: Ancient Extents.
E. 149: Inquisitions *post mortem*.
E. 159: Memoranda Rolls (K.R.).
E. 163: Exchequer Miscellanea.
E. 213: Ancient Deeds (Series R.S.).
E. 329: Ancient Deeds (Series B.S.).
E. 357: Escheators' Accounts.
E. 358: Miscellaneous Accounts.
E. 368: Memoranda Rolls (L.T.R.).
E. 401: Receipt Rolls.
E. 403: Issue Rolls.
E. 404: Wardrobe Debentures and Warrants for Issues.

Justices Itinerant

J.I. 1: Assize Rolls.

King's Bench

K.B. 27: Coram Rege Rolls.

Public Record Office

P.R.O. 31/9: Vatican Transcripts.

Special Collections

S.C. 1: Ancient Correspondence.
S.C. 7: Papal Bulls.
S.C. 8: Ancient Petitions.

B. OTHER REPOSITORIES

Bodleian Library

Dodsworth MSS. 8, 94: Volumes of Yorkshire and Northern charters.
Dugdale MSS. 12, 15, 17, 18, 20: Original notebooks of William Dugdale containing a wide variety of material.
Latin MS. Hist. C. 5: Daily account roll of royal Household, 2 Edward II.
Laud Miscellaneous MS. 529: Chronicle of English history, 1066–1390.
Tanner MS. 90: A Miscellaneous collection of mainly sixteenth-century material.
Kent Rolls 6: A fourteenth-century roll of documents from Tonbridge priory, Kent.

British Museum

   Additional MSS.

MS. 7965: Wardrobe Book of 25 Edward I.
MS. 9951: *Liber Cotidianus Garderobae*, 14 Edward II.
MS. 15568: Newent priory cartulary.
MS. 17362: Wardrobe Book of 13 Edward II.
MS. 28024: Beauchamp cartulary.
MS. 35093: *Liber Cotidianus Garderobae*, 1 Edward II.

Cotton MSS.

Julius E. I: Register of Gascon Documents.
Tiberius C. VII: Chronicle of Henry Knighton.
Claudius A. XIV: Poem of James Nicholas of Dacia, 1363, in honour of Aymer de Valence, Earl of Pembroke.
Claudius E. III: Chronicle of Henry Knighton.
Claudius E. VIII: Chronicle of Adam Murimuth.
Nero C. III: Includes a letter from the Younger Despenser to John Inge, 21 Mar. 1321.
Nero C. VIII: *Liber de compotis diversorum reddituum in garderoba Regis,* from 4 Edward II.
Nero D. X: Incomplete chronicle, 1287–1323, attributed to Nicholas Trivet.
Galba E. IV: Register of Henry of Eastry.
Vespasian F. VII: Includes a letter of the Younger Despenser, 21 Sept. 1319.
Cleopatra C. III: Extracts from chronicle of Dunmow priory.
Cleopatra D. III: Hales abbey chronicle.
Faustina B. V: Historia Roffensis.
Faustina B. VI: Croxden abbey chronicle.

Harleian MSS.

MS. 530: Miscellaneous collection including extracts from chronicle of Dunmow priory.
MS. 636: *Polistorie del Eglise de Christ de Caunterbyre.*
MS. 1240: Mortimer cartulary.

Lansdowne MSS.

MS. 229: Collection of Robert Glover.

Royal MSS.

MS. 16. E. V: Text of *Miroir de l'Ame* made for Marie de Saint-Pol, Countess of Pembroke.
MS. 20. A. III: A text of the French *Brut.*

Stowe MSS.

MS. 553: Account book of the Wardrobe, 15–17 Edward II.

Charters and Rolls

Additional Ch. 19835: Letters patent of Earl and Countess of Pembroke, 1312.
Cotton Ch. II. 26: Bundle of 48 original letters, temp. Edward II.
Cotton Ch. XVI. 58: Notarial certificate of the appointment of the Ordainers, March 1310.
Cotton Ch. XVI. 59: Letter of Seneschal of Gascony, 1323.
Cotton Ch. XXVII. 29: Acquittance to Chamberlain of Earl of Pembroke, 1312.
Egerton Roll 8724: Roll of Badlesmere and Mortimer muniments.

Harleian Ch. 43. C. 46: Agreement between the Earls of Lancaster and
Pembroke, 1314.
Harleian Ch. 48. G. 39: Charter of Elizabeth Comyn, 1325.
Harleian Ch. 56. F. 40: Letters of attorney of John de Stuteville, 1315.
Harleian Ch. 57. B. 43 and 47: Letters patent of Joan de Valence, 1302–3.
Sloane Ch. XXXII. 14: Grant by Philip de Angulo, 1298.

Cambridge University Library

MS. Dd. V. 5: Breviary of Marie de Saint-Pol, Countess of Pembroke.
MS. Ee. V. 31: Register of Henry of Eastry, Prior of Christ Church,
Canterbury.
MS. Ff. II. 33: Register of abbey of Bury St. Edmunds.

Cambridge, Pembroke College

MS. life of Marie de Saint-Pol, Countess of Pembroke, by G. Ainslie, 1847.

Cambridge, Trinity College

MS. R. 5. 41: Chronicle of A.D. 303 to 1385, originating in Canterbury.

Canterbury Cathedral

Register I.

Cardiff Central Public Library

Pembrokeshire deeds.

Foljambe Charters, Osberton Hall, Worksop

Appendix 4.

Guildhall Record Office, London

Hustings Roll 53.

Lambeth Palace

Register of Archbishop Walter Reynolds.
MS. 1213: Collection of documents on the major political events of the
reign of Edward II.

Lincoln Cathedral

Dean and Chapter Muniments, D. II/56/1, no. 39.

National Library of Wales

Chirk Castle Documents.
Haverfordwest Deeds.
Muddlescombe Deeds.
Picton Castle Papers.
Slebech Papers and Documents.
Microfilm 30: Chronicle of Wigmore Abbey (Univ. of Chicago Ms. 224.
Formerly known as Univ. of Chicago Ms. CS. 439. f. M.82. W.6).

Norfolk and Norwich Record Office
Institutions Register of John Salmon, Bishop of Norwich.

Society of Antiquaries of London
MS. 120: Wardrobe Book of 10 Edward II.
MS. 121: Wardrobe Book of 11 Edward II.
MS. 122: Chamber Account Book, 18 Edward II.

Swansea Corporation Records
Charter of Edward II, 1312.

Westminster Abbey Muniments
Nos. 1376, 5110.

French Archives
Archives Nationales, Series J. 374, J. 633, J. 918, KK. 909, PP. 19 *bis*.
Archives départementales de la Charente, Bundle G. 138.

2. PRINTED SOURCES

A. CALENDARS AND TRANSCRIPTS

Actes du Parlement de Paris, 1st series, 1254–1328, ed. M. E. Boutaric (Paris, 1863–7).
Anglo-Scottish Relations, 1174–1328, ed. E. L. G. Stones (London, 1965).
Antient Kalendars and Inventories of His Majesty's Exchequer, ed. F. Palgrave, 3 vols. (London, 1836).
Archives historiques du Poitou, La Société des Archives historiques du Poitou (Poitiers, 1872–1963).
The Black Book of St. Davids, ed. J. Willis-Bund, Cymmrodorion record series, no. 5 (London, 1902).
Calendar of Bodleian Charters and Rolls, ed. W. H. Turner (Oxford, 1878).
Calendar of Chancery Warrants, 1244–1326 (London, 1927).
Calendar of Charter Rolls, 1226–1326 (London, 1903–8).
Calendar of Close Rolls, 1227–1399 (London, 1902–27).
Calendar of Documents relating to Ireland, 1293–1307, ed. H. S. Sweetman, 2 vols. (London, 1881–6).
Calendar of Documents relating to Scotland, 1272–1357, ed. J. Bain, 2 vols. (Edinburgh, 1884–7).
Calendar of Entries in the Papal Registers relating to Great Britain and Ireland: Papal Letters, 1305–42, ed. W. H. Bliss *et al.* (London, 1895).
Calendar of Fine Rolls, 1272–1337 (London, 1911–13).
Calender of Hereford Cathedral Muniments, 3 vols., typescript made at National Library of Wales (Aberystwyth, 1955).
Calendar of Inquisitions Post Mortem, vols. 4–10, 1291–1361 (London, 1913–21).
Calendar of the Justiciary Rolls of Ireland, 1295–1314, ed. J. Mills, 3 vols. (Dublin, 1905–14).
Calendar of the Letter-Books of the City of London: B, D, and E, ed. R. R. Sharpe (London, 1900–3).

Calendar of the Letters and Papers of the Reign of Henry VIII, vol. 11, ed. J. Gairdner (London, 1888).

Calendar of the Memoranda Rolls, 1326–1327 (London, 1968).

Calendar of Miscellaneous Inquisitions, 1219–1349 (London, 1916).

Calendar of Patent Rolls, 1216–1399 (London, 1901–9).

Calendar of the Public Records relating to Pembrokeshire, ed. H. Owen, 3 vols., Cymmrodorion record series, no. 7 (London, 1911–18).

Calendar of the Treaty Rolls, vol. 1, *1234–1325*, ed. P. Chaplais (London, 1955).

Calendar of Wills Proved and Enrolled in the Court of Husting, London, 1258–1410, ed. R. R. Sharpe, 2 vols. (London, 1889–90).

Cartae et Alia Munimenta de Glamorgan, vol. 3, c. *1271–1331*, ed. G. L. Clark (Cardiff, 1910).

Cartulary of St. Peter's, Gloucester, ed. W. H. Hart, 3 vols., Rolls Series (London, 1863–7).

Catalogue of Ancient Deeds, 6 vols. (London, 1890–1915).

Chartae Privilegia et Immunitates, Irish Record Commission (Dublin, 1889).

Collectanea of John Leland, ed. Th. Hearne, 6 vols. (London, 1770).

Concilia Magnae Britanniae et Hiberniae, ed. D. Wilkins, 4 vols. (London, 1737).

'Deeds Enrolled on the De Banco Rolls, Edward II', ed. E. A. Fry, Public Record Office typescript (1927).

Description of Pembrokeshire by Geo. Owen of Henllys, ed. H. Owen, 4 vols., Cymmrodorion record series, no. 1 (London, 1892).

Descriptive Catalogue of the Charters and Muniments at Berkeley Castle, ed. I. H. Jeayes (Bristol, 1892).

Documents Illustrating the History of St. Pauls, ed. W. S. Simpson, Camden Society, new series, vol. 26 (London, 1880).

Documents Illustrative of English History in the Thirteenth and Fourteenth Centuries, ed. H. Cole (London, 1844).

Edward II, the Lords Ordainers, and Piers Gaveston's Jewels and Horses, ed. R. A. Roberts, Camden 3rd series, vol. 41 (London, 1929).

Foedera Conventiones Litterae et Cuiuscunque Generis Acta Publica, ed. Th. Rymer, Record Commission edition, 4 vols. (London, 1816–30).

The Gascon Calendar of 1322, ed. G. P. Cuttino, Camden 3rd series, vol. 70 (London, 1949).

Gascon Rolls (Rôles Gascons), 1307–17, ed. Y. Renouard (Paris, 1962).

The Glastonbury Cartulary, vol. 1, ed. A. Watkin, Somerset Record Society, vol. 59 (Frome, 1947; published for 1944).

Henry of Pytchley's Book of Fees, ed. W. T. Mellows, Northamptonshire Record Society, vol. 2 (Kettering, 1927).

Historical Manuscripts Commission, *Reports* 1, 3, 7, 9, 10; *Various Collections*, vol. 1; *Wells*, vol. 1.

Inventaire-sommaire des archives départementales de la Charente antérieures à 1790, ed. G. Babinet de Rancogne, etc. (Angoulême, 1880–1906).

Inventaire-sommaire des archives départementales de la Haute-Vienne antérieures à 1790, ed. M. A. Leroux, etc. (Limoges, 1882–1931).

Inventaire-sommaire des archives départementales de la Meuse antérieures à 1790, ed. A. Marchal, etc. (Bar-le-Duc, 1875–1949).

Layettes du Trésor des Chartes, ed. A. Teulet, etc. (Paris, 1863–1909).
Letters from Northern Registers, ed. J. Raine, Rolls Series (London, 1883).
Letters of Edward Prince of Wales, 1304–5, ed. H. Johnstone, Roxburghe
   Club, vol. 194 (Cambridge, 1931).
Lettres communes de Jean XXII, vol. 5, ed. G. Mollat (Paris, 1909).
Liber Albus of Worcester Priory, ed. J. M. Wilson, Worcestershire Historical
   Society (London, 1919).
Liber de Antiquis Legibus, ed. Th. Stapleton, Camden Society, vol. 34
   (London, 1846).
Liber Epistolaris of Richard of Bury, ed. N. Denholm-Young, Roxburghe Club
   (London, 1950).
Liber Quotidianus Garderobae, 28 Edward I, ed. J. Topham, Society of Anti-
   quaries (London, 1787). (The original MS. is Soc. of Antiqs. MS. 119.)
Litterae Cantuarienses, ed. J. B. Sheppard, 3 vols., Rolls Series (London,
   1887–9).
Monumenta Franciscana, ed. J. S. Brewer, Rolls Series (London, 1858).
Parliamentary Writs and Writs of Military Summons, Edward I and Edward II,
   ed. F. Palgrave, Record Commission (London, 1827–34).
Placitorum Abbrevatio, Record Commission (London, 1811).
Records of the Trial of Walter Langton, 1307–1312, ed. A. Beardwood, Camden
   4th series, vol. 6 (London, 1969).
Register of Walter Stapledon, Bishop of Exeter, 1307–26, ed. F. C. Hingeston-
   Randolph (London, 1892).
Register of William Greenfield, Archbishop of York, 1306–15, ed. W. Brown and
   A. Hamilton Thompson, 5 vols., Surtees Society, vols. 145, 149, 151–3
   (Durham, 1931–8).
Registers of John de Sandale and Rigaud de Assier, Bishops of Winchester, 1316–23,
   ed. F. J. Baigent, Hampshire Record Society (Winchester, 1897).
Régistres du Trésor des Chartes, vols. 1 and 2, ed. R. Fawtier (Paris, 1958–1966).
Registrum Ade de Orleton, Bishop of Hereford, ed. A. T. Bannister, Canterbury
   and York Series, vol. 5 (London, 1908).
Registrum Palatinum Dunelmense, ed. T. D. Hardy, 4 vols., Rolls Series
   (London, 1873–8).
Registrum Radulphi Baldock, etc., Bishops of London, ed. R. C. Fowler, Canter-
   bury and York Series, vol. 7 (London, 1911).
Registrum Ricardi de Swinfield, Bishop of Hereford, ed. W. W. Capes, Canterbury
   and York Series, vol. 6 (London, 1909).
Registrum Simonis de Gandavo, Bishop of Salisbury, ed. C. T. Flower and
   M. C. B. Dawes, Canterbury and York Series, vol. 40 (London, 1934).
Rotuli Parliamentorum, 1272–1326, ed. J. Strachey *et al.* (London, 1767).
Rotulorum Patentium et Clausorum Cancellarie Hiberniae Calendarium, vol. 1,
   part 1, ed. E. Tresham, Irish Record Commission (Dublin, 1828).
Statutes of the Realm, Record Commission (London, 1810–28).
Titres de la maison ducale de Bourbon, ed. Huillard Bréholles (Paris, 1867–82).
The War of St. Sardos, ed. P. Chaplais, Camden 3rd series, vol. 87 (London,
   1954).
Year Books of Edward II: 4 Edward II, 1311, ed. G. J. Turner, Selden Society,
   vol. 42 (London, 1926).

B. NARRATIVE SOURCES

Annales of John Trokelowe, ed. H. T. Riley, Rolls Series (London, 1866).
Annales Cambriae, ed. J. Williams ab Ithel, Rolls Series (London, 1860).
Annales of Henry Blaneford, ed. H. T. Riley, Rolls Series (London, 1866).
Annales Londonienses: Chronicles of the Reigns of Edward I and Edward II, vol. 1, ed. W. Stubbs, Rolls Series (London, 1882).
Annales Paulini: Chronicles of the Reigns of Edward I and Edward II, vol. 1, ed. W. Stubbs, Rolls Series (London, 1882).
Annals of Tewkesbury: Annales Monastici, vol. 1, ed. H. R. Luard, Rolls Series (London, 1864).
The Bruce of John Barbour, ed. W. M. Skeat, Early English Text Society, 2 vols. (London, 1870, 1889).
The Brut, ed. F. Brie, Early English Text Society, 2 vols. (London, 1906–8).
Chronicle of England of John Capgrave, ed. F. C. Hingeston, Rolls Series (London, 1858).
Chronicon de Lanercost, ed. J. Stevenson, Bannatyne Club, vol. 65 (Edinburgh, 1839).
Chronicon Galfridi le Baker of Swynbroke, ed. E. M. Thompson (Oxford, 1889).
Chronicon Henrici Knighton, ed. J. R. Lumby, 2 vols., Rolls Series (London, 1889–95).
Chronicon monasterii de Melsa, ed. E. A. Bond, 3 vols., Rolls Series (London, 1866–8).
Chroniques de Sempringham: Le Livere de Reis de Britannie, etc., ed. J. Glover, Rolls Series (London, 1865).
Continuatio Chronicarum of Adam Murimuth, ed. E. M. Thompson, Rolls Series (London, 1889).
Flores Historiarum, ed. H. R. Luard, 3 vols., Rolls Series (London, 1890).
French Chronicle of London, ed. G. J. Aungier, Camden Society, vol. 28 (London, 1844).
Gesta Edwardi de Carnarvon of a canon of Bridlington: Chronicles of the Reigns of Edward I and II, vol. 2, ed. W. Stubbs, Rolls Series (London, 1883).
Grandes Chroniques de France, vol. 8, ed. J. Viard, Société de l'Histoire de France (Paris, 1934).
Historia Anglicana of Thomas Walsingham, 2 vols., ed. H. T. Riley, Rolls Series (London, 1863–4).
Historiae Dunelmensis Scriptores Tres, ed. J. Raine, Surtees Society, vol. 9 (Edinburgh, 1839).
Johannis de Fordun Chronicon Gentis Scotorum, 2 vols., ed. W. F. Skene (Edinburgh, 1871–2).
Nicolai Triveti Annalium Continuatio, ed. A. Hall (Oxford, 1722).
Polychronicon of Ranulph Higden, ed. C. Babington and J. R. Lumby, 9 vols., Rolls Series (London, 1865–86).
Recueil des Historiens des Gaules et de la France, vol. 23, ed. H. Welter (Paris, 1894).
Scalacronica of Thomas Gray of Heton, ed. J. Stevenson, Maitland Club, vol. 40 (Edinburgh, 1836).
Vita Edwardi Secundi, ed. N. Denholm-Young (London, 1957).

Vita et Mors Edwardi Secundi: Chronicles of the Reigns of Edward I and Edward II,
vol. 2, ed. W. Stubbs, Rolls Series (London, 1883).
Walter of Guisborough, ed. H. Rothwell, Camden 3rd series, vol. 89 (London,
1957).

3. SECONDARY WORKS

Altschul, M., *A Baronial Family in Medieval England: The Clares* (Baltimore,
1965).
Baldwin, J. F., 'The Household Administration of Henry Lacy and Thomas
of Lancaster', *E.H.R.*, vol. 42 (London, 1927).
Barnes, P. M. and Barrow, G. W. S., 'The Movements of Robert Bruce
between September 1307 and May 1308', *Scottish Historical Review,* vol.
49 (Edinburgh, 1970).
Barrow, G. W. S., *Robert Bruce and the Community of the Realm of Scotland*
(London, 1965).
Beardwood, A., 'The Trial of Walter Langton', *Trans. of the American
Philosophical Association,* vol. 54, part 3 (Philadelphia, 1964).
Bellamy, J. G., 'The Coterel Gang: An Anatomy of a Band of Fourteenth-
Century Criminals', *E.H.R.*, vol. 79 (London, 1964).
Bevan, G. P., 'Kidwelly Charters', *Archaeologia Cambrensis,* 3rd series, vol. 2
(London, 1856).
Boissonade, P., 'L'ascension, le déclin et la chute d'un grand état féodal
du Centre-Ouest', *Bulletins et mémoires de la Société archéologique et historique
de la Charente,* 1943 (Angoulême, 1948).
Bridges, J., *The History and Antiquities of Northamptonshire* (London, 1791).
Brooke, R., *Catalogue of the Succession of the Kings, Princes, etc., from the Norman
Conquest to 1619* (London, 1619).
Burias, J., 'Géographie historique du comté d'Angoulême, 1308–1531',
Bulletins et mémoires de la Société archéologique et historique de la Charente,
1955 (Angoulême, 1957).
Butler, R., 'The Last of the Brimpsfield Giffards and the Rising of 1321–22',
Trans. Bristol and Gloucestershire Archaeological Society, vol. 76 (Gloucester,
1957).
Clementi, D., 'That the Statute of York is No Longer Ambiguous', *Album
Helen Maud Cam,* vol. 2, Studies Presented to the International Commis-
sion for the History of Representative and Parliamentary Institutions,
no. 25 (Louvain and Paris, 1961).
Colvin, H. M., *A History of Deddington* (London, 1963).
Complete Peerage, ed. G. E. Cokayne, new edition (London, 1910–59).
Davies, J. C., *The Baronial Opposition to Edward II* (Cambridge, 1918; new
impression, London, 1967).
—— 'The Despenser War in Glamorgan', *T.R.H.S.*, 3rd series, vol. 9
(London, 1915).
Delisle, L., *Recherches sur la librairie de Charles V, Roi de France, 1337–80*
(Amsterdam, 1967).
Denholm-Young, N., *History and Heraldry, 1254–1310* (Oxford, 1965).
—— *The Country Gentry in the Fourteenth Century* (Oxford, 1969).
Dictionary of National Biography, 1st edition (London, 1885–1900).

Du Chesne, A., *Histoire de la maison de Chastillon sur Marne* (Paris, 1621).

Dugdale, W., *The Baronage of England*, 2 vols. (London, 1675).

—— *Monasticon Anglicanum*, 6 vols. (London, 1817–30).

Dunham, W. H., 'Lord Hastings' Indentured Retainers, 1461–83', *Trans. of Connecticut Academy of Arts and Sciences*, vol. 39 (1955, and published separately by Yale, 1955).

Edwards, J. G., 'The Negotiating of the Treaty of Leake, 1318', *Essays in History Presented to R. L. Poole*, ed. H. W. C. Davis (Oxford, 1927).

—— 'Sir Gruffydd Llwyd', *E.H.R.*, vol. 30 (London, 1915).

Edwards, K., 'The Political Importance of the English Bishops during the Reign of Edward II', *E.H.R.*, vol. 59 (London, 1944).

Fairbank, F. R., 'The Last Earl of Warenne and Surrey', *Yorkshire Archaeological Journal*, vol. 19 (Leeds, 1907).

Fraser, C. M., *A History of Anthony Bek* (Oxford, 1957).

Fryde, E. B., 'The Deposits of the Younger Despenser with Italian Bankers', *Econ. Hist. R.* 2nd series, vol. 3 (London, 1950–1).

Fuller, E. A., 'The Tallage of 6 Edward II and the Bristol Rebellion', *Trans. Bristol and Gloucestershire Archaeological Society*, vol. 19 (Gloucester, 1894–5).

Gachard, M., 'Notice d'une collection de documents concernant le comté de Chiny', *Compte-rendu des séances de la Commission royale d'Histoire*, vol. 10 (Brussels, 1869).

Galbraith, V. H., 'A New Life of Richard II', *History*, vol. 26 (London, 1941–2).

Gibbs, V., 'The Battle of Boroughbridge and the Boroughbridge Roll', *Genealogist*, new series, vol. 21 (London, 1905).

Glover, R., *Nobilitas Politica et Civilis* (London, 1608).

Goffinet, H., 'Les comtes de Chiny', *Annales de l'Institut archéologique de la province de Luxembourg*, vols. 10, 11 (Arlon, 1878, 1879).

Gough, —, *Sepulchral Monuments*, 2 vols. (London, 1786–96).

Haskins, G. L., 'A Chronicle of the Civil Wars of Edward II', *Speculum*, vol. 14 (Cambridge, Mass., 1939).

—— 'The Doncaster Petition of 1321', *E.H.R.*, vol. 53 (London, 1938).

Holinshed, R., *Chronicles of England, Scotland and Ireland*, ed. J. Johnson, etc., 6 vols. (London, 1807–8).

Holmes, G. A., 'A Protest against the Despensers, 1326', *Speculum*, vol. 30 (Cambridge, Mass., 1955).

—— *The Estates of the Higher Nobility in XIV Century England* (Cambridge, 1957).

Hunter-Blair, C. H., 'Members of Parliament for Northumberland, 1258–1327', *Archaeologia Aeliana*, 4th series, vol. 10 (Newcastle, 1933).

—— 'Mitford Castle', *Archaeologia Aeliana*, 4th series, vol. 14 (Newcastle, 1937).

Ingpen, A. R., *An Ancient Family: Genealogical Study of the Family of Ingpen* (London, 1916).

Jeantin, —, *Manuel de la Meuse*, 3 vols. (Nancy, 1861–3).

Jenkinson, H., 'Mary de Sancto Paulo, Foundress of Pembroke College, Cambridge', *Archaeologia*, vol. 66 (London, 1915).

Bibliography 349

Johnstone, H., 'The Parliament of Lincoln of 1316', *E.H.R.*, vol. 36 (London, 1921).

Jones, F., 'The Subsidy of 1292', *Bulletin of Board of Celtic Studies*, vol. 13 (Cardiff, 1948–50).

Jones, M. C., 'The Feudal Barons of Powys', *Collections relating to Montgomeryshire*, vol. 1 (London, 1868).

Keen, M., 'Treason Trials under the Law of Arms', *T.R.H.S.*, 5th series, vol. 12 (London, 1962).

Lehugeur, P., *Histoire de Philippe le Long* (Paris, 1897).

Le Neve, J., *Fasti Ecclesiae Anglicanae, 1300–1541*, vol. 6, *Northern Province*, ed. B. Jones (London, 1963).

Levallois, H., 'Recherches à propos d'une liste des vassaux de Bar, de l'an 1311, sur le début du règne du comte Édouard I', *Bulletin mensuel de la Société d'archéologie lorraine et du Musée historique lorrain* (Nancy, 1901).

Lewis, F. R., 'William de Valence', *Aberystwyth Studies*, vol. 13 (Aberystwyth, 1935).

Lewis, N. B., 'An Early Fourteenth Century Contract for Military Service', *B.I.H.R.*, vol. 20 (London, 1943–5).

—— 'The Organization of Indentured Retinues in Fourteenth-century England', *T.R.H.S.*, 4th series, vol. 27 (London, 1965).

—— 'The English Forces in Flanders in 1297', *Studies in Medieval History Presented to F. M. Powicke*, eds. R. W. Hunt, W. A. Pantin, R. W. Southern (Oxford, 1948).

Liénard, M. L., *Dictionnaire topographique de la France: Meuse* (Paris, 1872).

Lucas, H. S., 'The Great European Famine of 1315, 1316, and 1317', *Speculum*, vol. 5 (Cambridge, Mass., 1930).

Lyubimenko, I. A., *Jean de Bretagne, Comte de Richmond* (Lille, 1908).

Maddicott, J. R., *Thomas of Lancaster, 1307–1322* (Oxford, 1970).

McFarlane, K. B., 'Bastard Feudalism', *B.I.H.R.*, vol. 20, 1943–5 (London, 1947).

—— 'The Wars of the Roses', *Proceedings of the British Academy*, vol. 50 (London, 1964).

—— 'Had Edward I a "Policy" towards the Earls?', *History*, vol. 50 (London, 1965).

McKisack, M., *The Fourteenth Century, 1307–1399* (Oxford, 1959).

—— 'Edward III and the Historians', *History*, vol. 45 (London, 1960).

Middleton, A. E., *Sir Gilbert de Middleton* (Newcastle, 1918).

Moor, C., *The Knights of Edward I*, Harleian Society, 5 vols. (London, 1929–32).

Nicolas, N. H., *The Siege of Caerlaverock* (London, 1828).

Owen, R., 'Welsh Pool and Powys-Land', *Collections relating to Montgomeryshire*, vol. 29 (London, 1896).

Painter, S., 'The House of Lusignan and Châtellerault, 1150–1250', *Speculum*, vol. 30 (Cambridge, Mass., 1955).

—— 'Castellans of the Plain of Poitou in the Eleventh and Twelfth Centuries', ibid., vol. 31 (Cambridge, Mass., 1956).

—— 'The Lords of Lusignan in the Eleventh and Twelfth Centuries', ibid., vol. 32 (Cambridge, Mass., 1957).

350   *Bibliography*

Phillips, J. R. S., 'The Career of Aymer de Valence, Earl of Pembroke, with special reference to the Period from 1312 to 1324', Ph.D. (London, 1967/8). (See also summary of thesis in *B.I.H.R.*, vol. 41 (London, 1968).)

Pole-Stuart, E., 'Some Aspects of the Political and Administrative History of Gascony, 1303–27', Ph.D. (London, 1927).

Pollock, F., and Maitland, F. W., *History of English Law*, 2 vols. (Cambridge, 1911).

Powicke, F. M. and Cheney, C. R., *Councils and Synods*, vol. 2 (Oxford, 1964).

—— and Fryde, E. B. (eds.), *Handbook of British Chronology*, Royal Historical Society Guides and Handbooks, no. 2 (2nd edn., London, 1961).

Prince, A. E. 'The Indenture System under Edward III', *Historical Essays in Honour of James Tait*, eds., J. G. Edwards, V. H. Galbraith, E. F. Jacob (Manchester, 1933).

Rees, W., *Historical Map of South Wales and the Border in the Fourteenth Century* (Ordnance Survey, London, 1933).

Renouard, Y., 'Édouard II et Clément V d'après les rôles gascons', *Annales du Midi*, vol. 67 (Toulouse, 1955), and *Études d'histoire médiévale*, vol. 2 (Paris, 1968).

Richardson, H. G., 'The English Coronation Oath', *Speculum*, vol. 24 (Cambridge, Mass., 1949).

—— and Sayles, G. O., 'The Parliament of 1316', *B.I.H.R.*, vol. 12 (London, 1934–5).

—— *The Administration of Ireland, 1172–1377*, Irish MSS. Commission (Dublin, 1963).

Rothwell, H., 'Edward I and the Struggle for the Charters, 1297–1305', *Studies in Medieval History Presented to F. M. Powicke*, eds. R. W. Hunt, W. A. Pantin, R. W. Southern (Oxford, 1948).

Russell, J. C., *British Medieval Population* (Albuquerque, 1948).

Salisbury, E., 'A Political Agreement of June 1318', *E.H.R.*, vol. 33 (London, 1918).

Sayles, G. O., 'The Formal Judgements on the Traitors of 1322', *Speculum*, vol. 16 (Cambridge, Mass., 1941).

Schnith, K., 'Staatsordnung und Politik in England zu Anfang des 14 Jahrhunderts', *Historisches Jahrbuch*, vol. 88 (Munich, 1968).

Smith, J. B., 'The Lordship of Glamorgan', *Morgannwg*, vol. 2 (Cardiff, 1958).

Smyth, J., of Nibley, *The Lives of the Berkeleys*, ed. J. Maclean, 3 vols., Bristol and Gloucestershire Archaeological Society (Gloucester, 1883–5).

Snellgrove, H. S., *The Lusignans in England* (Albuquerque, 1950).

St. Joseph, J. K., 'The Castles of Northumberland from the Air', *Archaeologia Aeliana*, 4th series, vol. 28 (Newcastle, 1950).

Stones, E. L. G., 'The Date of Roger Mortimer's Escape from the Tower', *E.H.R.*, vol. 61 (London, 1951).

—— 'The Folvilles of Ashby-Folville and their Associates in Crime, 1326–47', *T.R.H.S.*, 5th series, vol. 7 (London, 1957).

Storey, R. L., *The End of the House of Lancaster* (London, 1966).

Stubbs, W., *Constitutional History of England*, 3 vols. (Oxford, 1875).

Surtees, R., *History of Durham*, 4 vols. (Durham, 1816–40).

Tanner, L. E., 'The Countess of Pembroke and Westminster Abbey', *Pembroke College, Cambridge, Annual Gazette*, vol. 33 (Cambridge, 1959).

Taylor, A. A., 'The Career of Peter of Gaveston', M.A. (London, 1939).

Thomas, A. A., *Le Comté de la Marche et le Parlement de Poitiers*, École pratique des hautes études (Paris, 1910).

Thomas, A., Olivier-Martin, 'Un document inédit sur la procédure accusatoire dans la châtellanie de Bellac au XIVᵉ siècle', *Revue historique de droit français et étranger*, 4th series, vol. 14 (Paris, 1935).

Tout, T. F., *The Place of the Reign of Edward II* (Manchester, 1914 and 1936).

—— *The Political History of England, 1216–1377* (London, 1905).

—— *Chapters in Medieval Administrative History*, 6 vols. (Manchester, 1923–35).

Turner, T. H., 'The Will of Humphrey de Bohun, Earl of Hereford and Essex', *Archaeological Journal*, vol. 2 (London, 1845).

Walker, R. F., 'Richard Marshal and the Rising of 1233–34', M.A. (Wales, 1950).

Ward, J. C., 'The Estates of the Clare Family, 1066–1317', Ph.D. (London, 1962).

Watson, G. W., 'The Families of Lacy, Geneva, Joinville and La Marche', *Genealogist*, new series, vol. 21 (London, 1905).

—— 'Geoffrey de Mortemer and his Descendants', ibid., vol. 22 (London, 1906).

—— 'Marriage Settlements', ibid., vol. 35 (London, 1919).

—— 'Alice de la Marche, Countess of Gloucester and Hertford', ibid., vol. 38 (London, 1922).

Wilkinson, B., *Constitutional History of Medieval England*, 3 vols. (London, 1948–58).

—— 'The Negotiations Preceding the "Treaty" of Leake, August 1318', *Studies in Medieval History Presented to F. M. Powicke*, eds. R. W. Hunt, W. A. Pantin, R. W. Southern (Oxford, 1948).

—— 'The Sherburn Indenture and the Attack on the Despensers, 1321', *E.H.R.*, vol. 63 (London, 1948).

Williams, G. A., *Medieval London, from Commune to Capital* (London, 1963).

Index

Abbot, Philip, 291
Abel, John, 304
Achurch (Northants.), 77
Acre, Joan of, 16
Addingsley, John de, 304
Airmyn, William, 187
Alard, Henry, 62
Albret, Amanieu de, 60, 64
Aldwinkle (Northants.), 77
Alexander, Walter, 91, 259
Alnwick (Northumb.), 90
Altofts (Yorks.), 334
Alton castle (Staffs.), 134
Amiens, 61–2, 192
Amiens, Mise of (1264), 41
Amyot, John, 265
Ancona, Marquis of, *see* Got, Bertrand de
Anestey (Herts.), 310
Angoulême, Bishop of, 3
Angoulême, county of, 3, 5; *see also* Lusignan, Counts of La Marche and Angoulême; Lusignan, family of
Angoulême, Isabella of, 2
Angus, Earl of, *see* Umfraville, Robert de
Annales Londonienses, 33
Anvers, Thomas de, 291
Aquitaine, 60, 64, 86–7, 188, 232; *see also* Gascony
Argentein, Giles de, 74
Argentein, John de, 303
Arnold, Cardinal of St. Prisca, 41, 54–9, 61
Arnold, Bishop of Poitiers, 41, 57, 61
Arundel, Earl of, *see* FitzAlan, Edmund
Ashburne-in-the-Peak (Derbs.), 121
Aspremont, Goberd de, 114
Athol, Earl of, *see* Strathbogie, David de
Audley, Hugh, the Elder, 93, 122, 222
Audley, Hugh, the Younger: career of, 12–13, 20, 131–2; royal favourite (1317), 13, 132, 276; marriage to Margaret de Clare, 16, 132–3, 263; hostile to Lancaster, 131, 133; agreement with other enemies of Lancaster, 133; possible indenture with Pembroke, 146; contract to

serve King, 149, 314; safe conduct for Lancaster (1318), 164, 321; attitude to settlement with Lancaster, 169, 175; grants restored to, 173; pays compensation to Lancaster, 131, 174; removed from court, 174–6; in Scottish campaign (1319), 185; hostile to Younger Despenser (1320–1), 199–200, 283; breaks contract with King (1321), 151; lands seized by King, 207; ordered to give up Despensers' lands, 216, 218; flees to join Lancaster (1322), 222
Audley, Nicholas, 51
Audley, Nicholas, of Cemaes, 248–9
Aumale, Count of, 116
Aure (Somerset), 309
Autun, Bishop of, 5
Avesnes, John de, 2, 15
Avignon, 29, 107–11, 115, 117–18, 138, 142, 145, 259, 273, 277, 280, 324, 329

Bacon, Edmund, 93
Badlesmere, Bartholomew de: career of, 12, 20–1, 144, 261; links with Marchers, 15, 208; contracts with retainers, 255; appointed constable of Bristol (1312), 50–1; and defence of Berwick (1314), 76; dispute with Bristol (1315), 85, 87, 144; and defence of Scottish border, 88, 90–1; releases widow of Robert Clifford, 94; member of reform commission (1316), 95, 143–4; member of Council, 96, 102, 104, 106, 276; appointed to negotiate with Scots, 101; besieges Bristol, 102–3, 145; and Avignon mission (1317), 108, 110–11, 116, 138–9, 145, 277; prominent councillor, 121, 145; at Nottingham council, 121–2; brings armed force to King, 125; mediates between King and Lancaster, 131, 147, 153, 277; makes indenture with Roger Damory, 134–41, 151, 213, 277,

Index

371

Templars, 51, 72 n.
Tenby (Pembs.), 231, 335
Testa, William, 71
Thanet (Kent), 216
Thièvre, 7
Thornbury (Gloucs.), 263
Thorp, Walter de, 58
Thorpe Waterville (Northants.), 77–82, 127, 143, 227, 238, 242, 245
Thorrington (Essex), 242
Thundersley (Essex), 330
Tickhill castle (Yorks.), 54
Tilbury (Essex), 216
Titchmarsh (Northants.), 82
Tonbridge castle (Kent), 207, 233
Tours-en-Vimeu, 7, 234
Tout, T. F., 107, 135, 137–40, 143, 171, 176, 178, 206–7, 211, 225, 270, 287
Towcester (Northants.), 79, 242
Tower of London, 44–5
Tregaer, 244
Trivet, Nicholas, continuation of chronicle of, 124, 128
Trivet, Nicholas, chronicle ascribed to, 208 n.
Trokelowe, John, chronicle of, 156
Trumwyn, Roger, 54
Tuchet, William, 77–81
Tutbury (Staffs.), 160, 165–7, 173, 223, 333
Tweedmouth, 231
Tweng, William de, 304
Twynham, Walter de, 303
Tybetot, Payn, 26
Tybetot, Richard, 47 n.
Tynemouth (Northumb.), 32
Tyngewyk, Elias de, 51

Umfraville, Robert de, Earl of Angus (1307–25), 128, 188, 225–6, 228, 284
Umfraville, Thomas de, 299
Uvedale, Peter de, 255

Valence, Agnes de, 2, 15, 242
Valence, Aymer de, Bishop of Winchester (1250–60), 9
Valence, Aymer de, Earl of Pembroke (1307–24): birth and family background of, 1–2, 8–9, 15; character and abilities of, 1, 11, 21, 269–82 *passim*; marriages of, 5–7, 200, 202, 206; connections with France,

1–8, 13, 271; career as diplomat, 8; heirs of, 2, 18, 234–7; place among English magnates, 9–13, 15–16, 271; family relationship with King, 16; loyalty to King, 11, 23, 26–8, 36–7, 141–2, 210–12, 215, 239, 270–2; King's reliance on, 31, 42, 101, 110, 115–16, 142, 190–1, 193, 232, 238, 272, 317; attitudes of contemporaries to, 269–70; modern opinions of, 135–40, 270
Under Edward I: at Cambrai (1296), 9; inherits French lands, 3, 240; knighted (1297), 22; serves in Flemish campaign, 22–3; serves in Scotland and on embassies (1298–1307), 24–5; does homage for French lands (1300), 3; given Scottish lands (1301), 24; summoned to serve French King in Flanders (1303–4), 3; charged with welfare of future Edward II (1307), 24
Under Edward II:
— in 1307: appointed Keeper of Scotland, 25; inherits earldom of Pembroke, 9, 22, 25; negotiates King's marriage contract, 25
— in 1308: present at King's marriage, 26; part in Boulogne agreement on reform, 26–8, 273, 316–17; relations with Gaveston, 25, 27 n, 28–9; royal favours to, 29
— in 1309: assists return of Gaveston from exile, 29, 273–4
— in 1310: opposition to Gaveston, 30, 273–4; forbidden to bring armed retainers to Parliament, 30; elected an Ordainer, 30; refuses to serve in person in Scottish campaign, 31; refuses to rejoin King, 31
— in 1311: work on Ordinances, 31–2, 274
— in 1312: prevents Walter Langton acting as Treasurer, 32; appointed to pursue Gaveston, 32, 274; besieges Scarborough, 32; receives surrender of Gaveston, 33–4, 274; Gaveston seized from his custody, 35; rejoins King, 36–7, 274;